Germany and the Ottoman Empire

1914-1918

ERRATA
Germany and the Ottoman Empire, 1914-1918

BY ULRICH TRUMPENER

1) Because of last-minute changes in pagination, several index entries and cross-references in the footnotes refer erroneously to a page either behind or in front of the correct page.

2) In many footnotes the word "and" was erroneously printed in front of "*passim.*"

3) In some parts of the book the umlaut sign in "Jäckh" was omitted.

p. 19, note 33, line 2	insert period after "Feb"
p. 76, line 17	"Glotz" should be "Goltz"
p. 79, note 33, line 1	"Bd. 33" should be "Bd. 34"
p. 101, note 88, line 1	"Külhmann" should be "Kühlmann"
p. 159, lines 21-22	"nonannexionist" should be "nonannexationist"
p. 179, line 3	insert comma after "Hertling"
p. 217, note 43, line 8	delete "*Deutschland,*"
p. 223, note 56, line 1	delete "*Deutschland,*"
p. 251, lines 20 and 22	"SPD" should be "USPD"
p. 294, lines 17-22	should be "Although on June 19 Bethmann Hollweg . . . payments without collateral, Helfferich . . . to follow through."
p. 311, line 21	delete hyphen between "Reich" and "Ottoman"
p. 355, line 7	insert "the" after "from"
p. 414	transpose lines 5 and 6 under "Egypt"

Princeton University Press, 1968

Germany and the Ottoman Empire

1914-1918

By Ulrich Trumpener

Princeton, New Jersey

Princeton University Press 1968

327.430561
1871g
1968

To my parents

PREFACE

For almost exactly four years, the Ottoman empire participated in the First World War as an ally of the Central Powers. The Turks'[1] intervention on the side that lost the war destroyed their empire and opened the door to drastic political changes throughout the Near and Middle East. However, before they suffered defeat and the dismemberment of their empire the Turks played a remarkably active role in the European war and contributed, at least indirectly, to both its prolongation and intensification. By their military efforts and promotion of a potentially dangerous program of subversion in the Asian and African possessions of the Entente, the Turks tied down sizable British, Russian, French, and Italian forces which might otherwise have been used against the Central Powers in Europe. More important, the Ottoman army and navy successfully prevented the use of the Black Sea Straits for communications between Russia and her Western allies and thereby contributed substantially to the weakening and eventual collapse of the Russian war effort. Though they came to depend increasingly on financial and other assistance from Germany and, to a lesser extent, the Dual Monarchy, the Turks' cobelligerency was of great advantage to the Central Powers and perhaps even a decisive factor in enabling them to hold out as long as they did.

While the military developments on the Turkish fronts and the wartime policies of the Entente regarding the Ottoman empire have been treated in numerous well-documented studies, the Central Powers' general relationship with their Ottoman ally has so far received little scholarly attention. This study

[1] Although "Osmanlis" would be a more appropriate designation for the heterogeneous population of the Ottoman empire (and especially for its ruling elite), the term "Turks" will be used instead throughout this book in conformity with prevailing Western practice. As for the terms "Ottoman empire" and "Ottoman," I have taken the liberty of using them interchangeably with "Turkey" and "Turkish."

Preface

seeks to narrow the existing historiographic gap. It is concerned *primarily* with the nature and results of Germany's wartime policies in and with regard to the Ottoman empire. It also attempts to offer some insights into the character and achievements of the *Ittihad ve Terakki* (Union and Progress) Party which ruled the Ottoman empire from 1913 to 1918. Austria–Hungary's and Bulgaria's Turkish policies are dealt with only in passing, though an effort has been made to record those instances when they impinged directly on the German–Ottoman relationship.

The central question to which this book addresses itself is whether the Germans were really as influential or dominant in the Ottoman empire as most traditional works have suggested. Did Berlin, on the eve of and during World War I, have a decisive voice in the formulation of the Porte's policies? To what extent did the Germans control the Ottoman armed forces? What economic power did they hold in the Turkish lands and what gains did they make during the war? What long-range plans did the Reich government and German economic interests develop with regard to the Ottoman empire? Was the ruthless persecution of the Ottoman Armenians during the war inspired or condoned by Germany? These and related issues are the major concern of this study. No attempt has been made to describe the military events in the various Turkish theaters of war in detail. Historiographically, that is well-covered ground, and I have therefore purposely kept my references to frontline developments, naval engagements, etc., to a minimum.

My interest in the subject was first aroused when I looked through the newly opened wartime records of the German foreign office. The bulk of the documentation is taken from these and various other German government files, some of which are presently held in East German archives. In addition, I have consulted the wartime records of the Austro–Hungarian foreign ministry and the private papers of several contemporary figures. Permission to use the Turkish government archives

Preface

was not granted; it was therefore necessary to rely on translated, Turkish scholarly monographs and other secondary sources for information on the highly involved policy-making processes at the Porte. Wherever the available evidence was of dubious quality, the tentative nature of my conclusions has been indicated. Several topics have been omitted from the discussion. German subversive activities in Persia and Afghanistan and various frictions between Germans and Turks in connection with these enterprises have been exhaustively treated in a recently published study by Ulrich Gehrke; thus I have excluded that subject altogether. Similarly, no attempt has been made to deal with the Zionist Question. For a review of this issue the reader may refer, among others, to Saadia Weltman's article, "Germany, Turkey, and the Zionist Movement, 1914-1918," in the *Review of Politics* (1961). I have also ignored Germany's wartime propaganda and cultural programs in the Ottoman empire; let it be noted that the Germans themselves concluded at the end of the war that these programs had been of minimal political value.

In the initial stages of my research, my thesis adviser at the University of California, Professor Raymond J. Sontag, gave me much valuable guidance and assistance. I also profited from the advice of Werner T. Angress, Charles Jelavich, and Paul Seabury while I was a student at Berkeley and, more recently, from conversations or correspondence with Fritz T. Epstein, Hans Herzfeld, Gotthard Jäschke, Henry Cord Meyer, Dankwart A. Rustow, and Gerhard Weinberg. I am, of course, solely responsible for all errors of fact and judgment in this book.

My debts to librarians and archivists are heavy. I was given efficient assistance at the University of California Library at Berkeley, the Hoover War Memorial Library at Stanford, the National Archives, the Library of Congress, the New York Public Library, and the Yale University Library. At the Uni-

Preface

versity of Iowa Library, Mr. Dale M. Bentz, Mr. Frank Hanlin, and others satisfied my various requests with extraordinary understanding and kindness. My research in Europe was made both more profitable and enjoyable by the courteous assistance I received at the *Bundesarchiv* in Koblenz, the *Oesterreichisches Staatsarchiv* in Vienna, the Friedrich Meinecke Institute at the *Freie Universität*, Berlin, and, most particularly, at the *Deutsches Zentralarchiv*, Potsdam.

A travel grant from the Woodrow Wilson Foundation, an Old Gold Faculty Research Fellowship from the University of Iowa, and other financial assistance from that institution and from the University of Alberta facilitated the completion of this book. I also want to record my gratitude to Dr. Sedat Sami, who expertly translated a variety of Turkish publications for me, and to Mr. Joseph W. Baker for his help in copying documents from barely legible microfilms. The final copy was typed by Mrs. Mary R. Lyon.

My wife, Mary, helped me at every stage of my work and gave me much needed encouragement. I owe my greatest debt of gratitude to her and to Katherine, John, and Elizabeth, who patiently put up with the prolonged absences of their father.

Edmonton, Alberta, Canada   U.T.
February 1967

CONTENTS

ABBREVIATIONS

Archival Material

Identification of depositories in footnotes.

FO	German Foreign Office Archives, 1867-1920, Auswärtiges Amt, Bonn (American and British microfilm holdings)
AHFM	Austro-Hungarian Foreign Ministry Archives, Oesterreichisches Staatsarchiv, Vienna
DZA	Deutsches Zentralarchiv, Potsdam
Jackh Papers	The Papers of Ernst Jackh, Yale University Library
Kanner Papers	The Papers of Dr. Heinrich Kanner of Vienna, Hoover War Library, Stanford

Other abbreviations in footnotes

FO	Berlin Foreign Office
AHFM	Vienna Foreign Ministry
OHL	German Supreme Army Command
Dt	*Deutschland* (file citation)
Bd., Bde.	*Band, Bände* (volume[s] of German files)

Abbreviated Titles Used

As a rule, book titles have been omitted in all but the first footnote citation of each item. The following abbreviated titles are used where it is necessary to distinguish between several works of one author:

Fischer, *Weltmacht*	Fritz Fischer, *Griff nach der Weltmacht*
Lepsius, *Deutschland*	Johannes Lepsius, *Deutschland und Armenien 1914–1918*
——, *Bericht*	*Bericht über die Lage des Armenischen Volkes in der Türkei*

Abbreviations

Mühlmann, *Deutschland*	Carl Mühlmann, *Deutschland und die Türkei, 1913-1914*
———, *deutsch-türkische Waffenbündnis*	*Das deutsch-türkische Waffenbündnis im Weltkriege*
———, *Oberste Heeresleitung*	*Oberste Heeresleitung und Balkan im Weltkrieg 1914-1918*
Rathmann, *Stossrichtung*	Lothar Rathmann, *Stossrichtung Nahost 1914-1918*
Steglich, *Bündnissicherung*	Wolfgang Steglich, *Bündnissicherung oder Verständigungsfrieden*
———, *Friedenspolitik*	*Die Friedenspolitik der Mittelmächte 1917/18,* Bd. 1

Unless otherwise noted, all footnote references to Howard, Smith, and Wheeler-Bennett pertain to their works, *The Partition of Turkey, The Russian Struggle for Power: 1914-1917,* and *Brest-Litovsk,* respectively.

NOTE ON SPELLING AND
PLACE NAMES

Except in direct quotations from Western-language sources and similar special cases, all Ottoman personal names are spelled in consonance with modern Turkish usage. Thus Talaat Pasha appears as Talât Paşa, Djavid (or Javid) Bey as Cavid Bey, Mustapha Kemal as Mustafa Kemal, and so forth. The following notes on pronunciation may be helpful to the reader:

c "j" as in "job"
ç "ch" as in "child"
ş "sh" as in "shut"
ö French "eu" as in "peu"
ü French "u" as in "tu"

A circumflex over a vowel indicates a broadened sound.

The place names cited are generally those of the Ottoman period and rendered in the most customary English mode of spelling, for example, Constantinople instead of Istanbul, Smyrna instead of Izmir, Erzinjan instead of Erzincan. I apologize, particularly to Turkish readers, for taking these liberties.

Germany and the Ottoman Empire

1914-1918

CHAPTER I

The Eve of World War I

THE DECLINE of the vast and polyglot Ottoman empire after the 16th century and the concomitant appearance of numerous politically malleable spots in the Balkan peninsula, North Africa, and parts of western Asia may be termed one of the most important developments in the diplomatic history of modern Europe. As the once powerful state of the Ottoman sultans weakened and shrank because of administrative ineptitude, economic, intellectual, and technological stagnation, and the rebelliousness of some of its subject peoples, the Russian and Habsburg empires, as well as Britain and France, were drawn increasingly into Ottoman affairs—and into mutual competition for political and economic influence in the Near and Middle East. After the Napoleonic Wars these four great powers occasionally worked together, especially when it came to assisting some disaffected ethnic or religious group in the Sultan's realm, but usually their relationship in and along the edges of the Ottoman empire was marked by friction or outright animosity. Determined to prevent each other from gaining undue advantages from the weakness and possible collapse of the Ottoman state and intent on securing certain political or economic objectives in the Near and Middle East, the four great powers were repeatedly drawn, in various alignments, into conflict with each other. The clash of great power interests after 1815 was characterized by periodic Austro-Russian friction in the Balkans, several Anglo-Russian confrontations in the Straits region, intermittent Anglo-French quarrels over Egypt, and, most spectacularly of all, by the Crimean War in the 1850s.[1]

[1] For general introductions to the "Eastern Question" see Jacques Ancel, *Manuel historique de la question d'Orient* (4th edn., Paris, 1931); J.A.R. Marriot, *The Eastern Question* (4th edn., Oxford, 1940);

The Eve of World War I

During the last two decades of the 19th century the rivalry of the great powers in the Near and Middle East assumed a new dimension with the appearance of imperial Germany on the scene. Initially, the newly founded Reich had proved most reluctant to become actively involved in the "Eastern Question," but during the 1880s, and more particularly after Bismarck's dismissal, Berlin gradually abandoned its policy of restraint. Prussian military reformers and agents of Germany's armaments industry made their appearance in Constantinople, the latter soon outbidding some of the traditional foreign suppliers of the Sultan's army and navy. In addition, German banks, industrial firms, and railroad interests moved into the underdeveloped lands of Sultan Abdülhamid II and secured concessions, markets, and spheres of influence for themselves. Although German governmental support of many of these ventures was initially rather fitful, it became more and more pronounced as time went by. Kaiser Wilhelm II himself twice journeyed to the Ottoman empire before the turn of the century and during the second visit (in 1898) delivered pointedly pro-Ottoman and pro-Islamic speeches. Simultaneously, some

---

L. S. Stavrianos, *The Balkans since 1453* (New York, 1958); and the excellent new study by M. S. Anderson, *The Eastern Question, 1774-1923* (London, 1966).

The entrenchment of foreign capital in the Ottoman empire, especially after the 18th century, is well covered in D. C. Blaisdell, *European Financial Control in the Ottoman Empire* (New York, 1929); and Nasim Sousa, *The Capitulatory Regime of Turkey* (Baltimore, 1933).

On Russia's aspirations at the Straits and the counter-moves of the other European powers—especially Britain—useful summaries may be found in James T. Shotwell and Francis Deák, *Turkey at the Straits* (New York, 1940); Ettore Anchieri, *Constantinopoli e gli Stretti nella politica russa ed Europea* (Milan, 1948); B. A. Dranov, *Chernomorskiye prolivy* [The Black Sea Straits] (Moscow, 1948); and Egmont Zechlin, *Die türkischen Meerengen–Brennpunkt der Weltgeschichte* (Hamburg, 1964).

nationalistic groups in Germany, particularly the Pan-German League, began to talk openly of the need for expanding German influence in the Ottoman empire.[2]

Germany's *pénétration pacifique* of the Sultan's lands, crowned by the initiation of the "Bagdad Railroad" project, naturally provoked misgivings in Russia, Britain, and France, each of them having "traditional" interests in the Ottoman empire or adjacent regions. There is no need here to enumerate the various strategic, political, and economic interests of these countries which were hurt, or at least threatened, by Wilhelmian Germany's ventures into the Near and Middle East, or to discuss the diplomatic frictions which resulted from this clash of interests. Suffice it to note that from the 1890s on Germany's efforts to extend its economic, political, and military influence in the Ottoman empire put a serious strain on its general relations with Russia and Britain, and, to a lesser extent, with France. On some issues, notably the Bagdad railroad, tensions were ultimately reduced by a series of compromise settlements (the last one, with Britain, being concluded in the summer of 1914), but it is generally agreed today that the frictions between Germany and the Entente powers in and

---

[2] Cf. Hajo Holborn, "Deutschland und die Türkei 1878-90," *Archiv für Politik und Geschichte,* v (1925), 111-59; Mary E. Townsend, *The Rise and Fall of Germany's Colonial Empire 1884-1918* (New York, 1930), pp. 208-19; W. O. Henderson, *Studies in German Colonial History* (London, 1962), pp. 74-79; George W. F. Hallgarten, *Imperialismus vor 1914,* 2 vols. (rev. edn., Munich, 1963), i, 223-49, 266-70, 306-308, 474-83, 595-610, and *passim;* and the recent Marxist interpretations in A. S. Jerussalimski, *Die Aussenpolitik und die Diplomatie des deutschen Imperialismus Ende des 19. Jahrhunderts* (2d edn., Berlin, 1954), *passim,* especially pp. 265ff.; and Lothar Rathmann, *Berlin-Bagdad* (Berlin, 1962), pp. 5-63.

On Pan-German agitation for the eventual acquisition of living space in the Ottoman lands during the 1890s, see Alfred Kruck, *Geschichte des Alldeutschen Verbandes 1890-1939* (Wiesbaden, 1954), pp. 38-40.

along the edges of the Ottoman empire contributed substantially to the general atmosphere of distrust which made the First World War possible.[3]

The troubled relations between Germany and the Entente powers in the Near and Middle East prior to the outbreak of World War I have been analyzed and elucidated in numerous excellent studies. The prewar relationship between Germany and the Ottoman empire itself, on the other hand, has remained relatively obscure, and historical opinion on that subject is still very much divided. While some scholars have suggested that Germany's general influence in the Ottoman empire on the eve of World War I was not extraordinary, perhaps even on the decline,[4] others have concluded that by 1914 the Ottoman empire was little more than a satellite of the Reich.[5]

[3] Most of the standard histories on the origins of World War I (S. B. Fay, B. E. Schmitt, Luigi Albertini, A.J.P. Taylor, etc.) offer excellent coverage of these subjects. See also Christopher Andrew, "German World Policy and the Reshaping of the Dual Alliance," *Journal of Contemporary History*, 1:3 (1966), 137-51.

On the international repercussions of the Bagdad railroad project the pioneering study by Edward Mead Earle, *Turkey, the Great Powers, and the Bagdad Railway* (New York, 1923) has been supplemented and partly superseded by several more recent works, among them John B. Wolf, *The Diplomatic History of the Bagdad Railroad* (Columbia, Mo., 1936); Louis Ragey, *La question du chemin de fer de Bagdad* (Paris, 1936); Maybelle K. Chapman, *Great Britain and the Bagdad Railway, 1888-1914* (Northampton, Mass., 1948); E. R. J. Brünner, *De Bagdadspoorweg . . . 1888-1908* (Groningen, 1957); and Hallgarten, *Imperialismus vor 1914.*

[4] See, for example, Henry Cord Meyer, *Mitteleuropa in German Thought and Action, 1815-1945* (The Hague, 1955), p. 72; Fritz Fischer, "Weltpolitik, Weltmachtstreben und deutsche Kriegsziele," *Historische Zeitschrift*, 199 (1964), pp. 265-346, and *passim*, especially 308-22.

[5] For emphatic support of this thesis in recent monographic works, see W. W. Gottlieb, *Studies in Secret Diplomacy During the First World War* (London, 1957), p. 33; Lothar Rathmann, "Zur Legende vom 'anti-kolonialen' Charakter der Bagdadbahnpolitik in der wil-

The Eve of World War I

In order to clarify this issue and thus put the evolution of German-Ottoman relations during the war years into proper perspective, it will be necessary to review briefly the economic, political, and military ties that linked the two countries in the summer of 1914.

In many ways Germany's involvement in the internal affairs of the Ottoman empire during the prewar decades was most noticeable in the economic sphere. In fact, the search for markets, raw materials, and lucrative investment opportunities was practically the only constant in Germany's prewar activities in the Sultan's realm. What had the Germans accomplished by 1914?

As far as their most ambitious venture, the construction of a railroad from the Bosporus to Bagdad, is concerned, it is essential to remember that this project was only partially completed by the summer of 1914.[6] While the main line from Haydar Pasha, on the Bosporus, theoretically extended to a point just beyond the Euphrates River, there were still two unfinished sections in the Taurus and Amanus ranges which dras-

helminischen Aera des deutschen Monopolkapitalismus," *Zeitschrift für Geschichtswissenschaft, Sonderheft IX. Jahrgang* (1961), p. 253; and A. F. Miller, *Pyatidesyatiletye mladoturetskoi revolutsii* [The Fiftieth Anniversary of the Young Turkish Revolution] (Moscow, 1958), pp. 44-45. Miller's assertion that "German imperialism" had gained "full domination over Turkey" by 1914 has been incorporated verbatim into the most recent Soviet world history. See E. M. Shukov, editor-in-chief, *Vsemirnaya istoriya* [Universal History] 10 vols. (Moscow, 1955-65), VII, 360.

[6] The technical and financial aspects of the construction project up to the outbreak of World War I are covered in Hermann Schmidt, *Das Eisenbahnwesen in der asiatischen Türkei* (Berlin, 1914); Carl Mühlmann, "Die deutschen Bahnunternehmungen in der asiatischen Türkei, 1888-1914," *Weltwirtschaftliches Archiv*, 24 (Oct. 1926), pp. 121-37, 365-99; Orhan Conker, *Les chemins de fer en Turquie et la politique ferroviaire turque* (Paris, 1935); and Herbert Pönicke, "Heinrich August Meissner-Pascha und der Bau der Hedschas- und Bagdadbahn," *Die Welt als Geschichte*, 16 (1956), pp. 196-210.

tically limited the usefulness of the railroad. The track laid from the eastern terminal, Bagdad, on the other hand, had not quite reached Samara by the beginning of World War I, and even this stretch was of limited use because of its remoteness from the major sections of the line.[7] As will be shown later, the truncated state of the Bagdad line not only occasioned serious military problems during the war years, but also gave rise to a multitude of squabbles between Germans and Turks. For the moment, it should be noted that contrary to widespread contemporary charges, the Bagdad railroad enterprise was as yet neither capable of dominating the economic life of the Ottoman empire nor a suitable instrument for exerting political pressure on the Porte. On the contrary, by 1914 the railroad faced grave financial problems, and after 1914 it fell increasingly under the control of the Ottoman military authorities and provincial government agencies.[8]

Aside from the promotion of the Bagdad railroad project, German economic activity in the Ottoman empire in the prewar decades was characterized by heavy investment in the areas of municipal transportation, electric utilities, agriculture, and mining, and by a steadily mounting volume of trade between the two countries. Among the German companies doing business in or with the Ottoman empire, particularly important were: the *Deutsche Bank* of Berlin, the *Deutsche Orientbank*, the *Deutsche Palästina Bank*, the Krupp and Mauser com-

[7] Contrary to the data given in most modern literature on the Bagdad railroad, a large part of the track from Tell el Abyad to Ras el Ain (a stretch of 103 kilometers along the present Turkish-Syrian border) had not been laid by the outbreak of World War I. The total length of missing trackage between Haydar Pasha and Bagdad as of August 1, 1914 was therefore about 825 km (roughly 500 American miles). Cf. Richard Hennig, *Die deutschen Bahnbauten in der Türkei, ihr politischer, militärischer und wirtschaftlicher Wert* (Leipzig, 1915), p. 9; and FO, *Türkei 152*, Bd. 79, Rössler to Bethmann Hollweg, 20 Oct 1914; Rosenberg to Zimmermann, 27 Nov 1914.

[8] See Chapter IX.

The Eve of World War I

panies, the *Siemens Bau A.G.*, the *Hamburg-Amerika* steamship company, the *Deutsch-Levantinische Baumwoll-bau-Gesellschaft*, and the *Anatolische Handels- und Industriegesellschaft*. But there were numerous other firms which also profited from the progressive opening up of the Ottoman market.[9] However, despite the steady increase of German investments in and trade with the Ottoman empire from the 1880s to 1914, the Reich did not secure a controlling position in the Ottoman economy. On the eve of World War I several other European countries, notably France and Britain, were still firmly entrenched economically and even ahead of Germany in several areas.[10]

As the following table indicates, Germany was still lagging behind Britain, France, and Austria-Hungary in terms of imports from the Ottoman empire and almost equally far behind

[9] For detailed information on the various German enterprises in the Ottoman empire prior to the war, see Gottlieb, pp. 21-24; Henderson, pp. 77-82; Hallgarten, I and II, *passim*; Kurt Hassert, *Das Türkische Reich* (Tübingen, 1918), pp. 201-202; and Rathmann, *Berlin-Bagdad, passim*.

[10] On the influx of European capital and the expanding control of foreign interests over broad sectors of the Ottoman economy in the prewar decades, cf. Blaisdell, pp. 1-184; Gottlieb, pp. 19-27; Hallgarten, I and II, *passim*; Herbert Feis, *Europe, the World's Banker, 1870-1914* (New Haven, 1930), pp. 313-60; Orhan Conker and Emile Witmeur, *Redressement économique et Industrialisation de la Nouvelle Turquie* (Paris, 1937), pp. 41-53; Osman Nebioglu, *Die Auswirkungen der Kapitulationen auf die türkische Wirtschaft* [Probleme der Weltwirtschaft, Universität Kiel, v. 68] (Jena, 1941), part 2, *passim*; and Edwin Borchard and William H. Wynne, *State Insolvency and Foreign Bondholders*, 2 vols. (New Haven, 1951), II, 393-481.

The extent of foreign control over the Ottoman economy by 1914 can be gauged by the fact that out of a total of 244 industrial enterprises in the Ottoman empire only 54 were Turkish. Similarly, of the total Ottoman railroad trackage of 5,443 km, 3,910 km were operated by foreign concessionaires. See Nebioglu, p. 60; and Reinhard Hüber, *Die Bagdadbahn* (Berlin, 1943), p. 49.

both Britain and Austria-Hungary in the volume of exports to the Ottoman empire.[11]

Value of Ottoman Exports in 1913
(in Turkish pounds gold [T£])

TO	
Britain	4,661,000
France	4,294,000
Austria-Hungary	2,238,000
Germany	1,234,000

Value of Ottoman Imports in 1913
(in Turkish pounds gold [T£])

FROM	
Britain	8,128,000
Austria-Hungary	6,146,000
Germany	4,688,000
France	3,591,000

Similarly, Germany's total capital investments in the Ottoman empire were still considerably smaller than those of France. While French investments by 1914 amounted to at least 800 million gold francs (and possibly exceeded 900 million), the total of German investments lay somewhere between 500 and 600 million.[12] A major portion of the German capital, roughly 340 million francs, was invested in the Ottoman rail-

[11] Nebioglu, p. 64. These data, which are based on official Turkish statistics, may be misleading in that some of the German trade was handled by Austro–Hungarian middlemen and hence listed as Austrian, but there can be no doubt whatever that Britain's share in the foreign trade of the Ottoman empire was still much larger than that of Germany. Cf. Hassert, pp. 194-95; and Gottlieb, p. 21. Meyer's conclusion, p. 72, that Germany had only eight percent of Turkey's trade in 1914 is, on the other hand, not entirely convincing.

[12] Cf. Nebioglu, p. 69; Conker and Witmeur, p. 53; Feis, pp. 319-20; and Pierre Renouvin, *Le XIXe Siècle: II. De 1871 à 1914* [Histoire des relations internationales, v. 6] (Paris, 1955), 274.

road system, particularly in the Bagdad line, compared with about 320 million francs the French had put into this sector of the Ottoman economy.[13]

The French share in the "Ottoman Public Debt," which was administered by an international agency on behalf of the Porte's creditors, by 1914 amounted to approximately 59 percent, while Germany and Britain were holding about equal shares of most of the remainder.[14] The financial influence of France and Britain in the prewar Ottoman empire can also be gauged by the position of the *Banque Impériale Ottomane* (BIO), the leading Franco-British bank in Constantinople. Aside from controlling the Tobacco Monopoly and a large number of business enterprises in the Ottoman empire, the BIO still enjoyed the prerogatives of a state bank; that is, it had a legal monopoly on the issue of bank notes in the empire. Although bank notes and other types of paper money were used on only a modest scale in the Ottoman empire prior to the war, the privileged status of the BIO in the monetary sphere was by no means unimportant, as events after July 1914 were to show.[15]

[13] Hüber, p. 49. Cf., however, Nebioglu, p. 69, and Feis, p. 320, who list the French railroad investments as about 235 million and over half a billion francs, respectively.

[14] The exact size of the Ottoman public debt and the proportionate shares held by French, German, and British creditors have never been firmly established. However, there is reasonable certainty that the French share amounted to about 2.4 billion francs and that this constituted at least 59 percent of the total debt. Cf. Sousa, p. 77, note 23; Feis, p. 320, note 8; Borchard and Wynne, II, 479; Gottlieb, p. 20; Adib Roumani, *Essai historique et technique sur la Dette Publique Ottomane* (Paris, 1927), pp. 321-23; and Rondo E. Cameron, *France and the Economic Development of Europe, 1800-1914* (Princeton, 1961), p. 264.

[15] On the background and functions of the BIO prior to the war cf. Feis, pp. 320-21; Borchert and Wynne, II, 400ff.; Gottlieb, pp. 20-21; Cameron, pp. 187-89, *passim*; Hallgarten, I and II, *passim*; Ahmed Emin, *Turkey in the World War* (New Haven, 1930), p. 161; and David S. Landes, *Bankers and Pashas* (Cambridge, Mass., 1958), pp. 6off.

Finally, note should be taken of the implications of the Capitulatory System. Under this system, which had evolved through the centuries into a veritable economic strait jacket for the Porte, all the great European powers enjoyed a variety of special privileges in the Ottoman empire, among them the right to veto any changes in the external tariff rates of that country.[16] During the pre-1914 period this right was used repeatedly by one or the other great power to restrict the Porte or another European state which, for reasons of its own, wished to see the customs revenues of the Ottoman empire increased— as Germany, for instance, desired after the turn of the century.[17]

Altogether, it is clear that despite the great advances the Germans had made since the 1880s, their economic and financial power in the Ottoman empire at the beginning of World War I was still effectively counterbalanced by that of the other European powers.

As for Germany's political influence in Constantinople in 1914, it is true that Berlin's diplomatic relations with the *Ittihad ve Terakki* regime—as with most previous Ottoman governments—were generally cordial. However, the Porte had by no means abandoned the traditional Ottoman policy of maintaining a balance between the great powers, as is amply demonstrated by the twists and turns of its diplomacy in the pre-July period.[18] It has often been alleged that by that time the Turks

[16] See Sousa, *passim*; Walther Lehmann, *Die Kapitulationen* (Weimar, 1917), *passim*; Max Kunke, *Die Kapitulationen der Türkei* (Munich, 1918), part II. Nebioglu's conclusion, p. 74, that by 1914 the capitulatory system had reduced the Ottoman empire "economically to a colony of virtually all of Europe" is justified.

[17] On Britain's and Russia's resistance to an increase of Ottoman customs duties from 8 to 11 percent ad valorem, which was desired by the Porte and Germany in connection with the Bagdad railroad project, see Blaisdell, pp. 158-70; and Chapman, pp. 43ff.

[18] While most of the standard works on the origins of World War I and a few specialized studies, such as Harry N. Howard, *The Partition of Turkey. A Diplomatic History, 1913-1923* (Norman, Okla.,

were no longer masters of their own house because of the entrenchment of German officers in their army, but the evidence hardly supports the conclusion. While it is certainly true that the dispatch in 1913 of a new military mission under Gen. Otto Liman von Sanders resulted in a substantial increase of Germany's general influence in the Ottoman empire, this did not convert that country into a reliable ally of the Reich, let alone a helpless satellite. Gen. Liman's mission, which grew to about 70 members before August 1914, was given a great deal of latitude in the modernization and reform of the Ottoman army, but since virtually all command functions were retained by the Turks, it is simply not true that the Germans controlled the Sultan's military establishment and hence the country at large. It should be noted, moreover, that from 1908 on the Porte was employing high-ranking British officers as advisers on naval matters, which included the defense of the Straits. By 1914 the British naval mission in Constantinople, headed by Rear Adm. Sir Arthur H. Limpus, had in fact almost as many members as the German military mission.[19]

1931), include useful surveys of Ottoman prewar diplomacy, a more thorough treatment of that subject is definitely needed. 'The domestic situation in the Ottoman empire on the eve of the war is covered most authoritatively in Yusuf H. Bayur, *Türk inkilâbi tarihi* [History of the Turkish Reform], 3 [9] vols. (Istanbul and Ankara, 1940-57), II, *passim*; and Bernard Lewis, *The Emergence of Modern Turkey* (London, 1961), *passim*. For information on the organization and programs of the *Ittihad ve Terakki* Party Tarik Z. Tunaya's compendium, *Türkiyede siyasî partiler 1859-1952* [The Political Parties of Turkey, 1859-1952] (Istanbul, 1952), is particularly useful.

[19] On the international repercussions of Liman's dispatch to Constantinople and the prewar activities of his mission, cf. Carl Mühlmann, *Deutschland und die Türkei 1913-1914* (Berlin, 1929), pp. 1-27; "Die deutsche Militär-Mission in der Türkei," *Wissen und Wehr*, XIX (1938), 847-55; Hans Herzfeld, "Die Liman-Krise und die Politik der Grossmächte in der Jahreswende 1913/14," *Berliner Monatshefte*, XI (1933), 837-58, 973-93; Hallgarten, II, 429-46; and Liman's own ac-

Some foreign observers in Constantinople, among them the American ambassador to the Porte, Henry Morgenthau, were impressed and disturbed in the prewar months by the apparent Prussianization of the Sultan's army, especially after they had witnessed a parade of goose-stepping Turkish troops.[20] Germany's own military leaders, on the other hand, were generally sceptical about the strength and preparedness of the Ottoman army. Only six weeks before the Sarajevo incident the chief of the Prussian general staff, Gen. Helmuth von Moltke, concluded that it was most inappropriate to reckon with "Turkey in the foreseeable future as an asset [*zugunsten*] for the Triple Alliance or Germany."[21] In connection with this remark, it should be added that in 1913, when it had sent Liman and his men to Turkey, Berlin had explicitly reserved the right to recall the entire mission in the event of a European war, a provision which hardly supports the conclusion that Ottoman belligerency on Germany's side, and the direction of the Ottoman army by German officers, were taken for granted in Berlin from late 1913 on.[22]

How little the German government was actually counting on the Ottoman empire as a natural ally in the foreseeable future was demonstrated most clearly during the weeks follow-

---

count, *Five Years in Turkey* (Annapolis, Md., 1927), pp. 1-21. For an influential statement of the thesis that Liman's mission had the effect of delivering "Turkey into German hands," see Robert J. Kerner, "The Mission of Liman von Sanders," *Slavonic Review*, vi (1927-28), 12-27, 344-63, 543-60, vii (1928), 90-112. On the British naval mission see Arthur J. Marder, *From the Dreadnought to Scapa Flow. The Royal Navy in the Fisher Era, 1904-1919* (London, 1961-), i, 302.

[20] See Henry Morgenthau, *Ambassador Morgenthau's Story* (New York, 1918), pp. 46-47. As will be shown later on, Morgenthau's memoirs (which have been used as a major source by many Western authors) are of uneven quality.

[21] See Carl Mühlmann, *Das deutsch–türkische Waffenbündnis im Weltkriege* (Leipzig, 1940), pp. 13-14.

[22] See Liman's contract with the Porte in Mühlmann, *Deutschland*, pp. 88-92.

The Eve of World War I

ing the Sarajevo incident. Although the international horizon was steadily darkening—not least of all because of Berlin's own policy—the German government did little if anything to assure itself of Ottoman assistance in the event the Austro-Serbian conflict erupted into a European war. Instead, it was a group of Ottoman government figures who first proposed a closer relationship between the two countries, and even these overtures (presented by the war minister, Enver Paşa, on July 22) were initially turned down by the German ambassador to the Porte, Hans von Wangenheim.[23] His negative reaction may conceivably have been influenced by his personal conviction that the Ottoman armed forces were as yet a negligible quantity, but all available evidence points to the conclusion that he acted in accordance with standing policy directives. As has long been known, the Kaiser personally overruled the ambassador on July 24 with the explanation that "at the present moment" (the Austrian ultimatum to Serbia had been delivered the previous evening) Ottoman interest in a connection with the Triple Alliance should be taken advantage of "for reasons of expediency."[24]

As a result of this sudden change in Berlin's policy—obviously made in response to the threat of imminent war—negotiations concerning the scope and nature of the proposed Ottoman alignment with the Triple Alliance were initiated in Constantinople, and on July 28 a formal Ottoman alliance proposal was presented to Berlin.[25] It should be emphasized that even after the German government had secured the agreement of the Ottoman negotiators to certain modifications in the original

[23] *Die deutschen Dokumente zum Kriegsausbruch*, collected by Karl Kautsky, 4 vols. (Berlin, 1919), No. 117. See also Luigi Albertini, *The Origins of the War of 1914*, 3 vols. (London, 1952-57), III, 607-12.

[24] *Die deutschen Dokumente zum Kriegsausbruch*, Nos. 141, 144. Mühlmann, *Deutschland*, pp. 40-41, emphasizes that Berlin had just previously learned from Liman that four or five Turkish army corps were sufficiently equipped for use in the field.

[25] *Die deutschen Dokumente zum Kriegsausbruch*, No. 285.

draft treaty, the leading statesmen in Berlin proved remarkably hesitant to make a final commitment. As Chancellor Theobald von Bethmann Hollweg wired to the Constantinople embassy on the evening of July 31, Wangenheim was to sign the alliance only if it was certain that "Turkey either can or will undertake some action against Russia worthy of the name."[26]

For reasons to be discussed below, the ambassador decided two days later that this condition was met. In the early afternoon of August 2 he and the Ottoman grand vizier, Prince Mehmed Said Halim Paşa, affixed their signatures to the treaty document. Reflecting the delays occasioned by Berlin's hesitant attitude, some sections of the treaty text were already obsolete at the moment it was signed. Articles 1 and 2 provided for Ottoman intervention on Germany's side if the latter became involved in a war with Russia in connection with the Austro-Serbian conflict—an eventuality which, of course, had already become reality. Under Article 3 Germany agreed to leave the Liman von Sanders mission "at the disposal of Turkey," while the Porte, in turn, assured the mission "an effective influence on the general direction of the [Ottoman] army." The treaty further obligated Germany to help protect the territorial integrity of the Ottoman empire and stipulated that the alliance was "secret" and would remain in effect beyond December 31, 1918 unless formally renounced by either party.[27]

The German-Ottoman alliance of 1914 was not the logical culmination of carefully laid German plans; it was a hastily made arrangement.[28] Much has been written about the fact

[26] *Ibid.*, No. 508. Interestingly enough, Bethmann Hollweg made this point once again the following day (*ibid.*, No. 547).

[27] The alliance terms were first published in *ibid.*, No. 733. The original treaty may be found in FO, *Verträge 94.*

[28] For detailed analyses of the alliance negotiations, cf. Mühlmann, *Deutschland*, pp. 28-43; and Albertini, III, 605-15. See also Fritz Fischer, "Weltpolitik, Weltmachtstreben und deutsche Kriegsziele," p. 340. That Berlin's willingness in July 1914 to risk a general war stemmed at least partly from its concern about Germany's economic and political

that the alliance negotiations were initiated and brought to fruition by a small clique of Ottoman ministers, and that several members of the Ottoman cabinet were neither aware of nor agreeable to the formal alignment of their country with the Reich. It has been suggested that the furtive activities of the pro-alliance group were not only highly improper but also indicative of the spell which the Germans had cast on some of the leading figures of the *Ittihad ve Terakki* regime.[29] It would appear, though, that Germanophile sentiments actually had very little to do with the decisions of the pro-alliance group at the Porte.

Of the three Ottoman cabinet ministers who were most directly involved in the alliance negotiations, two—the grand vizier, Prince Said Halim (who simultaneously also served as the minister of foreign affairs), and the minister of interior, Mehmed Talât Bey—had never shown any particular pro-German orientation. To be sure, Said Halim, the cultivated scion of an Egyptian princely family, was an indecisive man and allowed himself to be manipulated by his colleagues throughout much of his tenure as grand vizier (1913-17), but there is no evidence that his association with the pro-alliance group in July 1914 was involuntary or, for that matter, the result of German bribes or blandishments. As for Talât Bey, the ex-telegraph operator who had become one of the most power-

---

prospects in the Balkans and Turkey (*ibid.*, pp. 342-43 and *passim*) is quite possible. But the recent assertion by Karl-Heinz Janssen, *Der Kanzler und der General. Die Führungskrise um Bethmann Hollweg und Falkenhayn 1914-1916* (Göttingen, 1967), p. 144 and *passim*, that Germany and Austria-Hungary ventured into war "only" because of their "Oriental interests and power positions," appears rather farfetched.

[29] For representative samples of the thesis that many figures in the Ottoman government had been "bought" or otherwise turned into minions of Berlin, see Sir James E. Edmonds, *A Short History of World War I* (London, 1951), p. 104; Gottlieb, pp. 32-33; or Sydney N. Fisher, *The Middle East* (New York, 1959), p. 361.

ful figures in the *Ittihad ve Terakki* Party organization and, hence, in the cabinet as well, it has been conceded even by hostile critics that he was intensely nationalistic and personally incorruptible. The idea that German inducements had anything to do with his option for an alliance with the Reich should therefore be dismissed as well.[30]

The situation is less clear-cut with regard to the third main figure of the pro-alliance clique, the war minister Enver Paşa. It is well known that this youthful general (he was 32 at the beginning of World War I) admired Germany, which he knew from a two-year tour of duty in Berlin as Ottoman military attaché (1909-11).[31] However, even though Enver was definitely impressed by the spirit and might of the German army and even wore a mustache after the style of Wilhelm II, his reputation as the "Kaiser's man" is not altogether valid. In particular, there is now evidence to show that the onetime friendship between Wilhelm II and Enver had cooled considerably by the summer of 1914. Their estrangement had its origin in the *coup d'état* of January 1913 in Constantinople, which had returned the *Ittihad ve Terakki* Party to power, and during which the Ottoman war minister, General Nazim Paşa, had been shot dead in Enver's presence.[32] Wilhelm II reacted very unfavorably to this incident. Since he also sus-

[30] On the background and political careers of Said Halim and Talât see Ibnülemin Mahmud Kemal Inal, *Osmanli devrinde son sadriazamlar* [The Last Grand Viziers of the Ottoman Period], 14 vols. (Istanbul, 1940-53), XII-XIII, 1893-1972; Lewis, pp. 221-22; and their *curricula vitae* in FO, *Türkei 152 Nr. 2*, Bd. 18.

[31] The best brief survey of Enver's career is Dankwart A. Rustow's article "Enwer Pasha," *Encyclopaedia of Islam*, rev. edn. (Leiden, 1960-), II, 698-702. See also Enver's *vita* in FO, *Türkei 152 Nr. 2*, Bd. 18; and, for the opinions of contemporaries, Morgenthau, pp. 30-34, *passim*; Capt. H. Seignobosc, *Turcs et Turquie* (Paris, 1920), pp. 39-48; or Joseph Pomiankowski, *Der Zusammenbruch des Ottomanischen Reiches* (Vienna, 1928), pp. 38-41, *passim*.

[32] An excellent brief summary of the events leading up to the coup is given by Lewis, pp. 206-21.

pected that Enver was sympathetic to the promotion of an anti-dynastic policy in the Ottoman empire, he emphatically ordered that Enver be kept from returning to Berlin.[33] Moreover, there are indications that the Kaiser subsequently became very cordial with the new Ottoman ambassador in Berlin, General Mahmud Muhtar Paşa, a bitter rival of Enver. Even after Enver had taken over the Ottoman war ministry in January 1914, thus assuming a pivotal position in the government, the Kaiser continued to make critical remarks about him, many of which were gleefully communicated to the Porte by Muhtar.[34]

Although Enver's motives in supporting an alliance with Germany cannot be established with any certainty, his initial proposals to Berlin (on July 22) strongly suggest that both he and his like-minded colleagues at the Porte were guided primarily by sober calculations of Ottoman self-interest. As Enver explained to Wangenheim with remarkable candor, the domestic reforms planned by the Young Turks could be carried out only if the Ottoman empire were "secured against attacks from abroad," that is, if it won "the support of one of the groups of Great Powers." While some elements in the *Ittihad ve Terakki* Party favored an alliance "with France and Russia," he continued, a majority of the Party's committee, headed by Said Halim, Talât, himself, and the President of the Chamber of

[33] See FO, *Dt 127 Nr. 6*, Bd. 3, Jagow to embassy Constantinople, 1 Feb 1913, No. 38; Chelius to FO, 1 Feb Gottlieb, p. 32, has pointed out that "German High Finance" had "spurred on" the coup and concludes that Enver's success "was a victory for the Kaiser," but this is a rather oversimplified version of what actually happened. Cf. Hallgarten, II, 371-73.

[34] FO, *Dt 127 Nr. 6*, Bd. 3, Wangenheim to Bethmann Hollweg, 8 May 1913, No. 139; Jagow to Wilhelm II, 8 Jan 1914; Mutius to FO, 8 Jan, No. 14; Jagow to embassy Constantinople, 9 Jan, No. 7; Mutius to Bethmann Hollweg, 14 Jan, No. 16; Wangenheim to FO, 4 March, No. 105. See also Jackh Papers, No. 3, "Auszug aus einem Brief des Kapitän Humann . . . ," 1 May 1915; and Kanner Papers, II, 295, "Unterredung mit Professor Lepsius am 4. Oktober. . . ."

The Eve of World War I

Deputies, Halil Bey, preferred a closer alignment with the Triple Alliance; for they did not wish to become the "vassals of Russia" and furthermore were convinced that the "Triple Alliance was stronger militarily than the Entente, and would prove the victor in case of a world war." The alliance proposal was thus quite bluntly presented from the very start as a matter of Ottoman self-interest, a point underscored by Enver's explicit warning that if Germany did not respond favorably, the Porte, "with heavy hearts," would have to associate itself with the Entente.[35]

Since the Kaiser immediately accepted the alliance proposal, it is, of course, impossible to tell whether Enver's warning was merely a bluff. What does seem clear, though, is that the pro-alliance group at the Porte made its choice for the Triple Alliance—that is, for Germany—primarily (and probably exclusively), on the basis of strict *raison d'état*. Although their decision for the Triple Alliance turned out to be a catastrophic mistake, it was the product of miscalculations regarding the actual strength of Germany and her allies rather than of unpatriotic submission to German wishes or pressures. This interpretation, it should be added, appears all the more warranted in view of the fact that between May and mid-July 1914 the Porte had made both an alliance proposal to Russia (through Talât) and a bid for closer relations with France (through navy minister Ahmed Cemal Paşa), only to be politely rebuffed in either case.[36]

[35] See *Die deutschen Dokumente zum Kriegsausbruch*, No. 117.

[36] Cf. B. E. Schmitt, *The Coming of the War, 1914*, 2 vols. (New York, 1930), I, 91; Gottlieb, pp. 34-35; I. V. Bestuzhev, "Russian Foreign Policy February-June 1914," *Journal of Contemporary History*, 1:3 (1966), 110-11 and *passim*. See also *Die Internationalen Beziehungen im Zeitalter des Imperialismus. Dokumente aus den Archiven der Zarischen und der Provisorischen Regierung. . .*, M. Pokrovski, ed., ser. 1, 5 vols. (Berlin, 1931-34), II, Nos. 295, 312, *Beilage* and *passim*; and *Documents diplomatiques français (1871-1914)*, 42 vols. (Paris, 1929-59), ser. 3, x, No. 504.

CHAPTER II

From Alliance Treaty to Intervention

AR FROM signaling the beginning of "complete" or "almost complete" German domination of the Ottoman empire,[1] the alliance treaty of August 2, 1914 was from the outset an arrangement between diplomatic equals, notwithstanding the enormous disparity between the two countries in terms of military, economic, and financial power. The failure of the Germans to convert their alliance with the Turks into a "rider-horse" relationship will be demonstrated in detail in the course of this book. However, it might be noted here that throughout the war the Germans were handicapped most decisively in their policy toward the Turks by the simple fact that they considered Ottoman military assistance essential for their own war effort. While there were some German officials, notably in the diplomatic service, who had grave doubts about the worth of the Ottoman alliance, virtually all of the top military and political figures in the Reich came to regard the Ottoman ally as an indispensable partner in the struggle for survival and ultimate victory. It was, above all, this prevailing attitude in German government circles that gave the Turks the means to stand up to or even exploit their more powerful ally right up to the end of the war.

It has often been suggested that the Germans were not particularly interested in active Ottoman assistance as long as their own invasion of France seemed to be going well.[2] Such

[1] Allegations that the Ottoman empire fell increasingly under German control after the outbreak of the war are common in Soviet publications, but may also be found in many Western works. See, for example, A. D. Novichev, *Ekonomika Turtsii v period mirovoi voini* [Turkey's Economy During the World War] (Moscow, 1935), pp. 139-40; Shukov, VII, 572; Howard, pp. 102, 114; Gottlieb, pp. 57-60; Fisher, p. 363.

[2] For a rather melodramatic version of this thesis, see Gottlieb, pp. 57-58.

From Alliance Treaty to Intervention

a conclusion is erroneous. Ottoman military help against both Russia and Britain was desired by Berlin from the very first week of the war. While the Prussian general staff and the Wilhelmstrasse had been remarkably hesitant in getting the Turks lined up on the side of the Central Powers, they radically changed their attitude once hostilities actually began. Confronted with the reality of a two-front war and a formal offer of assistance from the Turks, both Moltke and the civilian leaders at the Wilhelmstrasse during the first days of August abandoned their previous reserve and called for immediate Ottoman intervention against Russia. Moreover, even though the German-Ottoman alliance treaty of August 2 was formally directed against Russia alone, Moltke by August 5 began demanding prompt Ottoman assistance against the Western Entente powers as well.[3]

The desirability of stirring up trouble in and of launching military operations against Britain's Middle East possessions in the event of an Anglo-German conflict had long been publicly discussed in Germany and was a recurring theme in the Kaiser's famous marginalia, but there is no evidence that Berlin had any coherent action plans on hand when World War I broke out. Neither the correspondence between the Wilhelmstrasse and the German embassy in Constantinople, nor that between the Prussian general staff and Liman von Sanders' military mission, contains the slightest reference to any kind of contingency plan. The measures which were initiated in August 1914 to carry the war into Britain's Middle East possessions bore all the earmarks of hasty improvisation.[4]

[3] *Die deutschen Dokumente zum Kriegsausbruch*, Nos. 662, 836, 876.
[4] According to Fritz Fischer, *Griff nach der Weltmacht* (Düsseldorf, 1961), pp. 132-38, *passim*, Berlin had been interested in "revolutionizing the Islamic world" since the mid-1890s. On the other hand, he concedes that the "decisive concretization" of such a program, that is, the formulation of specific action plans concerning the various Moslem regions under Entente control, did not occur until September 1914.

From Alliance Treaty to Intervention

The only known plan for German-Ottoman action against the Entente that predated the conclusion of the alliance consisted of an oral agreement between Wangenheim, Liman, and Enver on August 1—the day Germany declared war on Russia. Meeting in the German embassy the three men agreed that once the alliance treaty was signed the Turks should assume a basically defensive posture on their Transcaucasian border and assemble the bulk of their land forces in Thrace for a joint offensive with the Bulgarian army against Russia, or, possibly, for operations against Greece. Since there was as yet no assurance whatever that Bulgaria would throw in its lot with the Central Powers or that Rumania would permit the use of its territory for the projected Turco-Bulgarian advance into Russia's flank, this agreement of August 1 had little more than symbolic value, *i.e.*, it at least put the Turks on record that they would actively support Germany's war effort.[5]

Wangenheim, though fully aware that the Turks would need at least a month just to get their forces in Thrace assembled, decided that under his latest instructions from Berlin he was now justified in signing the alliance treaty. As previously mentioned, he did so on the afternoon of August 2. Within the next 24 hours the Porte ordered full mobilization, but also issued an official declaration of Ottoman neutrality in the rapidly broadening European war.

Although it is difficult to establish exactly what went on at the Porte during the first days of August, a few salient points are clear. First, several Ottoman ministers were still altogether unaware of the fact that an alliance had been concluded with Germany. Second, those who had conducted the negotiations with Berlin, except for Enver, were obviously having second

Cf. Egmont Zechlin, "Friedensbestrebungen und Revolutionierungsversuche," *Aus Politik und Zeitgeschichte*, B20/61, B24/61, B25/61 (1961), pp. 329, 361, 363-64, and *passim*.

[5] See FO, *Dt 128 Nr. 5 secr.*, Bd. 3, Wangenheim to FO, 2 Aug 1914, Nos. 406, 407.

thoughts about the advisability of prompt intervention. As Said Halim explained to Wangenheim on August 3, he was opposed to any overt action as long as Ottoman mobilization was not completed and Bulgaria's attitude remained in doubt. Moreover, there was acute danger that Britain would commandeer the battleship *Sultan Osman*, which was about to be delivered to the Turkish navy by an English shipyard.[6] Ironically, the very same day (August 3) the London government did requisition this ship and another, the *Reshadiye*, without any tangible provocation from Constantinople. However, it is now clear that Britain's action was more justified than has hitherto been assumed, for two days earlier, on August 1, Enver and Talât had offered to direct the *Sultan Osman* to a German North Sea port, a proposal immediately accepted by Berlin.[7]

Two days after the Porte had issued its declaration of neutrality, on August 5, Enver initiated talks with the Russian military attaché in Constantinople concerning a possible alignment of the Ottoman empire with the Entente. He told the attaché that the recently ordered mobilization of the Ottoman army was by no means directed against Russia. Indeed, the Porte was prepared to withdraw troops from Transcaucasia, to use the Ottoman army for the neutralization of "this or that Balkan state which might intend to move against Russia," and even to assist other Balkan countries "against Austria," provided that Saint Petersburg could arrange a reconciliation of the various Balkan states with each other and with the Ottoman empire. Such a reconciliation, Enver concluded, might be achieved if the Aegean Islands and Western Thrace were re-

[6] Bayur, III:1, 62-69, 99; *Die deutschen Dokumente zum Kriegsausbruch*, No. 795.

[7] See FO, *Türkei 142*, Bd. 39, Wangenheim to FO, 2 Aug 1914, No. 404; Tirpitz to FO, 2 Aug; Zimmermann to Wangenheim, 3 Aug, No. 302; AHFM, *Türkei, Berichte 1913 X-XII, 1914*, Pallavicini to AHFM, 2 Aug, No. 386.

turned to Turkey, while Greece and Bulgaria (as well as Serbia) could receive territorial compensations elsewhere.[8]

There can no longer be any doubt that these curious overtures by Enver, which he repeated a few days later, were insincere. Quite aside from the fact that Enver's proposals provided a perfect cover story for the intended concentration of Ottoman troops in Thrace, it is now also clear that he kept the German embassy informed about his talks with the Russians.[9] Moreover, there is considerable evidence that he was working hard to speed up Ottoman intervention *against* the Entente.

Enver's commitment to the alliance with Germany expressed itself most concretely in connection with the so-called *Goeben* and *Breslau* affair. The dramatic escape of these two cruisers of the German Mediterranean Squadron (*Mittelmeer-Division*) from Sicilian waters to the Turkish Straits has been described by many authors, and no attempt will be made here to recount this colorful story in full detail.[10] However, inasmuch as there was a direct causal relationship between the progress of the German cruisers toward the Dardanelles and certain political developments in Constantinople, it will be necessary to delve rather deeply into some parts of the story.

The dispatch of the Mediterranean Squadron, and particu-

[8] On Enver's overtures and St. Petersburg's lukewarm responses cf. Howard, pp. 96-102; F. I. Notovich, *Diplomaticheskaya borba v godi pervoi mirovoi voini* [The Diplomatic Struggle During the Years of the First World War] (Moscow, 1947), I, 283-87; Albertini, III, 618-20; and C. Jay Smith, Jr., *The Russian Struggle for Power, 1914-1917* (New York, 1956), pp. 69-76.

[9] See FO, *Wk*, Bd. 19, Wangenheim to FO, 10 Aug 1914, No. 471; and *Dt 128 Nr. 5 secr.*, Bd. 3, same to same, 18 Aug, No. 529.

[10] For a fairly reliable account see Hermann Lorey, *Der Krieg zur See 1914-1918: Der Krieg in den türkischen Gewässern*, 2 vols. (Berlin, 1928-38), I, 1-28. Among the reminiscences by former crew members Georg Kopp, *Das Teufelsschiff und seine kleine Schwester* (Leipzig, 1930) is quite useful. See also Marder, II, 20-41, for a review of British blunders.

From *Alliance Treaty to Intervention*

larly of the *Goeben*, to the Straits had been requested by both Wangenheim and Liman after their August 1 conference with Enver. In their messages to Berlin they pointed out that the two cruisers would greatly enhance the capabilities of the Ottoman fleet in the Black Sea, where, according to Liman, a "free hand" was highly important for all future military operations. As a result of these requests the German admiralty on August 3 dispatched instructions to the commander of the Mediterranean Squadron, Rear Admiral Wilhelm Souchon, to take his ships to the Straits "at once." The wireless message reached Souchon at 0235, August 4, at which time his squadron was heading for the Algerian coast to disrupt the transfer of troops from North Africa to France. Being close to his target area, Souchon decided not to turn back immediately. Instead he shelled the ports of Bône and Philippeville, then set course for Messina, where he intended to refuel his ships. Since the *Goeben* was slowed down by defective boilers, the squadron did not reach Messina until the morning of August 5.[11]

In Constantinople, meanwhile, the whole project of moving the Mediterranean Squadron into Turkish waters had run into an unexpected political snag. While Enver, in his capacity as war minister, had already issued instructions to the military authorities at the Dardanelles to keep the Straits open for Souchon's ships, the grand vizier notified Wangenheim on August 4 that the uncertain attitude of Bulgaria and Rumania was causing him "the greatest concern," and that the *Goeben* and *Breslau* would therefore have to stay out of the Straits for the time being.[12]

Impressed by the grand vizier's objections Berlin on August

[11] *Die deutschen Dokumente zum Kriegsausbruch*, Nos. 652, 712, 775; FO, *Dt 128 Nr. 5 secr.*, Bd. 3, Wangenheim to FO [Liman to Moltke], 2 Aug 1914, No. 406; same to same, 2 Aug, No. 407; Alfred von Tirpitz, *Erinnerungen*, rev. edn. (Leipzig, 1920), p. 302; Lorey, I, 1-13.

[12] FO, *Wk*, Bd. 14, Wangenheim to FO, 4 Aug 1914, No. 426; *Dt 128 Nr. 5 secr.*, Bd. 3, same to same, 4 Aug, No. 429.

5 dispatched a telegram to Souchon: "At the present time [your] call on [*Einlaufen*] Constantinople not yet possible for political reasons." The admiral received this imprecise warning at 1100, August 6, but decided to sail to the Dardanelles anyway. According to the official German Naval History, Souchon sensed that the appearance of his squadron in Turkish waters would greatly strengthen the German position vis-à-vis the Porte, and assumed, in any case, that the "political" difficulties cited by Berlin did not necessarily apply to his squadron's entry into the Dardanelles (as distinct from a call on Constantinople itself). So on the same afternoon the *Goeben* and *Breslau* steamed out of Messina on the first leg of their eastward journey. With superior Anglo-French naval forces practically all around him, Souchon might of course still have tried to reach an Adriatic port of the Dual Monarchy, but since the Austro-Hungarian fleet was in no way prepared to come to his assistance, he wisely abandoned that alternative plan.[13] It should be noted in this connection that for the sole purpose of facilitating Souchon's escape into the Adriatic Berlin had urged Vienna on August 5 to declare war on Britain and France—the request being promptly rescinded three days later, when it became clear that Austrian assistance was no longer needed by the Mediterranean Squadron.[14]

Souchon's decision on August 6 to ignore Berlin's advisory telegram was a veritable stroke of luck, for the Porte had in fact already abandoned its negative stand by this time. Indeed, the German agencies in Constantinople had first learned of the

[13] See Lorey, I, 14-15; Hans Sokol, *Oesterreich-Ungarns Seekrieg 1914-1918*, 3 vols. (Vienna, 1929-33), I, 67-73; Tirpitz, p. 302; [Georg A. von Müller], *Regierte der Kaiser? Kriegstagebücher, Aufzeichnungen und Briefe des . . . Admiral Georg Alexander von Müller, 1914-1918*. Walter Görlitz, ed. (Göttingen, 1959), p. 44; FO, *Wk*, Bd. 15, Pohl to Wilhelm II, 5 Aug 1914.

[14] FO, *Wk*, Bde. 15-18, Tirpitz to FO, 4 Aug 1914; Jagow to Tschirschky, 5 Aug, Nos. 249, 250; Tirpitz to FO, 6 Aug; Jagow to Tschirschky, 8 Aug, No. 268.

Turkish policy switch in the predawn hours of August 6, but due to persistent communications problems, Berlin did not receive word of this development until the next afternoon, and Souchon himself apparently got no message at all.[15] Wangenheim was first apprised of the good news at 1 a.m., when the grand vizier called him to his office. Said Halim informed him that the cabinet had just "unanimously" decided to open the Straits to both Souchon's squadron and any Austrian warships which might come along, though the Ottoman empire would definitely continue to maintain its neutral status. Obviously sensing an opportunity for striking a hard bargain, the grand vizier then asked Wangenheim whether he was prepared to pledge Germany's acceptance of the following six proposals:

1. Germany promises its assistance in the abolition of the capitulations.
2. Germany agrees to lend its support in regard to the indispensable understandings with Rumania and Bulgaria, and it will see to it that Turkey secures a fair agreement with Bulgaria with reference to possible spoils of war.
3. Germany will not conclude peace unless [all] Turkish territories which may be occupied by its enemies in the course of the war shall be evacuated.
4. Should Greece enter the war and be defeated by Turkey, Germany will see to it that the [Aegean] islands are returned [to the Turks].
5. Germany will secure for Turkey a small correction of her eastern border which shall place Turkey into direct contact with the Moslems of Russia.
6. Germany will see to it that Turkey receives an appropriate war indemnity.

[15] On the futile efforts of the Constantinople embassy to establish radio contact with the *Goeben* and *Breslau*, see FO, *Dt 128 Nr. 5 secr.*, Bd. 3, Wangenheim to FO, 6 Aug 1914, No. 437.

From Alliance Treaty to Intervention

Fearful lest he endanger the rescue of Souchon's squadron by "protracted discussions," Wangenheim immediately accepted the deal and later in the day confirmed the agreement in writing. As he subsequently pointed out to the Wilhelmstrasse, most of the promises he had made could obviously be fulfilled only if the Central Powers won the war "decisively," and Berlin thereupon formally approved his action.[16]

The deal of August 6 marked a definite improvement in the Porte's diplomatic bargaining position. Unlike the alliance treaty signed four days earlier, the new agreement formally assured the Turks of some tangible gains after victory if they entered the war on the side of the Central Powers. More importantly, the pledges extracted from Wangenheim were soon to be used by the Porte as a lever for securing further commitments from Berlin, a process which it thoroughly exploited during the next four years.

Though the Porte was now formally committed to admit Souchon's cruisers into the Straits, Wangenheim and his superiors in Berlin soon found out that the Ottoman cabinet had no intention of abandoning the course of neutrality. On August 9 the grand vizier informed Wangenheim that the Rumanian government had proposed the conclusion of an Ottoman–Greek–Rumanian neutrality pact, and that under certain circumstances the Porte might decide to accept such an arrangement. In that case, he added, the secret alliance with Germany would, "of course, remain in effect," though it would be necessary to institute a "formal" disarmament of the *Goeben* and to

[16] See *ibid.*, Wangenheim to FO, 6 Aug 1914, No. 438; Jagow to Wangenheim, 7 Aug, No. 330; Mühlmann, *Deutschland*, pp. 44-46, 96-97; Bayur, III:1, 98-99. Regarding the abortive project by Berlin to have the Austrians move their fleet to the Straits cf. FO, *Wk*, Bd. 17, Zimmermann to Tschirschky, 7 Aug, No. 260; Sokol, I, 73-74; Franz Conrad von Hötzendorf, *Aus meiner Dienstzeit 1906-18*, 5 vols. (Vienna, 1921-25), IV, 186, 190, 197, 206, and *passim*.

convert her into an Ottoman ship "by means of a fictitious sale."[17]

On August 10 Bethmann Hollweg wired back to Wangenheim that Germany had no use for the grand vizier's plans and that every effort should be made to secure prompt Ottoman and Bulgarian intervention. Once the Mediterranean Squadron had arrived, the chancellor added, the chances for getting results in this matter would undoubtedly improve.[18]

Bethmann Hollweg's optimistic prognostication proved entirely mistaken. When Souchon's cruisers appeared off the Dardanelles on the afternoon of August 10 utter confusion erupted both at the headquarters of the Dardanelles command and in Constantinople itself. Judging from the best available evidence, the Turkish military authorities at the Dardanelles were not at all sure what they were expected to do about the approaching German ships, and when they wired to the capital for instructions, Enver at first refused to respond. Finally, after some German officers on his staff had pleaded with him that time was of the essence, he agreed to act without prior consultation with his colleagues and wired to the Dardanelles command to admit Souchon's ships into the Straits.[19]

A few hours after the *Goeben* and *Breslau* had been guided by a Turkish torpedo boat to a temporary anchorage well inside the Dardanelles, Wangenheim was summoned to the grand vizier. In the presence of the entire cabinet, Said Halim angrily informed the ambassador that he objected to Souchon's premature arrival. The Porte, he emphasized, had made no

[17] FO, *Dt 128 Nr. 2 secr.*, Bd. 13, Wangenheim to FO, 9 Aug 1914, No. 463. For background information see same to same, 8 Aug, No. 457; Waldthausen to FO, 10 Aug, No. 102, 11 Aug, No. 107.

[18] *Ibid.*, *Dt 128 Nr. 8 secr.*, Bd. 1, Bethmann Hollweg to Wangenheim, 10 Aug 1914, No. 350.

[19] Cf. Lorey, I, 20-21; Kopp, pp. 65-73; Hans Kannengiesser Pasha, *The Campaign in Gallipoli* (London [1928]), pp. 25-27; Friedrich Kress von Kressenstein, *Mit den Türken zum Suezkanal* (Berlin, 1938), p. 18; and Bayur, III:1, 78-81.

progress in its talks with Bulgaria, and if the Entente powers should now declare war because of the cruisers' presence in the Straits there was a very definite chance that the Bulgarians would "exploit Turkey's engagement elsewhere and march on Constantinople." "Surely," he said, "Germany would not want Turkey to commit suicide." Wangenheim, mindful of Berlin's persistent demands for Ottoman intervention and the grand vizier's own statements four days earlier, responded "energetically" to these complaints and announced that neither the withdrawal nor the disarmament of the two cruisers would be acceptable to Germany. Moreover, he made it clear that Germany expected to use the ships for operations against Russia in the near future. After prolonged discussions among themselves the members of the cabinet ultimately agreed to the continued presence of Souchon's ships, but attached several conditions to their "concession": the cruisers were to be anchored "at a remote spot" in the Sea of Marmara; they were to be transferred to the Sultan's navy by a fictitious sale; and they were not to enter the Black Sea until the Porte had obtained a firm Bulgarian commitment for common action against Russia.[20]

Before Berlin had time to react to these demands, the Porte unilaterally issued a public declaration that it had "bought" the two German cruisers for "eighty million Marks." Wangenheim promptly registered his displeasure over the *fait accompli*, but there was nothing else he could do.[21] As he informed the Wilhelmstrasse on August 14, it was impossible to contest the phony sale, for Turkish public opinion was elated over the "acquisition" of the two cruisers and might easily turn against Germany if Berlin should try to disavow it. Moreover, given the anti-interventionist sentiments of most of the Ottoman min-

[20] FO, *Wk*, Bd. 19, Wangenheim to FO, 11 Aug 1914, No. 473. Cf. Bayur, III:1, 81-82.

[21] FO, *Wk*, Bde. 19-20, Jagow to Wangenheim, 11 Aug 1914, No. 366; Wolffs Telegraphisches Bureau to FO, 11 Aug; Wangenheim to FO, 12 Aug, No. 485; Bayur, III:1, 82-83.

isters—only Enver was standing "like a rock for Germany"— and the dilapidated condition of the Dardanelles defenses, any immediate use of the *Goeben* and *Breslau* against the Russians was out of the question anyway.[22]

As a result of Wangenheim's warnings Berlin raised no objections to a solemn ceremony near the Golden Horn on August 16, during which Navy Minister Cemal Paşa officially received the *Goeben* and *Breslau* into the Ottoman navy. The cruisers were formally renamed *Yavuz Sultan Selim* and *Midilli*, the German crews donned fezzes, and Admiral Souchon himself was officially (but not actually) installed as commander of the Ottoman fleet.[23]

In the long run the bogus incorporation of the Mediterranean Squadron into the Sultan's navy proved to be a boon to the Germans, but the immediate repercussions were rather less satisfactory from Berlin's point of view. Contrary to its hopes, the Entente governments did not turn the presence of Souchon's ships in the Straits into a cause for war, and since the Porte was obviously disinclined to open hostilities on its own initiative Berlin could do nothing more than to continue its exhortations that the Turks should honor their alliance obligations.

[22] FO, *Wk*, Bd. 22, Wangenheim to FO, 14 Aug 1914, No. 499. On the initial reactions of the Entente governments to the presence of Souchon's cruisers in Ottoman waters and Berlin's appeals to the Porte to stand firm on this issue, see Notovich, I, 299-304; Albertini, III, 621-23; Gottlieb, pp. 45-46; and FO, *Dt 128 Nr. 5 secr.*, Bd. 3, Jagow to Wangenheim, 12 Aug 1914, No. 370; *Wk*, Bd. 20, Zimmermann to Wangenheim, 13 Aug, No. 384.

[23] Mühlmann, *Deutschland*, p. 66; Lorey, I, 31-32; Djemal Pasha, *Memories of a Turkish Statesman, 1913-1919* (London [1922]), pp. 121-22. On Cemal's background and career see Dankwart A. Rustow, "Djemal Pasha," *Encyclopaedia of Islam*, rev. edn., II, 531-32. Since Souchon's ships actually remained German until 1918 their original names will be used throughout the book. The *Goeben* was handed over to the Turks at the end of the war, and after over 40 years of additional service under the name of *Yavuz*, was recently offered to a West German shipyard for scrapping. See Lorey, I, 373; and *Der Spiegel*, 29 July 1964, p. 16.

From Alliance Treaty to Intervention

It would appear that neither Wangenheim nor his Austro-Hungarian colleague, Ambassador Johann Margrave von Pallavicini, were overly happy with Berlin's persistent demands for action. Both of them recognized that the Porte's procrastination was at least partly related to the unfinished state of Ottoman mobilization, the slow progress in the Turkish alliance talks with Sofia, and a number of other concrete problems, and they so informed their superiors in Berlin and Vienna.[24] Gen. Liman, on the other hand, saw little excuse for the Turks' continued refusal to intervene and became daily more impatient and cantankerous. To Wangenheim's dismay, the general even began talking of challenging both Enver and Cemal to duels and finally, on August 19, sent a request to the Kaiser that he and his officers be allowed to return to Germany. In justification of his unusual request, Liman asserted that Enver's recent statements and military dispositions made it very obvious that the Turks would not enter the war in the foreseeable future (certainly not until Russia had been "decisively beaten" by the Central Powers); that the Ottoman army was bound to "collapse" for lack of money and food if it were kept much longer in a state of mobilization inside the Ottoman empire; and that the whole atmosphere in Constantinople made it almost unbearable for German officers to continue their service there.[25]

Wangenheim, who had had plenty of trouble with the excitable military mission chief in the prewar period, initially reacted rather mildly to Liman's unreasonable conduct.[26] He requested the dispatch of an imperial note to the general, "in which he should be instructed, with a simultaneous acknowl-

[24] See FO, *Dt 128 Nr. 8 secr.*, Bd. 2, Wangenheim to FO, 15 Aug 1914, No. 505; *Wk*, Bd. 26, same to same, 19 Aug, No. 553.

[25] *Ibid., Türkei 139*, Bd. 33, Wangenheim to FO, 19 Aug 1914, No. 546; same to same [Liman to Wilhelm II], 19 Aug, No. 547. Cf. Liman, p. 23.

[26] See Hallgarten, II, 439-46, 561-74; Fischer, "Weltpolitik, Weltmachtstreben und deutsche Kriegsziele," pp. 315-17; and Ulrich Trumpener, "Liman von Sanders and the German-Ottoman Alliance," *Journal of Contemporary History*, 1:4 (1966), 179-81.

edgment of his accomplishments so far, . . . not to worry about political matters, but to defend *to the last* the post on which His Majesty the Kaiser has placed him."[27] The ambassador's expressed hope that Liman would mend his ways once it was made clear to him that his work in the Ottoman empire was just as meritorious as a combat assignment in the German army was quickly dashed a few hours later, when Liman cabled to the Kaiser's headquarters that Enver was generally agreeable to the withdrawal of "myself and of one-third to one-half of the military mission."[28]

This piece of news really exasperated Wangenheim. As he informed the Wilhelmstrasse in a follow-up dispatch, Enver had not agreed to any such arrangement; indeed, he had just made it clear that even a partial withdrawal of the military mission was completely out of the question, and that Liman's political obtuseness and impatience were "simply incomprehensible" to him. As might be expected, the Kaiser immediately turned down Liman's request and admonished him to work in harmony with Enver. Wangenheim, on the other hand, received an oblique reminder that he should try harder to secure the Turks' entry into the war.[29]

Considering the ambassador's lukewarm attitude regarding the desirability of prompt Ottoman intervention, Berlin's exhortation was by no means superfluous, but it is also clear that even a more determined man than Wangenheim would have been unable to dissuade the Porte from its neutralist course. For one thing, the Turks were getting nowhere in their efforts to align Bulgaria in a common front against Russia. The only result of their negotiations with the Sofia government was a fairly innocuous defensive pact signed by Talât and the Bul-

[27] Wangenheim's dispatch No. 546, *Türkei 139*, Bd. 33.

[28] FO, *Türkei 139*, Bd. 33, Wangenheim to FO [Liman to Lyncker], 20 Aug 1914, No. 556.

[29] *Ibid.*, Wangenheim to FO, 20 Aug 1914, No. 555; Bethmann Hollweg to FO, 20 Aug, No. 17.

garian premier, Vasil Radoslavov, on August 19. In its main clauses, the treaty provided for mutual assistance against foreign aggression but said nothing about any offensive collaboration against a third party. All subsequent efforts by both the Porte and the governments of Berlin and Vienna to transform this defensive arrangement into an offensive alliance against Russia ended in failure, since Sofia insisted on a written pledge of Rumanian friendship and neutrality which the Bucharest government, in turn, proved unwilling to give.[30]

While the failure to obtain Bulgaria's assistance for an attack on Russia was in itself sufficient excuse for the Porte to continue its procrastination, the lack of military preparedness further hardened the resistance in the Ottoman cabinet to Berlin's demands for action. As far as most Ottoman leaders were concerned, the poor condition of the Dardanelles defenses alone precluded any kind of overt action in the foreseeable future. Even Souchon and other German officers at the scene had to admit that the Turks had a point.[31] While an improvement of the situation could be expected after the arrival of German coastal defense experts, mines, and ammunition (requested by Souchon a few days after his arrival at the Straits),[32] it was generally agreed in Constantinople that in the meantime Ottoman intervention was definitely out of the question.

The cautious attitude adopted by most German representatives in Constantinople met with little understanding among the military and political authorities in the Reich. Throughout the last half of August the question of how soon the *Goeben* and *Breslau* could be withdrawn from the Dardanelles

[30] See Bayur, III:1, 99-101, 103-33, and *passim*; and Glenn E. Torrey, "German Policy toward Bulgaria, 1914-1915," unpubl. M.A. thesis (Univ. of Oregon, 1957), pp. 1-34, which offers much new evidence. Albertini's account, III, 615-17, contains several factual errors.

[31] See FO, *Dt 128 Nr. 5 secr.*, Bd. 3, Wangenheim to FO, 24 Aug 1914, No. 595.

[32] See Lorey, I, 36; Ulrich Trumpener, "German Military Aid to Turkey in 1914," *Journal of Modern History*, 32 (1960), pp. 146-47.

and launched against Russia became a major bone of contention—Berlin advocating prompt action in the Black Sea, the Turks and most of the German representatives in Constantinople counseling delay and caution.[33] The impatience in the Reich increased sharply at the beginning of September, when about 700 German sailors and coastal defense specialists (the so-called *Sonderkommando Usedom*) under the command of Admiral Guido von Usedom arrived at the Straits and began to overhaul the badly neglected fortifications at the Dardanelles. On September 4 Gen. von Moltke sent a reminder to Liman that speedy Ottoman intervention was highly desirable, and the Austro-Hungarian general staff went even further by stipulating the exact form of support which it expected from the Turks, namely an amphibious landing of about 50,000 men in the Odessa region.[34]

Neither Enver nor most of the German officials in Constantinople felt that such action was feasible under the prevailing military and political circumstances. Wangenheim advised Berlin on September 6 and 8 that Enver's hands were tied by the unwillingness of his colleagues to support his interventionist policy and a variety of technical problems (the lack of agreement with Bulgaria, the weakness of the Dardanelles defenses, and the tactical impossibility of launching any large-scale operations across the Black Sea). Not even the invasion of Egypt was as yet feasible, Wangenheim emphasized, despite strenuous efforts by Germans and Turks alike to get a suitable expeditionary force organized.[35]

An Ottoman attack on Egypt and the incitement of native

[33] See FO, *Wk*, Bde. 24-26, Krupp Co. to FO, 17 Aug 1914; Zimmermann to Wangenheim, 19 Aug, No. 433; *Dt 128 Nr. 5 secr.*, Bd. 3, Wangenheim to FO, 26 Aug, No. 609; Bethmann Hollweg to FO, 28 Aug, No. 26; Wangenheim to FO, 30 Aug, No. 645.

[34] *Ibid., Wk*, Bd. 33, Zimmermann to Wangenheim, 3 Sept 1914, No. 584; Mühlmann, *deutschtürkische Waffenbündnis*, p. 20.

[35] FO, *Dt 128 Nr. 5 secr.*, Bd. 4, Wangenheim to FO, 6 Sept 1914, No. 725, 8 Sept, No. 752. See also Trumpener, "Liman von Sanders and the German-Ottoman Alliance," pp. 186-87.

revolts against the Entente throughout North Africa had been of major interest to Berlin from the very beginning of the war, but the difficulties in implementing that program were stupendous.[36] Aside from the logistical problems attending any offensive move against the Suez Canal, there were formidable political obstacles to be overcome. Foremost among these was the sensitivity of the Italian government to any type of military or propagandistic activities by the Central Powers or the Turks in North Africa which might undermine Italy's already precarious position in Libya. From the very beginning of the war Rome had sent periodic admonitions to the Porte not to intervene on the side of the Central Powers.[37] By early September the Austro-Hungarian representatives in Constantinople were openly turning against any Egyptian venture for fear it might propel Italy into the camp of the Entente.[38]

Although these Austro-Hungarian objections were officially dropped by the middle of September, concern over possible Italian countermeasures if the Turks started marching lingered on both in Vienna and Constantinople. In Berlin, however, official insistence on prompt Ottoman intervention continued, with high priority being given to the "Egyptian campaign."[39] As Undersecretary of State Arthur Zimmermann explained to

---

[36] See Mühlmann, *deutschtürkische Waffenbündnis*, pp. 23-27, 88-89; Fischer, *Weltmacht*, pp. 93, 103, 132-38, 142-44.

[37] See *I Documenti Diplomatici Italiani*, ser. 5, 1, Augusto Torre, ed. (Rome, 1954), Nos. 437, 551, 554, 568, 569, 578, 632, 659; FO, *Dt 128 Nr. 1 secr.*, Bd. 33, Flotow to FO, 7 Aug 1914, No. 189; *Dt 128 Nr. 5 secr.*, Bd. 3, Wangenheim to FO, 12 Aug 1914, No. 486; *Wk*, Bd. 25, same to same, 17 Aug, No. 524.

[38] AHFM, *Krieg 21a, Türkei*, Pallavicini to AHFM, 6 Sept 1914, No. 548; 8 Sept, No. 544 [sic]; same to Berchtold, 9 Sept, No. 55/P; FO, *Dt 128 Nr. 5 secr.*, Bd. 4, Wangenheim to FO, 8 Sept, No. 752; 9 Sept, No. 767; 12 Sept, No. 791. Cf. Pomiankowski, pp. 79-80.

[39] FO, *Dt 128 Nr. 5 secr.*, Bd. 4, Bethmann Hollweg to FO, 14 Sept 1914, No. 43; Zimmermann to Wangenheim, 14 Sept, No. 691; Wangenheim to FO, 15 Sept, No. 819; AHFM, *Krieg 21a, Türkei*, Berchtold to Pallavicini, 14 Sept, No. 486; Pallavicini to AHFM, 16 Sept, No. 596.

Wangenheim, a Turkish march on Egypt and the incitement of Moslem unrest would really be an asset, rather than a liability, in terms of keeping Italy out of the Entente.[40]

In the meantime, while Germans and Austro-Hungarians had been arguing about the merits of prompt Ottoman action against Egypt, the Porte had pulled a political coup of the first magnitude. To the complete surprise and consternation of its two allies,[41] it informed the world on September 8 that it had decided to abrogate the capitulatory privileges of all foreign powers.[42] Confronted with the necessity of placating Turkish public opinion and hostile reactions in the neutral countries at one and the same time, Wangenheim and Pallavicini took the unprecedented step of joining the ambassadors of Britain, France, Russia, and Italy in a formal protest note against the Porte's extralegal resort to unilateral action, but intimated to the Turks at the same time that the Central Powers would not really press the issue for the time being.[43]

Although both Berlin and Vienna refused to agree formally to the Porte's unilateral action until much later in the war, the Turks went ahead with their abrogation measures. On October 1, 1914 they raised their traditionally foreign-controlled customs

[40] FO, *Dt 128 Nr. 5 secr.*, Bd. 4, Zimmermann to Wangenheim, 13 Sept 1914, No. 686. Cf. *Dt 128 Nr. 1 secr.*, Bd. 34, Jagow to Zimmermann, 6 Sept.

[41] According to Cavid's memoirs Wangenheim literally threw a fit when he got the news, and announced to Cavid that he and the military mission would leave Constantinople immediately. See Bayur, III:1, 166-69. Cf. FO, *Dt 128 Nr. 5 secr.*, Bd. 4, Wangenheim to FO, 9 Sept 1914, No. 764; AHFM, *Türkei LII/1*, Pallavicini to AHFM, 10 Sept, No. 567.

[42] See Howard, pp. 103-104; Sousa, pp. 189-90, 328-31; Bayur, III:1, 161-62.

[43] Cf. Pomiankowski, p. 78; Sousa, pp. 193-94; Bayur, III:1, 164-71; AHFM, *Türkei LII/1*, AHFM to Pallavicini, 11 Sept 1914, No. 470; Pallavicini to AHFM, 12 Sept, No. 576; *I Documenti Diplomatici Italiani*, ser. 5, 1, Nos. 630, 635, 651, 698, 790, 815, 816.

duties by 4% and closed all foreign post offices in the empire. Most of the other rights and privileges traditionally enjoyed by foreigners under the capitulatory system were officially canceled shortly thereafter.[44]

Whether this act of liberating the Ottoman empire from a major foreign shackle could be made permanent was, of course, another question, but the Porte had at least made a promising start. In fact, from the Turkish point of view, a new opportunity for playing both sides against the middle now existed, for while the Germans were already committed since August 6 to "help" in the abolition of the capitulations if the Turks helped the Central Powers to victory, the Entente governments were continuing to intimate to the Porte that the permanent abolition of the capitulatory system might be accepted by them as well if the Ottoman empire remained neutral.[45]

The prospect of Entente concessions in the capitulations question may well have reinforced the neutralist disposition of the grand vizier and most of the other cabinet members,[46] but it is clear that the vague Entente offers did not make any impression on Enver. On the contrary, heartened by the steady improvement of the Dardanelles defenses, the war minister actually intensified his efforts to create a cause for war with Russia. On September 14 he authorized Adm. Souchon to take his ships into the Black Sea and attack any Russian vessels he might encounter.[47] However, before Souchon could take advantage of this opening, the grand vizier forced a showdown on the issue in the cabinet and emerged triumphant. Faced with the practically unanimous opposition of his colleagues,

[44] Sousa, pp. 196-201; Kurt Ziemke, *Die neue Türkei* (Berlin, 1930), pp. 31-32.

[45] Howard, pp. 104-105.

[46] See AHFM, *Krieg 21a, Türkei*, Pallavicini to AHFM, 17 Sept 1914, No. 602; 19 Sept, No. 611.

[47] *Ibid.*, Pallavicini to AHFM, 15 Sept 1914, No. 589; FO, *Dt 128 Nr. 5 secr.*, Bd. 4, Wangenheim to FO, 19 Sept, No. 834.

Enver grudgingly agreed to cancel the authorization given to Souchon.[48]

With Wangenheim's approval, Souchon, frustrated by the veto of the Porte, lodged a passionate protest with the Ottoman government against its vacillating attitude and demanded a free hand in the Black Sea. He intimated, furthermore, that if the Porte refused to allow nonprovocative "training" maneuvers for his ships, he might be forced to conduct such maneuvers even without formal authorization. Although the Porte promptly reissued its veto, Souchon, again with Wangenheim's approval, carried out his threat the very next day by sending the *Breslau* into the Black Sea for a cruise of several hours' duration. As Wangenheim explained to the grand vizier shortly afterwards, Souchon's cruisers had come to the Straits to serve the interests of both Germany and the Ottoman empire. Even though they were now flying the Ottoman flag, the ships had not relinquished their German character, and the *Breslau* had entered the Black Sea because it was contrary to the spirit prevailing on German ships to be afraid of imaginary dangers. It was outright "shameful," he said, that they and the Ottoman fleet should hide from the Russians, especially since the latter were obviously averse to any hostile encounters in the Black Sea. Quite understandably, Said Halim was not at all impressed by Wangenheim's specious reasoning and expressed the suspicion that Souchon was eager to involve the Porte in the war. The ambassador countered that Souchon would never presume to act without the approval of the Ottoman military high command—a rather meaningless assurance from the grand vizier's point of view, considering Enver's unashamed advocacy of prompt intervention. Wangenheim concluded with a warning that the Porte could expect no preferential treatment after the war if it continued to procrastinate, and declared that the initiation of "naval demonstrations" in the Black Sea, the continuation of pan-Islamic propaganda, and the maintenance

[48] *Ibid.*, Wangenheim to FO, 19 Sept 1914, No. 836.

of full mobilization were the very least Germany could expect from her tardy ally.[49]

While Wangenheim was thus putting formal diplomatic pressure on the chief of the Ottoman cabinet, the ambassador's right-hand man, the "acting" naval attaché, Lt. Comdr. Hans Humann, simultaneously presented to Enver a much more straightforward résumé of German feelings and intentions. Humann had been a personal friend of Enver's since childhood, and, knowing that the war minister was sincerely committed to intervention anyway, he could afford to be frank. He reminded Enver that Souchon's attachment to the Ottoman navy was merely a pretense and that the admiral, as a German officer, could hardly be expected to slight his patriotic duties because of the whims of the Porte. Since the Ottoman government had hitherto refused to honor its alliance obligations and was even permitting the continued use of the Straits by enemy ships, it was unlikely that the admiral and his German crews would accept their enforced idleness much longer.[50]

Faced with Wangenheim's and Humann's protests and the unauthorized cruise of the *Breslau* on the previous day, the Ottoman cabinet decided to offer the Germans a compromise solution. As Enver informed Wangenheim on September 21, his colleagues were now willing to concede that Souchon had the right to maintain "German interests, even if these collide with Turkish interests." If the admiral wished to take his two cruisers into the Black Sea, he could do so, but the Ottoman government would formally disassociate itself from any war-

[49] See Wangenheim's dispatch No. 834, *Dt 128 Nr. 5 secr.*, Bd. 4; and Wangenheim to FO, 20 Sept 1914, No. 848, *ibid.* Wangenheim's move had been preceded by a more moderate appeal to the grand vizier on the part of the Austro-Hungarian ambassador. See AHFM, *Krieg 21a, Türkei*, Pallavicini to AHFM, 18 Sept, No. 605; 19 Sept, No. 611.

[50] Jackh Papers, No. 9, "Besprechung mit Enver Pascha am 20.9. 1914." On Humann's background and career see FO, *Dt 135 Nr. 1*, Bd. 5, Humann to Jackh, n.d.; and Ernest Jackh [Ernst Jäckh], *The Rising Crescent* (New York, 1944), pp. 118-20.

like acts he might commit. Moreover, the Porte was prepared to formalize Souchon's status in the Ottoman navy and to make him the head of a yet to be created naval mission, in which case even the purely Ottoman ships of the fleet would be allowed to enter the Black Sea for nonbelligerent purposes.[51]

Although outwardly this curious offer looks like a major retreat on the part of the anti-interventionists in the Ottoman cabinet, it would appear that the proposal was actually intended to ensure continued Ottoman neutrality. As the Germans learned confidentially about two weeks later, the Porte's offer was predicated on the assumption that any warlike acts perpetrated by Souchon on his own initiative could be disavowed much more convincingly if the admiral was a bona fide member of the Sultan's officer corps and could thus be depicted as an "insubordinate" troublemaker to the outside world.[52]

While one may conceivably question whether such specious and unrealistic arguments were, indeed, used in the deliberations of the Ottoman cabinet, the fact remains that the curious compromise solution was officially presented to the German government through regular diplomatic channels. On September 23 Ambassador Mahmud Muhtar Paşa informed Zimmermann that his government wished to formalize Souchon's current status by giving him a one-year appointment in the Ottoman naval service at the rank of vice-admiral. According to Muhtar, such an appointment would entail for Souchon both the "actual command" of the entire Ottoman fleet and the general supervision of a naval reform program by a mission of German officers and technicians.[53] The Kaiser immediately ac-

[51] FO, *Dt 128 Nr. 5 secr.*, Bd. 4, Wangenheim to FO, 21 Sept 1914, No. 847.

[52] Jackh Papers, No. 10, "Vertrauliche Mitteilungen vom 5. Oktober 1914."

[53] FO, *Türkei 139*, Bd. 33, Zimmermann to Jagow, 23 Sept 1914, No. 533. In connection with the Turkish proposals it should be noted that the British naval mission had been called home a few days before. See Marder, II, 231.

cepted the Ottoman proposal[54] and on September 24 Souchon, accompanied by Humann, presented himself to his new chief, Navy Minister Cemal. On being reminded of his obligations as an admiral of the Ottoman navy Souchon solemnly promised not to involve any Turkish ships in belligerent acts without proper authorization from the Ottoman high command.[55]

Meanwhile, at the very time when the Ottoman fleet was thus officially turned over to a German commander, Gen. Liman decided once again to get himself and his officers out of the Ottoman army. Angered and frustrated by the continued procrastination of the Porte the general informed his superiors in Germany that he and the other members of the military mission were obviously wasting their time in the Ottoman empire and that they might be put to better use on the battlefields of France or Russia. To Wangenheim, of course, Liman's desire to withdraw the mission from Ottoman service made no sense at all, and he did not hesitate to express his disgust with the general's naïve and shortsighted attitude. In a lengthy message to German imperial headquarters the ambassador pointed out that the Ottoman empire was not properly prepared for effective military action and that therefore "benevolent Turkish neutrality" was really much more valuable than a "premature Turkish declaration of war." To withdraw the military mission was tantamount to abandoning most of the influence Germany was at that time able to wield in the Ottoman empire, and would ruin the prospects for eventual Ottoman intervention. Wangenheim hastened to add that in his opinion such

[54] See FO, *Dt 128 Nr. 5 secr.*, Bd. 4, Jagow to FO, 24 Sept 1914, Nos. 191 and 193. In approving Souchon's appointment as Ottoman vice-admiral the Kaiser stipulated that Souchon would of course retain his status as a German rear admiral "on active duty."

[55] *Ibid., Türkei 139*, Bd. 33, "Besprechung mit Djemal Pascha am 24.9.1914." According to Pallavicini Wangenheim later confirmed Souchon's oral promise in a letter to the grand vizier, but there is no record of this in the German files. See AHFM, *Krieg 21a, Türkei*, Pallavicini to Berchtold, 28 Sept 1914, No. 58/P.

intervention was merely a matter of time, especially if Germany made some headway in the European theaters of war. Wangenheim's message dispelled all hesitations which the German military high command may have had with regard to Liman's request, and on September 26 the general was notified in a sharply worded message that he was expected to remain at his assigned post.[56]

Wangenheim's cautious optimism with regard to eventual Ottoman intervention was at least partially warranted by a gradual diminution of neutralist sentiments among some of the governmental and party leaders in Constantinople. According to confidential information obtained by the German embassy at this time the situation in the Ottoman cabinet was characterized by a three-way split, with Enver and Cemal as proponents of intervention, Said Halim and influential Finance Minister Mehmed Cavid Bey heading the anti-interventionists, and Talât acting as mediator between the two groups. In the central committee of the *Ittihad ve Terakki* Party (which may well be termed the real power in the government) the majority of members were reported to be "pro-German," but the anti-intervention minority was by no means negligible in terms of political influence, including among its members the prominent party ideologue and "inner circle member," Dr. Nazim Bey, and the powerful Police Prefect of Constantinople, Bedri Bey, who was also a close friend of Talât.[57]

[56] FO, *Dt 128 Nr. 5 secr.*, Bd. 4, Wangenheim to Jagow, 24 Sept 1914, No. 3; *Türkei 139*, Bd. 33, Jagow to Zimmermann, 27 Sept. Cf. Liman, p. 23, where the sharpest part of the Kaiser's message to him is understandably not reproduced.

[57] FO, *Dt 128 Nr. 5 secr.*, Bd. 4, Jäckh to Zimmermann, 26 Sept 1914, re "Unterredungen mit türkischen Vertrauensleuten." Reliable information on the composition of the central committee or "general council" of the *Ittihad ve Terakki* Party is scarce. It appears that the central committee had about 40 members in 1914, including most, but not all, ministers of the cabinet. Tunaya, p. 199, speaks of a "general directorate" (*Merkezi Umumî*) of about 12 men (with Said

From Alliance Treaty to Intervention

While this intelligence report on the major factions within the ruling Ottoman circles probably presents an oversimplified picture, there is ample evidence that at least with regard to the continued division between Enver and the grand vizier it is wholly accurate. By the end of August the deadlock between Enver and Said Halim had given rise to some talk, both in German and in Ottoman interventionist circles, concerning the desirability and feasibility of a coup d'état which might give Enver full control of the Ottoman government.[58] However, there is no evidence that German government agencies ever formulated a specific program for the attainment of that end, notwithstanding the steadily growing impatience with which Berlin reacted to the evasive tactics of the grand vizier and his supporters. Ernst Jackh, the well-known Turcophile journalist-scholar and arch-proponent of German-Ottoman collaboration both before and during World War I, has mentioned in one of his books that in September 1914 a scheme for kidnapping the grand vizier and other anti-interventionists was presented to the Wilhelmstrasse by Muhtar Paşa, but of course this fantastic proposal of Turkish provenance was not acted on.[59] In fact, while some leading figures in the German government were by now ready to push the hesitant ally into the war even against his will,[60] they were not prepared to get involved in, let alone

---

Halim and Talât being the only cabinet ministers among them), but this was probably a kind of politburo inside the Party's central committee.

I am indebted to Professors Roderic H. Davison of George Washington University and Gotthard Jäschke of Münster, Germany, for their advice on this matter.

[58] See FO, *Wk*, Bd. 32, Wangenheim to FO, 30 Aug 1914, No. 645; *Dt 128 Nr. 5 secr.*, same to same, 6 Sept, No. 725, 8 Sept, No. 752, 19 Sept, No. 834; and Jäckh Papers, No. 9, "Anlage zur Besprechung mit Enver Pascha am 20.9.1914."

[59] Jackh, *Rising Crescent*, pp. 114-16.

[60] AHFM, *Krieg 21a, Türkei*, Haymerle to AHFM, 19 Sept 1914, No. 533.

to sponsor, a coup in Constantinople. The inevitable result of this restraint was that the grand vizier and his faction were able to delay Ottoman intervention for several more weeks, but in the long run the Germans gained more than they lost.

With the official appointment of Souchon as commander of the Sultan's fleet the Porte had simultaneously canceled its previous veto against the entry of Ottoman warships into the Black Sea. As might be expected, Souchon promptly used his new authority to conduct naval maneuvers outside the Bosporus, but neither Enver nor Wangenheim gave him any encouragement to use his Black Sea cruises for the provocation of a Russian declaration of war. In fact, while Enver was willing to accommodate the Germans in a number of other matters, he was chastened enough by his humiliating defeat in mid-September not to issue a second carte blanche to Souchon behind the cabinet's back. Wangenheim, on the other hand, was drifting more and more into a position of watchful waiting, so much so that by the beginning of October Berlin decided to send a special emissary, Richard von Kühlmann, to Constantinople to try and stir the ambassador out of his embarrassingly passive attitude.[61]

The first indication that Enver's commitment to the alliance had not weakened (even though he refused to authorize naval action against Russia) came on September 26, when the war minister personally ordered the Dardanelles to be closed to all foreign ships. The sealing off of the still operative navigation channel through the Dardanelles had long been demanded by Souchon, Usedom, and other German admirals in Turkey,[62]

[61] See *ibid.*, Hohenlohe to AHFM, 1 Oct 1914, No. 575; FO, *Dt 128 Nr. 5 secr.*, Bd. 4, Zimmermann to Wangenheim, 4 Oct, No. 862; Mühlmann, *Deutschland*, pp. 72-73; and Richard von Kühlmann, *Erinnerungen* (Heidelberg, 1948), pp. 440-41.

[62] Cf. FO, *Dt 128 Nr. 5 secr.*, Bd. 4, Wangenheim to FO, 8 Sept 1914, No. 752; Jackh Papers, No. 9, "Besprechung mit Enver Pascha am 20.9.1914." Wangenheim, in contrast to the admirals, had very mixed feelings about closing the Straits, fearing above all that such a

but the actual closure on September 26 was certainly not an underhanded move by the Germans as has sometimes been alleged. While German officers were indeed in charge of the closure operations, they acted on a contingency plan previously approved by Enver. There is evidence that neither Wangenheim nor the German "inspector general" of the Ottoman coastal defense system, Usedom, even knew about the closure until the following day.[63]

Whether Enver's colleagues in the cabinet knew of and approved the sealing of the Straits is uncertain; at any rate, they did little or nothing to reverse the war minister's action. True, the grand vizier repeatedly assured the Entente ambassadors that the Straits would be reopened as soon as Britain and France withdrew their warships from the vicinity of the Dardanelles, but it is doubtful whether Said Halim really believed this himself.[64] From September 27 to 30 additional mine fields and antisubmarine nets were laid at the Dardanelles, and on October 2 Talât reassured the German embassy that the Straits would remain closed, Allied protests and threats notwithstanding.[65] A few days later Enver himself told the Germans that the grand vizier's conciliatory messages to the Entente should not be taken too seriously since Said Halim was no longer actually in charge of the situation.[66]

---

move would antagonize the neutral world and produce catastrophic bottlenecks in the provisioning of Constantinople. See Wangenheim's dispatch No. 752, *Dt 128 Nr. 5 secr.*, Bd. 4; and Wangenheim to FO, 11 Sept, No. 779, *ibid.*

[63] *Ibid.*, Wangenheim to FO, 27 Sept 1914, No. 906; AHFM, *Krieg 21a, Türkei*, Pallavicini to AHFM, 27 Sept, No. 656.

[64] FO, *Dt 128 Nr. 5 secr.*, Bd. 4, Wangenheim to FO, 28 Sept 1914, No. 915; 29 Sept, No. 921; *Wk*, Bd. 45, Quadt to FO, 4 Oct, No. 517; Howard, pp. 107-108.

[65] Lorey, II, 21; FO, *Dt 128 Nr. 5 secr.*, Bd. 4, Wangenheim to FO, 29 Sept 1914, No. 931; *Wk*, Bd. 44, same to same, 1 Oct, No. 951; Jackh Papers, No. 10, "Vertrauliche Mitteilung, 2.10.14."

[66] FO, *Dt 128 Nr. 5 secr.*, Bd. 4, Wangenheim to FO, 8 Oct 1914, No. 995.

Enver's claim that he, Talât, and Halil would henceforth be the true policy-makers at the Porte may initially have been received with scepticism by Wangenheim, but by October 9 he received definite proof of the realignment of forces in the Ottoman cabinet.

On that day, Enver informed Wangenheim that Talât and Halil had meanwhile committed themselves to back his intervention policy. Their first task would be to obtain Cemal's unconditional support, failing which they would force the grand vizier to choose between prompt intervention or the breakup of the cabinet. With the "overwhelming" majority of the Party central committee allegedly lined up on his side already, Enver was sure that a new cabinet of pro-interventionists could then be formed without delay. In fact, Ottoman intervention by the middle of October was for all intents and purposes assured, he concluded, provided that adequate gold supplies for the conduct of war were made available by Germany without further delay.[67]

Enver's call for German financial assistance was no surprise to the Berlin government. As early as September 30 the Porte had officially requested a gold loan of five million T£, but so far neither Bethmann Hollweg nor Zimmermann had thought it advisable to commit the German government to such an outlay unless the Turks intervened first.[68] As Zimmermann had informed Wangenheim on October 5, Berlin was willing to make an advance payment of T£ 250,000, but the balance of the requested loan (T£ 4.75 million) could be disbursed only after the Ottoman empire was fully involved in the war.[69]

[67] *Ibid.*, Wangenheim to FO, 9 Oct 1914, No. 1,010.

[68] On this official loan request from the Porte, which was most likely made with Said Halim's approval, and the initial reaction in Berlin, see especially FO, *Türkei 110*, Bde. 72-73, Zimmermann to Jagow, 30 Sept 1914, No. 613; Bethmann Hollweg to FO, 1 Oct, No. 65. Cf. Wangenheim to FO, 4 Oct, No. 965.

[69] *Ibid.*, Zimmermann to Wangenheim, 5 Oct 1914, No. 874.

From Alliance Treaty to Intervention

Wangenheim himself had mixed feelings about the renewed demand for German financial assistance. His reaction to Enver's conspiratorial plan of action was even less positive. Though he dutifully reported to Berlin the gist of Enver's proposals, Wangenheim bluntly reminded his superiors that he was personally not in favor of involving the Ottoman empire in the war "prematurely." The ambassador's cautionary remarks made no impression whatever in the Wilhelmstrasse, except to confirm Zimmermann's view that Wangenheim was losing his grip.[70]

Exhorted by Berlin to promote Ottoman intervention with all means at his disposal, Wangenheim had no choice but to go along with the implementation of Enver's general plan. The first step, previously suggested by Enver, was to call a secret meeting with the war minister and his followers in the German embassy building. The meeting, held on October 11, has been known to historians from Cemal Paşa's memoirs, but on this issue, as on a good many others, the navy minister's memory was none too good. To begin with, there were only four Ottoman participants at the conference—Enver, Talât, Halil, and Cemal himself (the latter having joined the conspiracy the preceding day). The grand vizier, contrary to Cemal's account, was not present; quite understandably he had not been invited to discuss a plot directed against himself and the other proponents of neutralism.

According to reports by both Wangenheim and Humann the four Ottoman statesmen concluded the conference with the declaration that they and "their group in the committee" were committed to war, that Souchon would be authorized to attack the Russians as soon as the German government had deposited T £ 2 million in Constantinople, and that they would

[70] FO, *Dt 128 Nr. 5 secr.*, Bd. 4, Wangenheim to FO, 9 Oct 1914, No. 1,010; Zimmermann to Wangenheim, 10 Oct, No. 920; AHFM, *Krieg 21a, Türkei*, Hohenlohe to AHFM, 7 Oct, No. 587.

induce the grand vizier to resign if he refused to agree to Ottoman intervention.[71]

There is some evidence that Enver's faction was momentarily disturbed by the sudden death of Rumania's Germanophile King Carol, but within a few days the interventionists came to the conclusion that a possible alignment of Rumania with the Entente was all the more reason to speed up the preparations for war. As Talât explained to the Germans on October 14, a shift in Rumania's attitude might easily persuade Sofia to abandon its reserve with regard to a joint Turco-Bulgarian program of action. That the Ottoman interventionists were not just passively waiting for a Bulgarian change of heart is attested to by a secret communication from Enver to the German embassy, according to which he was stepping up Moslem guerrilla activities in Serbian Macedonia. Enver explained that "his" guerrillas, about 1,500 men in all, had been instructed to provoke incidents between the Serbian authorities and the Bulgarian communities in Macedonia, and there was hope that this and similar measures would eventually produce a break between Belgrade and Sofia and propel the latter into the arms of the Central Powers.[72]

In light of the assurances given by Enver's faction Berlin had meanwhile decided to respond to the Ottoman call for financial assistance without any further discussion about the terms of the loan. On October 12 a hastily assembled shipment of one

[71] FO, *Dt 128 Nr. 5 secr.*, Bd. 4, Jagow to FO, 11 Oct 1914, No. 254; Wangenheim to FO, 11 Oct, No. 1,022; Jackh Papers, No. 10, "Bericht über die Beratung beim Botschafter am 11.10.14"; Djemal, p. 129.

[72] Jackh Papers, Nos. 10 and 11, Humann to Enver, 10 Oct 1914; "Bericht über die Beratung beim Botschafter am 11.10.14"; "Mitteilungen von Enver Pascha, 13.10.14"; "Vertrauliche Mitteilungen vom 14. Oktober 1914." On the background story of Ottoman guerrilla activities in Macedonia see Dankwart A. Rustow, "The Army and the Founding of the Turkish Republic," *World Politics*, 11 (1959), pp. 518-19.

million Turkish pounds in gold coins was put on a special train carrying the Kaiser's aide-de-camp, Prince Karl von Wedel, and the Rumanian minister to Berlin, Alexander Beldiman, for a ceremonial visit to Bucharest. Unlike many other German shipments consigned to Constantinople, this gold transport was allowed speedy transit through Rumania and reached its destination in near record time, that is, on the evening of October 16. Heartened by the safe arrival of the first shipment Berlin dispatched another million on October 17, though the German Treasury Department was none too happy about the whole venture. Despite Russian diplomatic efforts in Bucharest to block their transit through Rumania the two railroad cars carrying the second shipment arrived safely in the Ottoman capital on October 21. In the Berlin Foreign Office the "incredible" success of the gold transfer operation produced tremendous enthusiasm, while the Russian Foreign Office glumly put out an alert that an Ottoman attack might occur "within the next few days."[73]

The safe arrival of the gold eliminated the last obstacle to the implementation of the interventionists' plan of October 11 and Enver promptly got in touch with the German embassy to discuss the final preparations for war. At the same time, he submitted a general plan of action for transmittal to German imperial headquarters. As had been planned for a long time the opening move was to be an attack on the Russian Black Sea fleet "without [a] declaration of war." Wangenheim explained to Berlin in an accompanying commentary that the war minister had already prepared the requisite orders to both Souchon and the Ottoman naval officers serving under the admiral,

[73] FO, *Türkei 110*, Bd. 73, Zimmermann to Bussche, 12 Oct 1914, No. 528; same to Jagow, 14 Oct, No. 742; same to Tschirschky, 17 Oct, No. 814; Wangenheim to FO, 14 Oct, No. 1,031; 17 Oct, No. 1,051; 22 Oct, No. 1,076; *Die Internationalen Beziehungen im Zeitalter des Imperialismus. Dokumente. . . .* M. Pokrovski, ed., ser. 2, 6 vols. (Berlin, 1934-36), VI:1, 320-21.

though he had seemingly not yet cleared this matter with either Cemal or Talât.[74]

Items 2 through 6 of Enver's war plan were primarily concerned with the deployment and proposed objectives of the Ottoman land forces. It is here that Wangenheim's previous warnings against a "premature" intervention by the Turks receive more than ample justification. As Enver put it, the Ottoman army in Transcaucasia would have as its primary mission to contain the opposing Russian forces; no word here about any offensive action. The advance against Egypt, on the other hand, would require at least another six weeks of preparation and in any case would involve at most two army corps. The bulk of the Ottoman land forces would be kept in readiness in Thrace, but again there was no immediate prospect of using them offensively. As Enver explained,

> If agreement with Bulgaria can be reached, Turkish main forces are partly to advance with Bulgaria against Serbia, partly to secure this advance, if necessary, against Greece and Rumania. . . . Should Rumania join us too, Turkish main forces are to advance in conjunction with [the] Rumanian army against Russia.

Moreover, there was no possibility for the time being of a major amphibious assault in the Odessa region, a project in which the Austro-Hungarian general staff was still particularly interested.[75]

To Zimmermann, his patience long exhausted by Ottoman procrastination, Enver's rather sketchy outline of what the Turks could, would, or might do after intervention was better than no plan at all. He therefore urged speedy and unconditional acceptance of Enver's plan by the German Supreme Army Command (OHL). The new chief of the OHL, Gen.

[74] FO, *Dt 128 Nr. 5 secr.*, Bd. 4, Wangenheim to FO, 22 Oct 1914, No. 1,087.

[75] *Ibid.*; and AHFM, *Krieg 21a, Türkei*, Berchtold to Pallavicini, 21 Oct 1914, No. 637.

Erich von Falkenhayn, obliged with an appropriate telegram to Enver, but before his message arrived, the situation in Constantinople had once again deteriorated.[76] As Pallavicini had warned Vienna on October 22, the unity of Enver's faction was more apparent than real, and the next day the war minister himself had to inform the Germans that both Talât and Halil had become unsure of the appropriateness and desirability of immediate intervention.[77] The sudden "faintheartedness" of the two men was possibly nourished by Italian warnings and Bulgarian exhortations against any precipitate action by the Porte, but the limited military choices that offered themselves to the Turks if they intervened were probably just as important in provoking second thoughts among Enver's associates. Moreover, there is extensive evidence that neither Wangenheim nor his Austro-Hungarian colleague had yet abandoned his belief that "premature" action by the Turks was useless or even dangerous, and though they officially pushed the conspirators toward war, their personal scruples and hesitations may well have shown through their formal representations.[78]

Despite Talât's and Halil's backtracking Enver assured Wangenheim that things were going to be all right, especially since he could still count on Cemal's cooperation. Enver explained that he intended to dispatch the fleet into the Black Sea as quickly as possible and to equip Souchon with a sealed order which would authorize him to open hostilities without a formal declaration of war. In the event he could not obtain a

[76] See Zimmermann's marginal comments on Wangenheim's dispatch No. 1,087, *Dt 128 Nr. 5 secr.*, Bd. 4; Jagow to FO, 24 Oct 1914, No. 305, *ibid.*; and AHFM, *Krieg 21a, Türkei*, Hohenlohe to AHFM, 24 Oct, No. 626.

[77] *Ibid.*, Pallavicini to Berchtold, 22 Oct 1914, No. 62/P; Jackh Papers, No. 11, "Besprechung mit Enver Pascha am 23. Oktober 1914."

[78] Cf. FO, *Dt 128 Nr. 5 secr.*, Bd. 4, Wangenheim to FO, 24 Oct 1914, No. 1,094; Jackh Papers, No. 12, Humann to Busse, 25 Oct; AHFM, *Krieg 21a, Türkei*, Pallavicini to Berchtold, 29 Oct, No. 63-B/P; Bayur, III:1, 229-32, and *passim*; Kühlmann, pp. 448-55.

majority decision for war from his colleagues Enver would radio to Souchon not to open the sealed order, which would serve as a signal that the admiral must manufacture a suitable incident on his own. Understandably, Wangenheim was not satisfied with this complicated arrangement and demanded a "clear, written order from Enver to Souchon" which would place the responsibility for Ottoman intervention where it belonged: on a member of the Porte.[79]

Shortly before midnight of October 24-25 Enver sent word to Humann that most of the problems had been solved in the meantime. Although Halil was still not convinced that the time for intervention had come and intended to present his objections in person to the Berlin government, Talât had now swung back to the side of Enver and Cemal. Moreover, the latter three were certain that Halil would collaborate with them once hostilities started. To allay Wangenheim's misgivings Enver had meanwhile also drafted a more precise authorization for Souchon. The order in question, which was transmitted to the admiral on the morning of October 25, explicitly called for Black Sea maneuvers with the "entire fleet" and an attack on the Russian fleet if a "suitable opportunity" presented itself.[80] Simultaneously, Cemal issued a secret directive to the

[79] FO, *Dt 128 Nr. 5 secr.*, Bd. 4, Wangenheim to FO, 24 Oct 1914, No. 1,094, 25 Oct, No. 1,107. The "sealed order" in question had originally been drafted on October 22 and read as follows: "The Turkish fleet is to achieve naval supremacy in the Black Sea. Seek out the Russian fleet and attack it wherever you find it without declaration of war." Cf. *ibid.*, Wangenheim to FO, 22 Oct, No. 1,087; Mühlmann, *Deutschland*, p. 102; Jackh, *Rising Crescent*, p. 117; Bayur, III:1, 233.

[80] While this new order made the previously mentioned sealed order (of October 22) essentially superfluous, the latter apparently was given to Souchon as well, with the proviso that he should open it before initiating hostilities. Cf. Jäckh Papers, No. 11, Enver to Humann, 24 Oct 1914; Wangenheim's dispatch No. 1,107, *Dt 128 Nr. 5 secr.*, Bd. 4; and Gotthard Jäschke, "Mitteilungen: Zum Eintritt der Türkei in den Ersten Weltkrieg," *Die Welt des Islams*, n.s., 4 (1955), p. 51.

senior officers of the Ottoman fleet that Adm. Souchon was entitled to receive their compliance with his orders.[81]

Two days later, October 27, the Ottoman fleet steamed out of the Bosporus, ostensibly to engage in another round of training maneuvers in the Black Sea. Once the ships were at sea, Souchon informed the German and Ottoman senior officers under his command that they were on a mission of war. Deviating from his original plan, which had called for a high seas encounter with the Russian fleet in advance of any attacks on the Russian coast, Souchon now ordered an immediate assault on the enemy's coastal installations as the first order of business. His decision in this matter was probably sound tactically, but it produced needless political embarrassment for Enver's faction, which had counted on a much less provocative initiation of hostilities, namely, a manufactured incident at sea.[82]

By and large, the coastal raids were carried out in accordance with Souchon's instructions. In the early morning hours of October 29 several harbors and points on the Russian coast were shelled, mines were dropped in major shipping lanes, and a number of Russian vessels were destroyed either in port or at sea. A few hours later Souchon radioed to Constantinople that in response to continuous Russian interference with the maneuvers of the Ottoman fleet on the preceding day, "hostilities have been opened today."[83]

The news of Souchon's raid provoked a major crisis in the

[81] *Ibid.*; and AHFM, *Krieg 21a, Türkei*, Pallavicini to Berchtold, 29 Oct 1914, No. 63 A-D/P. Regarding Cemal's involvement in the preparations for the attack see also Bayur, III:1, 235-37; and Ali Ihsan Sâbis, *Harb Hâtiralarim* [My War Memoirs], 3 vols. (Istanbul and Ankara, 1943-52), II, 40ff.

[82] See Wangenheim's dispatch No. 1,107, *Dt 128 Nr. 5 secr.*, Bd. 4; AHFM, *Krieg 21a, Türkei*, Pallavicini's dispatch No. 63 A-D/P; Pallavicini to AHFM, 31 Oct 1914, No. 762; Lorey, I, 46-50, Bayur, III:1, 237-39.

[83] Lorey, I, 50-56; Bayur, III:1, 239; FO, *Dt 128 Nr. 5 secr.*, Bd. 4, Wangenheim to FO, 29 Oct 1914, No. 1,146.

ranks of the Ottoman cabinet. Both the grand vizier and Cavid protested vigorously and demanded the immediate cessation of the operation. Enver obliged outwardly by sending a ceasefire order to the fleet, but as he himself explained to Wangenheim, a "hint" had been included that Souchon need not take the order literally. Moreover, according to Enver, he and his supporters were agreed to dislodge both the grand vizier and Cavid unless they abandoned their opposition to intervention by the following evening.[84]

This was apparently the last information the Germans (or for that matter, the Austro-Hungarian embassy) managed to obtain about the situation at the Porte until the evening of October 31. What happened in the intervening day and a half has to be reconstructed on the basis of imprecise statements made later by Enver, Talât, and other Ottoman leaders, but certain, salient facts seem to be well established. To begin with, it seems clear that around noon on October 30 the grand vizier, Cavid, and three other ministers opposed to war announced their resignations from the cabinet but reversed their decision later on in the day at the request (or perhaps behest) of the central committee of the Party. It is also fairly certain that the central committee itself had two stormy meetings on October 30. During the first meeting, apparently held in the morning, a 17 to 10 vote in favor of intervention was reportedly cast. The second meeting, called in response to the resignation of the five cabinet members, was characterized by renewed debate on the question of war or peace during which Cemal presented a highly garbled account of the origins and purposes of Souchon's raid. The result of the meeting was a formal reconciliation of the various factions, highlighted by the reconstitution of the original cabinet. There is strong circumstantial evidence that the grand vizier's return to his post was causally related to a promise by Enver and his followers that they would not

[84] FO, *Dt 128 Nr. 5 secr.*, Bd. 4, Wangenheim to FO, 30 Oct 1914, No. 1,160. Cf. Emin, pp. 75-76; Bayur, III:1, 239-44.

object to the dispatch of conciliatory notes to Petrograd and the other Entente governments.[85]

As previously mentioned, neither Wangenheim nor his Austro-Hungarian colleague had any part in these deliberations at the Porte. It was only during the evening of October 31 that they were informed of the sentiments and plans of the Ottoman leaders.[86] Among other things, it was only then that they learned of the decision by Enver's faction not to dispense with the grand vizier's services even though the latter was still as opposed to intervention as ever. As Talât explained to Pallavicini, it was most desirable to keep Said Halim in office, "particularly in deference to public opinion." Talât intimated furthermore that he and everyone else in the cabinet, "except for Enver," were highly displeased with the form

[85] Cf. *ibid.*, pp. 245-52; Jackh Papers, No. 12, "Vertrauliche Mitteilungen vom 31. Oktober 1914"; FO, *Wk*, Bd. 55, Wangenheim to FO, 1 Nov 1914, No. 1,183. It appears from the two German reports that Cemal's speech in the committee meeting dwelled at length on the charge that the Russians had planned to mine the Bosporus. This was a trumped-up charge which apparently originated with Souchon or his chief-of-staff, Lt. Comdr. Wilhelm Busse. It is not clear whether Cemal was aware of its phoniness when he addressed the committee. On this issue see especially FO, *Dt 128 Nr. 5 secr.*, Bd. 4, Wangenheim to FO, 30 Oct, No. 1,163; *Wk*, Bd. 54, same to same, 31 Oct, No. 1,174; Jackh Papers, No. 12, "Aussagen russischer Gefangener von Pruth. . . . 29 Oktober 1914"; "J." to Enver, 30 Oct; and Lorey, I, 51.

[86] It would appear that at this juncture even the most experienced "intelligence agent" of the German embassy, Paul Weitz, was unable to secure any information from his various Turkish contacts. Weitz, the permanent correspondent of the *Frankfurter Zeitung* in Constantinople during much of the Wilhelmian period, was later attached to the Foreign Ministry of the Weimar Republic as a *"Wissenschaftlicher Hilfsarbeiter."* On his role as a political informant and adviser of the Constantinople embassy before and during the war, cf. FO, *Nachlass Paul Weitz, passim*; *Dt 135 Nr. 1 secr.*, Bd. 1, Weitz to Zimmermann, 15 Dec 1916; Hallgarten, I and II, *passim*; Pomiankowski, p. 50.

Souchon's attack had taken, that is, his failure to restrict hostilities to the high seas as he had been expected to.[87]

The dissatisfaction among his colleagues was confirmed by Enver who called Humann to a meeting in his office on the evening of October 31. According to the war minister, he and his followers had managed to restore a semblance of unity in the cabinet but only by making a concession to the grand vizier who, after all, had been "duped" rather badly by Enver's faction. The concession in question was the dispatch of "a kind of excusatory note to Russia," but, as Enver hastened to add, such a last minute gesture would surely have "no real effect." Humann was greatly upset by this revelation. He denounced the Turkish plan as dangerous and contrary to prior agreements and even intimated that a last minute disavowal of the alliance by the Porte might force Berlin to make a deal with Russia at Ottoman expense, but Enver insisted that his hands were tied, since he was isolated in the cabinet.[88]

The following day, November 1, the excusatory note conceded to the grand vizier was duly delivered to the Russian government, but the conciliatory language of the message was more than offset by the unwarranted assertion that the hostilities in the Black Sea had been provoked by the Russian fleet. Quite understandably, Foreign Minister Serge Sazonov rejected the Ottoman claims but intimated that a state of war between the two countries was not necessarily inevitable, provided that the Turks expelled all German military personnel at once.[89]

In Constantinople, meanwhile, both Wangenheim and Pallavicini were desperately trying to counteract the centrifugal tendencies in the Ottoman cabinet. Mindful of Talât's insist-

[87] AHFM, *Krieg 21a, Türkei,* Pallavicini to AHFM, 31 Oct 1914, No. 762.

[88] Jackh Papers, No. 12, "Vertrauliche Mitteilungen vom 31. Oktober 1914."

[89] *Die Internationalen Beziehungen . . . ,* ser. 2, VI:1, 355-56. Cf. Bayur, III:1, 254-58.

ence that the continued presence of Said Halim in the cabinet was politically necessary, Pallavicini, in agreement with Wangenheim, called on the grand vizier during the morning of November 1 and urged him to collaborate with Enver's faction. Said Halim, resentful of the game which had been played behind his back, refused to listen and declared that he was determined to resign. In view of the grand vizier's attitude, Pallavicini and Wangenheim thereupon agreed to throw their weight in the opposite direction, to push for the immediate appointment of either Talât or the former grand vizier, Ibrahim Hakki Paşa, to the head of the cabinet. However, before they got around to implementing their new strategy, Wangenheim received warning from Enver, Halil, and Talât himself that they still considered the continued presence of Said Halim at the helm of the cabinet indispensable. Whereas Talât had previously cited "public opinion" as the primary factor in this matter, the three now admitted that the resignation of Said Halim might cause "a split in the committee," aside from provoking unfavorable impressions both at home and abroad.[90]

There is no indication how Wangenheim reacted to this new twist, but it would appear from circumstantial evidence that he did nothing, leaving it to Enver's men to solve the cabinet crisis in their own way. Pallavicini, it should be noted, was by this time so confused about what was going on in the Ottoman cabinet that even several days later he could offer little more than conjectures on this subject to his superiors in Vienna.[91]

[90] AHFM, *Krieg 21a, Türkei*, Pallavicini to AHFM, 1 Nov 1914, No. 766; FO, *Dt 128 Nr. 5 secr.*, Bd. 5, Wangenheim to FO, 2 Nov, No. 1,205.

[91] See AHFM, *Krieg 21a, Türkei*, Pallavicini to Berchtold, 5 Nov 1914, No. 64/P. It might be mentioned, parenthetically, that the confusion of Wangenheim and Pallavicini was seemingly shared by Cemal and Talât; for their postwar remarks on the October cabinet crisis are well-nigh incoherent. Cf. Djemal, pp. 130-32; "Posthumous Memoirs of Talaat Pasha," *Current History*, xv (1921-22), 292-94.

From Alliance Treaty to Intervention

The tug-of-war between the grand vizier and Enver's faction was formally ended in a dramatic cabinet meeting at the grand vizier's house during the night of November 1-2. As Halil informed Wangenheim the next day, Talât had used this meeting to express "on behalf of the Party" his dissatisfaction with Said Halim's attitude. Talât reminded the grand vizier that he himself had signed the alliance treaty with Germany and that he would therefore have to accept "the responsibility for all consequences arising therefrom." According to Halil the grand vizier had thereupon agreed to stay on, but it appears that an implicit threat against his life rather than the persuasiveness of Talât's arguments was ultimately responsible for Said Halim's about-face.[92]

Although outwardly the settlement with the grand vizier marked a triumph for the war party, Halil took pains to warn the Germans that the rift in the Ottoman leadership was by no means completely cured. He argued, in particular, that he and the rest of the interventionists were still in a precarious position vis-à-vis their other colleagues, especially Cavid, who were vociferously denouncing the terms of the existing alliance treaty. According to Halil, Cavid and his "friends" were particularly incensed that the existing treaty with Germany offered the Ottoman empire no advantages whatsoever, especially in terms of long-range protection. They demanded above all that the mutual alliance obligations should apply for a longer period of time, at least 10 years, and that the Ottoman empire should receive formal German guarantees not only against Russia but against Britain, France, and "a coalition of smaller states" as well. As Halil explained to Wangenheim, a prompt revision of the existing German-Ottoman treaty along these lines would be appreciated by Enver's faction, so that it could cope

[92] Wangenheim's dispatch No. 1,205, *Dt 128 Nr. 5 secr.*, Bd. 5; Jackh Papers, No. 13, "Vertrauliche Mitteilungen vom 3. November 1914"; Pallavicini's dispatch No. 64/P, AHFM, *Krieg 21a, Türkei.* Cf. Bayur, III:1, 258-59.

more effectively with the oppositional elements arrayed behind Cavid. Moreover, it would be "desirable" for Germany to confirm that she did not intend to push for the restoration of her capitulatory rights even if other powers should try to regain theirs after the war. In return, the Porte would obligate itself to give special treatment to Germany (a most-favored-nation status under some circumstances) and to assist the Central Powers militarily if they became involved in another war.[93]

In view of the fact that Cavid and three other anti-interventionist ministers gave up their portfolios within the following 48 hours,[94] Halil's claim that the proposed treaty revisions were necessary to strengthen Enver's faction in the cabinet and central committee of the Party appears dubious. Indeed, there is reason to suspect that *all* of the Ottoman leaders wanted the revision of the alliance treaty, and that the need to satisfy "the opposition" was purposely exaggerated by Enver's men to frighten Berlin into prompt acceptance of the new Ottoman demands. Be that as it may, the Ottoman proposals met with little enthusiasm in Berlin (and even less in Vienna), and it took over two months of hard bargaining before the Porte got its way.[95]

[93] Wangenheim's dispatch No. 1,205, *Dt 128 Nr. 5 secr.*, Bd. 5.

[94] The resignations of Cavid; the minister of posts, Oskan Efendi; the minister of commerce, Süleyman el-Bostanî Bey; and the public works minister, Çürüksulu Mahmud Paşa, were publicly announced on November 3 and 4. See the brief bulletins in the Constantinople paper *Le Moniteur Oriental*; and Bayur, III:1, 259.

[95] See Chapter IV.

CHAPTER III

The German Generals in the Ottoman War Effort, 1914-18

ON NOVEMBER 2, 1914, four days after Souchon's provocative attack on the Russian Black Sea coast, the Tsarist government formally declared war on the Ottoman empire. The British and French governments followed suit a few days later, as did Serbia and the other smaller countries fighting on the Entente side. Already on November 3—that is, before London's and Paris's official declarations of war —an Anglo-French naval squadron subjected the outer forts at the Dardanelles to a brief but massive bombardment, while at about the same time skirmishes between Ottoman and Entente troops erupted along some of the eastern and southern frontiers of the Turkish empire. Full-fledged Ottoman participation in the great European war had thereby become an irrevocable fact.

The course of the war in the Near and Middle East during the next four years has been depicted in numerous general and specialized studies, and no attempt will be made in this book to cover the military developments in the various Turkish theaters of war.[1] Suffice it to say that the Turks fought (either alone or with the support of German and Austro-Hungarian troops) on over half a dozen widely scattered fronts, on most of which they held their own quite remarkably throughout much of the war.

In Transcaucasia and eastern Anatolia, the Ottoman Third Army, which was later assisted by another Turkish army, campaigned with limited success against strong Russian forces

[1] The most informative general surveys of the military events in the Near and Middle East are found in the pioneering study of Commandant Maurice Larcher, *La guerre turque dans la guerre mondiale* (Paris, 1926), and in Mühlmann, *deutsch-türkische Waffenbündnis*. On naval developments see especially Lorey.

until the summer of 1917, both sides sustaining heavy losses in what was much of the time a war of maneuver. In 1916 the Russians penetrated deep into Ottoman territory and stayed there until late 1917. In 1918 the Turks exploited the revolutionary turmoil in Russia to advance into the Transcaucasian provinces of the old Tsarist empire, where they planned to establish their rule either directly or indirectly.[2] As will be shown later on, this expansionist drive not only produced very serious tensions between the Turks and their German allies but also weakened the Ottoman military effort at some of the other Asiatic fronts.

In Mesopotamia the Turks from November 1914 on faced a slow but steady British advance from the Persian Gulf. Although the Ottoman troops in the Euphrates-Tigris region (eventually known as the Sixth Army) won a temporary respite through their victory at Kut-el-Amara in 1916, they lost Bagdad to the British in the following spring and were on the point of withdrawing from Mosul when the war ended.[3]

Incursions of Ottoman troops and German agents into Persian territory during and after the winter of 1914-15 led to the opening of a new front. Sporadic fighting between Turks and Russians in Persia continued until the spring of 1917, when their reverses in Mesopotamia forced the Turks to withdraw. However, following the evacuation of Russian troops from Persia, the Turks in early 1918 reinvaded the northern provinces of that unhappy country and maintained there a pre-

[2] Useful specialized studies of the war in Transcaucasia include Felix Guse, *Die Kaukasusfront im Weltkrieg* (Leipzig, 1940); N. G. Korsun, *Pervaya mirovaya voina na Kavkazkom fronte* [The First World War on the Caucasian Front] (Moscow, 1946); and the relevant chapters in W.E.D. Allen and Paul Muratoff, *Caucasian Battlefields* (Cambridge, 1953). See also Firuz Kazemzadeh, *The Struggle for Transcaucasia, 1917-1921* (New York, 1951).

[3] On the Mesopotamian campaigns see especially F. J. Moberly, *History of the Great War: The Campaign in Mesopotamia*, 4 vols. (London, 1923-27).

carious foothold against native opposition and British troops until the end of the war.[4]

In the Palestinian area the military situation until the summer of 1916 was characterized by sporadic offensive activities on the part of the Ottoman Fourth Army and of German and Austro-Hungarian units attached to it. Between January 1915 and August 1916 the Turks launched two major advances and several smaller raids to the Suez Canal; after September 1916 the British assumed the offensive. They cleared the Turks out of the Sinai Desert and advanced into southern Palestine, where they were held up in the first two battles of Gaza, but broke through in the Third Gaza Battle and captured Jerusalem in December 1917. Resuming their offensive in 1918 the British, assisted by Arab insurgents, won several overwhelming victories in northern Palestine and Syria and were driving the remnants of the Ottoman and German defenders into Anatolia when the Armistice of Mudros terminated the hostilities.[5]

In the Arabian peninsula, which was only tenuously controlled by the Turks, the British-sponsored Arab revolt in the summer of 1916 opened yet another theater of war in the Middle East. Most Ottoman garrisons east of the Jordan River and in the Hejaz were dislodged or annihilated in the ensuing two years, though the Turks held on to a few fortified places until the end of the war. In 1918 the Arab insurgents provided effective assistance to the British army in its northward advance through Palestine and Syria.[6]

[4] Ulrich Gehrke, *Persien in der deutschen Orientpolitik während des Ersten Weltkrieges*, 2 vols. (Stuttgart [1960]), offers much new material on this subject.

[5] See especially Sir George MacMunn and Cyril Falls, *History of the Great War: Military Operations, Egypt and Palestine*, 3 vols. (London, 1928-30).

[6] See George Antonius, *The Arab Awakening* (Philadelphia, 1939), pp. 126-275; Z. N. Zeine, *Arab-Turkish Relations and the Emergence of Arab Nationalism* (Beirut, 1958); M. S. Lazarev, *Kruchenye turet-*

German Generals in the Ottoman War

While Ottoman military operations in most of these Asian theaters were of considerable importance in terms of diverting Allied manpower and equipment from the major fronts in Europe, the most valuable contribution the Turks made to the war effort of the Central Powers was their successful defense of the Black Sea Straits.[7] By their dogged resistance to the British (and French) at the Dardanelles in 1915 the Ottoman army and navy not only prevented the opening of a badly needed supply route between Russia and her Western allies but also contributed indirectly to a stabilization of the Balkan situation which benefited the Central Powers. In particular, the successful defense of Gallipoli by the Turks played an indirect role in Bulgaria's decision to join the Central Powers in the autumn of 1915, and conversely, helped to lessen Rumania's interest in coming in on the side of the Entente.[8]

Finally, it should be mentioned that in addition to tying down sizable Entente military forces throughout the Near and Middle East, the Ottoman empire contributed several army divisions to the European campaigns of its allies. This "loaning" of Ottoman troops began in the summer of 1916 and con-

---

skogo gospodstva na Arabskom vostoke, 1914-18 gg. [The Shattering of Turkish Rule in the Arabic East, 1914-18] (Moscow, 1960).

[7] Cf. État-major général Turc, *Campagne des Dardanelles*: Historique des opérations ottomanes dans la guerre mondiale (Paris, 1924); Carl Mühlmann, *Der Kampf um die Dardanellen*: Schlachten des Weltkrieges, vol. 16 (Oldenburg, 1927); C. F. Aspinall-Oglander, *History of the Great War: Military Operations, Gallipoli*, 2 vols. (London, 1929-32); Reichsarchiv, *Der Weltkrieg 1914 bis 1918,* ix (Berlin, 1933), 173-93; Lorey, ii, 46-170; and Alan Moorehead, *Gallipoli* (New York, 1956). See also Trumbull Higgins, *Winston Churchill and the Dardanelles* (New York, 1963).

[8] On the Balkan situation in 1915 and the effects on it of the military stalemate in the Straits, cf. Notovich, *passim*; Carl Mühlmann, *Oberste Heeresleitung und Balkan im Weltkrieg, 1914-1918* (Berlin, 1942), pp. 52-149; Smith, pp. 282-350, and *passim*.

tinued until March 1918, when the last Ottoman divisions returned to Turkey. At least for a short time, late in 1916, close to 100,000 Ottoman soldiers fought on European fronts—three divisions in Rumania, two divisions in Galicia, and another two in Macedonia.[9]

During most of the war the Ottoman war effort at sea was restricted almost exclusively to the Black Sea and the Straits region. In both areas operations of the German-Ottoman fleet were essentially defensive in character, though occasional sorties into Russian coastal waters were undertaken. Despite numerous technical and tactical problems, among them an almost chronic shortage of fuel, the fleet gave valuable assistance to the defenders of Gallipoli in 1915 and to the Ottoman army operating in eastern Anatolia. South of the Dardanelles naval action against the vastly superior fleets of the Allies was limited until 1918 to sorties by German submarines and small Turkish vessels. An attempt by the *Goeben* and *Breslau* in January 1918 to initiate cruiser warfare in the Aegean ended quickly with the sinking of the *Breslau* and the crippling of the *Goeben* in an Allied mine field.[10]

Aside from the fact that the Ottoman empire had barely recovered from its previous armed conflicts with Italy and the Balkan states, the Turkish war effort from 1914 to 1918 was seriously hampered by a number of unique problems. One major handicap, of course, was the general economic backwardness and financial debility of the Ottoman empire. Practically without heavy industry and with a notoriously empty state treasury, the Turks were singularly ill-prepared to conduct war against some of the major powers of the world.[11] However,

[9] Mühlmann, *deutsch-türkische Waffenbündnis*, pp. 106-108, 119-24, 179-80, 349.

[10] See *ibid.*, pp. 108-12, 181-83, 234-35; and the more detailed treatment in Lorey, I, 57-374, and II, 20-216.

[11] On the economic and financial debility of the Ottoman empire at the beginning of World War I see especially Bayur, III:1, 181-93.

due to massive transfusions of gold and money from Germany and Austria-Hungary and, after 1915, of war materiel and other supplies, the Turks managed to keep their ragged armies in the field and their tottering economy going until the autumn of 1918.[12]

A second major problem facing the Ottoman empire throughout the war derived from the heterogeneity of its population and the doubtful loyalties of some of the ethnic and religious minorities. While dissatisfaction with the *Ittihad ve Terakki* regime in general and its war policy in particular was not limited to the non-Turkish population groups, it was certainly most pronounced among the Ottoman Greeks, the Armenians, and the Arabs. However, it is clear that in almost all cases the repressive wartime measures the Porte and the Ottoman military authorities initiated against these groups were out of proportion to the objective needs of internal security. In fact there is considerable evidence that the repressive programs frequently had the opposite effect, fanning latent discontent into open opposition or outright revolt, as in the case of many Arab tribes. Moreover, it is now fairly clear that the Porte's ruthless campaign against its Armenian subjects in 1915 and thereafter was intended primarily to decimate, and to disperse the remnants of, an "unwanted" ethnic minority and only incidentally concerned with providing security against uprisings, espionage, sabotage, or any other interference with the Ottoman war effort. Through its persecution or harassment of the Armenians, Greeks, and other minorities the *Ittihad ve Terakki* regime seriously hurt the general war effort of the Ottoman empire, especially by eliminating the very people who had the skills and experience to keep the economy going.[13]

A third major impediment to the Ottoman war effort between 1914 and 1918 was the empire's woefully underdeveloped transportation network. To appreciate the difficulties facing the Turks the reader should recall that the only link between Con-

[12] See Chapter VIII.   [13] See Chapter VII.

stantinople, the administrative and economic heart of the empire, and the various Asian theaters of war was the badly truncated line of the Bagdad railroad. Since west of the Euphrates River alone there were two gaps in the line, one in the Taurus and another in the Amanus range, all shipments to the eastern fronts in the first years of the war had to be unloaded twice and moved to the next section of track over primitive mountain roads. From Aleppo southward a number of rail lines —with varying gauges—extended into Palestine and the Hejaz, but the Ottoman forces in Mesopotamia and Persia found themselves several hundred miles removed from the end of the unfinished Bagdad line. The situation in eastern Anatolia, on the Russo-Ottoman front, was even more critical. Average distances between the fighting troops and the nearest railheads were three to four hundred miles, with much of the intervening terrain mountainous. Although this serious logistic handicap on the Transcaucasian front was initially overcome by the use of sea transports along the Anatolian Black Sea coast, Russian naval interference increasingly cut off this source of supplies, at least until the fall of 1917.[14]

As Carl Mühlmann in his valuable studies of the German–Ottoman war effort has shown, both the German Supreme Army Command (OHL) and the Austro–Hungarian general staff endeavored throughout the war to direct the military energies of the Turks toward tasks which would most effectively supplement their own operations at the various European fronts. To this end the OHL in particular strove, with limited success, to secure a strong voice in the general direction of the Ottoman armed forces. It is true that between 1914 and 1918 most Ottoman operations corresponded quite closely to what the OHL deemed desirable or necessary, but this general har-

[14] Mühlmann, *deutsch-türkische Waffenbündnis*, pp. 30-35. For a discussion of Ottoman and German efforts to expand the railroad network during the war, particularly in regard to the Bagdad line, see Chapter IX.

mony was primarily due to the fact that the Ottoman military leaders usually shared the strategic views held by the Germans. Whenever such agreement was lacking—as happened several times—the Ottoman High Command had no compunction about pursuing an independent course of action. Even Gen. Erich Ludendorff, the most energetic of Germany's military leaders, was to learn very soon after his entry into the OHL that imperiousness would get him nowhere in his dealings with the Ottoman ally.

To understand the basic limitations of German (and Austro–Hungarian) influence on the general conduct of Ottoman military operations, it should be remembered that throughout the war the central direction of all Ottoman armed forces, including the navy, was in the hands of Enver, who had assumed the title of "vice-generalissimo" (or "deputy commander-in-chief") on October 21, 1914.[15] As the de facto head of the Ottoman armed forces (the constitutional status of the Sultan, Mehmed V, as supreme commander was a mere formality), Enver was beholden to no one but some of his fellow ministers and the dominant faction in the central committee of the Union and Progress Party. Though his headquarters staff after 1914 was full of German officers, none of them, including Generals Fritz Bronsart von Schellendorff and Hans von Seeckt, who successively served as his chief-of-staff, had any command authority over the Ottoman armed forces other than that explicitly delegated to them by Enver.[16]

Under article 3 of the alliance treaty of August 2, 1914 the German military mission in Turkey had been formally assured "an effective influence on the general direction of the army," but the provision remained largely inoperative. While Gen. Liman and a good many other members of his mission were

[15] *Schulthess Europäischer Geschichtskalender* (Munich, 1860ff.), v. 55, p. 877. Cf. Pomiankowski, p. 88.

[16] On the distribution of German personnel at Enver's headquarters as of January 1918 see Appendix A.

German Generals in the Ottoman War

entrusted with the command of individual Ottoman armies, divisions, or regiments, they were only rarely in a position to influence the entire military effort of the Ottoman empire. It should be added that the same generalization applies to those German generals who were transferred to Turkey in the course of the war and who did not belong to the military mission, such as Field Marshal Colmar von der Goltz and Gen. von Falkenhayn.[17]

While the degree of German influence on the general conduct of the war varied considerably between 1914 and 1918, with Enver retaining ultimate control in all important questions, there was at least one sphere in which the Germans were actually given considerable freedom of action: the navy. Undoubtedly the prolonged absence of Navy Minister Cemal from Constantinople (he served as an army commander and military governor of the Syrian provinces from November 1914 until the end of 1917), explains to a large extent why Admiral Souchon, and after August 1917, his successor von Rebeur-Paschwitz, enjoyed somewhat greater latitude in the direction of the fleet than did the German officers holding field commands in the Ottoman army. It should be added, however, that all major decisions concerning naval operations required clearance from the Ottoman High Command, that is, from Enver, and it would be an error to assume that either Souchon or Rebeur-Paschwitz were ever absolute masters of the Sultan's fleet.[18]

Finally, a few words must be said about the peculiar structure of the *Ittihad ve Terakki* regime after October 1914. According to most traditional accounts of Turkish wartime history the Ottoman empire was ruled dictatorially by a triumvirate com-

[17] For a list of major Ottoman field commands (above division level) held by German generals during the war years see Appendix B.

[18] For brief summaries of Souchon's and Rebeur-Paschwitz's wartime activities see Mühlmann, *deutsch-türkische Waffenbündnis,* pp. 280-81; and Wilhelm Wolfslast, *Der Seekrieg 1914-1918* (Leipzig, 1938), pp. 108-11, 260-65, 365-70.

posed of Enver, Talât, and Cemal (or possibly even by Enver alone), but such generalizations are at best half-truths. From the evidence now available it must instead be concluded that from November 1914 to early October 1918 the direction of Ottoman policy lay in the hands of a sizable group of Union and Progress Party functionaries, among whom Enver and Talât were at most "first among equals" while Cemal did not even qualify for that distinction.

Especially in regard to foreign policy matters the post-October 1914 decisions of the Porte were usually the product of compromises among various factions in the upper echelons of the *Ittihad ve Terakki* Party organzation. While there was considerable fluidity in the alignment of Party leaders on various policy issues it is possible to distinguish at least two groups which regularly disagreed on matters of foreign policy. One group, that sided with Enver on most occasions, seems to have held a majority of seats in the central committee, but the other faction, usually headed by Cavid and including Said Halim among its members, proved itself a rather effective counterforce during much of the war period. Despite his ostentatious resignation from the cabinet after Turkey's intervention and his evident pro-French orientation, Cavid retained the confidence of many of his interventionist party colleagues, particularly Talât, and was thus able to influence the course of Ottoman policy on a variety of important issues. In fact, it was Cavid who handled many of the financial, economic, and political negotiations with the Central Powers during the war years, notwithstanding that officially he remained outside the cabinet until February 1917 (when Talât replaced Said Halim as grand vizier and formally brought Cavid back into the government as minister of finance).[19]

[19] On Cavid's important role in the Ottoman government throughout the war period see especially Chapters v, viii-x. Regarding major changes in the Ottoman cabinet between 1914 and 1918 consult Appendix E.

German Generals in the Ottoman War

FRICTIONS AND COMMAND PROBLEMS

Reference has already been made to the fact that in August and September of 1914 the ranking German officer in the Ottoman empire, Gen. Liman von Sanders, had become so frustrated by the procrastination of the Porte that he attempted twice to have himself and the other members of the German military mission recalled from Turkey. Far from becoming one of the masters of the Ottoman empire during the pre-intervention period (as has recently been asserted), the chief of the military mission actually wielded little influence of any sort outside of the Ottoman First Army, to whose command he had been assigned shortly after the outbreak of war in Europe. It is true that Liman frequently participated in top-level conferences at Ottoman GHQ, but his role there was clearly that of an adviser rather than policy-maker. In fact his recommendations on general strategic issues were repeatedly ignored or rejected by Enver and other high-ranking Ottoman and German military leaders. At the same time, Liman's relationship with the German embassy in Constantinople deteriorated rapidly because of his periodic interference with Wangenheim's own dispositions. By mid-October 1914, at the latest, the chief of the military mission found himself all but isolated from most of his German colleagues. In light of the evidence now available there is no longer any reason to question Liman's later claim that he was actually not even informed of Souchon's Black Sea raid until after it had been launched.[20]

Liman's undiplomatic complaints about the prolonged passivity of the Turks, his disagreements with Enver and some of the German officers on the latter's staff, and above all his high-handed attempts to get the military mission withdrawn from Turkey, had long since aroused the ire of Wangenheim. As soon as Ottoman participation in the war was assured the am-

[20] See Liman, Chapters iv-v; and Trumpener, "Liman and the German-Ottoman Alliance," pp. 181-89. Cf. Gottlieb, p. 58.

bassador took steps to get rid of the troublesome general. On October 31, two days after Souchon's raid, Wangenheim sent a note to Bethmann Hollweg asserting that Liman's continued presence in Constantinople would produce intolerable strains between Germans and Turks, as well as among the Germans themselves. The ambassador accused Liman in particular of "great nervousness" and a tendency "to judge everything from a personal point of view," and urged the chancellor to arrange as quickly as possible for the general's transfer to another duty post. According to Wangenheim the most suitable man to re-place Liman was obviously Field Marshal von der Goltz, who had spent many years in Turkey during the preceding three decades.[21]

Much to Wangenheim's chagrin, his proposal met with only lukewarm response at German Imperial Headquarters. While generally sympathetic with the ambassador's case, it notified him that the Turks themselves would have to apply for Liman's recall. Wangenheim was forced to inform Bethmann Hollweg that he could not possibly ask the Turks to issue such a blunt request, and that, in any case, Enver had meanwhile indicated that he needed Liman as the commanding general of the First Army. According to the ambassador there was hope, though, that Liman would soon move into "the field" with his troops, in which case an official Ottoman invitation to Goltz could probably be arranged quite easily.[22]

There are indications that Wangenheim's requests for Li-

---

[21] FO, *Türkei 139*, Bd. 33, Wangenheim to FO, 31 Oct 1914, No. 1,178. On Goltz' previous service in the Ottoman empire see [Colmar von der Goltz], *Denkwürdigkeiten*, Friedrich von der Goltz and Wolfgang Foerster, eds. (Berlin, 1932), pp. 106-63, 311-22; Hallgarten, *passim*; General Pertev Demirhan, *General-Feldmarschall Colmar von der Goltz. . . . Aus meinen persönlichen Erinnerungen* (Göttingen, 1960), pp. 15-198, *passim*.

[22] FO, *Türkei 139*, Bd. 33, Bethmann Hollweg to Wangenheim, 3 Nov 1914, No. 25; Wangenheim to FO, 5 Nov, No. 1,240; Goltz, p. 378.

man's recall (which continued) aroused growing consternation at German Imperial Headquarters, but Bethmann Hollweg was sufficiently impressed by the ambassador's complaints to call Goltz (who was then serving as German Military Governor of Belgium) for an interview. The elderly field marshal, who was none too happy with his current assignment, readily agreed to accept a new duty post in the Ottoman empire even if Liman, his junior in rank, were not placed under his authority.[23] When Bethmann Hollweg notified Constantinople of the field marshal's availability the Turks at first proposed to make Goltz an "adjutant general" in the Sultan's retinue, but since this offer was linked with the proposal to attach an Ottoman general to the Kaiser's personal staff in return, the latter rejected the "bargain" out of hand. However, a few days later, on November 25, Wangenheim was able to inform Berlin that despite the rebuff on the "exchange" proposal Enver had made it clear that he wanted and needed Goltz in Turkey. As Wangenheim explained, the vice-generalissimo was thinking of placing Liman in command of the Transcaucasian front and would therefore need another German "strategic adviser" at his Constantinople headquarters.[24] Simultaneously Wangenheim informed Zimmermann privately that the replacement of Liman by Goltz would be a godsend for all concerned. Liman, he wrote, "has completely severed his personal relations with me and persecutes the entire staff of the embassy with the most incredible chicanery. . . . Goltz would be a relief [*eine Erlösung*] for Turkey, the embassy, and the military mission itself."[25]

In response to Wangenheim's official message, the Kaiser on

[23] FO, *Türkei 139*, Bd. 33, Jagow to FO, 7 Nov 1914, No. 347; Goltz, p. 378.

[24] FO, *Türkei 139*, Bd. 33, Wangenheim to FO, 18 Nov 1914, No. 1,371; Zimmermann to Wangenheim, 22 Nov, No. 1,314; Wangenheim to FO, 25 Nov, No. 1,425.

[25] *Ibid.*, Wangenheim to Zimmermann, 25 Nov 1914, No. 1,426 ("Private").

November 28 ordered Field Marshal von der Goltz transferred to Constantinople. A few hours later an irate protest message from Liman arrived at German Imperial Headquarters. Addressing himself to Gen. Moritz von Lyncker, the chief of the Kaiser's *Militärkabinett*, Liman pointed out that Enver was well satisfied with him and had not the slightest intention of granting Goltz any influence at Ottoman GHQ. Moreover, Liman was by no means willing to accept command of the "Caucasus Army," that is, the Ottoman Third Army, as had recently been suggested to him. As he explained to Lyncker, large-scale operations on the Transcaucasian front were ruled out by the approach of winter; there was no need to replace the present Ottoman commander there; and he himself was fully occupied with directing the troops presently entrusted to his command. Finally, he was "particularly" opposed to changing duty posts inasmuch as the whole idea had obviously originated with Wangenheim: "I am not going to have myself removed from here [Constantinople] by the ambassador unless this becomes necessary in connection with the deployment of the Army that is presently under my command." Liman hastened to add that his decision in this matter had been accepted by Enver and that, in any case, only the Kaiser had the authority to deprive him of his post as military mission chief.[26]

Liman's refusal to leave Constantinople resulted in a further heightening of tensions between him and the German embassy staff. More importantly, it provided Enver with an excuse for assuming personal command of the Caucasus army and launching the first major offensive of the war. Heedless of Liman's warnings that a winter campaign in the mountains of northeastern Anatolia would be extremely difficult and risky, Enver and his German chief-of-staff, Gen. Bronsart von Schellendorff, left Constantinople on December 6 for the Transcau-

[26] *Ibid.*, Stumm to FO, 28 Nov 1914, No. 414; Lyncker to Bethmann Hollweg, 9 Dec (contains copy of Liman's message, dated 27 Nov 1914).

casian front. As Wangenheim cabled to Berlin on the same day, the vice-generalissimo had decided that a "major strike" against the Russians was possible and, since Liman had refused to go, Enver would now personally direct that offensive. This dénouement, according to the ambassador, was "extraordinarily deplorable" since Enver was needed in the capital to provide leadership and direction in case of "external complications" and to "regulate Liman's status vis-à-vis Goltz," Goltz being on his way to Constantinople by this time.[27]

Given the pivotal position of Enver in the Ottoman government Wangenheim's concern over the vice-generalissimo's departure for the remote Transcaucasian front was justified, but it is also clear that the ambassador regarded this development as a personal defeat in his long feud with Liman. The latter, in fact, started almost immediately after Enver's departure to assert himself, especially by meddling in the intelligence operations conducted by Wangenheim's staff.[28] Glotz' arrival in Constantinople on December 12 brought little improvement in the situation, for the field marshal possessed no formal authority to intervene in the squabbling between the embassy and the chief of the military mission.[29] In fact, nobody in Constantinople seemed to know what Goltz' actual status and functions as the Sultan's "adjutant general" should be, and it was only after Enver's return to the capital in January 1915 that the field marshal was formally posted as a "special adviser" to the Ottoman High Command.

Until that time Wangenheim was pretty much on his own in coping with the troublesome Liman. The extent of the am-

[27] *Ibid.*, Wangenheim to FO, 6 Dec 1914, No. 1,542; Liman, pp. 37-39; Goltz, pp. 379-80.

[28] See FO, *Türkei 139*, Bd. 33, Wangenheim to FO [Laffert to Falkenhayn] 11 Dec 1914, No. 1,580.

[29] On the frigid reception given Goltz by Liman see Pomiankowski's report in Conrad, v, 937. Wangenheim stayed away from the official welcome ceremony, partly to avoid meeting Liman in public; see FO, *Türkei 139*, Bd. 33, Wangenheim to FO, 14 Dec 1914, No. 1,611.

bassador's frustrations is reflected in a dispatch to the Wilhelmstrasse of December 16, in which he once again demanded Liman's removal from Constantinople, preferably by an order from the Kaiser posting the general to the Transcaucasian front:

> The fact that Enver, instead of Liman, is in charge of the Caucasus Command entails increasing difficulties for the promotion of our business here. Many important military questions call for a decision by Enver who cannot easily be reached by telegraph. His functions here are presently taken care of by various personages. At [Ottoman General] Headquarters Liman seems to exercise decisive influence. Due to [our] tense relations an exchange of opinions with him is impossible. He regards also the [German] military attaché as his enemy, while he confides in the Austrian military attaché. As a result the Austrian embassy is far better informed than our own. Under these circumstances I can for the time being no longer accept responsibility for the implementation of our politico-military objectives. . . .[30]

To Wangenheim's chagrin his superiors in the foreign office reacted with complete indifference to his complaints. As Jagow put it, the first order of business for the ambassador would have to be the reestablishment of a modus vivendi with Liman, a suggestion Wangenheim heatedly rejected as totally unrealistic. Deserted by his superiors in Berlin Wangenheim next tried to secure Enver's return to Constantinople, but since the latter was deeply involved in directing a seemingly successful offensive against the Russians, his efforts were in vain.[31]

[30] *Ibid.*, Wangenheim to FO, 16 Dec 1914, No. 1,629. Liman's hostility toward the German military attaché, Maj. von Laffert, was understandable in view of the fact that Laffert had played a prominent role in the embassy's program of dislodging Liman. See especially *ibid.*, Wangenheim to FO, 21 Dec, No. 1,683.

[31] See *ibid.*, Jagow to Wangenheim, 16 Dec 1914, No. 1,545; Wangenheim to FO, 21 Dec, No. 1,683; and *Türkei 150*, Bd. 9, same to same, 24 Dec, No. 1,715.

On December 30 Wangenheim addressed a long, personal letter to an unidentified "friend" in the Wilhelmstrasse (probably Zimmermann) in which he characterized the prolonged absence of Enver and the resultant increase of Liman's influence as matters of gravest political import. First of all, he complained, Enver's absence made it increasingly difficult to keep the "military" in check, that is, to prevent the implementation of various measures by the army authorities which would produce adverse political effects.

> As probably in all belligerent countries, we have here a military and a diplomatic faction; the military men demand the most severe measures against all elements that hamper the military operations. They call for draconic action against Greek espionage, for internment camps for Frenchmen and Englishmen, and so forth.
>
> I have had to speak out against such measures for the most part because Turkey would be denounced as barbaric if she used the same methods England and France do; because we would be held accountable by not only our enemies but also the neutrals for Turkish fury, whose scope cannot always be predicted given the uncivilized state of the populace; and because there is the acute danger that the neutrals may succumb eventually to the influence of English and French intrigues and thereby be moved to intervene against Turkey and, consequently, against us.[32]

According to Wangenheim he had previously been able to avert a series of "extremist measures" through his influence on Enver, but now that Liman was occupying Enver's place at

[32] FO, *Türkei 139*, Bd. 34, Wangenheim to "Dear Friend," 30 Dec 1914. On Wangenheim's successful fight to prevent the execution of a soldier attached to the Greek legation in Constantinople who was accused of espionage, see *Türkei 168*, Bde. 12-13, Quadt to FO, 11 Dec 1914, No. 780; Wangenheim to FO, 13 Dec, No. 1,601; 4 Jan 1915, No. 30; Quadt to FO, 12 Jan, No. 43; and Wangenheim to FO, 14 Jan, No. 121.

Ottoman GHQ, he was condemned to impotence. Liman's refusal to inform the embassy of what the military intended to do had in fact created an intolerable situation, and it was only to be hoped that Goltz would manage to keep an eye, and to exert a restraining influence, on Liman's activities. As for Jagow's recent suggestion that the embassy should establish a working arrangement with the military mission chief, Wangenheim concluded that Liman was widely believed to be close to insanity and that he, Wangenheim, was neither willing nor able to assume the role of a psychiatrist.[33]

Thanks to strenuous efforts by Goltz and a number of other German officers in Constantinople, but seemingly also because of a note of censure from the Kaiser, Liman agreed in early January 1915 to resume personal relations with the embassy. The rapprochement was however rather artificial from the very beginning, especially since Liman had meanwhile managed to secure the transfer of the German military attaché, Maj. von Laffert, to the Western front, thus depriving the ambassador of one of his most loyal supporters in the previous quarrels with the military mission chief.[34] As events were to show, the truce patched up in early January was merely a temporary solution.

While Wangenheim and Liman were quarrelling in Constantinople, Enver had led the Third Army into a frightful disaster. After impressive initial gains his ambitious offensive in the Armenian mountains bogged down in snow and ice. By early January 1915 his troops, decimated by frostbite, hunger, disease and enemy action, were forced to retreat, and only a remnant, perhaps 10 to 20 percent, of the Third Army survived the campaign. With his dream of a big victory over the Russians rudely shattered the vice-generalissimo surrendered com-

---

[33] Wangenheim to "Dear Friend," 30 Dec 1914, *Türkei 139*, Bd. 33. Cf. *Dt 128 Nr. 5 secr.*, Bd. 5, Jäckh to Zimmermann, 2 Jan 1915.

[34] See FO, *Türkei 139*, Bd. 34, Wangenheim to "Dear Friend," 6 Jan 1915; AHFM, *Türkei, Berichte 1915*, Pallavicini to Berchtold, 7 Jan, No. 2 D/P.

mand of the ruined army to a general staff officer, Col. Havis Hakki Bey, and made his way back to Constantinople, where he arrived in mid-January.[35]

All news about the catastrophic rout in Transcaucasia was carefully withheld from the public, but within the higher echelons of the Ottoman army Enver's fiasco sparked an unpleasant row. Liman, who had consistently warned against any kind of winter offensive at the Transcaucasian front, reacted to the disaster by demanding the resignation of Enver's chief-of-staff, Gen. Bronsart von Schellendorff.[36] Probably Liman's move against the latter was only partially connected with the abortive offensive, and a number of other grievances may have contributed to his desire for Bronsart's dismissal. Bronsart had a few weeks earlier informed the German embassy that Liman should not be decorated with the Iron Cross, and a number of other directives annoying to Liman had come from or via Bronsart.[37] Whatever the case, Enver decided to stand squarely behind his chief-of-staff while making it clear that if anybody resigned it would have to be Liman himself.[38]

Anxious to avoid the escalation of this quarrel into a political crisis Wangenheim made a personal appeal to Liman to drop the matter. He pointed out to the general that among other things the dismissal of Bronsart would merely serve to add credibility to charges that the Germans on Enver's staff had been responsible for the disaster in Transcaucasia. Liman fi-

[35] On the abortive Transcaucasian campaign, see especially Larcher, pp. 367-89; Mühlmann, *deutsch-türkische Waffenbündnis*, pp. 63-65; and Guse, pp. 34-55. Cf. Liman, pp. 37-40; Pomiankowski, pp. 102-104; and the not always reliable account in Allen and Muratoff, pp. 249-85.

[36] FO, *Türkei 139*, Bd. 34, Wangenheim to FO, 23 Jan 1915, No. 200; Pomiankowski, p. 104; Liman, p. 43. See Reichsarchiv, *Der Weltkrieg 1914 bis 1918*, IX, 171, for the assertion that Bronsart had counseled against Enver's ambitious campaign plan, but without success.

[37] See FO, *Türkei 139*, Bd. 33, Wangenheim to FO, 21 Dec 1914, No. 1,683; and Liman, pp. 40-43.

[38] Wangenheim's dispatch No. 200, *Türkei 139*, Bd. 34.

nally relented but not without first obtaining assurance from Enver that he would henceforth consult with him on any and all matters which involved a member of the military mission.[39] In reasserting his authority over all the officers of his mission, including Bronsart, Liman was well within his rights under the provisions of his contract of 1913, but inasmuch as many of the German officers in question had a Turk as their immediate superior, Liman's claims were to cause endless complications.

No doubt Enver was aware of the potential for trouble. A few weeks after the compromise settlement between them Enver suggested to Liman that he should accept command of the leaderless Third Army (Havis Hakki having meanwhile died), but Liman once again refused to be shunted off to the Transcaucasian front.[40] In retrospect his decision was wise, for only a few days later, on February 19, the long expected Allied attack on the Dardanelles opened with a massive bombardment by an Anglo-French task force.

The battle for the Straits, which assumed a new dimension in April with the landing of Allied troops on Gallipoli, has been described innumerable times and need not be recounted in any systematic fashion.[41] Here it is intended merely to indicate briefly how this battle affected the general relationship between the Turks and their German allies.

First, during the major part of the battle for the Straits (February to November 1915), the hard-pressed Turks were physically isolated from the Central Powers and unable to get much material assistance from them. Due to Rumania's refusal to permit the transit of military personnel and materiel, and the failure of the Austrians and Germans until the fall of 1915 to pry open an alternate supply route through Serbia, only a few hundred German soldiers and a mere trickle of equipment

[39] FO, *Türkei 139*, Bd. 34, Wangenheim to FO, 26 Jan 1915, No. 226.
[40] Liman, p. 49.
[41] See above, note 7. The most recent study, Robert R. James, *Gallipoli* (New York, 1965), contributes little that is new.

reached Constantinople before November 1915. As a result the defenders of the Dardanelles were chronically short of ammunition and other supplies, which caused much bitterness in Constantinople.

Rumania's decision in early October 1914 to close its borders to all German and Austrian munitions shipments destined for Turkey had initially given rise to various German attempts to eliminate that roadblock by bribery, subterfuges, etc.,[42] but already by November 1914 it had become obvious that an alternate route through Serbia would have to be opened up by military action. Spurred on by Wangenheim, the Berlin Foreign Office therefore directed several urgent pleas to the OHL for the conquest of northeast Serbia (the Negotin district), but neither Falkenhayn nor his Austrian counterpart, Gen. Franz Conrad von Hötzendorf, saw his way clear to launch such an offensive.[43]

Throughout the following months the embassy and other German agencies in Constantinople sent periodic warnings to Berlin that the need for German aid was growing; with the initiation of Allied naval attacks on the Dardanelles in mid-February of 1915 the calls for supplies grew in intensity. Again and again Wangenheim, Usedom, Goltz, and others reminded Berlin that the Turks would need ammunition and other equipment from the Central Powers, but all to no avail. On March 8 Wangenheim and his new military attaché, Col. von Leipzig, jointly sent emphatic warnings to Berlin that unless

[42] See Trumpener, "German Military Aid to Turkey in 1914," p. 149.
[43] Mühlmann, *Oberste Heeresleitung*, pp. 52-65; Janssen, pp. 41-48. Aside from citing the threat to Germany's investments and long-range prospects in the Ottoman empire if it were to be overwhelmed by the Allies, Zimmermann and Bethmann Hollweg, in their pleas to the OHL and the Kaiser, eventually went so far as to characterize the possible loss of Turkey as an irreparable blow: "The outcome of the world war would thereby be decided against us." (Neither this or similar hyperbolic statements by the "civilians" in later months seem to have made much of an impression on Falkenhayn or his staff.)

the shrinking ammunition supplies of the Turks were replenished from Germany, the Straits were most likely to be lost.

Already now [Wangenheim wrote] the situation is extremely critical. Should the Dardanelles actually be forced because of Germany's and Austria's failure to live up to all their promises concerning the supply of ammunition, the effect on the attitude of the Turks would be incalculable.[44]

Put off with platitudes from the OHL, the ambassador dispatched another warning on March 12 in which he pointed out that the Turks were fighting magnificently, but that the defense was likely to break down for lack of ammunition. Wangenheim emphasized that such a catastrophe would be the exclusive fault of Germany and the Dual Monarchy which were leaving their ally in the lurch.[45]

Fortunately for the Central Powers the laboriously prepared attempt by the Anglo-French fleet to blast its way through the Dardanelles on March 18 not only failed but also convinced the Allies (quite without cause) that a continuation of purely naval attacks would be futile.[46] With the decision to call in the army and invade the Gallipoli peninsula, an operation that required several weeks' preparation, the British unwittingly gave the Turks a desperately needed breathing spell during which they could improvise the replenishment of their exhausted ammunition stock and deploy additional troops on either side of the Straits.[47]

Undeceived by the temporary lull at the Dardanelles and bombarded by pleas from Constantinople, the Wilhelmstrasse,

[44] FO, *Türkei 142*, Bd. 45, Wangenheim to FO, 8 March 1915, No. 568; Mühlmann, *deutsch-türkische Waffenbündnis*, pp. 38-45.

[45] See FO, *Türkei 142*, Bd. 45, Treutler to FO, 11 March 1915, No. 155; *Türkei 150*, Bd. 10, Wangenheim to FO, 12 March, No. 610.

[46] On the great battle of March 18 see especially Lorey, II, 84-93. Cf. *History of the Great War. Naval Operations,* Sir Julian S. Corbett and Sir Henry Newbolt, eds. 5 vols. (London, 1920-31), II, 213-30.

[47] See Liman, pp. 56-62; Higgins, pp. 157-79; Marder, II, Chapter x.

and Chancellor Bethmann Hollweg himself, Falkenhayn attempted on March 21 to impress upon Conrad von Hötzendorf the need for a joint Austro-German offensive against Serbia which would among other things open a secure supply route to the embattled Turks. Conrad, convinced of the primacy of the Russian front, reacted only lukewarmly, and by the beginning of April Constantinople was notified that no immediate relief should be expected. Diplomatic efforts in the second half of March to break down the Rumanian veto on transit shipments to Turkey failed, as did various other projects to get German ammunition through to the Straits.[48]

While the continued isolation of Turkey from its allies was producing considerable nervousness among the German political and military figures in Constantinople, tensions there were heightened by mounting disagreements between Enver and Liman. Judging from the available evidence the new quarrel started in February with their disagreements over how to react to the Allied naval attacks. Shortly after their onset Enver had ordered a general deployment of forces in the Straits area to the effect that the First Army, commanded by Liman, would defend the European side of the Straits while another, the Second Army, would be generally responsible for the Asiatic shores. This arrangement and various other directives issued by Enver's headquarters were considered unsound by Liman who vigorously protested. Within a few days their disagreements on strategy turned into a full-blown personal quarrel. As a result Enver finally informed Wangenheim that Liman's insubordinate attitude made it "impossible" to work with him and that he expected the Kaiser to remind the military mission chief that he must "obey" the Ottoman vice-generalissimo "unconditionally."[49]

[48] Mühlmann, *Oberste Heeresleitung*, pp. 90-101; Janssen, pp. 95-104; Glenn E. Torrey, "Rumania and the Belligerents, 1914-16," *Journal of Contemporary History,* 1:3 (1966), 182.

[49] FO, *Türkei 139,* Bd. 34, Wangenheim to FO, 25 Feb 1915, No. 459. Cf. Liman, pp. 53-54.

Liman, on his part, lodged an official complaint with Wangenheim over Enver's recent directives, and when that did not produce any results, he turned directly to German Imperial Headquarters by wiring to Lyncker on March 2: "I herewith report to Your Excellency that there has been a rash of military blunders and precipitate measures here, while I—contrary to my contract and the alliance treaty—am not being consulted at all." Liman was particularly incensed by the "willful" refusal of Enver's chief-of-staff, Gen. Bronsart, to keep him posted on what was being planned by the Ottoman High Command. Moreover, he asserted, Goltz was constantly meddling in business concerning Liman's own army, and there was great danger that such a "deliberate undermining" of his authority would eventually lead to a "catastrophe for the [First] Army."[50] The extent of Liman's resentment can be gauged by a supplementary, special report from Col. von Leipzig, according to which Liman and Enver, though they worked in the same building, were no longer talking to each other, while Liman's relationship with Bronsart had become "well-nigh untenable." Leipzig pointed out that the tensions between the two German generals were primarily due to Liman's "nervousness, jealousy, and suspiciousness," and that Bronsart was really doing his best to meet his dual obligations as Enver's associate and as a subordinate of the military mission chief.[51]

Shortly after the dispatch of Liman's and Leipzig's messages to Germany Enver himself wired to the Kaiser and informed him that he needed Bronsart more than Liman, and that if any personnel changes were deemed necessary the military mission chief should be removed.[52] German Imperial Headquarters thereupon chose to ignore the whole issue for the time being.

[50] *Ibid.*; and FO, *Türkei 139*, Bd. 34, Wangenheim to FO [Liman to Lyncker], 2 March 1915, No. 502.

[51] *Ibid.*, Wangenheim to FO [Leipzig to Lyncker], 2 March 1915, No. 503.

[52] *Ibid.*, Wangenheim to FO [Enver to Lyncker], 2 March 1915, No. 509.

According to his memoirs Liman devoted the next few weeks to impressing on the Ottoman High Command that a separate army should be formed at the Dardanelles to cope with a "large landing" of Allied forces, a landing which was certain to come once the British realized that "the road to Constantinople could not be opened by action on the water alone." Given Liman's strained relations with both Enver and Bronsart it is not surprising that his proposals were at first ignored. However, a week after the great Allied naval attack, on March 24, Enver suddenly agreed to the creation of a special Dardanelles defense group, henceforth to be known as the Fifth Army, and simultaneously offered its command to Liman. The general "assented at once." The next day he left Constantinople for his new command post on the Gallipoli Peninsula, taking with him a small number of German officers and his trusted Ottoman chief-of-staff, Lt. Col. Kâzim Bey.[53] For the next 10 months Liman was to serve uninterruptedly as the commander-in-chief at the Gallipoli front (a position which gained him worldwide recognition), but despite his prolonged absence from Constantinople no real relaxation of tensions between him and the Ottoman High Command, or for that matter, the German embassy, ever came.

In accepting his new position on Gallipoli Liman seems to have believed that he would retain some authority over the troops of the First Army as well. Instead of surrendering his command over the latter army to Goltz as a matter of course, as Liman suggests in his memoirs, he actually objected emphatically to being succeeded by the field marshal. However, both the Sultan and the Kaiser ignored his protests, and in mid-

---

[53] Liman, pp. 56-57; Pomiankowski, pp. 125-26. One of the divisions assigned to Liman's new army was commanded by Lt. Col. Mustafa Kemal (the future Atatürk), who was to play a decisive role in the Gallipoli campaign. In 1918, by then a general, he would serve again under Liman's command.

April Goltz was officially installed as the commanding general of the First Army.[54]

About two weeks later the British landings on Gallipoli began, and Liman, in his capacity as Fifth Army commander, became the man primarily responsible for the defense of the peninsula. During the initial stages of the bloody fighting on Gallipoli, in May and June of 1915, Liman's capable direction of the defense seems to have silenced his numerous critics in Constantinople, but by July new tensions developed between him and the German representatives in the capital. The new crisis was triggered by Liman's growing dissatisfaction with and subsequent dismissal of several German officers under his command. Particularly serious was Liman's decision in early July to dismiss the German commander at the Sedd-el-Bahr front, Col. Weber, and to appoint the Turkish general, Ferid Vehib Paşa, in his place. Wangenheim wired to Berlin a few days later that this incident was highly deplorable in view of Weber's proven merit, but even more so because it would confirm the Turks in their chauvinistic belief that their own officers were just as capable of running the campaign as the German experts among them. In fact, Wangenheim continued, Liman's action had further undermined the prestige and authority of the German military mission and encouraged the growth of an intransigent Turkish nationalism, which in itself was a growing "danger for our present and future tasks in Turkey."[55]

While Liman was making himself extremely unpopular among the German representatives in Constantinople, his next move—his refusal to employ a Lt. Col. Schwabe as a division

---

[54] Cf. Liman, p. 57; Goltz, p. 405; FO, *Türkei 139*, Bd. 35, Wangenheim to Treutler, 15 April 1915, No. 892; Wangenheim to FO, 16 April, No. 895; Treutler to FO [Lyncker to Wangenheim], 17 April, No. 289.

[55] FO, *Türkei 139*, Bd. 36, Wangenheim to FO, 15 July 1915, No. 1,603. Cf. Liman, p. 78.

commander—got him temporarily in trouble with the Ottoman High Command as well. As Wangenheim wired to Berlin, he was caught in the middle between Liman and Enver's headquarters, which insisted on Schwabe's appointment; and the general confusion was heightened by the fact that there was no military attaché to arbitrate the issue—Col. von Leipzig having been killed two weeks earlier in a shooting accident.[56]

Wangenheim's desire for the speedy appointment of a new military attaché was met quite promptly by the German High Command, which dispatched Col. Otto von Lossow, a veteran of Turkish service, to Constantinople.[57] Hardly had von Lossow installed himself at the embassy when Bronsart suggested to the OHL that Lossow be sent to Gallipoli. As Bronsart put it, it was most desirable to get rid of Liman's Turkish chief-of-staff, Kâzim Bey, and to appoint a German trench warfare expert like Lossow in his place, for, in Bronsart's opinion, Liman's direction of the Fifth Army left much to be desired. Moreover—and this was perhaps the crux of Bronsart's message—Lossow possessed all the qualifications to "replace" Liman if that should become "necessary" in the future.[58]

Wangenheim's report about Liman's apparent partiality for Turkish officers and Bronsart's thinly veiled attack on the general's competence seem to have convinced Falkenhayn that Liman was too much of a liability in his present post. Falkenhayn sent word to Enver and the Porte that Liman was needed in Germany to provide firsthand information on the "military situation at the Dardanelles," and that during his absence

[56] Wangenheim's dispatch No. 1,603, *Türkei 139*, Bd. 36. On Col. von Leipzig's death see Pomiankowski, p. 143. The story, repeated by Howard, p. 436, note 159, that Leipzig was "murdered by the Turks" is probably without foundation.

[57] Lossow, shortly to be promoted to major general, served as military attaché (*Militärbevollmächtigter*) in Constantinople until the autumn of 1918. He later gained notoriety as Reichswehr commander in Bavaria, especially in the events leading up to Hitler's beer hall putsch of 1923.

[58] FO, *Türkei 139*, Bd. 36, Treutler to FO, 25 July 1915, No. 232.

Goltz, assisted by Lossow, might take over command at the Gallipoli front. Liman reacted with predictable anger. Fully aware that a roundabout attempt was being made to dislodge him permanently from his position, he fired back a message to Lyncker in which he challenged the need for his personal appearance in Germany and bluntly inquired whether the Kaiser wanted him to apply for retirement from the service.[59]

Before Falkenhayn had a chance to react to this challenge, Liman received an unexpected boost from Enver, who was by his own admission impressed by Liman's willingness to put Turkish officers in key positions. In a lengthy conversation with Humann Enver made it clear that he was quite satisfied with Liman's latest dispositions on Gallipoli and did not want him recalled, notwithstanding the fact that the general was indeed a very difficult man to get along with. Enver pointed out, furthermore, that he was not overly impressed by the leadership qualities of Goltz, whom he described as "too old, quite especially too soft, [and] a poor judge of men," and that consequently only a man like Lossow would qualify as Liman's successor if the OHL insisted on recalling the military mission chief.[60]

Exhorted by Bethmann Hollweg not to act precipitously and faced with Enver's opposition, Falkenhayn canceled the recall order on August 1, but insisted that Lossow be attached to Fifth Army Headquarters, so that his "rich experiences in modern defensive warfare will be utilized by Liman to the widest extent."[61] Lossow dutifully appeared at Liman's headquarters shortly thereafter, but as Liman caustically remarks in his

[59] Cf. *ibid.*; Hohenlohe to FO [Liman to Lyncker], 29 July 1915, No. 1,682; and Liman, p. 81.

[60] FO, *Türkei 139*, Bd. 37, "Besprechung mit Enver Pascha am 30. Juli 1915," signed by Humann. See also Bd. 36, Treutler to FO, 1 Aug 1915, No. 248, for a direct plea from Enver to Falkenhayn not to recall Liman in the midst of the campaign.

[61] See *ibid.*, Bethmann Hollweg to Treutler, 30 July 1915, No. 932; Treutler to Bethmann Hollweg, 30 July, no No.; Treutler to FO, 1 Aug, Nos. 248 and 251.

memoirs, he "did not stay long, as I had absolutely no official work for him."[62]

Having repelled all attempts to dislodge him from his position, Liman continued in command of the Gallipoli fronts to the end of the campaign in January 1916, when the last British troops withdrew from the embattled peninsula. This triumph for the defending Turks was somewhat darkened by the success with which the bulk of the British forces were evacuated from the various bridgeheads, a success which triggered renewed tensions and recriminations between Liman and the Ottoman High Command.

After the surprise evacuation of the British from all but the Sedd-el-Bahr sector during the second half of December 1915, Liman made extensive preparations to launch a massive attack against the remaining British positions. In the midst of these preparations, on January 5, 1916, several divisions earmarked for the attack were ordered withdrawn by the Ottoman High Command. As might be expected Liman reacted to this interference with his own dispositions in impassioned fury. In a telegram to the new German ambassador in Constantinople, Paul Count von Wolff-Metternich (Wangenheim had died a few months earlier), Liman vigorously protested the renewed violation of his contractual rights and announced that he was sending his resignation from all of his positions to both Enver and the Kaiser.[63]

Enver seems to have recognized the validity of Liman's pro-

[62] Liman, p. 82. Cf. Pomiankowski, p. 135. Regarding a subsequent quarrel of Liman with Goltz see FO, *Türkei 139*, Bd. 37, Hohenlohe to Treutler, 9 Sept 1915, No. 78; Treutler to Hohenlohe, 10 Sept, No. 36.

[63] Liman, pp. 100-102; FO, *Türkei 139*, Bd. 39, Wolff-Metternich to FO, 10 Jan 1916, No. 47; Liman to Wolff-Metternich(?), 10 Jan [Wolff-Metternich to Bethmann Hollweg, 18 Feb, No. 80, Enclosure No. 3]. Cf. Pomiankowski, pp. 141-43. On the various personnel changes at the Constantinople embassy and the German foreign office during the war, consult Appendix D.

test against the untimely depletion of his forces, for he quickly modified the initial order sent to the Fifth Army.[64] At the same time, though, the vice-generalissimo proved no longer willing to put up with Liman's imperiousness. (With the Gallipoli campaign over, Liman was less indispensable than he had been the previous summer.) On January 10 Enver wrote Falkenhayn that he would accept the general's resignation and that Bronsart, because of his position and personal qualities, was the most suitable man to assume command of the German military mission. As for Liman's contention that Enver's intervention in the affairs of the Fifth Army constituted a breach of Liman's contractual rights, Enver explained to Falkenhayn that he interpreted the basic status and functions of the military mission chief quite differently:

> The chief of the Mission is entitled only to participation [*Mitwirkung*] in all larger questions, [but] never to co-determination [*Mitbestimmung*]. The latter would violate the foundations of our constitution, since the Mission chief can never be held accountable for his actions or decisions by the organs of the state. The very assignment of Marshal Goltz and Marshal Liman to responsible positions places me in a difficult situation vis-à-vis the government and parliament. I would have to answer personally for possible mistakes or failures of these non-Ottoman army commanders.
>
> Nevertheless, I have gladly assumed that responsibility in response to the need of the hour. It is all the more impossible, and also unjustified by the special circumstances of a contract, that an army leader should claim the right to participate in, and to be consulted on, matters pertaining to the overall direction of the war which can be evaluated by me alone.[65]

[64] Liman to Wolff-Metternich, 10 Jan, FO, *Türkei 139*, Bd. 39; Liman, p. 102.

[65] FO, *Türkei 139*, Bd. 39, Enver and Humann to Falkenhayn, 10 Jan 1916 [Wolff-Metternich to Bethmann Hollweg, 18 Feb, No. 80, Enclosure No. 1].

Simultaneously, Enver sent a largely analogous letter to Liman and informed him that, pending the Kaiser's decision on Liman's future, he would hold back the letter of resignation which the general had addressed to the Sultan.[66]

Whereas in the preceding summer the OHL, in its concern over the "pro-Turkish" personnel policy of Liman, had been rather eager to recall the controversial general, Falkenhayn and the Kaiser this time reacted with remarkable ambivalence to the new quarrel. On January 12, 1916 Falkenhayn informed Enver that an equitable settlement of the whole issue would require some time, and a few days later the Kaiser conferred on Liman the oak leaf cluster to the *Pour le mérite* medal in public recognition of his successful defense of Gallipoli. Finally, on January 22, the Kaiser got around to the issue at hand. He informed Liman that he did not wish to get involved in a review of the general's contractual rights in the midst of the war and that Liman should adjust himself to Enver's wishes.[67]

Prodded by Wolff-Metternich, Liman thereupon called on the vice-generalissimo. According to Liman's account of this interview, he and Enver reached full agreement on all points at issue, whereupon Liman withdrew his request for release from the Fifth Army command.[68] In light of subsequent events, however, it would appear that Enver and Liman thoroughly misunderstood each other's positions—a misunderstanding which may very well have been caused by Enver's imperfect command of the German language and the fact that Liman was somewhat hard of hearing! In any event, a bare five days after the interview Enver notified the perplexed general that in his capacity as military mission chief Liman would henceforth have to do without a number of "rights," to wit:

[66] *Ibid.*, Enver to Liman, n.d. [Wolff-Metternich to Bethmann Hollweg, 18 Feb, No. 80, Enclosure No. 4].

[67] *Ibid.*, Falkenhayn to Enver, 12 Jan 1916 [Wolff-Metternich to Bethmann Hollweg, 18 Feb, No. 80, Enclosure No. 2]; *Norddeutsche Allgemeine Zeitung*, 16 Jan; Lyncker to Liman, 22 Jan.

[68] *Ibid.*, Wolff-Metternich to Treutler, 23 Jan 1916.

(a) Your Excellency will not have the right to issue orders to German officers who are not in Your Excellency's army regarding the performance of their duties, or to interfere in these same matters.

(b) Requests for German officers and enlisted personnel will be ... [initiated] by me and arranged by Your Excellency.

. . . .

(d) The assignment of the German officers, etc., and the distribution of [German] military supplies among the armies will be handled by me according to need.

(e) German officers assigned to ... [your] army will be sent back after I have given approval. Since I will inform the appropriate higher Turkish authorities of these changes regarding Your Excellency's position, I request that Your Excellency, in turn, notify the German officers.[69]

Predictably, Liman refused to accept this formal curtailment of his rights; for as he reminded both Enver and the Military Cabinet in Germany, his contract of 1913 had specifically accorded him full authority over all non-Ottoman officers serving in the Sultan's army.[70] On receiving word from Germany that the Kaiser did not wish to get involved in an "examination" of the dispute, Liman next sent an innocuous message to Enver to the effect that he would, as always, "endeavor" to cooperate with the vice-generalissimo and the Porte in all matters pertaining to the military mission.[71]

Enver, who was on an inspection tour in the eastern provinces at this time, replied on February 12 that he expected Liman to comply with his directives and to notify his German fellow officers accordingly. When this message was politely ignored by Liman, Enver dispatched a second telegram on

[69] *Ibid.*, Enver to Liman, dated "15.11.31" [Forwarded by Wolff-Metternich to Berlin FO, 16 Feb 1916, No. 251].

[70] See *ibid.*, Liman to Enver, 29 Jan 1916; Liman to Lyncker, 29 Jan.

[71] See *ibid.*, Wolff-Metternich to FO, 18 Feb 1916, No. 266.

February 17 in which he requested a clear-cut answer "whether Your Excellency has accepted my conditions or not." In a follow-up telegram Enver made it clear, moreover, that he was initiating a purge of those German officers in the Fifth Army who might not wish to comply with the directives in question. Unruffled by these thinly veiled ultimatums, Liman wired back on February 18 that he could under no circumstances accept the curtailment of his contractually fixed right to supervise the assignment of other German officers. According to Liman, any such basic revision of the original contract required the prior approval of the Kaiser, and since such approval had as yet not been given, the directives issued by Enver were obviously inoperative.[72]

It would appear that Liman's stubborn defense of his "rights" was not merely a matter of personal vanity, but also a reflection of his genuine conviction that without him at the helm the members of the military mission would find themselves in a very difficult situation. As Liman explains in his memoirs, the Turks were totally unqualified to judge for what employment the German officers were fitted, quite aside from the fact that care "had to be exercised so as not to assign German officers to offices controlled by Turkish commanders who were inimical to Germany." That Liman had reason to be concerned about the latter issue is borne out by one of his reports to the embassy, according to which many German officers had already complained about "unjustified denigrations" and "undignified treatment" from their Ottoman superiors.[73]

While Ambassador Wolff-Metternich seems to have sympathized with Liman, the Kaiser and his advisers decided that the crisis had become too serious to permit further procrastination. On February 20, Lyncker wired to both Wolff-Metternich and Bronsart that Enver's controversial directives should

[72] *Ibid.*

[73] Cf. Liman, pp. 114-15; FO, *Türkei 139*, Bd. 39, Wolff-Metternich to FO, 24 Feb 1916, No. 297.

be accepted in their entirety, for the preservation of the vice-generalissimo's good will was "absolutely indispensable."[74] A subsequent proposal by Liman to appeal the whole issue to Talât was rejected out of hand by Falkenhayn, and Wolff-Metternich was once again warned that Enver's continued collaboration was far more important than the satisfaction of Liman's wishes.[75]

Lyncker's message from the Kaiser was either not properly relayed to Liman or purposely ignored by him. Whichever, he and Enver got into a new row a few weeks later over the reassignment of a German officer, Lt. Col. Friedrich Kress von Kressenstein, and Liman reasserted his right to be consulted on such matters. On hearing of the new conflict the Kaiser on April 10 sent an impatient reminder to Wolff-Metternich that he had long since ordered full compliance with Enver's wishes, but for some reason the ambassador did not receive this imperial message until a full week later, or so he claimed later on. By the time he got in touch with Liman, the latter had already received an extremely blunt dispatch from Enver that his dismissal from the Sultan's service would be initiated unless he gave in at once.[76]

Furious over the vice-generalissimo's "insulting" ultimatum, Liman promptly applied for his recall to Germany. In Berlin Jagow reacted to the general's intention to quit with unmitigated alarm. He pointed out to the Kaiser's staff that the departure of Liman right after the death of Goltz (who had succumbed to spotted fever in Bagdad on April 19) would "make a bad impression in Turkey itself and be interpreted by our

[74] *Ibid.*, Lyncker to FO, 20 Feb 1916; same to Bethmann Hollweg, 21 Feb. See also Luckwald to FO [Falkenhayn to Jagow], 18 Feb, No. 9.

[75] *Ibid.*, Wolff-Metternich to FO, 24 Feb 1916, No. 297; Treutler to FO, 26 Feb, Nos. 108 and 109; Jagow to Wolff-Metternich, 27 Feb, No. 283.

[76] Cf. *ibid.*, Bd. 40, Wolff-Metternich to FO, 21 April 1916, No. 561; same to Bethmann Hollweg, 21 April, No. 181; and Liman, p. 115.

enemies as symptomatic for the collapse of our [alliance] policy."[77]

Jagow's plea for renewed efforts by Falkenhayn and others to avert an open break turned out to be unnecessary, for Enver, apparently under pressure from Talât and other Turkish leaders, suddenly adopted a more conciliatory attitude. Using Liman's trusted chief-of-staff, Kâzim Bey, as an intermediary, Enver assured the general on April 22 that he had not meant to insult him and that he would be most happy if Liman continued his meritorious service as commander of "a part of the Imperial Ottoman Army."[78]

At the behest of Wolff-Metternich Liman thereupon agreed to meet the vice-generalissimo again face to face. Unfortunately, only fragmentary information about the ensuing conference between the two men is available. All we know is that Liman obtained formal assurance from Enver that he would consult him on all assignments of German officers, while Liman, in turn, agreed to withdraw his request for recall.[79]

Needless to say, Liman's successful defense of his contractual rights constituted a humiliating experience for the proud vice-generalissimo. The resulting strains in their personal relationship were heightened in the following months by Liman's close association with Ambassador Wolff-Metternich, who had long since lost the confidence of Enver and other Turkish leaders because of his pointed opposition to the persecution and mistreatment of the Armenians.[80]

---

[77] See *ibid.*; and FO, *Türkei 139*, Bd. 40, Jagow to Treutler, 22 April 1916, No. 530.

[78] *Ibid.*, Enver to Liman, 22 April 1916 [enclosure in Wolff-Metternich to Lyncker and Bethmann Hollweg, 25 April, no No.]. Regarding the intercession of Talât and Intendant-General Ismail Hakki Paşa on Liman's behalf, cf. *ibid.*, Metternich to FO, 22 April, No. 567; and AHFM, *Krieg 21a, Türkei*, Pallavicini to Burian, 29 April, No. 34A-I/P.

[79] Cf. FO, *Türkei 139*, Bd. 40, Liman to Enver, 22 April 1916; Wolff-Metternich to FO, 22 April, No. 567; and Liman, p. 115.

[80] See Chapter VII.

German Generals in the Ottoman War

In mid-June 1916 Commander Humann, the German official closest to Enver, asserted in a private letter to Ernst Jäckh in Berlin that Liman was "conspiring" against the vice-generalissimo. About six weeks later Enver himself aired this charge in a formal communication to the German government. In particular Enver accused Liman of abetting Wolff-Metternich in his unfriendly attitude toward various Turkish policies and of intrigues against the vice-generalissimo himself:

For several months, he [Liman] has been intriguing against me; [he] asserts that my position is undermined and has but one goal: to topple me. Nobody knows why. With Wangenheim he did not get along at all. . . . With Metternich, who is our enemy, he has been on intimate terms from the start and provides [him] continuously—against all laws and regulations—with secret reports about the army.

A change in this state of affairs is very much in order and should be made as quickly as possible if a reorientation of Turkish policy is to be avoided.[81]

With Wolff-Metternich's recall to Germany and his replacement by the more Turcophile Richard von Kühlmann during the following two months, Enver's suspicion of Liman seems to have markedly subsided. There is no evidence that further complaints about him were sent to Berlin. It is clear, though, that the long series of disagreements with Liman since the beginning of the year made Enver more determined than ever to get rid of the general and the whole military mission system as soon as the war had been brought to a successful conclusion.

The first indication of Enver's determination to scrap the existing military mission system was contained in a programmatic outline of future German-Ottoman military relations which he presented to the military attaché, Gen. von Lossow, in

[81] Jackh Papers, No. 20, Humann to Jackh, 13 June 1916; DZA, Reichskanzlei, *Auswärtige Angelegenheiten 7, Türkei,* Bd. 1, "G.A.," 7 Aug 1916, signed by Wahnschaffe.

early November 1916. As Lossow subsequently informed the Berlin war ministry and other military authorities in Germany, Enver had made it clear that the postwar collaboration between the two allied armies would have to be organized on a new level. While he was willing and indeed eager to utilize German officers in the expansion and training of the Ottoman army and had earmarked many important staff and command positions for them, the Porte would not renew the existing contract with Liman or agree to any similar kind of arrangement. Instead, the Ottoman government would in the future insist on hiring each foreign officer individually, as had been the custom in the pre-1913 period.[82]

To Lossow, Enver's plans for the postwar era seemed entirely reasonable. As he explained to his superiors in Germany it was only natural in view of the steadily growing "national consciousness and self-esteem of the Turks" that they wished to scrap the privileged status of the German reformers, and it would be useless and imprudent for Berlin to insist on the perpetuation of the kind of rights that Liman had obtained in his original contract.[83]

Although Liman, during a brief visit to Germany in December 1916, did his best to convince the leaders there that "too much complaisance toward Enver" would erode the influence of his mission, Gen. Ludendorff informed Enver in early January 1917 that he was agreeable to a review of the conditions which had made for friction between Germans and Turks previously.[84]

As a result of Ludendorff's initiative a "temporary" agreement delineating the authority of the military mission was worked out during the following months which provided that

[82] FO, *Türkei 139*, Bd. 42, Lossow to Berlin war ministry *et al.*, 19 Nov 1916.

[83] See *ibid.*; and Lossow to General Staff, 20 Dec 1916.

[84] Cf. Liman, pp. 149-50; and FO, *Türkei 139*, Bd. 42, FO to Kühlmann [Ludendorff to Enver], 12 Jan 1917, No. 34.

the Ottoman High Command would "consult" the mission whenever it moved German personnel around. During the negotiations preceding this agreement Enver made it clear, however, that he wanted a more permanent settlement with regard to the future military collaboration between the two countries. His proposal for the conclusion of a formal military convention which would come into effect after the war was accepted by the German government, and after lengthy negotiations between Enver and the military attaché, Gen. von Lossow, a draft agreement was prepared in June 1917. Significantly, neither during these preliminary negotiations nor in the final polishing of the convention text was Liman ever consulted, and, predictably, he objected vehemently when he saw the finished product in October. In a grumbling letter to Berlin Liman took particular exception to a clause in the convention draft according to which after the war all German officers in Ottoman service would be assigned to their posts and supervised in the performance of their duties by the Ottoman war minister and their immediate superiors, but, also predictably, the general's objections were disregarded in Germany.[85]

Several members of the Ottoman cabinet were not at all satisfied with the convention draft either, but Enver and the Prussian war minister, Gen. Hermann von Stein, nevertheless signed the document on October 18, 1917 on behalf of their respective sovereigns.[86] The convention, which was to enter into effect "upon the conclusion of peace" and was to run for at least 10 years unless the German-Ottoman alliance treaty was previously abrogated, provided for the closest possible cooperation between the German and Ottoman armies. In nine lengthy

[85] See Mühlmann, *deutsch-türkische Waffenbündnis*, pp. 128-29; FO, *Dt 128 Nr. 5 secr.*, Bde. 6-7, Kühlmann to Bethmann Hollweg, 13 June 1917, No. 330; Memo, Berlin FO, 28 Sept; Lossow to General Staff, 29 Oct; Liman to Berlin war ministry, 10 Oct. Cf. Liman, pp. 187-88.

[86] FO, *Dt 128 Nr. 5 secr.*, Bd. 7, Bernstorff to FO, 14 Oct 1917, No. 1,258; Lossow to General Staff, 29 Oct.

articles the convention called for the establishment of uniform standards in the organizational structure, training, and equipment of the two allied armies and regulated in detail the methods by which common action and common planning for all contingencies would be ensured. With regard to the assignment of German personnel to the Ottoman army in the postwar period, the convention's stipulations accorded fully with Enver's often repeated demands for the elimination of the military mission system. Article 4 included the following provisions:

> The German army administration will make available, upon request by the Turkish administration, a stipulated number of selected officers for assistance in the expansion of the Ottoman army—provisionally for a period of five years. These officers will be given leave without pay by the German army administration; [they] will transfer into Turkish service and be paid by the Turkish Army administration. *In all matters relating to their official duties and assignments* these German officers will be *subordinates of the Turkish war minister and their superior officers.* Pending other arrangements between the two army administrations, they will, however, remain subject exclusively to the judicial and honor code and the disciplinary authority of their own country. . . .
>
> All further details on this subject will be regulated by a special agreement between the two army administrations and *by the contract which the Turkish war ministry will conclude with each German officer who transfers into Turkish service.*[87]

With the signing of this convention clear notice was given to Liman that his contractual rights in the Ottoman empire would be terminated automatically once the war was over. The way in which Berlin had consistently bypassed him in the

[87] *Ibid., Militärkonvention,* 18 Oct 1917 [italics added]. For other provisions of the convention, see Appendix C.

drafting of the convention indicated, moreover, that his advice on basic issues of military policy was no longer respected by his superiors in Germany. On the other hand, it is clear from subsequent developments that the OHL continued to think of Liman as a very capable strategist and tactician. In fact only a few weeks after they had ignored him on the question of the convention Field Marshal Paul von Hindenburg and Gen. Ludendorff recommended to Enver that he drop his long-time chief-of-staff, Bronsart, and appoint Liman in his place.[88]

By way of sketching in the background of this curious proposal, it should be pointed out that the OHL at this time was deeply disturbed by developments on the Palestinian front, where the "Third Battle of Gaza" was raging. The failure of the Turks to hold their lines convinced both Hindenburg and Ludendorff that serious mistakes had been made by Enver's staff, and Bronsart was made the scapegoat.[89]

Enver did not take very kindly to the OHL's suggestion that his own staff was to blame for the setbacks in Palestine, nor did he like the idea of having the strong-headed military mission chief entrench himself at his headquarters. However, after a few days' hesitation he accepted a compromise proposal to the effect that he would exchange Bronsart for Gen. von Seeckt, one of the best strategists the Germans had. The OHL, eager to remove Bronsart, promptly agreed to the arrangement, and Seeckt was shortly thereafter sent off to Constantinople. In early January 1918 he was formally installed in Enver's headquarters, while Bronsart was unceremoniously shunted off to the German Western front.[90]

[88] See FO, *Türkei 139*, Bd. 43, Külhmann to Bernstorff, 17 Nov 1917, No. 1,383; Mühlmann, *deutsch-türkische Waffenbündnis*, p. 180.

[89] See *ibid.*, pp. 172-80, 289.

[90] FO, *Türkei 139*, Bd. 45, Bernstorff to FO, 27 Nov 1917, No. 1,529; Lersner to FO, 2 Dec, No. 1,795; Mühlmann, *deutsch-türkische Waffenbündnis*, p. 180. Cf. [Hans von Seeckt], *Aus seinem Leben 1918-1936*, Friedrich von Rabenau, ed. (Leipzig, 1940), pp. 13-14.

German Generals in the Ottoman War

As might have been expected, friction between Liman and Enver's new chief-of-staff developed almost immediately, for Seeckt, like Bronsart before him, was disinclined to worry about the "autonomous" status of the military mission within the Ottoman armed forces. Seeckt's efforts to integrate various administrative functions hitherto exercised by the military mission's own bureaus into a more centrally controlled system quickly aroused Liman's ire, and in early February 1918 he once again applied for his recall to Germany.[91] The OHL this time simply ignored his request, an attitude which is rather understandable in view of the fact that another prominent German in Ottoman service, Gen. von Falkenhayn, had meanwhile gotten into trouble with Enver himself.

Falkenhayn, Hindenburg's predecessor at the OHL, had come to Turkey in May 1917 at the invitation of the Porte. Originally he had been assigned to direct an Ottoman-German offensive to recapture Bagdad from the British (Operation "*Yilderim*"), but when this project had to be abandoned Falkenhayn was placed in command of the Palestinian front instead (September 1917).[92] During the following five months Falkenhayn was reasonably successful in slowing down the advance of superior British forces, though he could not prevent the abandonment of Jerusalem and a number of other Palestinian districts. Falkenhayn's creditable performance was not generally acknowledged. Enver later blamed him for "using up" every Turkish general under his command, and Cemal, as military governor of the Syrian provinces, had continuous frictions with him. In February 1918 both Enver and Seeckt notified the OHL that Falkenhayn's perpetual disagreements with the Ottoman High Command and his inability to get along with the civilian authorities in Palestine made it advisable

[91] Liman, pp. 194-96; Seeckt, pp. 15-19, *passim*.

[92] See Werner Steuber, *Jilderim. Schlachten des Weltkrieges*, v. 5 (Oldenburg, 1922), *passim*; Mühlmann, *deutsch-türkische Waffenbündnis*, pp. 144-56, 168-70; FO, *Türkei 139*, Bd. 43, Lyncker to FO, 8 June 1917.

to relieve the general of his command. After some hesitation, the Kaiser accepted the inevitable and appointed Falkenhayn to an army command in occupied Russia. For Falkenhayn, erstwhile Prussian minister of war and, from 1914 to 1916, the man in charge of all German operations, this dénouement must have been a rather painful experience, though there are indications that the glamor of a Turkish desert command had long since worn off for him.[93]

Even before Falkenhayn left Enver had decided to give the Palestinian command to Liman. Seeckt avidly supported this decision, not least of all because it would at long last remove the quarrelsome military mission chief from Constantinople and thereby facilitate Seeckt's own work at Ottoman GHQ. The new German ambassador, Johann Count von Bernstorff, also approved of the arrangement, for in his opinion Liman was perhaps the only general who might yet be able to stabilize the Ottoman front in Palestine.[94] On his arrival there in early March Liman quickly found that he had been entrusted with a difficult and thankless task. The three Ottoman armies in Palestine, collectively known as "Army Group F," were woefully under-strength—the Fourth Army, for instance, comprised a total of about 3,500 combatants—and the logistic system was in utter disarray. Throughout the next six months Liman fought bitterly with Enver and Seeckt for replacements and supplies, but had only limited success. Facing the numerically superior and well-equipped forces of Gen. Allenby with generally undernourished and ill-clad troops, Liman was particularly outraged by the fact that the Turks were frittering away both soldiers and supplies in their Transcaucasian adventures.

[93] Mühlmann, *deutsch-türkische Waffenbündnis*, pp. 170-80, 213-14, 288; Seeckt, pp. 20-21; Djemal, pp. 185-93; Franz von Papen, *Der Wahrheit eine Gasse* (Munich, 1952), pp. 87-94, 98-103; FO, *Türkei 139*, Bd. 46, Bernstorff to FO, 2 Feb 1918, No. 166; Bayur, III:3, 374ff.

[94] Mühlmann, *deutsch-türkische Waffenbündnis*, p. 214; Liman, pp. 196-97; Seeckt, pp. 20-21; FO, *Türkei 139*, Bd. 46, Bernstorff to FO, 19 Feb 1918, No. 243.

German Generals in the Ottoman War

"The real reason," he wrote bitterly to Ludendorff in August, "why officers, troops, money, various materiel, clothing, coal, and many other things are in short supply here" was the "over-extension" of the Turks in Transcaucasia. Seeckt, strangely enough, neither then nor later accepted the validity of Liman's complaints, thus contributing to the general's wrath.[95]

By the beginning of September tensions between Liman and the Ottoman High Command, that is, Enver and Seeckt, once again reached the breaking point. Having received tactical advice instead of the troops and supplies he wanted Liman brusquely reminded Enver that without prompt support of his theater by the High Command there would be serious trouble. Enver replied with equal brusqueness, whereupon Liman threatened to take his case to the new Sultan, Mehmed VI—a somewhat more self-confident and active monarch than his recently deceased brother. However, before Liman's dispute with Enver could go any further, Allenby's forces launched their long-awaited major offensive. As Liman had warned all along, his troops were in no way prepared to offer more than temporary resistance and within a few days the battle turned into a rout of Army Group F. During the next six weeks, his last in Ottoman service, Liman directed as best he could the headlong retreat of his scattered forces toward the north. When the Porte signed the Armistice of Mudros, he was practically the only German general left in the Ottoman empire.[96]

IN REVIEWING the role Liman and other German generals played in the Ottoman war effort, certain general conclusions can readily be drawn. First, despite the phenomenal growth of the German military establishment in Turkey after 1915 (there were close to 25,000 officers and men in the Ottoman

[95] Mühlmann, *deutsch-türkische Waffenbündnis*, pp. 215-25; Liman, pp. 198-267, and *passim*.
[96] See Mühlmann, *deutsch-türkische Waffenbündnis*, pp. 225-30; and below, Chapter XI.

empire by the end of the war), the Ottoman armed forces remained exclusively an instrument of Turkish policy. Neither the members of Liman's mission nor any other German officers ever controlled the Ottoman army as a whole, for both the supreme command and a large proportion of the major unit commands in the field were in the hands of Turks.[97] Though Enver had a large number of German officers on his staff (including several generals) they were clearly his subordinates and wielded influence by advice and persuasion, not by dictation. Both Bronsart von Schellendorff and his successor, Seeckt, established a good working relationship with Enver and were therefore able on many occasions to mold his views on strategic and tactical issues. However, in order to retain his confidence they were also periodically forced to associate themselves with decisions by Enver which were objectionable to some of their German fellow generals or even to the OHL. Bronsart's relucant support of Enver's Caucasus offensive in 1914 (despite Liman's warnings) and Seeckt's spirited defense of the vice-generalissimo's Caucasus policy vis-à-vis his superiors in Germany during the last year of the war are two of the more obvious cases in point.[98]

Gen. Liman was one of the most capable field commanders the Turks had during the war. Although he made some mistakes during the Gallipoli campaign, his energy and ability to maintain the confidence of his Turkish subordinates account

---

[97] Until 1917 the Ottoman land forces comprised six armies, thereafter eight. Four of these had Turkish commanding generals throughout the war. Of the others, the Fifth Army was under German command for almost three years, the First for 14 months, the Sixth for half-a-year, and the Eighth for two months. It should be added, however, that from mid-1917 on several Turkish-commanded armies were placed under the overall control of Falkenhayn and then of Liman as components of Army Group F. Late in the war (June 1918), a Ninth Army was formally created in Transcaucasia, with a Turkish general, Y. Şevki Paşa, in command.

[98] On Seeckt see below, Chapter VI.

in no small part for the successful defense of the Straits in 1915. The defeat of Army Group F in the autumn of 1918 has associated Liman's name with one of the worst setbacks the Turks suffered during the entire war, but most students of the Palestinian fiasco agree that it was hardly Liman's fault, given the enormous difficulties under which he was laboring. Liman's record as chief of the military mission was rather less distinguished. While he deserves credit for achieving certain improvements in the training and organization of the Ottoman army his headstrong ways and undiplomatic conduct contributed in no small measure to the general erosion of German influence in Constantinople. Liman's inclination to go his own way repeatedly caused well-nigh chaotic conditions in the German camp, and his periodic quarrels with Enver put a severe strain on the alliance relationship itself. The determination of the Porte to revamp the system of German-Ottoman military collaboration at the end of the war, particularly its insistence on subordinating future military missions to rigid controls, was related to its unpleasant experiences with Liman. Altogether it is clear that Liman was not even remotely as powerful in the Ottoman army as has often been alleged, and his political usefulness to the German government was limited both before and during the war.

Among the other high-ranking German generals who served in the Ottoman empire during the war years, Field Marshal von der Goltz enjoyed by far the greatest esteem in the Turkish officer corps, but his influence on the man who counted, Enver, was virtually nil. Eventually sent off to the remote Mesopotamian theater of war the marshal had the personal satisfaction of leading troops in battle, but even in his geographically limited area of command—Mesopotamia and Persia—he never possessed absolute authority.[99] Gen. von Falkenhayn served approximately nine months in the Ottoman empire, most of

[99] Cf. Goltz, pp. 380-459; Mühlmann, *deutsch-türkische Waffenbündnis,* pp. 70-81, 287, and *passim;* Gehrke, *passim.*

the time under conditions which were truly frustrating. His authority as the commander of the Palestinian front was continuously challenged by officials of the Turkish administration in Syria and Palestine, his relationship with subordinate Turkish officers and eventually the Ottoman High Command was marked by a great deal of friction, and his recall from Turkey finally became inevitable. Kress von Kressenstein, who became a major general in the spring of 1917, made an excellent record during his three years' service in Palestine, initially as a staff officer with various units and later as an army commander. Like Liman he earned the respect of most of his Turkish colleagues and subordinates. As chief of the German Delegation in Tiflis during the summer and autumn of 1918, Kress was saddled with the difficult task of safeguarding German interests vis-à-vis the Turks. Despite his formerly close relations with prominent figures in the Ottoman military hierarchy, he accomplished relatively little in that regard and had to watch helplessly as the Turks pursued their expansionist drive toward the Caspian Sea.[100]

[100] On the activities of Gen. Kress in 1918 see Chapters VI and VII.

CHAPTER IV

Political Evolution of the
Alliance, 1914 to Early 1917

A s PREVIOUSLY mentioned, Turkish entry into the war in
early November 1914 had been accompanied by urgent requests for the modification of the existing German-Ottoman alliance treaty and for a formal pledge by the Reich that
it, for one, would under no condition insist upon the restoration of its capitulatory rights in the post-bellum period.[1] With
these requests the leaders of the *Ittihad ve Terakki* regime
made the opening move in what was subsequently to become
a highly successful campaign to extract far-reaching political,
financial, and economic concessions and pledges for their country from the two Central Powers. Despite German and Austro-
Hungarian reluctance the Porte almost invariably got most or
even all it wanted in the end. As will be shown in this and following chapters, the Turks owed their success above all to the
consummate skill with which they convinced Berlin and Vienna that the preservation of political stability in the Ottoman
empire and the continuation of the Ottoman war effort de-
pended directly on the extent to which the Central Powers
complied with the Porte's wishes.

GERMANY ACCEPTS NEW OBLIGATIONS,
WINTER 1914-15

While the Turkish request in early November 1914 for the
modification and extension of the German-Ottoman alliance
received a sympathetic hearing from Wangenheim and Pallavicini and some of their immediate superiors in Berlin and
Vienna, Chancellor Bethmann Hollweg initially was not at
all receptive to the Porte's proposals:

The current world conflict [he wired to the Wilhelmstrasse

---

[1] See above, pp. 60-61.

The Alliance, 1914 to Early 1917

and Constantinople] was provoked not least of all by the exaggeration and spread of the alliance system. After the restoration of peace . . . [we] should try as much as possible to get rid of the *cauchemar des coalitions*. Under these circumstances we decided only with great reluctance to conclude a formal alliance with Turkey and consider a further extension of it basically undesirable. An extension of the alliance against *all* states would create a new basis for a new general system of coalitions, which we wish to avoid as a matter of principle.

The preservation and protection of Turkey correspond to our own interests and belong to the basic principles of our policy which we *must* follow as previously, even without an extension of the alliance treaty. The current comradeship-in-arms increases the solidarity of our interests in any case. If our armies emerge victorious from the present war, Turkey will have nothing to fear in the foreseeable future, not even from England, for the stakes of the struggle are the destruction of England's world supremacy. Should we be defeated or weakened, we would probably be unable—*despite* the alliance treaty—to protect Turkey against all coalitions and eventualities. . . .

The alleged dissensions in the Ottoman cabinet, the chancellor continued, was no reason for Germany to accept additional obligations, for the grand vizier himself had committed the Ottoman empire to intervention by signing the original alliance treaty. All that Bethmann Hollweg was willing to concede was formal assurance to the Porte that Germany would not insist on the restoration of the capitulatory system.[2]

Bethmann Hollweg's blunt refusal to renegotiate the alliance treaty caused considerable dismay in Constantinople.

[2] FO, *Dt 128 Nr. 5 secr.*, Bd. 5, Wangenheim to FO, 2 Nov 1914, No. 1,205; Zimmermann to Jagow, 3 Nov, No. 927, 5 Nov, No. 960; Bethmann Hollweg to FO, 5 Nov, No. 97; Zimmermann to Wangenheim, 5 Nov, No. 1,141. See also Jagow to FO, 6 Nov, No. 343.

On November 7 Wangenheim wired to Berlin that the chancellor's decision should be reversed immediately, for unless Germany made some concessions the interventionist ministers would be in serious trouble. In fact, he added, they had already expressed resentment and doubt of Germany's sincerity,

> especially since they regard the treaty issue as a mere formality for us, while for them the unity of their Party and hence their position vis-à-vis the army and the people, in short the entire outcome of ... [their policy], are at stake.[3]

As a result of Wangenheim's intercession (and a note from Vienna that it for one had already indicated a willingness to negotiate), Bethmann Hollweg reluctantly abandoned his position and on November 10 authorized Wangenheim to open negotiations with the Porte.[4] The ensuing German-Ottoman talks in Constantinople, which were regularly attended by Pallavicini, bogged down repeatedly, and it was only in early December that a rough draft agreement could be forwarded to Berlin. In its essentials the agreement called for the formal incorporation of the Ottoman empire into the German-Austrian alliance system and for mutual military assistance in case either Germany or the Ottoman empire was attacked by Russia, France, or Britain, or a coalition of two or more Balkan states. Germany's obligation to support the Turks in case of a British attack was however to apply only if Britain were supported by a second European state. Finally, the draft treaty provided for the conclusion of a "special" post-bellum German-Ottoman military convention.[5]

Although Wangenheim proudly pointed out to Berlin that he had talked the Porte out of a demand for an explicit guar-

[3] *Ibid.*, Wangenheim to FO, 7 Nov 1914, No. 1,262.

[4] *Ibid.*, Zimmermann to Bethmann Hollweg, 8 Nov 1914, No. 80; Bethmann Hollweg to FO, 10 Nov, No. 100; FO to Wangenheim, 10 Nov, No. 1,194.

[5] *Ibid.*, Wangenheim to FO, 2 Dec 1914, No. 1,486, 4 Dec, No. 1,508; and same to Bethmann Hollweg, 3 Dec, No. 295.

antee of the Ottoman empire's territorial integrity, the Wilhelmstrasse was not overly pleased with the ambassador's handiwork. Above all, Berlin pressed for and eventually obtained the Porte's agreement that the *casus foederis* could not be invoked against Rumania (which was technically still allied with the Central Powers), nor against any Balkan state which had no common borders with the Dual Monarchy. A second counterproposal by Berlin—to have all treaty obligations apply explicitly only to wars in which either party had been the victim of an "unprovoked" attack—was energetically turned down by the Turks. As Halil pointed out to Wangenheim, to insert a clause about "unprovoked" attacks into the new treaty meant opening "the back door" for those who wished to evade their obligations, and the Porte suspected that the Dual Monarchy might someday try to do just that.[6]

Halil's uncomplimentary remark about Austria-Hungary, whose formal "adherence" to the German-Ottoman alliance dated from August 4, was obviously provoked by mounting evidence that Vienna had no interest in helping the Turks in the Balkans. In fact, after hesitating for several weeks the Austro-Hungarian Foreign Minister, Leopold Count Berchtold, notified Berlin on December 28 that because of the Dual Monarchy's special sensitivity to any "turbulence in the Balkans," all references to southeastern Europe should be deleted from the German-Ottoman draft treaty. Two days later Berchtold indicated that he was willing to compromise on the Balkan clause provided that the Porte agreed to the "unprovoked attack" stipulation in return.[7]

Confronted with impatient reminders from the Turks that the conclusion of the treaty was overdue, the Wilhelmstrasse rejected Berchtold's proposal. Zimmermann explained to

[6] *Ibid.*, Jagow to Wangenheim, 8 Dec 1914, No. 1,459; Wangenheim to FO, 12 Dec, No. 1,587; Bethmann Hollweg to Wangenheim, 14 Dec, No. 1,520; and Wangenheim to FO, 17 Dec, No. 1,642.

[7] *Ibid.*, Austro-Hungarian embassy, Berlin, to FO, 28 Dec 1914; same to same, 30 Dec.

Vienna on January 2, 1915 that it was too dangerous to reopen negotiations on the treaty in view of the tense political situation in Constantinople. Any further haggling about the treaty terms was liable to weaken the position of those "cabinet and committee members who are devoted to us," especially since there was still "a strong current against Turkey's participation in the war" in the Ottoman capital.[8]

Berchtold took several days to make up his mind, but finally agreed to withdraw his objections and on January 11, 1915 the new German-Ottoman treaty was formally signed by Said Halim and Wangenheim. Considering Bethmann Hollweg's distaste for any further treaty commitments the conclusion of the new pact was no mean achievement for the Turks. Scheduled to run concurrently with the German-Austrian Alliance Treaty (that is, at least until July 1920, and if the latter were renewed, until 1926), the new German-Ottoman pact assured the Turks of German military assistance in any defensive war against Russia, France, a coalition of Balkan states (with the exceptions noted above), or Britain (if the latter was supported by another European state).[9]

To Said Halim in particular the new treaty seems to have appeared as a definite improvement over the original alliance of August 1914, for he suggested right away that the older treaty should be torn up. Initially Berlin was more than happy to oblige, especially since the old treaty had contained an implicit guarantee of Ottoman territorial integrity, but the Germans' euphoria quickly faded when it became clear that the Turks would not formally renew their commitment to allow

[8] *Ibid.*, Zimmermann to Austro-Hungarian embassy, Berlin, 2 Jan 1915.

[9] *Ibid.*, Zimmermann to Wangenheim, 8 Jan 1915, No. 53; Wangenheim to FO, 11 Jan, No. 102; *Verträge 94 (IE)*, "Deutsch-türkischer Bündnisvertrag vom 11.1.15." The assertion by Mühlmann, *Deutschland*, p. 46, that Berlin had shared the Porte's desire to renegotiate the original alliance treaty is obviously wrong. For the text of the new treaty see *ibid.*, pp. 98-99.

the German military mission an "effective influence on the general direction of the army." As Enver explained to Wangenheim, he had accepted that "degrading" clause in the old treaty "merely for the sake of a quick agreement," and any formal reconfirmation of that clause was out of the question. As a result Berlin dropped the subject, and both sides seem to have agreed to leave the status of the treaty of 1914 in abeyance.[10] On March 21, 1915 Austria-Hungary formally declared its "adherence" to the revised German-Ottoman alliance.[11]

NORTH AFRICA, PAN-ISLAMISM, AND ITALY

During the three months of Ottoman neutrality the military and political leaders of Germany had become increasingly preoccupied with getting a Turkish advance on Egypt underway. Aside from the strategic advantages which such an operation would entail, particularly in terms of cutting Britain's lifeline to India, the march of Ottoman troops toward the Nile Valley was also expected to provoke popular uprisings in Egypt itself and in other Islamic areas under Entente control.[12]

The promotion of Moslem unrest in the British and French colonies and in the southern provinces of the Russian empire was one of the few subjects on which the Turks and the Germans could rather easily agree, at least in theory. While the Germans were primarily concerned with hampering the war effort of the Entente, the Turks seem to have been interested above all in reasserting Ottoman leadership in the Islamic

[10] FO, *Dt 128 Nr. 5 secr.*, Bd. 5, Wangenheim to FO, 14 Jan 1915, No. 126; Jagow to Zimmermann, 15 Jan, No. 47; Zimmermann to Wangenheim, 16 Jan, No. 43; Wangenheim to FO, 10 Feb, No. 338; Zimmermann to Wangenheim, 14 Feb, No. 290.

[11] Mühlmann, *Deutschland,* p. 46; FO, *Dt 128 Nr. 5 secr.,* Bd. 6, Tschirschky to FO, 17 Sept 1916, No. 327. See also Gerard E. Silberstein, "The Central Powers and the Second Turkish Alliance 1915," *Slavic Review,* 24 (1965), pp. 77-89, *passim.*

[12] Mühlmann, *deutsch-türkische Waffenbündnis,* pp. 24-27, 88-89, 261; Fischer, *Weltmacht,* pp. 140-48.

world and in securing political influence or perhaps even territorial gains in North Africa and western Asia. Although any
generalizations about the ambitions of the *Ittihad ve Terakki*
regime are risky, it seems fairly clear that the Porte had its eye
particularly on Egypt, Libya, parts of Persia, and the Caucasian
provinces of Russia. Moreover, some Ottoman leaders, including Enver, were definitely dreaming of expanding deeply into
Russia's central Asian provinces under the banner of Pan-
Turanianism.[13]

The implementation of the German and Ottoman plans,
both as regards the military advance into Egypt and the incitement of popular unrest there and elsewhere, required a great
deal more time, effort, and money than most of the German
leaders had expected. Although from August 1914 on both the
Germans and the Porte sent agents, propaganda material, and
money into some of the African and Asian possessions of the
Entente, few tangible gains had been made by the time the
Ottoman empire openly entered the war.[14] Similarly, the preparations for the military advance into Egypt were making very

[13] Cf. *ibid.*, pp. 132-55; and Fischer, "Deutsche Kriegsziele, Revolutionierung und Separatfrieden im Osten 1914-1918," *Historische Zeitschrift,* 188 (1959), pp. 249-93; Zechlin, "Friedensbestrebungen und
Revolutionierungsversuche," pp. 325-40, 352-57, and *passim*; Gehrke,
I, 1-6, 21-28, and *passim*.

On Turkish war aims and expansionist ambitions cf. Bayur, III:1,
65-67, *passim*; Gotthard Jäschke, "Der Turanismus der Jungtürken:
Zur osmanischen Aussenpolitik im Weltkriege," *Die Welt des Islams,*
23 (1941), pp. 9-28, *passim*; Serge A. Zenkovsky, *Pan-Turkism and
Islam in Russia* (Cambridge, Mass., 1960), pp. 106-11, 127-28, and
passim.

[14] Fischer, *Weltmacht,* pp. 140-48, 149-55; Zechlin, "Friedensbestre-
bungen und Revolutionierungsversuche," pp. 352-56, 363-64, and *passim*;
FO, *Wk 16*, Bd. 1, Wangenheim to FO, 6 Aug 1914, No. 443, 18 Aug,
No. 534, 20 Aug, No. 554, 22 Aug, No. 581; *Dt 128 Nr. 5 secr.*, Bd. 4,
Wangenheim to FO, 8 Sept, No. 752; Jäckh Papers, No. 10, "Be-
sprechung mit Enver Pascha am 2. Oktober 1914."

slow progress, despite extensive financial assistance from Berlin
and the assignment of several capable German staff officers to
the Palestine staging area.[15] To make matters worse from the
German point of view, the Pan-Islamic propaganda emanating
from Constantinople and the concentration of Ottoman troops
in southern Palestine were causing mounting irritation in
Rome. Both the German government and the Porte assured the
Italian government that their Pan-Islamic activities were not
and would not be directed against the Italian colonial empire,
but Rome remained on edge. In fact, it repeatedly sent warnings to Constantinople that Ottoman participation in the war
would put an unfortunate strain on Italo-Turkish relations.[16]

On October 27, the day the Ottoman fleet steamed out of the
Bosporus to attack the Russians, Enver notified Berlin that he
had instructed the Senussis in Libya to "prepare for war against
England," but not to molest the Italians (whom they had
fought intermittently ever since 1912, when Tripolitania and
Cyrenaica had been ceded to Italy by the Porte).[17] During the
following days, while the Ottoman drift into war became more
and more obvious, Berlin once again assured the Italian government that Italy's rights in Africa would be fully respected

[15] FO, *Wk*, Bd. 25, Wangenheim to FO, 18 Aug 1914, No. 530;
Dt 128 Nr. 5 secr., Bd. 4, same to same, 8 Sept, Nos. 745, 752; 11
Sept, Nos. 779, 785; 12 Sept, No. 791; 9 Oct, No. 1,010; Jagow to
FO, 13 Sept, No. 140; Bethmann Hollweg to FO, 14 Sept, No. 43;
Türkei 110, Bd. 72, Wangenheim to FO, 20 Sept, No. 850. See also
Liman, pp. 25-27; Kress, pp. 27-69; Pomiankowski, pp. 101-102.

[16] *I Documenti Diplomatici Italiani,* ser. 5, 1, Nos. 915, 930, 944; FO,
Dt 128 Nr. 1 secr., Bd. 34, Bethmann Hollweg to FO, 25 Oct 1914,
No. 80; *Dt 128 Nr. 5 secr.*, Bd. 4, Wangenheim to FO, 26 Oct, No.
1,113.

[17] FO, *Dt 128 Nr. 1 secr.*, Bd. 36, Wangenheim to FO, 27 Oct 1914,
No. 1,128. On the intermittent clashes between the Senussis and the
Italians after the conclusion of the Italo-Turkish War of 1911-12, see
especially E. E. Evans-Pritchard, *The Sanusi of Cyrenaica* (Oxford,
1949), pp. 104-24.

and promised adequate compensations in case some "territorial changes on the north coast of Africa" should materialize. Nevertheless, Rome remained "nervous." On October 31 Prime Minister Antonio Salandra told the German ambassador, Johannes von Flotow, that he hoped Italy could maintain her neutrality, but that any Ottoman interference with the operation of the Suez Canal would be regarded as a very serious matter by the Italians, who needed the canal to communicate with their east African colonies.[18]

The Austro-Hungarian government, which was of course particularly sensitive to any possible shift in Rome's attitude, sent a pointed reminder to Constantinople that Italy was Austria-Hungary's "ally," and that all violations of Italy's interests should be studiously avoided.[19] The Porte responded to this admonition on November 2 with the suggestion that Italy be invited to join the German-Ottoman alliance, at least as an inactive partner, but Wangenheim proposed instead that the Turks issue a formal declaration that they would "respect Italian interests to the fullest extent." In accordance with Wangenheim's suggestion the Porte four days later sent a formal note to Berlin to the effect that the Turks, once they had reached the Suez Canal, would not interfere with neutral shipping, and that they would "continue to observe very strictly" the provisions of the Lausanne Treaty with regard to Cyrena-

[18] FO, *Dt. 128 Nr. 5 secr.*, Bd. 4, Zimmermann to Flotow, 30 Oct 1914, No. 635; same to Tschirschky, 30 Oct, No. 951; Flotow to FO, 31 Oct, Nos. 588, 594.

[19] *Ibid.*, Stollberg to FO, 31 Oct 1914, No. 628. While insisting on a policy of extreme caution with regard to Libya, Vienna raised no objection to the incitement of unrest in Egypt. The request of the Khedive, Abbas Hilmi, to be accompanied by an Austro-Hungarian representative when he returned to Egypt "with the Turks" was approved by Berchtold. See AHFM, *Krieg 21a, Türkei*, Pallavicini to AHFM, 19 Oct 1914, No. 714; AHFM to Pallavicini, 20 Oct, No. 634; Pallavicini to Berchtold, 29 Oct, No. 63-C/P.

ica. Zimmermann immediately forwarded this note to the German embassy in Rome for appropriate use, noting that the Reich would guarantee the Ottoman pledge "as long as Italy remains neutral."[20]

While the German, Austro-Hungarian, and Ottoman ambassadors in Rome were doing their best to reassure the Italian government of Turkey's amicable intentions, final arrangements were being made in Constantinople for the proclamation of a *jihad*, a holy war of Islam, against the Entente nations. The declaration of a *jihad* by the Sultan-Caliph had been promised to Berlin on several occasions prior to the intervention of the Ottoman empire, and most of Germany's political and military leaders were eagerly looking forward to that event.[21] As the Wilhelmstrasse reminded Wangenheim on November 13, the forthcoming pronouncement (*fetva*) by the *sheik-ul-Islam* concerning the need for a holy war should be forwarded immediately to Berlin so that it could be translated into "Arabic and Indian" [sic] for leaflet propaganda among the "enemy Moslem soldiers in France."[22]

On November 14 formal proclamation of the *jihad* in Constantinople was followed by well-organized demonstrations in the streets. A large group of demonstrators, accompanied by a band, marched to the German embassy where Wangenheim received several "delegates." After being harangued by the prominent Union and Progress Party leader, Dr. Nazim, and a Turkish-speaking member of Wangenheim's staff, the demonstrators moved on to the Austro-Hungarian embassy—

[20] FO, *Dt 128 Nr. 5 secr.*, Bd. 5, Wangenheim to FO, 3 Nov 1914, Nos. 1,204, 1,215; Zimmermann to Flotow, 6 Nov, No. 678.

[21] Cf. *ibid.*, Bd. 4, Wangenheim to FO, 22 Oct 1914, No. 1,087; Jäckh Papers, No. 11, "J." (Lt. von Janson) to German embassy Constantinople, 22 Oct; Bayur, III:1, 317-48, *passim*; Mühlmann, *deutsch-türkische Waffenbündnis*, p. 24; Fischer, *Weltmacht*, pp. 132-37.

[22] FO, *Wk*, Bd. 59, Zimmermann to Wangenheim, 13 Nov 1914, No. 1,234.

though not without first issuing "ceaseless" cheers for the Kaiser and the German ally.[23]

While all this commotion and "enthusiasm" was no doubt good news to Berlin, neither Wangenheim nor his Austro-Hungarian colleague were overly pleased with the whole business. Wangenheim wired to the Wilhelmstrasse the same evening that the unleashing of religious passions among the Turks was liable to do more harm than good. There had already been anti-Armenian violence and other disorder in the city, and he was doing everything "to prevent further troubles for which we would be held responsible."[24] In contrast to Maj. Laffert, his military attaché, who seriously thought that the display of green flags by German troops would prevent the Moslems in the Entente armies from shooting at them, Wangenheim had little if any confidence in the efficacy of the Ottoman-sponsored *jihad*. As he wrote to Zimmermann in a private letter, the Sultan-Caliph's appeal was likely to "coax only a few Moslems from behind the warm stove."[25]

By and large the ambassador's scepticism was well justified. Only a small percentage of the world's Moslems heeded Constantinople's call for religious solidarity. In most Islamic regions where native unrest against the Entente did materialize (Libya, the Sudan, Persia), holy war sentiments seem to have played a relatively unimportant role. Nevertheless, it would be

[23] *Ibid.*, Bde. 59-60, Wangenheim to FO, 14 Nov 1914, Nos. 1,337, 1,338, 1,342; Emin, pp. 174-78.

[24] FO, *Wk*, Bd. 60, Wangenheim to FO, 14 Nov 1914, No. 1,342. The recent assertion by Fischer, *Weltmacht*, p. 138, that Wangenheim was an avid supporter of the "revolutionizing efforts" undertaken by Germany is obviously an overstatement. Regarding Pallavicini's misgivings about the *jihad* see AHFM, *Krieg 21a, Türkei,* Pallavicini to Berchtold, 29 Oct, No. 63B/P; same to AHFM, 2 Nov, No. 773; same to Berchtold, 5 Nov, No. 64/P; 19 Nov, No. 68/P. See also Liman, p. 35.

[25] Cf. FO, *Wk*, Bd. 60, Wangenheim to FO [Laffert to OHL], 14 Nov 1914, No. 1,341; *Türkei 110*, Bd. 73, Wangenheim to "Dear Friend" (Zimmermann), 13 Nov.

inappropriate to conclude that the Ottoman call for a *jihad* was completely useless, for there is considerable evidence that the Entente governments were seriously worried by the specter of Pan-Islamic unrest and kept sizable armies in most of their Moslem territories.[26]

The proclamation of the *jihad*, needless to say, provoked new misgivings in Rome. To allay Italian concern the German government instructed its consular representatives in Libya to promote good relations between the natives and their Italian overlords and to divert the warlike energies of the Libyans against the Entente. Simultaneously Berlin sent another appeal to the Porte to support the German efforts by appropriate messages to the Senussis.[27] In response to Berlin's appeal Enver offered to send his younger brother, Maj. Nuri Bey, on a "peace-keeping" mission to the Senussis—a proposal which he had made once before (in early November), but which had been rejected by Rome. As Wangenheim explained to Berlin on November 20, Enver was intent on getting his brother into Libya, since Nuri could be counted on not only to allay frictions between the natives and the Italians but also to direct the Senussis against the British in Egypt. A Senussi invasion from the west would in fact be an important precondition for the Ottoman conquest of Egypt, as the eastern approach to the Nile valley was much more strongly defended by the British.[28]

Although Enver openly admitted that he was determined to get his brother into Libya even if Rome persisted in its opposi-

[26] Cf. Larcher, pp. 528-29; Emin, pp. 177-79; Mühlmann, *deutsch-türkische Waffenbündnis*, pp. 282-85; George Lenczowski, *The Middle East in World Affairs*, 3rd edn. (Ithaca, N.Y., 1962), pp. 50-54.

[27] FO, *Dt 128 Nr. 1 secr.*, Bd. 37, Zimmermann to Flotow, 15 Nov 1914, No. 734; same to Wangenheim, 15 Nov, No. 1,249.

[28] *Ibid.*, Bd. 38, Wangenheim to FO, 20 Nov 1914, No. 1,393. On Enver's earlier offer and its rejection by the Italian foreign minister, Baron Sonnino, see *Dt 128 Nr. 5 secr.*, Bd. 5, Wangenheim to FO, 3 Nov, No. 1,217; *Dt 128 Nr. 1 secr.*, Bd. 37, Flotow to FO, 7 Nov, No. 633.

tion, Wangenheim concluded from his conversations with other Ottoman leaders that they were still hopeful of drawing Italy into the German-Ottoman alliance. Indeed, the ambassador gained the impression that the Porte would make all kinds of concessions to attain that objective, such as "ceding" the Egyptian town of Sollum to Italy or granting the latter a "sphere of influence in Asia Minor." At Wangenheim's suggestion Berlin subsequently informed Rome of the Turkish willingness to bargain, but the Consulta showed itself unimpressed.[29] In fact, only a few days later, Rome advised the Porte that it would have to insist on further pledges regarding Libya, namely a "solemn" Turkish appeal to the Libyans to abstain from *jihad* activities against Italy, along with a formal acknowledgment that all Libyans living in the Ottoman empire were subjects of the Italian state.[30]

Although the Porte was highly displeased by the Italian position (and blamed Berlin and Vienna for the increasing assertiveness of the Consulta), it agreed to accept both Italian demands if Rome in return withdrew its objection to Nuri's proposed mission. This Ottoman proposal, which was once again connected with an offer to "cede" Sollum to Italy, was turned down by Foreign Minister Sydney Sonnino and the negotiations between Constantinople and Rome soon petered out.[31] Undaunted, the Porte continued to spin its web in Libya. In February 1915 Nuri Bey managed to sneak into Cyrenaica aboard a smuggler's ship. Backed up by clandestine shipments of money and materiel he and other Ottoman and German agents subsequently instigated and organized Senussi attacks

[29] See Wangenheim's dispatch No. 1,393, *Dt 128 Nr. 1 secr.*, Bd. 38; Jagow to FO, 22 Nov 1914, No. 403; FO to Flotow, 22 Nov, No. 779; Flotow to FO, 23 Nov, No. 729; 24 Nov, No. 737, *ibid.* Cf. *Dt 128 Nr. 5 secr.*, Bd. 5, Memo by Zimmermann, 24 Nov.

[30] FO, *Dt 128 Nr. 1 secr.*, Bd. 38, Wangenheim to FO, 28 Nov 1914, No. 1,445.

[31] See *ibid.*; and Wangenheim to FO, 29 Nov 1914, No. 1,466; Flotow to FO, 1 Dec, No. 773.

on the Italians (after Rome's declaration of war on the Dual Monarchy in May 1915) and (later in the year) on the British forces in western Egypt as well. Skirmishes and occasional small-scale battles between the tribesmen and Italian and British troops continued well into the spring of 1917, when the hard-pressed Senussis agreed to a formal truce. Although the desert fighting in western Egypt and Cyrenaica between 1915 and 1917 was a sideshow, the Senussis and their Ottoman and German "advisers" did keep tens of thousands of British and Italian troops occupied for over two years.[32]

While Enver had initially intended to synchronize the projected Ottoman attack on Egypt with a Senussi invasion from the west, the German High Command persuaded the Turks in January 1915 to launch their offensive at once, that is, unilaterally.[33] Headed by Cemal Paşa and Lt. Col. Kress von Kressenstein an Ottoman expeditionary force of about 20,000 men made a forced march through the Sinai Desert and reached the Suez Canal in early February. Although some of the invaders managed to cross the waterway, mounting British resistance persuaded Cemal to call off the attack and to withdraw with the bulk of his forces to Palestine.[34]

The failure of the expeditionary corps to secure a permanent foothold at or near the Canal and the fact that the Ottoman advance had triggered neither a native uprising in Egypt nor any Senussi activities in the Western Desert caused considerable disappointment at the German High Command, though

[32] On the fighting in Libya and western Egypt from the summer of 1915 to the spring of 1917, see especially MacMunn and Falls, I, 101-45; Evans-Pritchard, pp. 125-45; Larcher, pp. 513-21. Extensive new evidence may be found in FO, *Tripolis 1,* Bde. 15-17; and *Wk 11u,* Bde. 1-3.

[33] Regarding Gen. von Falkenhayn's insistence on the prompt initiation of the offensive see Mühlmann, *deutsch-türkische Waffenbündnis,* pp. 89-90.

[34] Cf. Djemal, pp. 147-59; Kress, pp. 46-99; Pomiankowski, pp. 166-67; MacMunn and Falls, I, 28-52.

Falkenhayn was greatly relieved that the campaign had at least not ended with a rout such as the Turks had suffered in Trans-caucasia the preceding month. Moreover the Germans soon concluded that the Ottoman dash to the Suez Canal had served at least the limited purpose of alarming the British, for the latter subsequently moved additional troops into Egypt—troops which might otherwise have been available on the Western front. The Turks, in agreement with the OHL, did not resume any large-scale operations out of Palestine until the summer of 1916, but the sporadic appearance of smaller Ottoman troop units at or near the Suez Canal served to keep the British worried during much of the intervening period.[35]

THE PORTE SECURES FURTHER POLITICAL
CONCESSIONS, 1915-17

While the revised German-Ottoman alliance treaty of January 1915 had formally met the Turks' demands for security against the Entente in the postwar period, the Porte soon made it clear that it wanted further pledges and concessions from its allies. In April 1915 the grand vizier reminded Berlin and Vienna that they had not yet officially recognized the permanent abolition of the capitulations, and in November the Porte announced that it expected German and Austro-Hungarian support of Ottoman "compensatory" territorial demands on Bulgaria and Greece.[36] More important, the conquest of southern Mesopotamia by the British and—after January 1916—of large parts of eastern Anatolia by the Russians induced the Ottoman government to demand yet another revision of the

---

[35] Mühlmann, *deutsch-türkische Waffenbündnis*, pp. 90-91; Reichs-archiv, *Der Weltkrieg 1914 bis 1918*, IX, 173. Cf. MacMunn and Falls, I, 53ff.; Edmonds, pp. 370-71; Paul Guinn, *British Strategy and Politics, 1914 to 1918* (Oxford, 1965), p. 131, and *passim*.

[36] See AHFM, *Türkei, Berichte 1915*, Pallavicini to AHFM, 20 April 1915, No. 320; Jackh Papers, No. 17, "Streng vertrauliche Mitteilungen vom 11. Nov. 1915."

alliance treaty, namely the inclusion of a pledge that Germany would not make peace unless the terms were acceptable to the Porte. Finally, the Turks made it known in September 1916 that they expected their allies to acquiesce in the unilateral Ottoman abrogation of various international treaties, starting with the Paris Treaty of 1856, which curtailed or interfered with the sovereign rights of the Porte.[37]

Before discussing the settlement of these issues between the Central Powers and the Porte it is necessary to refer briefly to a number of personnel changes in Constantinople and Berlin that occurred in 1915 and somewhat altered the general political relationship between the two governments. The first change involved the Ottoman embassy in Berlin. It will be recalled that Ambassador Muhtar had never been on good terms with Enver. Moreover, his support of the alliance policy charted by Enver and his followers was at most lukewarm, and there were periodic complaints from Constantinople that he could not be trusted. Although the Kaiser was obviously fond of the ambassador, Enver's group in the central committee cautiously suggested to Berlin in March 1915 that Muhtar should be replaced, and by early July Wangenheim cabled to the Wilhelmstrasse that the "Turkish ministers' distrust" of Muhtar was growing steadily. A few days later Muhtar was recalled. His place was taken by Gen. Ibrahim Hakki Paşa, who was to preside over the Berlin embassy during the next three years.[38]

The change at the Berlin embassy was primarily the work of Halil Bey, who was increasingly being used by Enver's faction as a kind of diplomatic troubleshooter and foreign policy

---

[37] Mühlmann, *Deutschland*, p. 47; FO, *Türkei 204*, Bd. 1, Wolff-Metternich to FO, 5 Sept 1916, No. 204.

[38] *Ibid., Dt 127 Nr. 6*, Bd. 3, Wangenheim to FO, 10 March 1915, No. 585; Jagow to Treutler, 10 March, No. 93; Treutler to FO, 11 March, No. 150; Wangenheim to FO, 7 July, No. 1,556, 13 July, No. 1,588; Jagow to Wangenheim, 14 July, No. 1,338. Cf. Jäckh Papers, No. 3, "Auszug aus einem Brief des Kapitän Humann . . . an Dr. Jäckh," (dated 1 May 1915).

spokesman. Indeed, by the summer of 1915 Enver, Talât, and their followers presented their colleagues with the plan of making Halil officially the foreign minister, that is, to restrict Said Halim to his functions as grand vizier. This plan was strenuously opposed by Said Halim and his supporters, nor was the Sultan overly happy with having another "radical" added to the council of ministers. However, after three months of wrangling in the central committee, during which Said Halim repeatedly threatened to quit all his posts, the Enver-Talât group won out and Halil was formally installed as foreign minister in October 1915.[39]

The dislodgment of Said Halim from the foreign ministry and his replacement by Halil undoubtedly strengthened the ties between the Ottoman empire and the Central Powers, but there is no evidence that the Germans had anything to do with the change at the Porte. In fact, the German embassy in Constantinople had very mixed feelings about it. As the *chargé* of the embassy, Konstantin von Neurath,[40] wrote to Bethmann Hollweg on November 5, Halil was certainly one of "the most energetic and loyal supporters" of the alliance with the Central Powers and his appointment therefore was most valuable in terms of the common war effort, but this advantage was counterbalanced by the fact that Said Halim's moderating influence would now be missing in certain matters which were of great political importance. In particular, Neurath emphasized, Said Halim had hitherto sought courageously to limit

[39] See FO, *Dt 127 Nr. 6,* Bd. 3, Grünau to FO, 4 July 1915, no No.; *Türkei 159 Nr. 2,* Bde. 13-14, Hohenlohe-Langenburg to FO, 29 Sept, No. 2,210; Neurath to Bethmann Hollweg, 5 Nov, No. 654; AHFM, *Türkei, Berichte 1915,* Pallavicini to AHFM, 20 Oct, No. 797; Jäckh Papers, No. 17, "Konstantinopel, . . . Zur Lage am 4. Nov." Cf. *Schulthess,* v. 56, p. 1,162; Bayur, III:2, 398-401.

[40] Baron von Neurath later became a prominent figure in Germany, serving as foreign minister from 1932 to 1938 and subsequently as "Reichsprotektor Böhmen-Mähren." He was sentenced to 15 years imprisonment at the Nuremberg Trials.

the persecution of various ethnic and religious minorities in the empire, and although his efforts had been futile with regard to the Armenians, he had so far been successful in blocking the efforts of his radical colleagues to extend the brutal persecution measures to the Greek population element as well. Moreover, only recently he had spoken out against any harassment of the Christian-Syrian population, as was advocated by some of his colleagues. Altogether, Neurath concluded, it would be most unfortunate and politically harmful if Said Halim's position in Constantinople were undermined any further. Should he ever quit his post in disgust the already existing political tensions in Constantinople would definitely be aggravated, especially since the "left wing" of the Party, that is, the group around Talât, had more than enough enemies in the country already.[41]

The appointment of Halil as Ottoman foreign minister coincided with a highly important change at the German embassy in Constantinople. On October 25 Ambassador Wangenheim died unexpectedly. To fill the vacancy the Wilhelmstrasse first thought of picking Ernst Prince zu Hohenlohe-Langenburg, who had served during the summer of 1915 as a replacement for Wangenheim while the latter was taking a cure in Germany. However, the Porte made it clear that Hohenlohe-Langenburg would not be welcome inasmuch as his attitude regarding the Armenian question had been decidedly unfriendly.[42] Berlin thereupon chose Count von Wolff-Metternich.

Wolff-Metternich, a distinguished career diplomat who had served as ambassador to the Court of St. James from 1901 to

[41] FO, *Türkei 159 Nr. 2*, Bd. 14, Neurath to Bethmann Hollweg, 5 Nov 1915, No. 654. Cf. Jäckh Papers, No. 17, "Konstantinopel, . . . Zur Lage am 4. Nov." For a detailed discussion of the Armenian question see Chapter VII.

[42] *Schulthess*, v. 56, pp. 1,155; 1,157; 1,162; Pomiankowski, pp. 174-75; AHFM, *Türkei, Berichte 1915*, Pallavicini to Burian, 29 Oct 1915, No. 91A-C/P.

1912, from the moment he appeared in Constantinople antagonized the Turks. While some of his critics, especially Humann, later blamed Wolff-Metternich's difficulties on his aloofness, "excessive stinginess," and other personal idiosyncrasies, there is ample reason to conclude that the new ambassador's unpopularity with the Turks was primarily the result of his outspoken criticism of their Armenian policy. Said Halim recalled later on that Wolff-Metternich had used his first audience with him to reproach the Porte severely for its handling of the Armenian question. And Enver complained to Humann in December 1915 that the new ambassador was impossible to deal with inasmuch as he would not talk about anything but the Armenian persecutions.[43]

Although during the early months of 1916 both Wolff-Metternich and certain other German dignitaries who had been to Constantinople assured the Wilhelmstrasse that the working relationship between the embassy and the Porte was entirely satisfactory, it appears that the ill feelings between Wolff-Metternich and some of the leading Ottoman figures were never really eliminated. To make matters worse, Wolff-Metternich antagonized some of the German officials serving in Constantinople, especially Generals Bronsart von Schellendorff and Lossow, because of his friendly relations with Liman von Sanders.[44]

[43] See *ibid.*, Pallavicini to Burian, 18 Dec 1915, No. 103A-E/P; *Türkei, Berichte 1916,* same to same, 7 Oct 1916, No. 76C/P; Jäckh Papers, No. 4, "Zur Lage am 20. Dezember 1915"; and FO, *Dt 135 Nr. 1 secr.,* Bd. 1, Jagow to Solf, 24 Feb 1916; *Regierte der Kaiser?,* p. 197; Pomiankowski, pp. 175-76.

[44] FO, *Dt 135 Nr. 1 secr.,* Bd. 1, Solf to Jagow, 22 Feb 1916; Jagow to Treutler, 24 Feb, No. 156; Wolff-Metternich to FO, 24 Feb, No. 298; same to Jagow, 28 Feb (private); Jagow to Wolff-Metternich, 8 March, No. 321; and Wolff-Metternich to Jagow, 22 Aug (private). On Liman's quarrels with Enver and the latter's German advisers and on Wolff-Metternich's involvement in this matter, see above, pp. 90-97.

Having long since lost the support of Humann (whom he later characterized as an "arch-scoundrel"), Wolff-Metternich in the summer of 1916 was deserted by the senior member of his own staff as well. In two letters to Frédéric Hans von Rosenberg, the head of the Near East desk in the Berlin Foreign Office, Embassy Counsellor von Neurath pointed out that Wolff-Metternich had been quarreling with the Turks ever since his arrival in Constantinople and that he, Neurath, could no longer be expected to exhaust his strength in patching up relations with the Porte.[45] Almost simultaneously, Humann forwarded to the *Reichskanzlei* a memorandum by Talât and Enver in which they demanded Wolff-Metternich's immediate replacement. In listing their objections to the ambassador both Turks emphasized that he was totally devoid of sympathy for the innovations which the *Ittihad ve Terakki* regime was introducing in the Ottoman empire, a charge which referred quite obviously to Wolff-Metternich's opposition to the Porte's Armenian policies. As Talât put it, "the work that is to be done must be done *now*; after the war it will be too late." Enver added in his bill of particulars that Wolff-Metternich, aside from being old-fashioned and obstreperous, was playing a dangerous game in supporting Liman von Sanders, and concluded his remarks in the same vein as Talât's, namely that the Porte would no longer put up with that kind of an ambassador.[46]

Despite a veiled threat by Enver that the general political relationship between the Ottoman empire and Germany would be jeopardized unless Wolff-Metternich was recalled immediately, Berlin refused to be rushed. In fact, it was only after Enver, seconded by Lossow, had reiterated his demand during a visit to the Kaiser's headquarters at Pless in the second week

[45] FO, *Dt 135 Nr. 1 secr.*, Bd. 1, Neurath to Rosenberg, 4 Aug 1916 (private).

[46] DZA, Reichskanzlei, *Auswärtige Angelegenheiten 7, Türkei*, Bd. 1, "G.A.," signed by Wahnschaffe, 7 Aug 1916; and "Agenda für Bundesratsausschuss für auswärtige Angelegenheiten, 8 Aug 1916."

of September that serious steps were taken to get the unpopular ambassador out of Constantinople. Although it took Berlin another two weeks to pick a suitable successor (both Falkenhayn and Zimmermann were among those being considered), Bethmann Hollweg was finally able to inform the Turks that Richard von Kühlmann, well known to them from his earlier tour of duty in Constantinople, would take over the embassy. On September 29, 1916 the semi-official *Norddeutsche Allgemeine Zeitung* announced euphemistically that Wolff-Metternich had "been granted leave," and a few days later the ambassador left Constantinople.[47]

While the change of ambassadors was probably unavoidable, some German diplomats felt that a grave mistake had been made. Legation Counsellor von Radowitz (who had just replaced Neurath at the Constantinople embassy) wrote to Jagow on September 24 that it was unfortunate that "Enver's frowning" should be the undoing of a German ambassador whose political views and reports had been entirely acceptable to his superiors, that is, the chancellor and Jagow himself. Indeed, the result of the whole affair would surely be a strengthening of the military in both Germany and the Ottoman empire at the expense of the civilian leaders and, secondly, a hardening of the Turks' belief that they could get anything they wanted from the German government.[48]

RADOWITZ' complaint about the insatiable appetite of the Porte for concessions from Germany must be considered in light of

[47] FO, *Dt 135 Nr. 1 secr.*, Bd. 1, Bethmann Hollweg to Jagow, 29 Aug 1916; Jagow to Bethmann Hollweg, 30 Aug, No. 146; 1 Sept, No. 153; Bethmann Hollweg to Jagow, 12 Sept, No. 682; Jagow to Bethmann Hollweg, 12 Sept, No. 164; Bethmann Hollweg to Jagow, 20 Sept, No. 720; *Regierte der Kaiser?*, pp. 214, 217, 221; *Schulthess*, v. 57:1, pp. 447-48; Pomiankowski, p. 176.

[48] FO, *Dt 135 Nr. 1 secr.*, Bd. 1, Radowitz to FO, 24 Sept 1916, No. 242. Cf. AHFM, *Türkei, Berichte 1916*, Pallavicini to Burian, 29 Sept, No. 74B/P.

the frustrating negotiations which Berlin had been forced to conduct during the preceding half year. As previously mentioned, the Porte was not satisfied with the tacit acceptance of its anti-capitulation policy by the German and Austro-Hungarian governments, but insisted that the permanent abrogation of the capitulatory system be formally acknowledged by them. Throughout 1915 the Wilhelmstrasse managed to postpone a formal commitment on this matter, but by 1916 it became clear that the Porte could no longer be put off.[49]

There is no need to go into the prolonged and tedious negotiations on the capitulation question between Berlin and Constantinople during 1916. Suffice it to note that even though Berlin agreed in principle to abandon Germany's traditional capitulatory rights and to accept a new juridical relationship with the Ottoman empire on the basis of "mutual equality and the European law of nations,"[50] there were several matters of detail on which agreement proved extremely difficult. In particular, the Wilhelmstrasse held out for a long time against the Porte's demand that the special status and privileges of German religious and educational institutions in the Ottoman empire be eliminated along with all other capitulatory rights. Through most of the summer and fall of 1916 this issue was debated with increasing vehemence; at least on two occasions Talât let it be known that he would sooner resign from the cabinet than give in to the Germans. When this bit of "*chantage*," as Jagow called it, was followed by dire warnings from Enver that his own position at the Porte was being weakened by the continuing squabble on the capitulation question, Ber-

---

[49] In November 1915 Wolff-Metternich cautioned the Porte that the settlement of the capitulation issue would require time and careful preparation. See AHFM, *Türkei, Berichte 1915,* Pallavicini to Burian, 20 Nov 1915, No. 97A-G/P.

[50] See Zimmermann's announcement in the Reichstag on May 12, 1916, *Verhandlungen des Reichstags. XIII. Legislaturperiode. II. Session,* vol. 307, p. 1,046. Cf. Bayur, III:3, 469-77.

lin's opposition caved in.[51] In this connection it should be mentioned that the OHL had long since called for a more compromising German attitude. For, as Ludendorff put it, there was no justification for antagonizing the Porte and "thereby jeopardizing our entire future position in Turkey" on account of that "handful of [German] schools and churches" in the Ottoman empire.[52]

With Berlin's retreat on the school and religious issue the definite settlement so long desired by the Porte became feasible. On January 11, 1917 Ambassador Hakki and representatives of the Wilhelmstrasse signed a series of public treaties which formally abrogated all German capitulatory rights in the Ottoman empire and placed the juridical, consular, and commercial relationship between the two countries on the basis of mutual equality.[53] In addition, a secret treaty was initialed in Constantinople the same day in which the German government pledged its solidarity with the Porte if the latter should decide to reject Entente demands for the reestablishment of the capitulatory system at the end of the war.[54] Finally, in an exchange

[51] See AHFM, *Krieg 21a, Türkei,* Pallavicini to Burian, 19 Aug 1916, No. 63A-E/P; *Türkei LII/1,* Pallavicini to AHFM, 15 Aug, No. 370; 25 Oct, No. 507; 26 Oct, No. 510; Hohenlohe-Schillingsfürst to Burian, 30 Oct, No. 122A-B/P; Pallavicini to Burian, 31 Oct, No. 83A-E/P; *Türkei, Berichte 1916,* Pallavicini to Burian, 7 Oct, No. 76C/P; 18 Nov, No. 88C/P; FO, *Dt 135 Nr. 1 secr.,* Bd. 1, Bethmann Hollweg to Jagow, 12 Sept 1916, No. 682; Jagow to Bethmann Hollweg, 12 Sept, No. 164; Bethmann Hollweg to Wilhelm II, 25 Sept, No. 8; *Dt 128 Nr. 5 secr.,* Bd. 6, Wolff-Metternich to FO, 26 Sept, No. 246; Jäckh Papers, No. 5, Humann to Jäckh, 15 Nov 1916.

[52] FO, *Dt 135 Nr. 1 secr.,* Bd. 1, Grünau to FO, 26 Sept 1916, No. 750.

[53] These treaties, 10 in all, were subsequently ratified by the Ottoman parliament and German Reichstag. For the text of the treaties and the debate in the Reichstag preceding ratification, see *Verhandlungen des Reichstags,* v. 321, Anlage, Nr. 755; vol. 310, pp. 3,197-3,211; and *Schulthess,* v. 58:1, pp. 426-32, 530-36.

[54] See FO, *Dt 128 Nr. 5 secr.,* Bd. 6, "Geheimvertrag zwischen dem Deutschen Reich und dem Osmanischen Reiche wegen Beseitigung der Kapitulationen," signed by Kühlmann and Halil Bey.

of secret notes the two governments agreed to accord each other a most-favored-nation status with regard to religious, educational, medical, and charitable organizations and institutions; and Halil, Talât, and Enver "solemnly" gave their word to Kühlmann, "confirmed by a handshake" in the presence of two witnesses, that they would always "respect" the German institutions falling in those categories.[55]

The second major issue between Germany and the Ottoman empire which had to be threshed out in 1916 concerned the demand by the Porte that the alliance treaty of January 1915 be supplemented by a clause prohibiting either country to make a separate peace or to initiate negotiations for a general peace settlement without the consent of the other. As previously mentioned, the Turkish demand was causally related to the conquest of extensive Ottoman territory by the Russians and the British, but it would appear that the decisive factor was a rather unfortunate interview between Enver and Gen. von Lossow. On July 6, 1916 the OHL had approached the Ottoman High Command with the request that two Turkish divisions be made available for service in Galicia, where the Austro-Hungarian front was beginning to crack up under the impact of the Brussilov offensive. While Enver was quite willing to help out, both Liman and Wolff-Metternich registered strenuous objections to the proposed transfer of Ottoman troops; the former because the general military situation in Turkey was much too serious to denude it of troops, the latter because he suspected that the Turks would later cite their military assistance in Europe as a justification for new political demands on Germany. In particular, Wolff-Metternich warned Berlin that the requested military assistance in Central Europe would give the Turks a fairly good right to demand from their allies that they continue the war until all occupied Ottoman territory had been evacuated by the Entente. The am-

[55] *Ibid.,* Halil to Kühlmann, 11 Jan 1917; Kühlmann to Halil, 11 Jan; Memorandum, dated Pera, 11 Jan 1917, signed by Kühlmann, Lossow, Humann, Halil, Talât, and Enver.

bassador further pointed out that the Turks might also feel justified in raising their conditions for an acceptable settlement with Russia (particularly as regards the Straits question), thereby undercutting future German efforts to come to terms with Petrograd.[56]

Jagow, who was quite impressed by these warnings from Liman and Wolff-Metternich, immediately contacted the OHL and pointed out that the political reservations submitted by the ambassador should be seriously considered before the transfer of Ottoman troops to Galicia was put into effect. Rather naïvely Falkenhayn thereupon instructed Lossow to have a "frank talk" with Enver regarding the whole issue and to report his findings back to the OHL; the result was the unfortunate interview between Enver and Lossow. In a two-hour conversation on July 14 Lossow invited the vice-generalissimo to outline his views on a large number of topics, some of which Berlin had previously tried very hard not to talk about at all. As far as the Wilhelmstrasse was concerned the most serious *faux pas* by Lossow was probably his "frank" inquiry whether the Turks would object to the conclusion of peace as long as the "Caucasus and Iraq" had not been completely cleared of the enemy. To this, Enver replied with equal frankness that he and his colleagues at the Porte had always thought that the peace settlement would naturally be worked out in common and that Germany would see to it that the Ottoman empire regained its lost territories as much as that was possible. It was true, he continued, that no formal agreement had been made in this matter, but inasmuch as the question had now been raised by Lossow, he would be "grateful for a reply whether his and his colleagues' views were being shared in Germany."[57]

[56] Mühlmann, *deutsch-türkische Waffenbündnis*, pp. 107-108; Wolfgang Steglich, *Bündnissicherung oder Verständigungsfrieden* (Göttingen, 1958), pp. 110-11.

[57] See FO, *Türkei 150*, Bd. 1, Wolff-Metternich to FO, 15 July 1916, No. 49; *Dt 128 Nr. 5 secr.*, Bd. 6, same to same, 15 July, No. 48, Steglich, *Bündnissicherung*, p. 111.

Wolff-Metternich and his superiors in the Foreign Office were horrified by Lossow's undiplomatic conduct, but the damage was done. During the following weeks the Porte initiated formal diplomatic inquiries concerning Germany's attitude on the question of a common peace policy, and on September 5 Foreign Minister Halil Bey traveled to Berlin to settle the matter once and for all. Once there he presented a draft treaty to the Wilhelmstrasse which stipulated that (1) Germany and the Ottoman empire would use all their efforts to secure a peace which rewarded either country in accordance "with its sacrifices and its efforts"; (2) neither country would conclude peace without the consent of the other as long as the territory of either was in enemy hands; (3) neither would conclude a separate peace; and (4) the Ottoman empire would be entitled, under certain circumstances, to reclaim parts of Thrace from Bulgaria.[58] As Talât explained to Wolff-Metternich on September 19, the Porte had recently supplied its allies with troops and accepted German overall leadership in the war, so it could expect Germany in return to take care of Ottoman interests at the peace settlement. To the consternation of the ambassador, Talât illustrated his contention with the remark that if necessary Russia would have to be offered parts of occupied Poland to obtain her withdrawal from Turkish Armenia, and the same method would have to be used to get the British out of Iraq, that is, Germany "would have to evacuate parts of Flanders, so that the English give back Basra." As for the Ottoman claims in Thrace, Talât pointed out that close to 400,000 Moslems lived on the other side of the present Turco-Bulgarian border, and that their return to Ottoman rule would be a prerequisite for a permanent, amicable relationship with Bulgaria. Should the latter secure major territorial gains elsewhere in the Balkans, the cession of these Thracian border districts would

[58] FO, *Dt 128 Nr. 5 secr.,* Bd. 6, Wolff-Metternich to FO, 16 July 1916, No. 54; Jagow to Wolff-Metternich, 17 July, No. 12; Steglich, *Bündnissicherung,* pp. 112-14.

hardly involve an inordinate sacrifice for the Bulgarians; besides, the Ottoman empire needed a broader defensive belt to the west of its capital than it now possessed.[59]

After some hesitation Berlin accepted the Ottoman draft treaty except for the clause on Bulgaria, and on September 28, 1916 the revised document was signed by Jagow and Halil.[60] Although the Austro-Hungarian government was very reluctant to associate itself with the newly expanded German-Ottoman alliance treaty, the Turks insisted on a formal commitment which they eventually got in the form of a separate treaty signed March 22, 1917.[61]

ASIDE FROM pinning Germany down on the capitulations issue and the question of a common peace policy, the Porte initiated steps in late summer 1916 to secure the formal approval of the Central Powers for the abrogation of various international treaty obligations which the Ottoman empire had incurred during the 19th century. On this issue Berlin and Vienna, for once, remained firm.

The first inkling of what the Porte was after came to the Germans on September 5, 1916. Before boarding the train for

---

[59] FO, *Türkei 150*, Bd. 1, Wolff-Metternich to FO, 20 Sept 1916, No. 234. It should be noted that some of the Thracian territory claimed by the Porte had been ceded to Bulgaria in September 1915 to secure her entry into the war. See Arno Mehlan, "Das deutsch-bulgarische Weltkriegsbündnis," *Historische Vierteljahresschrift*, 30 (1935), pp. 778-82; Alexander Dallin *et al.*, *Russian Diplomacy and Eastern Europe, 1914-1917* (New York, 1963), pp. 230-33, *passim*; and Bayur, III:2, 475-81.

[60] FO, *Dt 128 Nr. 5 secr.*, Bd. 6, Jagow to Wolff-Metternich, 28 Sept 1916, No. 76; Steglich, *Bündnissicherung*, pp. 113-14. A copy of the treaty is in Mühlmann, *Deutschland*, pp. 99-101.

[61] See AHFM, *Türkei LII/2*, Memorandum, 20 Oct 1916; FO, *Dt 128 Nr. 5 secr.*, Bd. 6, Jagow to Wolff-Metternich, 27 Sept, No. 74; Wolff-Metternich to FO, 1 Oct, No. 251; Tschirschky to FO, 24 Oct, No. 373; Kühlmann to FO, 23 March 1917, No. 387; Steglich, *Bündnissicherung*, pp. 115-16, 121-23, 218, note 358.

Berlin Halil informed the perplexed Wolff-Metternich that the Ottoman cabinet had just decided to declare null and void the Paris Straits Treaty of 1856, the London Declaration of 1871, and the Berlin Treaty of 1878. As Halil explained, all three of these international treaties had imposed "political shackles" on the Ottoman state which the Porte intended to be rid of. Inasmuch as the state of war with the Entente powers had in effect eliminated all Turkish treaty obligations toward them, all that was left to be done was to arrive at an understanding with Germany and Austria-Hungary that the treaties in question were indeed no longer in effect.[62]

Neither the German nor the Austro-Hungarian government was eager to talk about this unorthodox proposal, for what the Turks were in fact suggesting was that the Central Powers should give up their prewar treaty rights as well. This became perfectly clear from a note which Halil presented to Jagow on October 7, 1916. Prefacing his communication with a lengthy historical survey of how "certain signatories" of the 1856 and 1878 treaties had "constantly violated" essential clauses pertaining to the Ottoman empire, Halil argued that these violations alone were sufficient cause for considering the treaties null and void. Moreover, the state of war with some of the signatory powers voided Turkish obligations toward them in any case. Finally, and this was the clinching argument, the Ottoman government was now allied with two great European powers "on a footing of perfect equality." Hence, Halil continued, the Ottoman empire

has freed itself very definitely from . . . the collective tutelage of the great powers under which some of the latter wish to keep it; it, therefore, enters the group of European powers with all the rights and prerogatives of a government which is entirely independent. . . .

[62] FO, *Türkei 204,* Bd. 1, Wolff-Metternich to FO, 5 Sept 1916, No. 204.

The totality of these various considerations renders the aforementioned Treaties [of 1856 and 1878] completely null and without any contractual value. Nevertheless, to leave no doubt on that point among those signatory states which have transformed their relations of friendship [with the Ottoman empire] into those of an alliance, the Imperial Government has the honor to inform the Imperial Government of Germany ([and] the Imperial and Royal Government of Austria-Hungary) that it denounces the aforementioned treaties of 1856 and 1878.[63]

As on several previous occasions both the German and Austro–Hungarian governments attempted to stall the Turks with simple passivity, by failing to make a formal reply to the Turkish note, a tactic that turned out to be of little use. On November 2, 1916 the Porte unilaterally made public the note it had directed to Berlin the previous month, a breach of diplomatic etiquette most distressing to the Wilhelmstrasse. When Radowitz and Pallavicini lodged complaints with Halil, Halil admitted he had been personally responsible for the publication and perhaps a bit rash. In self-defense he pointed out that he had understood from his recent discussions in Berlin and Vienna that the Central Powers were basically in agreement with the Porte's proposal, quite aside from the fact that the public in the Ottoman empire wished to know what he had accomplished in the allied capitals. According to Radowitz's subsequent report to Berlin, Halil "finally asked us that we give him a reply to the note soon, [a reply] which was bound to be of a positive nature anyway, so that he would have something pleasant for his parliament; for unfortunately he could not yet present it with the treaties regarding [the abrogation of] the capitulations." Radowitz immediately reminded Halil that the settlement of the capitulations question was held up

[63] *Ibid.*, "Notiz. Von Halil Bey . . . dem Herrn Staatssekretär am 7. Oktober überreicht."

solely by the uncompromising Turkish stand on the "school question," but remained noncommittal as to when and whether Berlin would act on the other issue.[64] As a result, Halil decided to increase the pressure. In analogous statements to the German and Austro–Hungarian embassies he announced on November 7 that at the reopening of parliament during the following week the government would have to "mention" in the speech from the throne that the Treaties of 1856 and 1878 had been canceled, and it would be "desirable" if one could announce as well that in this matter the Porte had "acted in agreement with the allied governments."[65]

Faced with the threat of another *fait accompli* if it continued to evade the issue, the Wilhelmstrasse finally was persuaded to respond to the Ottoman proposal formally. On November 11 Jagow directed a lengthy note to the Porte in which he acknowledged that it had a good case for renouncing its treaty obligations vis-à-vis the Entente countries. On the other hand, Germany and Austria-Hungary, as cosignatories of these 19th century treaties, could not accept a unilateral abrogation of their own rights, but would have to insist on being asked for consent. He continued:

> The German government will be ready to give that consent, in principle, as of now. In particular, it will be perfectly in accord with Turkey that the latter thus rids itself of the shackles which have been imposed by the Lebanon Statute and the arrangements on the passage of war ships through the Bosporus and the Dardanelles; but in giving this assurance it considers it understood that the Ottoman government will first reach an accord with its German ally concerning the disposition of the Straits Question at the peace settlement.
>
> Similarly, the German government must make a reserva-

[64] *Ibid.*, Radowitz to FO, 2 Nov 1916, No. 1,144; Zimmermann to Radowitz, 2 Nov, No. 1,245; Radowitz to FO, 6 Nov, No. 1,169; AHFM, *Türkei LII/2*, Memorandum, 20 Oct.

[65] FO, *Türkei 204*, Bd. 1, Radowitz to FO, 7 Nov 1916, No. 1,175.

tion with regard to the clauses of the two treaties which refer to commerce and navigation as well as to religious liberty; for as far as these clauses relate to the German empire and its nationals [*ressortessants*], they cannot be modified without prior, amicable understandings between the two governments. The German government must attach all the more importance to such a reservation inasmuch as in the renunciation of the rights in question it cannot avoid . . . [bringing the matter before the Reichstag].

Altogether, Jagow concluded, there was certainly good reason to expect that these problems could be settled "without difficulty." Two days later, on November 13, the Ballhausplatz followed Berlin's example and delivered a similar note to the Porte.[66]

As might be expected, the formalistic attitude shown by Berlin and Vienna was very much resented by the Porte. Although it deferred to their wishes and omitted all references to them in its announcement to Parliament concerning the unilateral Ottoman abrogation of the Treaties of 1856 and 1878, Halil left the Germans in no doubt that he and his colleagues had expected a different attitude from them.[67] As he told the departing Radowitz on November 21, it looked as though Germany had not yet fully understood that the Ottoman empire expected to be treated on a footing of equality. Contrary to Berlin's views there was absolutely no need for Germany to register a reservation regarding the ultimate settlement of the Straits question, for the Porte would "naturally" consult with its allies when it came to devising a "definite solution." As for the question of German commercial and navigation rights, these could and should be settled by ordinary trade agreements be-

[66] *Ibid.*, Jagow to Hakki Paşa, 11 Nov 1916; "Abschrift einer Note an den . . . ottomanischen Botschafter, Hussein Hilmi Pascha, ddo. Wien, 13 November 1916."

[67] See *ibid.*, Radowitz to FO, 13 Nov 1916, No. 1,188; Kühlmann to FO, 14 Nov, No. 1,196; *Schulthess*, v. 57:2, pp. 465-66.

tween the two countries. But what was most disturbing to him and his colleagues, Halil continued, was Jagow's suggestion that the question of religious liberty in the Ottoman empire should be regulated by a treaty with Germany: "No civilized nation was expected to make explicit commitments regarding principles of international law, such as the freedom of religion, by means of additional international treaties. By making such a demand, one placed Turkey outside the family of civilized powers and, thereby, injured its dignity." While the rulers of the Ottoman empire were determined to continue the close relationship with Germany, public opinion demanded that the latter prove its good will.

This could be accomplished only if Germany, without bargaining and without making reservations, granted with a grand gesture everything that Turkey required for its independence and for ridding itself of the shackles of international oppression. Turkey was fighting this war in order to achieve complete independence and had every reason to expect from its allies unconditional assistance in this regard.[68]

As previously noted, the commercial and religious relations between the Reich and the Ottoman empire were eventually regulated to the Turks' satisfaction by the public and secret agreements of January 1917, but Berlin steadfastly refused to sanction officially the unilateral abrogation of the 19th century treaties by the Porte. During the last two war years the Turks tried repeatedly to reopen discussions on that subject, but to no avail.[69]

[68] FO, *Türkei 204*, Bd. 1, Memorandum by Radowitz, 21 Nov 1916. Cf. Bayur, III:3, 487.

[69] See, for example, FO, *Türkei 159 Nr. 2*, Bd. 16, Kühlmann to FO, 20 April 1917, No. 499; *Türkei 204*, Bd. 1, "G.A." by Rosenberg, 14 July. Cf. Bayur, III:3, 488.

CHAPTER V

Peace Feelers and the Problem of
the Straits, 1914-17

EVER SINCE the Anglo-French bombardment of the Dardanelles forts on November 3, 1914 Turks and Germans alike had been working feverishly to reorganize and strengthen the defenses on both sides of the Straits. By the end of the year Wangenheim advised Berlin that it was "less likely than three months ago" that the Dardanelles could be forced by an Allied naval attack.[1] Nevertheless apprehension as to what would happen in the event of a sustained Allied effort lingered on in Constantinople, if only because of the limited supply of artillery ammunition available to the defenders. As Adm. Souchon confided to Ernst Jäckh during the latter's visit to Constantinople, the ammunition stock at the Dardanelles was sufficient for hardly more than "one engagement"; in fact, some of the Ottoman gunboats had only enough shells to fire for one minute.[2] Adm. von Usedom, since September 1914 officially in charge of all Ottoman coastal defenses, painted a similarly gloomy picture in a report to the OHL of early January 1915, pointing out that he could give no guarantee for the security of the Dardanelles beyond the first day of battle. Gen. Liman, on the other hand, seems to have been much more optimistic about the situation at the Straits, especially since he was convinced that a naval breakthrough to the Sea of Marmara and to Constantinople itself would be of limited value to

---

[1] FO, *Türkei 150*, Bd. 9, Wangenheim to FO, 24 Dec 1914, No. 1,715. On the military preparations at the Dardanelles after November 3, see especially Lorey, II, 25-31. Cf. Aspinall-Oglander, I, 34-35; Pomiankowski, pp. 109-15.

[2] FO, *Dt 128 Nr. 5 secr.*, Bd. 5, Jäckh to Zimmermann, 2 Jan 1915. Cf. *Türkei 142*, Bd. 42, Wangenheim to FO, 10 Dec 1914, No. 1,574.

the Allies unless and until they could occupy and control the shorelines as well.[3]

During the first six weeks of 1915 the Ottoman High Command received a number of intelligence reports about the probability of an Allied naval attack, but it was apparently only on February 15 that detailed information on the concentration of Anglo-French naval forces in the eastern Mediterranean reached Constantinople.[4] Four days later the expected Allied bombardment of the Dardanelles forts began, opening the first phase of the great battle at the Straits which was to drag on until the beginning of the next year.

Although the Russian High Command (*Stavka*) had requested Western military assistance against the Turks on several occasions (notably at the height of Enver's ill-fated Transcaucasian campaign), Britain's decision to launch an attack at the Dardanelles caused considerable misgivings at the Russian foreign office. Since the establishment of Russian control over the Straits constituted the most important Russian war aim, Sazonov in particular "intensely disliked the thought that the Straits and Constantinople might be taken by our Allies and not by the Russian forces."[5] With no Russian troops available to anticipate the British in their prospective drive to Constantinople Sazonov was forced to rely on purely diplomatic means to secure British and French recognition of Russia's postwar claims at the Straits. In March he obtained the necessary commitment from London, and in April, after consid-

[3] Mühlmann, *deutsch-türkische Waffenbündnis*, p. 43; Liman, pp. 47-48.

[4] Pomiankowski, p. 114; Lorey, ii, 46. For an intelligence report from Gibraltar see, for example, FO, *Dt 128 Nr. 1 secr.*, Bd. 43, *Admiralstab Berlin to FO, 20 Feb 1915.

[5] See Serge Sazonov, *Fateful Years* (New York, 1928), p. 255; Robert J. Kerner, "Russia, the Straits and Constantinople, 1914-15," *Journal of Modern History*, i (1929), 400-15; Gottlieb, pp. 63-90; Smith, pp. 185-207; Higgins, pp. 87-141.

erable wrangling, the French government agreed as well to Russia's acquisition of Constantinople and the Straits region after their common victory, though the consent of both Western governments was accompanied by several qualifying statements.[6]

It appears that the British and French decision to accommodate Russia in the Straits question was partly influenced by fear that the Central Powers might otherwise try to lure Russia out of the war through an attractive Straits offer of their own.[7] Such fear was not totally unwarranted, for by the spring of 1915 the Central Powers were indeed beginning to work on just such a proposition. The idea of offering Russia a new arrangement at the Straits in order to secure her withdrawal from the war seems to have occurred first of all to the Austrians in December 1914;[8] by February 1915 some circles at the Porte were beginning to think along similar lines.

The day after the Allies opened their naval attack on the Dardanelles—February 20, 1915—Ambassador Muhtar suggested to the chief of the Kaiser's Navy Cabinet (*Marinekabinett*), Adm. Georg A. von Müller, that "sooner or later" the Russians would have to be granted unhindered passage through the Straits anyway, and that timely concessions might produce a "Russo–German–Turkish alliance."[9] Although Müller's cryptic diary entry of this conversation does not indicate whether

---

[6] Cf. Notovich, Chapter xiv; Gottlieb, pp. 90-108, 112-31; Smith, pp. 207-41. On the frustration of Russia's designs on the Straits by Britain during the prewar years see Oswald Hauser, "Die englisch-russische Konvention von 1907 und die Meerengenfrage," in *Geschichtliche Kräfte und Entscheidungen. Festschrift Otto Becker* (Wiesbaden, 1954), pp. 233-65.

[7] Gottlieb, pp. 104-105. Cf. C. Jay Smith, Jr., "Great Britain and the 1914-1915 Straits Agreement with Russia: The British Promise of November 1914," *AHR*, 70 (1965), pp. 1,015-34.

[8] See Gerhard Ritter, *Staatskunst und Kriegshandwerk*, 3 vols. (Munich, 1954-64), iii, 78.

[9] Müller, *Regierte der Kaiser?*, p. 92.

Muhtar's remarks were official in nature, circumstantial evidence suggests that the ambassador was indeed speaking on behalf of the Porte. Wangenheim informed the German chancellor about three weeks later that it was apparent from informal talks he had had with the grand vizier that the latter was "by no means" averse to a rapprochement with Russia and a modification of the Straits regime for the latter's benefit. As far as the ambassador himself was concerned, the idea of detaching Russia from her Western allies in this way was definitely worth considering, especially since the war would probably have to be terminated by way of separate peace settlements anyway. Wangenheim noted that a tripartite settlement of the Straits question which would involve Germany, Russia, and the Ottoman empire had been of interest to some Russian diplomats before the war and might still hold some appeal to Petrograd—though only if the Russian empire received guarantees "that a Turkey strengthened by Germany" was not necessarily a stumbling block on its way to the Aegean Sea. Should Russia approach Berlin with "more precise" peace feelers in the future, the ambassador concluded, it would be altogether appropriate and unobjectionable to the Porte if Germany brought up the question of the Straits.[10]

By the time this report reached Berlin the first of the famous Vasilchikova letters to Tsar Nicholas II had already been written.[11] In it the Russian court lady, M. A. Vasilchikova, informed her sovereign from her place of internment in Austria that she had been approached by three prominent aristocrats, "two Germans and one Austrian" with connections to Wilhelm II and Emperor Francis Joseph, who had assured her the Central Powers wanted to make peace with Russia, and that

[10] FO, *Türkei 150 secr.*, Bd. 1, Wangenheim to Bethmann Hollweg, 10 March 1915, No. 146.

[11] The letters, dated 10 March, 30 March, and 27 May 1915, are reproduced in *Die Internationalen Beziehungen . . .* , ser. 2, VII:1, No. 347; VII:2, No. 454; and VIII:1, No. 22.

the Tsar only had to express the wish and the Straits would be opened to Russia. It has never been settled definitively whether the three aristocrats in question initiated this peace feeler on behalf of their respective governments (nor do we know for sure who they were), but it is unlikely that the Wilhelmstrasse played more than a tangential role in this entire episode.[12] That the officials in the German foreign office had as yet given little if any serious thought to a deal at the Straits is indicated by Berlin's tardy response to Wangenheim's report of March 10 and the questions Jagow put to the ambassador. Referring to Wangenheim's suggestion that the Russians be given the right of unhindered passage through the Straits, the state secretary first of all wished to know how practicable this would be, particularly if the Ottoman empire should be at war with a third power. And what exactly would the Turks expect in return if they granted Russia the right of free passage? But perhaps most crucial of all—was a tripartite agreement as proposed by Wangenheim really desirable, or would not Germany as a cosignatory be drawn into new conflicts with Russia once the latter resumed her traditional quest for control of Constantinople itself?[13]

The ambassador's reply to these questions deserves particular attention for two reasons. First, Wangenheim pointed out that the proposed concessions to Russia were feasible from the technical and political point of view. As far as Ottoman sentiments were concerned he was reasonably sure the Porte would

[12] Rudolf Stadelmann, "Friedensversuche im ersten Jahre des Weltkrieges," *Historische Zeitschrift*, 156 (1937), p. 520, feels the probe was essentially "private" and "Austrian" in origin. Otto Becker, *Der Ferne Osten und das Schicksal Europas, 1907-1918* (Leipzig, 1940), pp. 52-53, identifies the Grand Duke of Hesse as one of the three men who contacted Madame Vasilchikova and concludes that the Wilhelmstrasse must have been in on the project. Howard, p. 133, refers erroneously to an approach by "Austro-German diplomats."

[13] FO, *Türkei 150 secr.*, Bd. 1, Jagow to Wangenheim, 27 March 1915, No. 586.

"unconditionally acknowledge the Russian claims" for special shipping rights at the Straits ("joint use" with the Turks "under the exclusion of third powers," as Wangenheim defined it), if Petrograd in return recognized the independence of the Ottoman empire, agreed to the abrogation of all capitulations, and concluded a trade treaty with the Porte. Second, Wangenheim made it clear that he personally considered it more important to get Russia out of the war than to worry about the adverse consequences the proposed Straits deal might have in the long run. Even though there was a possible danger that the Russians would eventually exploit their new rights at the Straits to "seize Constantinople," such an eventuality should "hardly have any bearing on our decisions at the moment," and perhaps it was just as well if Germany did not become a party in the proposed Straits convention to begin with.[14]

While the leading men at the Berlin foreign office did not share Wangenheim's sense of urgency, they did agree to his suggestion that the proposed new order at the Straits be anchored in a purely bilateral agreement between the Porte and the Russian government. As Jagow put it, even if Germany did not formally figure as a guarantor of such an agreement, the continued presence of a German military mission in the Ottoman empire, as well as German help and advice in the upkeep and extension of the Straits defenses after the war, would enable the Reich to protect one side against "encroachments" by the other. But, Jagow continued, was the Porte really in earnest about the whole project in the first place?[15]

Replying to Jagow's sceptical inquiry, the ambassador wired back immediately that the Turks were indeed willing to deal. After the proclamation of a British "protectorate" over Egypt (which occurred on December 18, 1914) and the British

attacks on Smyrna and the Dardanelles [Wangenheim ex-

[14] *Ibid.*, Wangenheim to FO, 29 March 1915, No. 764.
[15] *Ibid.*, Jagow to Wangenheim, 30 March 1915, No. 628.

plained], the Turkish government has become more and more Anglophobic. I could notably perceive the changing mood in the grand vizier, who repeatedly made the point that one ought to make peace with Russia so that one could then hit England all the harder.

Moreover, Wangenheim continued, he had received unequivocal assurances from Said Halim that his colleagues in the Party were agreeable to a conciliatory policy toward Russia, that is, to grant her ships free passage through the Straits.[16]

It appears that the avowed willingness of the Porte to come to terms with Russia caused some uneasiness in Berlin. In his return message to Wangenheim, Jagow at any rate took pains to emphasize that "we are still desirous of holding out against all our enemies," but conceded at the same time that an understanding with Russia, as proposed by the Turks, might very well be of mutual benefit. Hence, even though no serious Russian peace feelers had yet materialized, it would be useful to have an explicit policy statement from the Porte on hand which would allow the Wilhelmstrasse to drop appropriate hints in Petrograd.[17]

Berlin's request for a formal commitment on the Straits question occasioned considerable debate in the Ottoman cabinet, but eventually Said Halim succeeded in establishing the necessary agreement. On April 18 he officially informed the German embassy that the Porte was agreeable to having Berlin transmit the following points to the Russian government once the latter approached Germany with a concrete peace feeler:

[16] *Ibid.,* Wangenheim to FO, 31 March 1915, No. 786.

[17] *Ibid.,* Jagow to Wangenheim, 2 April 1915, No. 653. Cf. Paul R. Sweet, "Leaders and Policies: Germany in the Winter of 1914-15," *Journal of Central European Affairs,* 16 (1956), pp. 229-52; and Fischer, *Weltmacht,* pp. 217-28, regarding the evolution of German governmental attitudes on the question of a separate peace with Russia and for a summary of German efforts prior to April 1915 to establish contacts with the Tsarist government.

The Problem of the Straits, 1914-17

The Turkish government recognizes that Russia, because of her geographic location, is entitled to joint economic and military usage of the Straits. It [the Porte] is prepared to work out this matter peaceably with the Russian government, but under the exclusion of other powers.

The former Straits conventions, which constituted a curtailment of Turkish sovereignty, must fall. Turkey would assure Russia free commercial shipping through the Straits even at a time when Turkey might be at war with a third power. The passage of Russian war ships could be allowed only under certain precautions for the security of the Turkish empire, but an understanding on this matter should be reached easily.[18]

Armed with this statement from the Porte, Berlin several times during the following months sent word to Petrograd that the Central Powers and the Turks themselves were prepared to accord Russia a new status at the Straits if she agreed to make peace.[19] Inasmuch as the Russians themselves had not extended any "concrete" peace feelers of their own, these German suggestions were technically in violation of the tacit agreement between the Wilhelmstrasse and the Porte that the Straits offer would be made in response to Russian soundings. However,

[18] See FO, *Türkei 150 secr.*, Bd. 1, Wangenheim to FO, 14 April 1915, No. 880, 18 April, No. 918; and Jagow to Bethmann Hollweg, 19 April, No. 143.
The assertion by Fischer, *Weltmacht*, p. 234, that the Porte's declared willingness to offer Russia a new status at the Straits was the result of "strong" German prodding is without foundation.

[19] On the various German peace feelers to Russia in the late spring and summer of 1915, most of which involved some references to the Straits, see Stadelmann, "Friedensversuche," pp. 521-27; Fischer, *Weltmacht*, pp. 232-35; C. V. Lafeber, *Vredes- en Bemiddelingspogingen uit het eerste jaar van Wereldoorlog I* (Leiden, 1961), pp. 95-114, *passim*; and Erwin Hölzle, "Das Experiment des Friedens im Ersten Weltkrieg 1914-1917," *Geschichte in Wissenschaft und Unterricht*, 8 (1962), p. 498. Cf. Janssen, Chap. XIII and *passim*.

this technical violation hardly warrants the charge that Berlin was trying to arrange an understanding with Russia "at the expense" of its Ottoman ally.[20] There is no evidence whatever that the Germans ever offered more to Russia than the Porte had explicitly agreed to concede in its statement of April 18. Parenthetically it should be added that the Turks themselves repeatedly sent word to the Russian government that they were ready to talk about the Straits, though it is not entirely clear exactly when they began these overtures.[21]

Somewhat more precise information is available on the contacts which the Porte established with France in the early spring of 1915. Toward the end of March, Cavid Bey, who was then negotiating a major German-Ottoman loan agreement in Berlin, traveled—with the knowledge of the German government—to Switzerland and there conferred at length with several French politicians who had asked to see him. While it is still not entirely clear whether his interlocutors,

[20] For a recent version of such a charge see W. M. Carlgren, *Neutralität oder Allianz. Deutschlands Beziehungen zu Schweden in den Anfangsjahren des ersten Weltkrieges* (Stockholm, 1962), p. 146, note 3.

A better case of "disloyal" inclinations can however certainly be made with regard to the Austro-Hungarian chief-of-staff, Conrad von Hötzendorf, who had proposed to the Ballhausplatz in early April that "undisputed, sole possession of the Dardanelles and the Bosporus" be offered to Russia as an inducement for a quick peace. It should be added however that this proposal was made by Conrad at a moment when he felt the imminent intervention of Italy would spell the ruin of the Habsburg Monarchy, that is, in an atmosphere of panic. See Ritter, III, 81.

[21] See FO, *Türkei 150*, Bd. 10, Kühlmann to FO, 5 April 1917, No. 436, which records the "confidential" statement of Foreign Minister Nessimi Bey that Russia had been advised "several times during the war" of the Porte's willingness to "talk about" concessions at the Straits.

Concerning one approach to Russia which the Turks seem to have made in April 1915 see *Die Internationalen Beziehungen* . . . , ser. 2, VII:2, No. 510.

among them apparently the former cabinet minister, Jean Dupuy, and the *député*, Georges Boussenot, acted in an official capacity, they did assure Cavid that the Entente would welcome a separate peace with the Ottoman empire.[22] According to one of the reports Cavid sent to the Porte, France was also prepared to "guarantee the integrity of the Turkish empire" if the Turks "cleared a lane for merchant ships through the mine fields" at the Straits—an interesting proposal (if it was actually made), since it bore no resemblance whatever to the stringent armistice terms France and Russia had previously agreed on.[23]

Although the Porte rejected the idea of a separate peace it did maintain the contact established by Cavid for at least two more months. The latter's sporadic conversations with various French emissaries seem to have continued into early June, when, according to President Poincaré's memoirs, the Porte became more and more evasive and the contacts were broken off.[24] However, there are some indications that secret probes from France or Britain did occur again shortly thereafter, and in early July Halil Bey casually mentioned to Pallavicini that if worse came to worst (presumably a reference to the tense situation at Gallipoli), the Turks might have "to save the situation

[22] Cf. Bayur, III:2, 158-66; Lafeber, pp. 159-62; Gottlieb, p. 110; André Scherer and Jacques Grunewald, eds., *L'Allemagne et les problèmes de la paix pendant le première guerre mondiale: Documents . . .* , I (Paris, 1962), Nos. 61, 65, 67, 72; and FO, *Dt 128 Nr. 5 secr.*, Bd. 5, Jagow to Bethmann Hollweg, 16 April 1916, No. 116.

[23] FO, *Orientalia Generalia 5*, Bd. 95, Wangenheim to FO, 12 April 1915, No. 862; E. Adamov, ed., *Die europäischen Mächte und die Türkei . . . : Konstantinopel und die Meerengen*, 4 vols. (Dresden, 1930-32), IV, Nos. 256-63; Friedrich Stieve, ed., *Iswolski im Weltkriege. Der Diplomatische Schriftwechsel Iswolskis aus den Jahren 1914-1917* (Berlin, 1925), No. 260.

[24] Cf. Wangenheim's dispatch No. 862; Gottlieb, pp. 111-12; Adamov, IV, Nos. 265-70; Scherer and Grunewald, I, No. 81; Raymond Poincaré, *Au service de la France*, VI (Paris, 1930), 227-31, 240-43, 254; Bayur, III:2, 166-73.

through an understanding" with the Allies, a solution which, as Halil intimated, would not be actively sought by the Porte but would rather derive from the initiative "of the other side."[25] A few months later, when the situation on Gallipoli had become much less critical from the Ottoman point of view, Pallavicini thought he detected a mounting assertiveness on the part of the Turks which unless treated with skill and tact might cause serious troubles in the future and perhaps even induce the majority of the Ottoman leaders to seek a deal with the Entente.[26] Pallavicini's disquietude was soon to be shared by the German ambassador, who wrote to Bethmann Hollweg on December 21, 1915 that the imminent Anglo-French withdrawal from Gallipoli might conceivably induce the Ottoman leaders to "raise anew the question for which purpose they were continuing the war against the English and French, and whether it was not more advisable to attempt the conclusion of a favorable peace."[27]

This message, coupled with an earlier report from the Ottoman capital that Enver's influence at the Porte seemed to be waning, caused considerable anxiety in German governmental circles, but by the beginning of the new year it became obvious that the proponents of an active war policy were still firmly in control.[28] Although the available evidence does not allow definite conclusions, there is good reason to assume that to-

---

[25] AHFM, *Krieg 21a, Türkei*, Pallavicini to AHFM, 3 July 1915, No. 516.

[26] See *ibid., Türkei, Berichte 1915*, Pallavicini to Burian, 20 Nov 1915, No. 97B/P; *Krieg 21a, Türkei*, same to same, 7 Dec, No. 75B/P; Pomiankowski, pp. 183-84. Cf. Lafeber, pp. 82-84.

[27] FO, *Dt 128 Nr. 5 secr.*, Bd. 6, Wolff-Metternich to Bethmann Hollweg, 21 Dec 1915, No. 727.

[28] See *ibid., Türkei 159 Nr. 2*, Bd. 14, Wolff-Metternich to FO, 21 Dec 1915, No. 3,009; Falkenhayn to Bethmann Hollweg, 22 Dec, No. 20,652 op.; Bethmann Hollweg to Luckwald, 23 Dec, No. 3; same to Wolff-Metternich, 23 Dec, No. 2,543; Wolff-Metternich to Bethmann Hollweg, 16 Feb 1916, No. 72.

ward the end of the Gallipoli campaign there were some Ottoman leaders (among them most certainly Cavid) who were
advocating a general reorientation of Ottoman policy but failed
to carry their colleagues with them. An unidentified German
official in Constantinople, probably Humann, noted a few
months later that the opponents of the present war policy
seemed to be fairly impotent and the likelihood of Turkey's
veering toward a separate peace consequently quite small.[29]

Although all German peace feelers, including those intimat-
ing the willingness of the Reich and her allies to grant Russia
a new status at the Straits, had been ignored or rebuffed by
the Tsarist government during the second year of the war,[30]
Berlin tried once again in 1916 to start a conversation with Petrograd on the Straits question. Following up an earlier effort
to establish contact with the Russian government through the
Swedish foreign minister, Knut A. Wallenberg, and his brother, Marcus,[31] Jagow authorized the German legation in Stock-

[29] See *ibid.*, Wolff-Metternich to Bethmann Hollweg, 14 Feb 1916,
No. 67; and Jackh Papers, No. 8, "Zur Lage am 8. März 1916 (Sonder-
frieden)." These reports confirm that, aside from Enver, Talât and
Halil were the most important proponents of continued collaboration
with the Central Powers. That Enver repeatedly talked to the American ambassador about Turkey's desire and need to get "an early
peace" (Morgenthau, pp. 386-90) does not necessarily invalidate the
conclusions reached by the Germans.

Concerning an alleged plot by Cemal Paşa at the end of 1915 to
march with Allied support on Constantinople, to depose both Mehmed
V and the government, and to declare himself hereditary Sultan, see
Smith, pp. 354-58. I have found no evidence to substantiate this story.
Cf. Bayur, III:3, 224.

[30] On the reception of the German feelers and the general attitude
of the Russian government in 1915, cf. Smith, pp. 273-347; Gottlieb,
pp. 112-31; and Dallin *et al., passim.* Fischer, *Weltmacht*, p. 235, suggests that by early August 1915 the futility of the German peace feelers
to Petrograd had become completely obvious to Berlin.

[31] On the earlier probe through the Wallenberg brothers, which was
initiated in July 1915, see FO, *Türkei 150 secr.*, Bd. 1, Jagow to Lucius,

holm in February 1916 to arrange for another probe via these Swedish intermediaries. In his instructions to the head of the legation, Hellmuth von Lucius, Jagow emphasized that Germany was not offering territorial cessions but better shipping rights at the Straits, and that this should be made clear to the Russians when the Wallenbergs resumed their contacts with them. Moreover, inasmuch as the Russian government had previously shown a proclivity for publicizing informal feelers from Berlin as full-fledged German peace offers (which was, of course, embarrassing in terms of Germany's avowed confidence in winning the war), the Wallenbergs should make sure that the renewed probe was presented as a Swedish move.[32]

There is some justification for the charge that a roundabout peace feeler of this type could hardly have much impact in Petrograd, but this does not mean that the Wilhelmstrasse was insincere in renewing its Straits offer.[33] The genuineness of the offer is amply confirmed by two memoranda on desirable peace conditions which were drawn up at the German foreign office in May 1916, both of them listing the "right of passage through the Straits for individual warships" as one of the concessions that should be made to Russia.[34] Moreover, there is good evidence that the Porte, at this time, was still agreeable to such a deal, though the Turks also felt that the

---

18 July 1915, No. 114; Lucius to FO, 21 July, No. 821; and Lucius to Bethmann Hollweg, 14 Feb 1916, No. 427.

[32] Scherer and Grunewald, 1, Nos. 200, 202, 203.

[33] On the question of whether the renewed German peace feelers to Russia in 1916 were insufficient in what they offered and perhaps not really meant to achieve any concrete results, cf. Erwin Hölzle, *Der Osten im ersten Weltkrieg* (Leipzig, 1944), p. 30; Hölzle, "Deutschland und die Wegscheide des ersten Weltkriegs," in *Festschrift Otto Becker*, pp. 277-81; and Hölzle, "Das Experiment des Friedens," especially pp. 497ff.; Fischer, *Weltmacht*, pp. 278-88, *passim*.

[34] The full text of these two memoranda, dated May 8 and May 17, 1916, is reproduced in Scherer and Grunewald, Nos. 242 and 252. On the background see Fischer, *Weltmacht*, pp. 282-87.

proper moment for a settlement with Petrograd had not yet come—primarily because Russian troops were deep in Anatolia.[35]

In early July 1916 the Hamburg banker, Fritz Warburg, in a "private" but officially authorized meeting at Stockholm with the Vice-President of the Duma, A. D. Protopopov, and another Russian politician, once again passed the message that Germany would agree to very far-reaching concessions in the "Bosporus question," but neither this feeler nor any of the subsequent efforts by Berlin to establish a line to Petrograd met with any success.[36] In November 1916 Russian minister to Sweden A. V. Nekludov informed the Germans via Knut Wallenberg that in his "personal opinion" Russia had to continue the war until she was given the "key to the Black Sea," and that this would necessarily require the surrender of at least "a small bit" of territory at the Dardanelles to Russia. In conformity with all his previous policy statements, Jagow immediately wired back to Stockholm that the cession of Straits territory was out of the question, and that the German-Ottoman proposals, now as in the past, pertained exclusively to granting Russia special shipping rights at the Straits.[37]

In February 1917 the Bulgarian minister to Germany, Dimiter Rizov, went to Stockholm and Christiana to establish

[35] Cf. FO, *Türkei 150,* Bd. 10, Wangenheim to FO, 8 June 1915, No. 1,330; *Dt 128 Nr. 5 secr.*, Bd. 6, Wolff-Metternich to FO, 15 July 1916, No. 48; *Türkei 204,* Bd. 1, same to same, 5 Sept, No. 204; and AHFM, *Krieg 21a, Türkei,* Pallavicini to Burian, 3 June, No. 43A-C/P.

The first indication that the Porte had developed second thoughts about granting Russian warships, as distinct from commercial vessels, special transit rights at the Straits was received in Berlin only in September 1916. See FO, *Türkei 150,* Bd. 10, Wolff-Metternich to FO, 7 Sept 1916, No. 211.

[36] Cf. Scherer and Grunewald, I, No. 281; Smith, pp. 409-10; Fischer, *Weltmacht,* pp. 287-88; Ritter, III, 265; and A. Nekludoff, *Diplomatic Reminiscences, 1911-1917* (New York, 1920), pp. 424-28.

[37] FO, *Türkei 150 secr.*, Bd. 1, Lucius to FO, 21 Nov 1916, No. 1,368; Jagow to Lucius, 23 Nov, No. 1,148.

contacts with his "Russian friends" there. In the course of his trip he talked to the heads of the Russian legations in both capitals and informed them, among other things, that concessions at the Straits, including the right for Russian warships to pass through, were still available to Petrograd, but no response was given by the Tsarist government. A few weeks later it was overthrown.[38]

In the meantime Prince Sixte of Bourbon-Parma had initiated his well-known negotiations with the Habsburg family. In trying to find out Vienna's attitude on the question of a separate peace he suggested on January 29 and again on February 13 that the Entente might be willing to treat with Austria-Hungary if the latter agreed, among other things, to disinterest itself in the fate of Constantinople and the Straits. In his initial reply to the prince Kaiser Karl indicated his acceptance of that condition, but in a more formal memorandum of February 19, drafted by Foreign Minister Ottokar Count Czernin, the issue of the Straits was studiously ignored. A month later Sixte came to Austria and met with Kaiser Karl at Schloss Laxenburg on March 23. The emperor made it clear that in view of the fluid political situation in Russia he did not wish to make any commitments with regard to Constantinople. Interestingly enough Sixte not only accepted that decision but also indicated that with the fall of the Tsarist regime France's support of the Russian claims at the Straits might cease, and that it obviously corresponded to French national interest to leave the Turks in control of Constantinople.[39]

The collapse of the Tsarist regime and the emergence of Prince Lvov's Provisional Government in Petrograd in mid-

[38] Cf. Becker, p. 91; Scherer and Grunewald, No. 478; Wolfgang Steglich, *Die Friedenspolitik der Mittelmächte 1917/18*, vol. 1 (Wiesbaden, 1964), 431-32.

[39] *Ibid.*, pp. 16-18, 35-39. Cf. Ritter, III, 453-64 and *passim*; and Robert A. Kann, *Die Sixtusaffäre und die geheimen Friedensverhandlungen Oesterreich-Ungarns im ersten Weltkrieg* (Munich, 1966), pp. 61-67 and *passim*.

March 1917 occasioned mixed reactions in Berlin, Vienna, and Constantinople. Although it was soon to become clear that the new Russian government was hardly in a position to disregard the sentiments of the Petrograd Soviet of Workers and Soldiers —which advocated, from the start, the conclusion of an anti-imperialistic peace—the well-known expansionistic orientation and the first official statements of the new foreign minister, Paul Miliukov, produced the impression abroad that Russia was not ready to quit the war or to abandon its claims to the Turkish Straits.[40]

While Germany's leaders were generally inclined to await further developments in Russia, King Ferdinand of Bulgaria and members of the Sofia cabinet made it known in Berlin during the last week of March that they wished to see conciliatory gestures and peace feelers initiated right away. Partly in response to these Bulgarian proposals Bethmann Hollweg and Count Czernin announced publicly at the end of the month that Russia could have an honorable peace. The Bulgarian premier, Radoslavov, echoed these announcements in a speech to the *Sobranje*, and on April 4 Talât (who had become grand vizier two months earlier) expressed himself in a similar vein in an interview published by *Tanin*. At the same time, however, Talât took care to emphasize that no settlement was possible unless the new Russian government repudiated Miliukov's views regarding the settlement of the "Turkish question" and abandoned the expansionist ambitions of the Tsarist era.[41]

In an effort to sound out the new Russian regime the Wilhelmstrasse agreed in the beginning of April to another round of conversations between Rizov and Russian officials in Scan-

[40] Steglich, *Friedenspolitik*, I, 59-60; Robert D. Warth, *The Allies and the Russian Revolution* (Durham, N. C., 1954), pp. 45-48; Robert Paul Browder and Alexander Kerensky, eds., *The Russian Provisional Government 1917: Documents*, 3 vols. (Stanford, 1961), II, 1,042-43.

[41] Steglich, *Friedenspolitik*, I, 61-62. Excerpts of Talât's statement in *Schulthess*, v. 58:2, 819-20.

dinavia. On April 11 the Bulgarian diplomat called on the Russian minister to Norway, K. N. Gulkevich, and told him that in view of Russia's announced willingness to grant autonomy to the Poles the German government was prepared to accept a return to the *status quo ante* in the east. Rizov declared, moreover, that he personally knew of no reason why Constantinople might not be assigned to Russia.

It is extremely doubtful that the Wilhelmstrasse had authorized Rizov to make such sweeping proposals. In any event, when the OHL learned of his renewed contacts with the Russians it sent a pointed reminder to Bethmann Hollweg that a *status quo ante* settlement was unacceptable to it for "military reasons."[42]

IN THE meantime, on April 6, the United States had formally entered the war, though only against Germany. Not altogether unreasonably Berlin thereupon called on the Porte to break off diplomatic relations with Washington. Enver agreed at once that such a gesture of "German-Ottoman solidarity" should be made, but Cavid and some other prominent *Ittihad ve Terakki* Party figures would hear nothing of it. The resulting discussions at the Porte appear to have become quite acrimonious; it took Talât almost two weeks to restore some semblance of unity in his cabinet. Finally, on April 20, he was able to inform Kühlmann that the rupture of relations with the United States had been approved "unanimously," and that appropriate notice had already been given to the American embassy.[43]

According to Kühlmann's subsequent report to Berlin the infighting at the Porte during the previous two weeks had

[42] Steglich, *Friedenspolitik*, I, 62-63. On Rizov's subsequent peace appeals to Russia see Browder and Kerensky, II, 1,073-75.

[43] Cf. FO, *Dt 128 Nr. 5 secr.*, Bd. 6, Zimmermann to Kühlmann, 1 April 1917, No. 314; *Türkei 159 Nr. 2*, Bd. 16, Grünau to FO, 14 April 1917, No. 488; Kühlmann to FO, 16 April 1917, No. 486, 20 April, No. 500; *Papers Relating to the Foreign Relations of the United States, 1917 Supplement 1*, pp. 598-606.

really worried him. He noted that all the Ententophile elements in the *Ittihad ve Terakki* Party had "banded together" in an attempt to reassert themselves in the government and simultaneously to undermine Enver's position. Fortunately these "intrigues" had finally been checked by "a few appropriate countermoves," and one of Cavid's most militant supporters, Ismail Canbulat Bey, had already been gotten out of the way by his appointment as Ottoman minister to Sweden. Indeed, Kühlmann concluded, the "Ententist circles" in Constantinople had suffered a defeat "during the American crisis [which they would] not so easily forget."[44]

Kühlmann's report about the continuing tensions in the *Ittihad ve Terakki* regime appears to have convinced Berlin that a more accommodating attitude toward the Porte was called for. When Talât arrived in the German capital a few days later for talks on a number of unresolved issues, Zimmermann and other German government figures agreed without much ado to accept most of his wishes. First, the grand vizier secured a written pledge that the Reich would sign no peace treaty which provided in any form for the restoration of the capitulatory system. Next he induced Zimmermann to agree in writing to an amendment of the Treaty of September 28, 1916 whereby the two allies committed themselves to share all gains they made from their common enemies "in proportion to their respective sacrifices and achievements." In accepting this formula Zimmermann took pains to point out that the Turks already had valuable enemy assets at their disposal (namely the British and French economic enterprises in the Ottoman empire), and that these would naturally have to be included in any inter-allied compensation arrangement, but Talât refused

---

[44] Kühlmann to FO, 20 April. No. 500. Canbulat, a former *vali* of Constantinople, spent only a few months at his new diplomatic post and returned to the Ottoman capital in the autumn of 1917. After withdrawing to Switzerland because of renewed frictions with Enver he was called into the Ottoman cabinet as minister of interior in July 1918.

to make any commitments. A third treaty change demanded by Talât, namely that the restricted *casus foederis* vis-à-vis Britain should be eliminated from the Alliance Treaty of January 1915, was temporarily sidetracked by Zimmermann with the excuse that Austria-Hungary's agreement would have to be obtained first. To demonstrate their good will the German negotiators promised on the other hand to supply the Ottoman navy with 12 submarines and 12 destroyers and to hand over the *Goeben* and *Breslau* as well after the end of the war.[45]

Talât's success in securing these new commitments from Germany seems to have strengthened his authority in Constantinople, or so it appeared to Kühlmann. As he reported to Berlin on May 10 the grand vizier's "popularity in all circles" had soared to unprecedented heights since his return from Berlin, and feelings toward the Reich had become "markedly warmer" as well. Apparently the Austro-Hungarian government was receiving rather different reports from Constantinople. On May 16 Czernin expressed concern to the Wilhelmstrasse that the Turks might try to desert the alliance, and the Austro-Hungarian ambassador in Berlin, Gottfried Prince zu Hohenlohe-Schillingsfürst, chimed in with the proposal that "financial inducements" to Cavid be used to counteract his Ententophile inclinations. There is no evidence that the Wilhelmstrasse acted on this proposal. According to Undersecretary Wilhelm von Stumm the Turks could hardly afford to desert the Central Powers in view of the dismemberment plans the Entente was forging against the Ottoman empire; indeed, Berlin and Vienna would always be in the position to offer, or at least promise, "far more" to the Porte than the other side possibly could.[46]

---

[45] FO, *Dt 128 Nr. 5 secr.*, Bd. 6, Zimmermann to Kühlmann, 28 April 1917, No. 411; 2 May, No. 437; same to Grünau, 4 May, No. 195. On the background of the naval deal see *ibid.*, Souchon to Capelle, 20 March; Hans Peter Hanssen, *Diary of a Dying Empire* (Bloomington, Ind., 1955), p. 186.

[46] FO, *Türkei 159 Nr. 2*, Bd. 17, Kühlmann to FO, 10 May 1917, No. 588; *Dt 128 Nr. 5 secr.*, Bd. 6, "Aufzeichnung über eine am 16. Mai 1917 . . . stattgehabte Besprechung."

Foreign Minister Miliukov's resignation under fire in mid-May appears to have persuaded the leaders of the Ottoman empire that Russia might soon agree to come to terms with its enemies. At the beginning of June Ahmed Nessimi Bey (who had replaced Halil as Ottoman foreign minister four months earlier), informed Berlin that the Porte was prepared to show the "greatest possible willingness to oblige in the Straits question" if a separate peace settlement with Russia should materialize. The other "basic" peace conditions would be the "restoration of Turkey's territorial integrity [and] the exchange of prisoners."[47]

On June 16 the *Norddeutsche Allgemeine Zeitung* published an officially inspired commentary on the war aims message President Wilson had sent to Petrograd two weeks earlier. In the concluding paragraph the German commentary contained a statement to the effect that the recently publicized Russian formula of peace without annexations and indemnities could definitely serve as a viable basis for terminating the war between the Quadruple Alliance and Russia. A few days later Talât suggested to Vienna and Berlin that the Quadruple Alliance should go a step further and officially offer a nonannexionist peace to *all* enemy governments. Simultaneously, he added, the Russian government should be invited to secure from its allies full acceptance of that proposal within a specified period of time, say a month.[48]

Initially both Zimmermann and Czernin responded negatively to Talât's suggestion, Czernin with the explanation that the Western Powers were not sufficiently interested in peace. Undaunted, Talât returned to his suggestion a week later, pointing out to Pallavicini that with his plan a wedge might be driven between Russia and her Western allies. How much Vienna's subsequent policy moves were affected by this com-

[47] Warth, pp. 49-63, *passim*; FO, *Türkei 150 secr.*, Bd. 1, Kühlmann to Bethmann Hollweg, 4 June 1917, No. 315.

[48] Ritter, III, 534-35; *Schulthess*, v. 58:1, 640-41; Steglich, *Friedenspolitik*, I, 103-107, *passim*.

munication from the Porte is uncertain, though it may have been more than coincidence that only a few days later Czernin contacted two prominent members of the German Reichstag (Matthias Erzberger and Albert Südekum) with the announcement that Austria-Hungary was prepared to renounce an annexationist peace and that they should induce the Reichstag and the German government to issue corresponding policy statements.[49]

Czernin's ostensible support of Talât's plan should not be construed as evidence that the Austro-Hungarian government was actually aiming at a nonannexationist peace, and that only Germany was still holding out for a victory peace. In fact, while Vienna sent soothing declarations to the Porte that the Dual Monarchy favored a nonannexationist separate peace with Russia and sympathized with Talât's original plan, Czernin simultaneously confided to Pallavicini, for his "purely personal and strictly secret" information, that under the prevailing circumstances the Dual Monarchy was actually not prepared "to renounce any and all annexations and reparations in a general peace settlement."[50]

In the meantime the newly appointed papal nuncio in Munich, Eugenio Pacelli, had called on Bethmann Hollweg, Kaiser Wilhelm, and Kaiser Karl to ascertain their views and sentiments on the question of peace. On July 23 Pacelli secretly returned to Berlin and presented to the Wilhelmstrasse a papal memorandum in which an agenda for a general peace conference was sketched out. Among the issues that were to be settled at such a conference were the "freedom of the seas," the curtailment of armament programs, and the judicial arbitration of international disputes. The memorandum proposed, furthermore, that Britain should surrender the German colonies she had conquered, while Germany was to evacuate the occupied parts of France and Belgium and acknowledge the "full military,

[49] Ritter, III, 556; Steglich, *Friedenspolitik*, I, 107-108.
[50] *Ibid.*, pp. 108-109.

political, and economic independence" of the latter country. In addition, the peace conference was to adjust economic conflicts among the nations; settle territorial disputes between Austro-Hungary and Italy as well as between the Reich and France; and make appropriate settlements with regard to Poland, Serbia, Rumania, and Montenegro.[51]

Although a formal German reply to the papal memorandum was naturally withheld pending a thorough study of the document, Zimmermann at once orally informed Pacelli that several items in the memorandum were unacceptable to Germany, including the omission of any reference to the Ottoman empire. During the next two and a half weeks the new German chancellor, Georg Michaelis, worked with Zimmermann and—after the first week of August—with the latter's successor as state secretary, Kühlmann, on the promised written reply to the Vatican. After consultation with the Vienna government and the OHL, the finished product was presented to Pacelli on August 12.[52]

It is not necessary here to enumerate the various objections to the papal program which the German government expressed in this note. Suffice it to say that the reply contained a specific reference to the interests of the Ottoman empire, namely, that a peace settlement would have to include the evacuation of occupied Ottoman territory and the acceptance by the enemy powers of the abolition of the capitulatory system. Formally the German government thereby lived up to the pledges it had given to the Porte, though there are some indications that the Wilhelmstrasse was not entirely sincere in its avowed support of the Ottoman demands. Thus when Michaelis on August 14 offered Count von Bernstorff the Constantinople ambassadorship (which had just been vacated by Kühlmann's appointment as state secretary), the chancellor made it clear that Bernstorff would face the "very difficult and unpleasant" task of wringing

[51] *Ibid.,* pp. 118-32, *passim.*
[52] *Ibid.,* pp. 132-39.

"concessions" from the Porte, as otherwise the chances for a general peace settlement would be slim indeed.[53]

At the time the German government delivered its formal reply to the secret memorandum from the Vatican, Pope Benedict XV had already issued his famous Peace Note to all the belligerents. Perhaps as a result of Zimmermann's complaints to Pacelli on July 24 the papal note did contain a fleeting reference to the Ottoman empire, though hardly the kind Berlin had expected. Appealing to all belligerents to settle outstanding territorial questions in a "conciliatory spirit" and with due regard for the "aspirations of the population," the Pope stressed that the "spirit of equity and justice" would be particularly important in handling the questions relative to "Armenia, the Balkan States, and ... Poland."[54]

This reference to "Armenia," as well as the Pope's suggestion that with the creation of a new international order of law it would be feasible to establish the "true freedom and community of the seas," naturally caused acute misgivings at the Porte. On August 11 Enver wrote directly to Hindenburg and appealed to him not to tolerate any longer the kind of talk about a peace without compensations in which German diplomatic and parliamentary circles had been engaged in recent months:

> In my opinion the decisions of our times are still lying in the hands of a few strong men in our countries. If we have so far succeeded with sword in hand to compensate for the very unfortunate political preparation of this war, the politicians should now also be willing to wait until the soldier has prepared for them the ground for renewed and, we hope, successful activity.

Hindenburg's reply to Enver, on August 17, expressed gen-

[53] *Ibid.*, pp. 137, 142.

[54] James Brown Scott, ed., *Official Statements of War Aims and Peace Proposals* (Washington, D.C., 1921), pp. 129-31; Steglich, *Friedenspolitik*, 1, 143-44.

eral agreement with the vice-generalissimo's views and assured him, also on behalf of Chancellor Michaelis, that there would be no "official" German appeal for peace.[55] The Austro-Hungarian government, on the other hand, notified the Porte (August 21) that it intended to declare its acceptance of the Pope's "concrete and practical proposals" as a "suitable foundation for the initiation" of peace talks. Although Vienna actually had several mental reservations about the papal proposals, the Turks quite naturally concluded from this announcement that their Austro-Hungarian ally was about to bargain away their rights in eastern Anatolia and at the Straits. Nessimi therefore formally notified Vienna on August 24 and 25 that the Porte could not accept the papal proposals in their entirety and demanded that any reply to the Vatican be drafted in proper consultation among all four allies. Czernin quickly agreed to the proposed procedure. On September 3 he arranged with the Ottoman ambassador in Vienna, Hüseyin Hilmi Paşa, that in any reply to the papal note no reference to Armenia would be made, and that the Central Powers' acceptance of the freedom of the seas would be worded in such a way as to protect the special rights of the Turks in the Straits area.[56]

After prolonged discussions among themselves and with Sofia and Constantinople, both the German and the Austro-Hungarian governments finally issued their formal replies to the Vatican on September 21. In deference to the Porte's wishes both replies spoke of the desirability to create true freedom of the "high seas" (a term designed to indicate that the Turkish Straits were excluded from this category). On the other hand neither the German nor the Austro-Hungarian reply made any specific reference to the determination of the Central Powers bloc to see all member governments restored to their sov-

[55] DZA, Reichskanzlei, *Kriegsakten 22*, Bd. 1, Enver to Hindenburg, 11 Aug 1917; Hindenburg to Enver, 17 Aug.

[56] Steglich, *Friedenspolitik*, 1, 150-51, 157-58, 169-71.

ereign rights within the prewar boundaries, a formula which the Porte had tried hard to get included in the two documents.[57]

Irritated by Berlin's and Vienna's decision to skip over the question of Ottoman territorial integrity in their notes to the Vatican, the Porte immediately let it be known in Berlin that it expected a formal pledge from Germany to the effect that it would not permit any infringements on the sovereign rights of the Ottoman empire. As Ambassador Hakki explained to the Wilhelmstrasse, his government wished to be formally assured of German support not merely against outright annexations of Ottoman territory, but also against the imposition of any indirect or covert foreign controls over certain outlying parts of the empire. Even if the German government had not actually promised such support heretofore (and the Porte felt that a promise of this kind had been made during Talât's visit to Berlin in April), the time for writing an appropriate treaty had now come. Indeed, if Berlin demurred, "one would come to the conclusion in Turkey" that the Reich intended to accept a peace settlement under which certain parts of the Ottoman empire, such as Armenia and Mesopotamia, would be converted into another Egypt.[58]

Although the Wilhelmstrasse was most reluctant to assume such an "additional, rather inconvenient extra burden," the Porte stated during the following two weeks that it expected prompt compliance, and Berlin's resistance collapsed. When Kaiser Wilhelm paid a state visit to Constantinople in mid-October, both Kühlmann and Rosenberg went along to negotiate the issue on the spot. On receiving rather oblique assurances from Talât that the Porte was merely concerned about maintaining its sovereign rights within the borders of 1914,

[57] *Ibid.*, pp. 171-75, 182-95 *passim*; Scott, pp. 137-41. See also Klaus Epstein, *Matthias Erzberger and the Dilemma of German Democracy* (Princeton, 1959), pp. 216-21.

[58] FO, *Dt 128 Nr. 5 secr.*, Bd. 6, Memorandum by Bussche, 18 Sept 1917. On the background story see also Steglich, *Friedenspolitik,* I, 156.

and that it expected no German commitments with regard to Egypt, Cyprus, the Aegean Islands, or other Ottoman lands which had been lost or alienated previously, Kühlmann initialed a preliminary agreement whereby Germany undertook to sign no peace which in any form curtailed the sovereign rights of the Porte. Together with Germany's earlier pledge to prevent the reintroduction of the capitulations the new agreement was incorporated in a formal treaty and signed by Bernstorff on October 27. Simultaneously the Alliance Treaty of January 1915 was formally amended to the Porte's satisfaction; that is, the restrictive clause concerning the *casus foederis* vis-à-vis Britain was officially deleted and the mutual obligations were explicitly extended by adding Italy to the states listed in Article 1 of the alliance.[59]

Inasmuch as British government officials, in particular, had repeatedly made it clear that the Entente intended to eliminate or curtail Ottoman sovereignty in several Asian regions, the German-Ottoman October Treaty raised a rather serious formal barrier against meaningful future talks between Germany and the Entente. How Berlin intended to get around that difficulty if it ever came to a negotiated peace is not entirely clear. According to Bernstorff's memoirs, the Wilhelmstrasse was not overly worried, and Kühlmann, particularly, subscribed to the consoling theory that once the chips were down the Porte would surely release Berlin of the obligations it had now assumed. Kühlmann's optimistic view that "Turkey would prove amenable on all questions" if at least the capitulatory question was ultimately settled to its satisfaction was soon to reveal itself as a highly unrealistic prognosis.[60] Within

---

[59] FO, *Dt 128 Nr. 5 secr.*, Bd. 6, Bernstorff to FO, 26 Sept 1917, No. 1,174; Bd. 7, Kühlmann to FO, 20 Oct, No. 179; *Türkei 110 Nr. 5, Handakten,* unsigned memorandum, Berlin, 23 Oct; Steglich, *Bündnissicherung,* pp. 115, 213-15; *Friedenspolitik,* 1, 195-96.

[60] Johann Bernstorff, *Memoirs* (New York, 1936), pp. 185-86. Concerning British announcements that the Porte's control over Arabia,

a few weeks after the Constantinople accords had been signed Russia sued for peace, and Berlin then received its first object lesson of how little "amenable" the Turks would actually be on questions relating to their territorial sovereignty.

Armenia, Mesopotamia, and other Asian areas was to be curbed or altogether eliminated, see, for example, Lord Cecil's statements in the House of Commons, 16 May 1917, *The Parliamentary Debates, Commons,* 5th ser., xciii (London, 1917), 1,668-70; or Lloyd George's Glasgow speech of June 29, 1917, *Schulthess,* v. 58:2, 304-305. For a critical analysis of Entente war aims in the Near and Middle East see Arno J. Mayer, *Political Origins of the New Diplomacy, 1917-1918* (New Haven, 1959), pp. 17-19, 70-71, 253, and *passim.*

TRANSCAUCASIA

Prewar frontiers ～⌣‒‒‒
Railroads ╫╫╫╫╫╫╫╫╫╫

CHAPTER VI

Dissension over Transcaucasia, 1918

WHEN THE Tsarist regime was toppled in March 1917 the Russian "Caucasian army" was deep in Ottoman territory, with such major towns as Trabzon, Erzurum, and Van lying well behind its lines. As war weariness and revolutionary propaganda spread through Russia in the following months, military discipline deteriorated. Following the example first set on the European front an increasing number of Russian soldiers in the Turkish theater of war resorted to "self-demobilization." In agreement with the OHL, which was content to let the demoralization and disintegration of Russia's armed forces run its natural course, the Turkish troops in eastern Anatolia made virtually no effort to exploit the thinning of the Russian lines for the reconquest of lost ground. In fact, from June onward hostilities on the Russo-Turkish front all but ceased.

During the autumn of 1917 more and more sections of the Russian front and much of the hinterland were taken over by various Transcaucasian volunteer units, including a large number of Armenian troops. After the Bolsheviks seized power in Petrograd these Transcaucasian formations and "a few hundred Russian officers" were practically the only elements the Russian theater commander, General Przhevalskii, could still rely on for holding the lines against the Turks.[1] But the Turks, well aware of the Bolsheviks' commitment to end the war and confident of obtaining a negotiated withdrawal of Russian troops from their soil before long, remained militarily passive in the weeks following Lenin's successful coup. On November

[1] See Mühlmann, *deutsch-türkische Waffenbündnis*, pp. 131-35; Allen and Muratoff, pp. 442-57; Kazemzadeh, *Struggle for Transcaucasia*, pp. 32-62, *passim*; Richard Pipes, *The Formation of the Soviet Union*, rev. edn. (Cambridge, Mass., 1964), pp. 98-102; and D. M. Lang, *A Modern History of Soviet Georgia* (New York, 1962), pp. 192-99.

26 the new rulers in Petrograd formally approached Germany and her allies with a ceasefire proposal, and a week later armistice negotiations opened at Brest-Litovsk, with Gen. Max Hoffmann acting as the principal spokesman for the Central Powers and Gen. Zeki Paşa attending as chief representative of the Ottoman empire.

As might be expected the Porte wished to have a provision for prompt Russian withdrawal from all occupied Ottoman territory included in the armistice terms, but Berlin was reluctant to support that demand. In his recommendations to the German delegates at Brest-Litovsk Kühlmann noted that he had no objection to an informal airing of the Turkish demand, but if the Bolsheviks should then come up with counterdemands, or if there was any indication that the conclusion of the armistice might be jeopardized because of the Porte's wishes, the matter should be dropped until regular peace negotiations were initiated. As a result of this German hesitancy no formal provisions regarding the evacuation of Turkish territory were written into the armistice agreement. Under Article III of the Brest-Litovsk Armistice, signed on December 15, the lines of demarcation in the "Russo-Turkish theaters of war in Asia" were to be determined by agreements between the military commanders on either side, the implication being that the existing front lines would serve as points of reference.[2]

While the armistice talks were still underway the Porte gave notice to Berlin and Vienna that in the impending peace negotiations with the Bolsheviks it would not merely insist on the restoration of the 1914 border but also lay claim to the Districts of Batum, Ardahan, and Kars which had fallen to Russia after the War of 1877-78. On December 15 Enver advised the Wilhelmstrasse in a personal letter that he and his colleagues at the Porte expected and counted on Germany's ener-

---

[2] Steglich, *Friedenspolitik,* I, 243-94, *passim*; Mühlmann, *deutschtürkische Waffenbündnis,* pp. 134-35, 194; John W. Wheeler-Bennett, *Brest-Litovsk. The Forgotten Peace* (London, 1938), pp. 75-93, 379-84.

getic support in the attainment of these Ottoman objectives. According to Enver Germany was committed to give such support both by the recently signed treaty on the full restoration of Ottoman territorial sovereignty and by one of the pledges which Wangenheim had given on August 6, 1914.[3]

Two days after Enver had dispatched this letter to Berlin Bernstorff advised the Wilhelmstrasse that he regarded the vice-generalissimo's demand for the restoration of the Transcaucasian frontier of 1877 as just a "typical Oriental" attempt to indulge in some bargaining with Germany. On the other hand, Bernstorff noted, all Turks were obviously determined to get back the lands they had lost to the Russians since the beginning of the war, as well as the Thracian area which they had ceded to Bulgaria in 1915. To ensure continued Turkish fidelity to the alliance and to manifest Germany's appreciation of the military contributions the Turks had made during the previous years, an accommodating attitude by the Reich would certainly be in order. The following day Berlin instructed Bernstorff to remain noncommittal and to point out to the Porte that the satisfaction of its various territorial wishes in the Transcaucasian area would be greatly facilitated if some popular demand for the return of Ottoman rule could be shown to exist. This proposition, which Bernstorff presented to Talât on December 20, was apparently not very welcome at the Porte. As Talât explained to Pallavicini the following day, the holding of plebiscites in the occupied Ottoman provinces was quite superfluous since only Turks happened to live there—"there were no Armenians left," and the Kurdish population had moved away at the time of the Russian invasion.[4]

On December 25, three days after formal peace negotiations

---

[3] See FO, *Wk 15*, Bd. 24, Bernstorff to FO, 12 Dec 1917, Nos. 1,619, 1,620; 13 Dec, No. 1,636; *Russland 97a*, Bd. 10, Enver to FO, 15 Dec.

[4] FO, *Türkei 110 Nr. 5, Handakten*, Bernstorff to FO, 17 Dec 1917, No. 1,653; *Wk 15*, Bd. 25, Bussche to Bernstorff, 18 Dec, No. 1,566; Bernstorff to FO, 20 Dec, No. 1,681; Steglich, *Friedenspolitik*, I, 294-95.

between the Quadruple Alliance and the Bolshevik government had opened at Brest-Litovsk, Kühlmann advised Enver in a personal letter that Germany sympathized with the Transcaucasian aspirations of the Porte, but that it would probably be necessary to demonstrate that the people in the areas claimed by the Turks wished to be reincorporated into the Ottoman empire. Echoing Berlin's advice of the previous week Kühlmann thus gave notice to the Porte that it would have to come up with a plausible case of popular self-determination if it wished Germany to back the Turkish territorial claims in Transcaucasia.[5]

Aside from calling for a nonannexationist peace settlement and the vindication of the principle of popular self-determination, the Bolshevik delegation at Brest-Litovsk had proposed from the start that mutual troop withdrawals from all areas conquered during the war should be effected. Since Germany did not want to pull back its armies for the time being, while conversely the Turks still had Russian troops on their soil and were impatient to get rid of them, the German negotiators at Brest-Litovsk were faced with the rather delicate task of satisfying the Porte's wishes without giving the Bolsheviks too much of an opening in the question of Russia's own occupied territories. Kühlmann solved the problem on December 27 with the proposal that the withdrawal of occupation troops after the signing of peace should be effected in all those areas where popular self-determination was not at issue. Since he listed "Poland, Lithuania, Courland, and portions of Estonia and Livonia" as the areas where the principle of self-determination was to become operative, his proposal seemed to imply that the Central Powers would evacuate all occupied White Russian and Ukrainian regions, while the Russians in turn should withdraw from the Anatolian provinces of the Ottoman empire. Although the Bolshevik delegates immediately

[5] FO, *Russland 97a*, Bd. 10, Kühlmann to Enver, 25 Dec 1917.

objected to the German definition of self-determination, they apparently accepted the other half of Kühlmann's proposal. The next day, before they returned to Petrograd for consultation, they advised the Ottoman delegation that all occupied Turkish territory would be evacuated.[6]

While these top-level negotiations between the Bolshevik government and the Quadruple Alliance had been going on at Brest-Litovsk, the political situation in Russian Transcaucasia had become increasingly fluid. At the end of November various political groups had formed an interim government for Transcaucasia, the *Zakavkazskii Komissariat*, which was to maintain order in the region until such time as the All-Russian Constituent Assembly established a new government for the entire Russian state. Headed by the Georgian Menshevik, E. G. Gegechkori, the *Komissariat* included two or three representatives of each major ethnic group in Transcaucasia—Armenians, Azerbaijanis (or Azeri Tartars), Georgians, and Russians. From the beginning the *Komissariat* refused to recognize Lenin's regime in Petrograd and steered a more or less anti-Bolshevik course, but could not prevent the spread of Bolshevik propaganda, which seems to have been particularly effective among the dispersing soldiers of the defunct Caucasian army.[7]

On December 18, shortly after the Bolshevik representatives at Brest-Litovsk had signed a general armistice with Germany and her allies, officers of the Caucasian army and delegates of the Tiflis *Komissariat* concluded a separate ceasefire treaty with the Turks at Erzinjan. There is some disagreement among historians whether the Erzinjan treaty was merely meant to implement Article III of the Brest-Litovsk Armistice

[6] Wheeler-Bennett, pp. 122-29; Steglich, *Friedenspolitik,* I, 313-16.

[7] Cf. Kazemzadeh, pp. 54-62, 80-81; Pipes, pp. 102-106, *passim;* and A. B. Kadishev, *Interventsiya i grazhdanskaya voina v Zakavkase* [Intervention and Civil War in Transcaucasia] (Moscow, 1960), pp. 28-33.

or whether it constituted a separatist act on the part of the *Komissariat*. Subsequent developments in Transcaucasia suggest that the latter interpretation is closer to the mark.[8]

In the second week of January 1918 the Bolshevik peace delegation, now headed by Leon Trotsky, resumed its negotiations with Germany and her allies at Brest-Litovsk. Simultaneously the Turks endeavored to open separate peace talks with the Tiflis *Komissariat*. In mid-January Gen. Vehib, the head of the Ottoman "Army Group Caucasus," sent two letters to Gen. I. Z. Odishelidze, the commander of the Georgian contingent within the Transcaucasian army, and informed him and the *Komissariat* that the Porte was prepared to recognize Transcaucasia as an independent state and to conclude peace with it. Only the first of these letters appears to have reached Tiflis immediately, and, after lengthy debate there, was left unanswered. Several other notes from Vehib, in which he protested the alleged maltreatment of the Moslem population by Armenian bands, were answered promptly and in conciliatory terms by Odishelidze.[9]

Toward the end of January suspicion grew in Tiflis that the Turks might use the alleged plight of their coreligionists on the eastern side of the armistice line as a pretext for resuming hostilities. The *Komissariat* therefore decided to respond to the Porte's earlier peace proposal which it had hitherto ignored. On January 28 the *Komissariat* informed the Turks that it was, in principle, agreeable to the conclusion of peace but would have to coordinate its policy with other autonomous governments on the territory of the old Tsarist empire. The next day Gegechkori invited the "governments" of the Ukraine

---

[8] Cf. Ministerstvo Inostranich Del SSSR, *Dokumenty vneishnei politiki SSSR*, 1 (Moscow, 1957), Nos. 30, 31, and note 8; and Lang, p. 201; Kazemzadeh, pp. 81-82; Kadishev, p. 41.

[9] Kazemzadeh, pp. 84-86; Kadishev, pp. 41-42. According to Kazemzadeh Turkish complaints about Armenian outrages against Moslems were not altogether groundless.

Dissension over Transcaucasia, 1918

and the so-called South-Eastern Union to send representatives to Tiflis for consultation on a common policy toward the Turks, but both governments declined. The *Komissariat* thus found itself in unenviable isolation when on February 12 the Ottoman army began a general advance across the demarcation lines fixed eight weeks earlier.[10]

Although Gen. Vehib assured the commander of the Transcaucasian forces that his troops had no hostile intentions and were advancing merely in order to protect the Moslem population behind the armistice lines against further harassment by marauding bands, the real object of the operation was to bring most of Transcaucasia under Turkish control. Enver admitted as much in a speech to the Ottoman Chamber of Deputies, and on February 14 intimated to Liman and Bernstorff that he meant to reach the shores of the Caspian Sea, from where a "connection" with Turkestan could be established.[11]

After occupying Erzinjan on February 13 Vehib's troops rapidly advanced eastward all along the line, encountering only sporadic and ineffective resistance from some Armenian units. On February 23 a newly constituted Transcaucasian parliament, the *Seim*, opened in Tiflis and immediately tackled the problems posed by the Turkish advance. After a week of lively debate the *Seim* in joint session with the *Komissariat* adopted a unanimous resolution that peace between Transcaucasia and the Ottoman empire should be secured; that it should be based on the restoration of the prewar Russo-Turkish border; and that an effort should be made to obtain "autonomy" for those

[10] Kazemzadeh, p. 86. The decision by Enver to send Vehib's forces across the armistice lines was communicated to Germany and apparently also to the "Russian Commander-in-Chief on the Caucasus front" almost a week in advance. See FO, *Russland 97a*, Bd. 11, Seeckt to OHL, 6 Feb 1918.

[11] See *ibid.*, Bernstorff to FO, 15 Feb 1918, No. 225; A. N. Kheifets, *Sovetskaya Rossiya i sopredelnye strani vostoka v godi grazhdanskoi voini, 1918-1920* [Soviet Russia and the Adjacent Countries of the East During the Civil War, 1918-1920] (Moscow, 1964), p. 34.

Armenian districts which would pass back to Ottoman rule.[12]

Before the *Komissariat* had a chance to open meaningful negotiations with the Porte, it learned to its dismay that the Petrograd government had meanwhile, on March 3, signed away Russia's rights in three districts east of the prewar frontier. Under the terms of the Brest-Litovsk Peace Treaty between the Quadruple Alliance and the Russian Federal Soviet Republic, the latter undertook "to ensure the immediate evacuation of the provinces of Eastern Anatolia and their lawful return to Turkey" and to withdraw, in addition, all Russian troops from the Districts of Ardahan, Kars, and Batum. These latter areas, according to Article IV, were to be reorganized with regard to their "national and international relations," and Russia was "to leave it to the population of these districts to carry out this reorganization in agreement with the neighboring States, especially with Turkey."[13]

Despite its ambiguous terminology this provision amounted to a practical guarantee that the Turks would be able to reincorporate these three districts into their empire and thus basically met one of the major demands they had raised in Berlin since December of the previous year.[14] In agreeing, after much hesitation, to support the Porte's claims to the Transcaucasian frontier of 1877,[15] Germany's leaders were motivated

[12] Allen and Muratoff, pp. 460-62; Kazemzadeh, pp. 87-91; Kadishev, pp. 44-45.

[13] The texts of the Brest-Litovsk Peace Treaty and of a supplementary Russo-Turkish convention may be found in Wheeler-Bennett, pp. 403-408; and J. C. Hurewitz, *Diplomacy in the Near and Middle East*, 2 vols. (Princeton, 1956), II, 31-33.

[14] The official annexation of the three districts by the Ottoman empire finally occurred in August 1918 after plebiscites had been held there under very dubious circumstances. See Ziemke, p. 51; *Schulthess*, v. 59:2, 523. Contrary to Wheeler-Bennett, p. 265, Turkish troops were not yet in physical control of Ardahan, Kars, or Batum when the Brest-Litovsk Treaty was signed. In fact the Turks did not cross the prewar borders until the end of March.

[15] On the last minute inclusion in the Brest-Litovsk peace terms of the

by the hope that the satisfaction of some of their ambitions in the east would distract the Turks from their increasingly bitter dispute with Bulgaria over the disposition of the Dobruja and the readjustment of their common border in Thrace. This hope proved illusory. To make matters worse, the Porte soon made it clear that it was not satisfied with the Brest-Litovsk settlement and had no intention of abiding by it.[16]

As soon as the terms of the Bolshevik peace settlement with the Quadruple Alliance became known in Tiflis, the *Seim* served formal notice to the major belligerent powers and to Petrograd that Transcaucasia did not consider itself bound by the Brest-Litovsk Treaty. In pursuance of its original plan the *Komissariat* instead sent a delegation to Trabzon to work out a separate agreement with the Ottoman government. After some procrastination the Turks received the delegation on March 12 and immediately made it clear that Transcaucasia had no right to dispute the validity of the Brest-Litovsk settlement since it had never officially declared its independence from Russia. Rather unwisely the *Komissariat* waited almost four weeks before yielding on that point, thereby giving the Turks a theoretical justification for continuing their military advance.[17]

---

clause regarding the 1877 frontier and the Wilhelmstrasse's refusal to support certain other, more far-reaching, Turkish claims in Transcaucasia, see FO, *Russland 97a*, Bd. 11, Bernstorff to FO, 21 Feb 1918, No. 251; Schüler to FO, 24 Feb, No. 486; Rosenberg to FO, 28 Feb, No. 534; same to same, 3 March (No. illegible); Kühlmann, pp. 549-50; Wheeler-Bennett, pp. 255-69, *passim*; Fischer, *Weltmacht*, pp. 733-34.

[16] Cf. *ibid.*, pp. 679-89 and *passim*; Ziemke, pp. 48-50; Mühlmann, *deutsch-türkische Waffenbündnis*, pp. 190-93.

[17] Kazemzadeh, pp. 91-99; Pipes, pp. 106-107; Kadishev, pp. 47-49. For more detailed information on this and subsequent developments see also FO, *Türkei 183*, Bd. 53, "Aperçu historique sur les pourparlers de paix de la Transcaucasie et de l'Arménie . . . ," compiled by Armenian officials later in the year.

Dissension over Transcaucasia, 1918

At the end of March Vehib's forces reached the prewar Turco-Russian border and crossed it at several points. By April 10, when the *Komissariat* finally acknowledged the validity of the Brest-Litovsk Treaty, Ottoman columns were closing in on both Kars and Batum. Three days later the Turks notified the *Komissariat* that the negotiations in Trabzon could not be continued unless Transcaucasia formally proclaimed its independence from Russia. The *Seim* responded to this new Turkish demand by a fiery declaration of war.[18]

For a few days it looked as though this gesture of defiance might have some meaning. Although the Turks captured Batum on April 14 without much trouble, they ran into strong and effective resistance from Armenian troops when they tried to take Kars a few days later. Apparently under the impact of this setback the Turks declared themselves willing to resume peace talks with Tiflis. On April 22 the *Seim* reversed its earlier stand and voted—over the protests of the Kadets and Social Revolutionaries—for the proclamation of an "independent Transcaucasian Federative Republic." During the next few days an uneasy armistice was arranged all along the "front," and Kars was surrendered to the Turks on April 24-25.[19]

With hostilities temporarily suspended the newly formed federal "government" in Tiflis, which was headed by the Georgian Menshevik, Akaki Chkhenkeli, accepted a Turkish proposal to transfer the peace negotiations to Batum. On May 11 the conference was formally opened in that city. The Ottoman delegation, which was headed by Halil Bey, informed the Transcaucasian representatives that the Porte was no longer

[18] Allen and Muratoff, pp. 462-65; Kazemzadeh, pp. 99-102; Kadishev, pp. 49-50.

[19] Allen and Muratoff, pp. 465-67; Kazemzadeh, pp. 102-108; Pipes, p. 107. Cf. Kadishev, pp. 51-52; Lang, pp. 203-204; and Vahe A. Sarafian, "The Formation of the Armenian Independent Republic [Part II]," *Armenian Review*, XII:3 (Oct 1959), 99-102.

satisfied with the Brest-Litovsk settlement and would claim some additional territories east of the 1877 border line. In a draft treaty the Turks had brought along they demanded the cession of several Armenian-populated districts, including the city and environs of Alexandropol. Two days later Halil also demanded temporary Ottoman control of the rail line running from there to Dzhulfa (on the Persian border). While the badly divided representatives of the Tiflis government were still pondering these demands, the Turks suddenly denounced the existing armistice and marched into the regions they claimed. On May 15 Ottoman troops occupied Alexandropol.[20]

Both the OHL and the Wilhelmstrasse were disturbed by this turn of events. For one thing, the Ottoman crossing of the lines fixed by the Brest-Litovsk Treaty raised the danger of complications with the Bolshevik government in Moscow. Moreover, while the OHL at this time had no particular objections to the spread of Ottoman influence in the Azerbaijani regions of Transcaucasia and was also agreeable to Ottoman control of the Alexandropol-Dzhulfa railroad (militarily of major importance for any operations in the north Persian area), the Porte's apparent determination to bring all of Transcaucasia under its influence posed a direct threat to Germany's own ambitions in that area. What both the military and civilian leaders of the Reich were aiming at was the preservation, under German tutelage, of some kind of Transcaucasian state, with Georgia forming the core. Such a state would provide the Reich with the long-sought-for "bridge to Central Asia" and Persia, as well as open up valuable economic opportunities for German business and industry. To make sure these German interests in Transcaucasia would be properly respected by the Turks Berlin had sent Gen. von Lossow to the Batum Con-

[20] Kazemzadeh, pp. 109-12; Allen and Muratoff, pp. 467-72, and *passim*; Sarafian, "Formation of the Armenian Independent Republic [Part II]," pp. 102-103; Kadishev, pp. 55-56.

ference, and it was to him that the distraught representatives of the Tiflis government, particularly the Georgian members, now turned for help.[21]

On May 15 Premier Chkhenkeli appealed to Lossow for German pressure on the Porte and intimated at the same time that his native Georgia might apply for affiliation with the German Reich if the Turks continued their drive into Transcaucasia. Lossow did not immediately pick up that idea, but endeavored instead to promote a settlement between the Porte and the Tiflis delegates which would entail the preservation of the Transcaucasian federative state. His efforts at mediation proved futile, however; especially since the Moslem Azerbaijanis refused to become involved in a German-sponsored settlement. By May 22 tensions between the Azerbaijanis and other groups in the Transcaucasian government had become so acute that the Georgian leaders decided on a radical solution—to disassociate Georgia from the Transcaucasian Federation and to apply formally for German protection. On May 26 the National Council of Georgia in Tiflis officially proclaimed the independence of Georgia as a "democratic republic," and Noi Ramishvili formed a new cabinet in which Chkhenkeli assumed the post of foreign minister. Two days later the Armenians and Azerbaijanis drew the consequences from the collapse of the Transcaucasian federative state and announced the formation of republics of their own.[22]

The disintegration of the Transcaucasian federative state and the continuing advance of Ottoman troops across the Russo-Turkish borders of 1877 were watched with growing alarm in Germany. Already, on May 15, Ludendorff had instructed Gen. von Seeckt to use all his influence on Enver to effect a halt in the Ottoman invasion of areas to which the Porte had no

[21] Cf. Mühlmann, *deutsch-türkische Waffenbündnis*, pp. 195-97; Fischer, *Weltmacht*, pp. 736-39.

[22] Kazemzadeh, pp. 113-24; Fischer, *Weltmacht*, pp. 740-42; Kadishev, pp. 62-63.

title whatever. Since neither this nor a similar appeal five days later produced any results, Ludendorff, in agreement with the new chancellor, Count Hertling adopted a sterner tone. The military developments in Mesopotamia and Persia, he wired to Seeckt on May 25, clearly called for the shift of all available Ottoman forces to those two theaters of war.

> If the Turkish government, in pursuit of political interests in other areas, neglects the defense of its own national territory and causes us troubles in the Caucasus, . . . it must not assume that we shall later recoup its own national territory at our expense.
>
> I must, moreover, sharply demand of Your Excellency that I shall be informed of the military situation in Turkey with [more] foresight and thoroughness.[23]

In contrast to Gen. von Lossow, who had repeatedly warned the OHL and the Wilhelmstrasse that the Turks were obviously attempting to gain control of the entire Caucasus region, Seeckt responded to Ludendorff's complaints with a spirited defense of the Porte's policies. According to him, the continuing eastward advance of the Ottoman army was based on "purely military" considerations. In the Azerbaijani areas, "about 300,000 Moslems" were prepared to make common cause with the Turks, and the Porte could certainly not be blamed for being interested in this manpower reservoir. As for the OHL's insistence that the Turks should concentrate on the military tasks in Mesopotamia and Persia, Seeckt asserted that operations in those areas required prior control of the Baku region—a task which the Turks would obviously have to handle themselves since no German troops were available.[24]

In compliance with instructions from Chancellor Hertling

---

[23] FO, *Russland 97a*, Bd. 15, Ludendorff to Seeckt, 25 May 1918, No. 31,767p. See also *ibid.*, Hertling to Berckheim, 24 May, No. 1,055; Ludendorff to Hertling, 25 May; Mühlmann, *deutsch-türkische Waffenbündnis,* pp. 198-99.

[24] *Ibid.,* p. 199.

Dissension over Transcaucasia, 1918

Bernstorff had meanwhile lodged a formal diplomatic protest with the Porte concerning its high-handed actions in Transcaucasia. The ambassador pointed out that, among other things, because of the existing treaty obligations toward the Soviet government in Moscow, the Reich could "neither approve of nor support a further advance of Turkish troops in the Caucasus or any Turkish propaganda outside the . . . Districts" of Ardahan, Kars, and Batum. He, furthermore, gave notice to the Porte that Berlin was prepared to recognize the independence of Georgia as soon as Soviet consent had been obtained and invited the "Imperial Ottoman Government to proceed in like fashion and to respect Georgia's borders." In the ensuing discussions Talât, Enver, and Nessimi denied that any violation of the Brest-Litovsk Treaty had occurred and assured Bernstorff that "a further advance of Turkish troops [into Transcaucasia] was by no means intended." According to Enver the military movements there were simply designed to open up secure communications routes to Persia and Mesopotamia.[25] Barely 24 hours later Ottoman troops marched into Karakilissa, a major point on the railroad line leading northward to Tiflis.

Faced with the ominous advance of the Turks the Georgian government hurriedly concluded a number of provisional treaties with Lossow, in which Germany was accorded extensive military and economic rights in the new state. Among other things, the Ramishvili cabinet agreed to place Georgia's railroads and mines under joint German-Georgian control and to channel all mineral exports to the Reich for the duration of the war. Lossow, in turn, pledged himself in writing to do everything in his power to mobilize Berlin's support of the young republic. Accompanied by Chkhenkeli and other Georgian politicians as well as by two representatives of the

[25] FO, *Russland 97a*, Bd. 15, Hertling to Bernstorff, 26 May 1918, No. 829; Bernstorff to FO, 27 May (No. illegible).

new Armenian Republic, Lossow then boarded a ship at Poti and hastened back to Berlin—much to the consternation of the Wilhelmstrasse which had expected him to stay in Transcaucasia.[26]

Shortly after Lossow's departure from Poti the Porte issued ultimatums to both the Georgian and the Armenian governments in which it demanded their immediate acceptance of the Turkish peace terms. Although two German battalions arrived at Poti on June 3 the Georgian government did not feel strong enough to defy the Turks and therefore authorized its representatives at Batum to sign the Porte's terms the following day. Also on June 4 the Armenian government in Yerevan and the Azerbaijani government, temporarily quartered in Elizavetpol (or Ganja), formally concluded preliminary peace treaties with the Ottoman empire at Batum.

In the Turco-Georgian treaty, the Tiflis government abandoned its claim to two districts east of the Russo-Turkish frontier of 1877 (the Akhaltsikhe-Akhalkalaki area) and accepted various limitations of its sovereign rights. The size of the Georgian army was to be determined by an agreement with the Porte. Moreover, the Turks reserved the right to use and if necessary "protect" with their own troops the railroad lines of Georgia. Since the Ramishvili cabinet had only a week earlier offered the use of Georgia's railroads to Germany, the June 4 treaty placed it in an uncomfortable position.[27]

The peace terms the Turks imposed on the Armenian government were considerably more severe. The territory they allotted to the infant Republic amounted to only about 12,000 square miles, with Yerevan itself being placed within artillery

[26] Kazemzadeh, pp. 122-23; Fischer, *Weltmacht*, pp. 743-44. Cf. Zourab Avalishvili, *The Independence of Georgia in International Politics, 1918-1921* (London [1940]), pp. 55-64, *passim*. Copies of the so-called Poti Agreements between Lossow and the Georgian government may be found in FO, *Verträge Nr. 103*.

[27] Kazemzadeh, pp. 125-27.

range from the newly drawn Turco-Armenian border. More-over, the Armenian government was forced to accept continued Ottoman control of the strategic Alexandropol-Dzhulfa rail-road line. Under these circumstances, the fact that the Turks had at least acknowledged the existence of an "independent" Armenian state could hardly be very encouraging to most Armenians.[28]

The third treaty which the Porte concluded on June 4, with Azerbaijan, was quite different in character, reflecting the spirit of solidarity the Turks wished to promote among the Moslem population of that region. Aside from acknowledging the in-dependence of the Azerbaijani Republic the Turks promised military and economic assistance to the new state. In a supple-mentary treaty it was further agreed that Ottoman troops could use the railroads and highways of Azerbaijan for an advance on Baku, the implication being that the conquest of the oil city would be a joint venture.[29]

Since Germany had neither sufficient military power in Transcaucasia nor any other means to prevent the Turks from pursuing their "imperialistic" designs, Kühlmann proposed to the OHL on June 4 that Germany should concentrate for the time being on the consolidation of the Georgian state. Lossow, who had just arrived back in Berlin, concurred, pointing out that once Germany had secured a firm foothold in Georgia the other areas of Transcaucasia would more or less "automati-cally" drop into her lap. Kühlmann insisted that the continuing Turkish advance toward Baku should be blocked at once, since

[28] See Sarafian, pp. 105-106; Kazemzadeh, p. 127. For the text of the Turco-Armenian treaty and several supplementary conventions, cf. A. Poidebard, "Chronique: Le Transcaucase et la République d'Arménie dans les textes diplomatiques . . . ," *Revue des Études Arméniennes*, iv:1 (1924), 37-53; and the copies in FO, *Türkei 183*, Bd. 52.

[29] Kazemzadeh, p. 127; Kadishev, pp. 63-64; Gotthard Jäschke, "Osmanisch-Aserbeidschanischer Zusatzvertrag vom 4. Juni 1918," *Welt des Islams*, n.s., vi (1961), 133-36.

otherwise serious complications with the Bolshevik government in Moscow were certain to develop.[30]

On June 8 Field Marshal von Hindenburg notified the Wilhelmstrasse that he agreed with the general approach it had counseled. Simultaneously Ludendorff dispatched an extremely gruff message to Enver.

> Without any consideration for its allies, Turkey has made light of the treaties concluded in Brest insofar as they pertain to Transcaucasia. The German government has already made clear its objections to this and indicated the consequences which arise from such conduct. I must not fail to impress upon Your Excellency that I am in complete agreement with the policy of the German government. . . .
>
> I call on Your Excellency once again to respect the borders fixed by the Brest Treaty; otherwise I must reserve the right to take further decisions. Treaties which were concluded between Turkey and the Transcaucasian states without reference to Germany, Austria, and Bulgaria, I cannot acknowledge at all. As Your Excellency knows, I have always warmly supported your interests and wishes. I must impress upon Your Excellency not only that I will not be able to do this from now on, but also that the conduct of Turkey in contravention of treaty obligations would make my cooperation with Your Excellency altogether impossible.[31]

The next day Hindenburg himself followed up with another message to Enver which was hardly less imperious in tone. Given the general situation, Hindenburg emphasized, the Quadruple Alliance could not afford to cause antagonism in

---

[30] Fischer, *Weltmacht*, pp. 744-45. Cf. FO, *Dt 128 Nr. 5 secr.*, Bd. 7, Kühlmann to Berckheim, 3 June 1918, No. 1,178.

[31] Fischer, *Weltmacht*, pp. 746-47; Mühlmann, *deutsch-türkische Waffenbündnis,* pp. 200-201; Johannes Lepsius, ed., *Deutschland und Armenien 1914-1918. Sammlung diplomatischer Aktenstücke* (Potsdam, 1919), No. 399.

the "Caucasian states," and it was particularly important that the population of the Baku oil region be spared any "disturbance by Turkish troops or Turkish-Tartar irregular forces." The OHL therefore expected the Ottoman army to withdraw forthwith to the borders fixed at Brest-Litovsk and to turn instead in full force against the British troops in Mesopotamia and northern Persia.[32]

Enver, who had meanwhile traveled to Batum to survey the Transcaucasian situation, replied to the OHL's messages with equal vehemence. He reminded Hindenburg and Ludendorff that a quick peace settlement in Transcaucasia had been Germany's expressed wish. That Lossow had left the Batum peace conference was not the Porte's fault, nor could the Ottoman empire afford to wait for renewed German participation in the peace negotiations. As for the territorial gains the Porte had secured by the treaties of June 4, they were the fruit of negotiated accords with the various governments of Transcaucasia and therefore did not contravene the spirit of previous German-Ottoman agreements. The OHL's demand for an Ottoman withdrawal to the Brest-Litovsk line, that is, the border of 1877, was not acceptable. If Germany persisted in her negative attitude, Enver added, he would probably hand in his resignation.[33]

Enver's threat had a sobering effect in Germany, for it was obvious that once he stepped down the alliance relationship between Germany and the Ottoman empire would become even more strained than it already was. Thus, despite the flare-up of outright hostilities between the advancing Ottoman troops and German sentries in some parts of Georgia, the OHL immediately moderated its complaints and instructed Seeckt to search for an accommodation. Apparently as a result of Seeckt's

[32] Mühlmann, *deutsch-türkische Waffenbündnis,* pp. 201-202; Seeckt, pp. 34-35.

[33] Mühlmann, *deutsch-türkische Waffenbündnis,* pp. 202-203; Seeckt, pp. 35-36.

efforts some of the Ottoman troops heading in the general direction of Tiflis were diverted onto a more easterly route and on June 20 arrived at Elizavetpol instead.[34] During the following week, Enver organized the formation of a mixed Ottoman-Azerbaijani task force for the conquest of Baku and placed it under the command of his brother Nuri, who had meanwhile returned from his mission with the Libyan Senussis. Designated the "Army of Islam," Nuri's forces—about 6,000 Turkish regulars and 10,000 to 12,000 Azerbaijani volunteers and militiamen—slowly fought their way eastward during the following weeks and reached Kurdamir, halfway between Elizavetpol and Baku, by the middle of July. Although Hindenburg once again reminded Enver that any action in Transcaucasia which might cause "political and military complications" for the Central Powers ought to be avoided, the vice-generalissimo refused to make any commitments with regard to his Baku plans.[35]

While the Germans were unable to do anything about the steady Ottoman advance toward the Caspian Sea, they worked all the more diligently at the consolidation of their position in Georgia. Late in June Gen. Kress von Kressenstein arrived in Tiflis as "Chief of the German Imperial Delegation in the Caucasus." His assignment was to mobilize both the economic and human resources of Georgia for the German war effort and, incidentally, to keep the Turks at bay. During the following weeks several additional German infantry battalions, along with some artillery units and technical troops, were moved into

---

[34] Cf. Mühlmann, *deutsch-türkische Waffenbündnis,* p. 203; Seeckt, p. 37; Pomiankowski, p. 365; Allen and Muratoff, pp. 477-79. On the efforts of Erzberger to push Hertling and Kühlmann into a more forceful attitude toward the Porte, see the minutes of the June 19 meeting of Reichstag deputies with the chancellor, in: Erich Matthias, ed., *Der Interfraktionelle Ausschuss 1917/18,* 2 vols. (Düsseldorf, 1959), II, 408-11.

[35] Allen and Muratoff, pp. 478-79, 484-89; Pomiankowski, p. 365; Mühlmann, *deutsch-türkische Waffenbündnis,* pp. 204-205; Seeckt, p. 39.

Georgia from the Crimea. On July 12 the Georgian government delegates who had come to Berlin with Lossow the previous month signed a number of agreements which cemented the German-Georgian tie even further. Among other things, a German financial consortium undertook to help the Georgian government with the issue of a new currency, while another consortium of industrial firms, including the Krupp company, contributed 50 percent of the capital for the formation of a corporation which would assume exclusive control of Georgia's manganese ore exports.[36]

That the "protection" of the Georgian Republic and the exploitation of its economic resources were regarded in Berlin as a mere interim solution is apparent from several German government documents. On June 28 the Wilhelmstrasse advised Bernstorff in Constantinople that in the long run it would be necessary to arrange for the restoration of a larger Transcaucasian state, since only then would Germany be able to tap the economic resources of the entire region. Four days later, at a conference with representatives of the Foreign Office at GHQ, Ludendorff emphasized that Germany needed both military personnel from Georgia and the oil resources of Baku. The following afternoon he and the state secretary of the Navy Department, Adm. Eduard von Capelle, reiterated the latter point. They noted that it was of vital importance for Germany's war effort to get hold of the Baku oil, and that it was therefore essential to keep the Turks from marching on that city. Simultaneously, diplomatic efforts should be made to secure an agreement with the Moscow government whereby Germany would be entitled to exploit the oil resources in return for guaranteeing "possession of Baku to the Russians." In any event, Ludendorff and Capelle concluded, the "oil question" was im-

---

[36] Mühlmann, *deutsch-türkische Waffenbündnis,* pp. 197, 205-206; Fischer, *Weltmacht,* pp. 747-48; Avalishvili, pp. 85-94; Günter Rosenfeld, *Sowjetrussland und Deutschland, 1917-1922* (Berlin, 1960), pp. 94-95.

portant enough to warrant the dispatch of German troops to Baku if "necessary."[37]

After prolonged strife in Baku between Armenians and Moslems, governmental power in the city and its environs had fallen in April 1918 into the hands of a Council of People's Commissars which was composed exclusively of Bolsheviks and left-wing Mensheviks. Headed by the Armenian Bolshevik, Stepan Shaumian, the Council looked to Moscow for direction and delivered large quantities of oil to Soviet Russia during its brief tenure in office. Early in June the Baku Soviet dispatched a "Red Army" toward Elizavetpol to block the advance of the Turks and "liberate" the Azerbaijanis from the forces of reaction. During the ensuing campaign the Baku army, which was composed mostly of Armenians, indulged in many acts of terror against the Moslem population along the way but had only brief success in holding up Nuri's Army of Islam. By the end of July the first columns of Nuri's force reached the Caspian Sea south of Baku and began to close in on the city.[38]

Faced with imminent assault by the Turkish-Azerbaijani army, the non-Bolshevik majority in the Baku Soviet voted to call in British help, the nearest British force, about 1,000 men under the command of Maj. Gen. L. C. Dunsterville, being only a few days' march away in northern Persia. On instructions from Moscow Shaumian and the other Bolshevik commissars refused to get involved in the proposed cooperation with the British "imperialists" and eventually, on July 31, left the city. They were quickly intercepted and brought back as quasi-prisoners by the newly created government of Baku, the "Centrocaspian Dictatorship." This new regime, organized by the Social Revolutionaries with the support of Armenian

[37] Fischer, *Weltmacht,* pp. 745-46; Hans W. Gatzke, "Dokumentation: Zu den deutsch-russischen Beziehungen im Sommer 1918," *Vierteljahreshefte für Zeitgeschichte,* III (1955), 84-92.

[38] See Kazemzadeh, pp. 128-37; Pipes, pp. 199-203. Cf. Kadishev, pp. 83-129, *passim.*

nationalists, immediately invited Dunsterville's force to come to the rescue of Baku, and the first British soldiers arrived there on August 4.[39]

The news of Nuri's penetration to the outskirts of Baku and of the demise of Bolshevik rule in the city caused a flurry of excitement in German government circles. Since the Wilhelmstrasse had meanwhile made considerable progress in its talks with Moscow concerning the delivery of Baku oil to Germany, the emergence of a pro-British regime in Baku was just as unwelcome in Germany as having the Turks themselves assume control of that city. Although Gen. von Seeckt tried to persuade the OHL that Ottoman possession of Baku would certainly be preferable to having the Armenians and British there, the OHL was not fully convinced. On August 4 Ludendorff ordered Seeckt to deliver the following message to Enver:

> Unless the [Turkish] advance on Baku is halted at once and the troops are withdrawn to their original positions (*Ausgangsstellung*), I shall have to propose to His Majesty the recall of the German officers in the Turkish High Command. I cannot tolerate that the threat of a new war with Greater Russia is conjured up by the patently treaty-violating conduct of responsible Turkish authorities.[40]

Since Enver refused to make any binding commitments the OHL shortly thereafter called Seeckt home "for consultations." By the time Seeckt departed from Constantinople (on August 6) Nuri's Army of Islam had already launched its first assault on Baku but had been driven back. Markedly impressed by the resistance his troops had encountered, Nuri decided to await the arrival of reinforcements. This gave the defenders a breath-

---

[39] Kazemzadeh, pp. 136-39; Richard H. Ullman, *Anglo-Soviet Relations, 1917-21* (1: *Intervention and the War*) (Princeton, 1961), pp. 305-10; Kadishev, pp. 123-31, *passim*. See also L. C. Dunsterville, *The Adventures of Dunsterforce* (London, 1932), pp. 207-209.

[40] Mühlmann, *deutsch-türkische Waffenbündnis*, p. 207. Cf. Seeckt, p. 41.

ing spell which permitted Gen. Dunsterville to move the bulk of his force into the city. By mid-August three British battalions, a field battery, and several armored cars had arrived in Baku, some of whom were immediately deployed along the city's defense perimeter. For a variety of reasons cooperation between the local defense forces and the British was rather poor from the beginning. Dunsterville recalls in his memoirs that "there was never a day or a night that there was not a gap of one or two miles in our line owing to the intentional failure of local battalions to reach their destination," but gradually this undisciplined conduct was largely curbed. Fortunately for the defenders of Baku, Nuri's troops remained fairly inactive until the end of August. The only major engagement occurred on August 26, when two Turkish battalions attacked a British outpost on Mud Volcano, about five miles north of the city.[41]

While the lull in the siege of Baku was initially welcome to Germany's military and political leaders, the influx of British troops into the oil city gradually forced them to reevaluate their stand on the Baku question. On August 17 Enver forwarded to Germany incontrovertible evidence that additional British forces had joined the defenders of Baku, and proposed prompt offensive action there, if possible in conjunction with German troops. His call for German-Ottoman cooperation in the capture of the city was backed by Ambassador Bernstorff as well as Gen. Seeckt, who was still in Berlin at this time. Ludendorff thereupon notified the Wilhelmstrasse that a military solution of the Baku question seemed, indeed, necessary and requested energetic efforts to secure Moscow's consent to a joint Ottoman-German occupation of the city:

> Given the threat of further British entrenchment in Baku, I must urgently repeat my proposal that we should come to terms with the Russians and the Turks on the following

[41] Mühlmann, *deutsch-türkische Waffenbündnis,* pp. 207-208; Allen and Muratoff, pp. 490-94; Seeckt, pp. 41-42; Dunsterville, pp. 209-78, *passim.*

basis: Baku shall remain Russian; the administration to be established there would have to guarantee the delivery of oil to Germany and Russia as well as take account of Turkish needs. The longer an agreement is delayed the more firmly will the English establish themselves [in Baku].[42]

Ludendorff's call for a quick settlement with Moscow on the Baku question posed a serious dilemma for the Wilhelmstrasse. Ever since May it had conducted negotiations with the Soviet government on a number of political and economic issues which had been left open by the Brest-Litovsk Treaty, and three "supplementary" treaties had already been initialed on August 10. In their main provisions these treaties called for payment of six billion marks in goods, bonds, and gold by Russia to Germany; the formal renunciation of Russian sovereignty over Livonia and Estonia; Soviet acceptance of Georgia's right to independence; and the expulsion of all Entente troops from northern Russia. Germany, on her part, undertook in these treaties to evacuate White Russia and certain parts of the Ukraine; to give the Bolsheviks access to the Baltic in several places; and to refrain from occupying any more Russian territory or encouraging the activities of separatist movements on Russian soil. With reference to Baku, one of the draft treaties already initialed guaranteed Russia continued possession of the city and called for sizable oil deliveries from there to the Reich. Moreover, Article 14 of that treaty specifically obligated Germany not only to deny assistance to the military operations of any "third Power" outside of Georgia or east of the 1877 Russo-Turkish border line but also to dissuade that "third Power" (the Ottoman empire) from advancing any further into specified areas of the Caucasus and Transcaucasia, including the vicinity of Baku.[43]

[42] Mühlmann, *deutsch-türkische Waffenbündnis*, pp. 208-209.

[43] Cf. Wheeler-Bennett, pp. 327-47; Fischer, *Weltmacht*, pp. 753-72; Rosenfeld, pp. 102-23; Gerald Freund, *Unholy Alliance* (London, 1957), pp. 12-28, *passim*.

Dissension over Transcaucasia, 1918

Since obviously neither a unilateral Turkish nor a joint German-Turkish occupation of Baku was permissible under the provisions of the draft treaties, Berlin was now forced to push Moscow into a modification of the agreed-upon settlement. In response to hastily made inquiries, the Soviet government promptly advised the Wilhelmstrasse that it might not object to the expulsion of the British from Baku by German forces, but that the Turks would have to stay out of the oil city. In fact, Moscow added, it would rather see the British remain there than have the Turks get possession of the city.[44]

Faced with a possible refusal by the Soviet government to sign the laboriously prepared draft treaties, the OHL once again called on Enver to keep his troops in the Baku area from advancing any further. Addressing himself to Gen. Seeckt, who had meanwhile returned to Constantinople, Ludendorff pointed out further that Germany was willing to liberalize its financial aid program to the Porte and to grant the Turks a fair share of the Baku oil if Enver at long last complied with the OHL's wishes.[45]

While the OHL was frantically trying to keep the Army of Islam immobilized, orders were dispatched to Gen. Kress in Tiflis to assemble as quickly as possible a German task force for use in the Baku area. Since Kress had only about 5000 German soldiers at his disposal and needed most of them to maintain security in Georgia, the assembly of the expeditionary force took several weeks—much too long as events were to show.[46]

Concurrently with ordering the concentration of German troops in Georgia and the transfer of some additional units

[44] Mühlmann, *deutsch-türkische Waffenbündnis*, p. 209; Freund, p. 28.

[45] Mühlmann, *deutsch-türkische Waffenbündnis*, pp. 209-10; Seeckt, p. 43. Soviet historians, for example, Kadishev, pp. 76 and 146, tend to depict Berlin's efforts to keep the Turks out of Baku as a more or less formal and insincere gesture, but this interpretation is hardly warranted.

[46] Mühlmann, *deutsch-türkische Waffenbündnis*, pp. 210, 322.

from the Ukraine to Kress's command, the OHL again appealed to the Wilhelmstrasse to secure a quick settlement with the Soviet government regarding the vexing Baku question. Thanks to the negotiating skill of the new state secretary, Paul von Hintze, and his associates at the Wilhelmstrasse, these efforts were eminently successful. On August 27 the Russo-German Supplementary Treaties to the Brest-Litovsk Peace were officially signed in Berlin by Soviet Ambassador Adolf Joffe. While the formal provisions of the principal *Ergänzungsvertrag* committed Germany to respect Russia's sovereignty in Baku and to oppose Turkish expansion there and elsewhere in Transcaucasia, the Soviet government in turn now agreed in a series of appended notes to give Germany a relatively free hand in the Baku question. In a confidential letter to Joffe, dated August 27 and acknowledged the same day, Hintze reemphasized Germany's intention to secure the withdrawal of the Ottoman army from the Baku area and simultaneously gave formal notice that German troops might be used to expel the British from the oil city if the Bolsheviks "should not be able" to do the job themselves.

> The German government assumes that Russia will not consider such action an unfriendly act but rather support it through the accommodating conduct of the authorities as well as through the enlightenment of the population. On its part the German government affirms that in the Russian areas which shall be occupied in the course of this action the Russian civil administration will remain in existence, and that this area will again be evacuated by the German troops upon demand of the Russian government; [however], such demand from the Russian side shall be made only after the danger of renewed British penetration has been eliminated.[47]

[47] FO, *Verträge Nr. 102*, "Deutsch-russischer Ergänzungsvertrag zu dem Friedensvertrag . . . d.d. Berlin, 27.8.18"; Appended note, Hintze to Joffe; Reply, Joffe to Hintze, 27 Aug 1918.

Dissension over Transcaucasia, 1918

Having obtained Moscow's tacit acceptance of a German march on Baku, Hintze committed the Reich in a second, appended note to several interesting concessions. He promised to arrange for the diversion of one-fourth of Georgia's manganese ore exports to Russia and allowed the Soviet government five weeks' time to make "proposals . . . concerning the size of minimal monthly quotas for the crude oil and crude oil products" which Russia had undertaken to deliver. More important, in an explanatory commentary on Article 14, Section 1 of the official treaty, Hintze affirmed that Germany would not assist the Turks in their Transcaucasian ventures even if these should "unfortunately" lead to hostile encounters between them and "troops of Russia." Indeed, such nonintervention by Germany would apply as long as the Russian troops did not cross the 1877 Russo-Turkish border line or violate the frontiers of Georgia.[48]

It appears that Berlin informed the Porte only of the provisions of the *Ergänzungsvertrag* itself and not of the appended secret notes, but the Turks were outraged in any case. While the Turkish press bitterly denounced Germany's meddling in Transcaucasia, Talât sent word to Berlin that Germany's arrangements with the "enemy of yesterday and the enemy of tomorrow" at the expense of its Ottoman ally might induce the Porte to go its own way altogether. Hintze was obviously impressed by the uproar in Constantinople, for on August 30 he anxiously inquired at the OHL what precautions it had taken to keep the Turks from opening the Dardanelles to the Allies. Ludendorff replied a few days later that the possibility of a Turkish betrayal had been studied by German naval authorities for quite some time, and they were confident that an Allied surprise attack at the Straits could be frustrated since the mine system there was German-controlled. However, in case of a "methodical" Allied attack and "possible total passivity

[48] *Ibid.*, Note, Hintze to Joffe; Reply, Joffe to Hintze, 27 Aug 1918. The text of this second note by Hintze may be found in Wheeler-Bennett, Appendix VIII.

of the Turks," the chances for successful resistance would indeed be small.[49]

On September 7 Talât arrived in Berlin to settle the Transcaucasian issue once and for all. As he explained to State Secretary von Hintze during their first meeting the recent Russo-German treaties had been a most unpleasant surprise to the Porte, but he was willing to forget about that matter if an acceptable arrangement on Transcaucasia could now be worked out. Indeed, he added jokingly, without such a settlement he could not possibly return to Constantinople. According to Talât the Porte envisaged the following solution: First, Georgia, Armenia, and Azerbaijan were to be made into "buffer states against Russia," and Georgia should cede "a few districts" to the Ottoman empire. Second, Baku was to be incorporated into the Azerbaijani Republic. Third, the 14 million Moslems in Turkestan were to be organized "militarily" with active German help, so that they could be used in the war against both the "English and Russia"(!). If Germany agreed to this program, Talât concluded, the Porte would restrict its claims in Europe to the return of the Thracian area which Bulgaria had acquired in 1915 and raise no further objections to Bulgaria's acquisition of the Dobruja.[50]

Three days later Talât reiterated these proposals in written form and suggested in addition that an independent state in the northern Caucasus be created and recognized. Hintze replied on September 12 in a conciliatory but essentially negative manner. Far from accepting the Turkish demand for additional Georgian land he proposed on the contrary that the Porte return some of the Georgian territory which it had acquired by the Batum peace treaty of June 4. As for Armenia, Azerbaijan,

---

[49] See Matthias, II, 515, note 81; FO, *Russland 97a*, Bd. 23, *Aufzeichnung,* 30 Aug 1918; *Türkei 150,* Bd. 1, Hintze to Berckheim, 30 Aug, No. 2,083; Berckheim to FO, 3 Sept, No. 2,030. Cf. Lorey, II, 210-11; Karl Helfferich, *Der Weltkrieg* (Karlsruhe, 1925), pp. 665-70.

[50] FO, *Russland 97a*, Bd. 24, Memorandum by Hintze, 7 Sept 1918.

and the northern Caucasus, Germany could not possibly recognize their independence without prior arrangements with the Soviet government. In the meantime, though, the Turks should withdraw their forces from the Baku area and leave it to German troops to drive the British out of the oil city. Once possession of Baku was secured Germany would of course see to it that the Turks, along with Austria-Hungary and Bulgaria, received a fair share of the oil resources there. Finally, "since Turkestan constitutes part of the Russian state area," Germany had to decline any participation in the proposed "political and military reorganization" of that area. On the other hand, if the Porte wished to carry out its plans in Turkestan "at its own risk and expense," Berlin would raise no formal objections.[51]

While the Wilhelmstrasse was thus fending off the Turks on the diplomatic front, the OHL did everything in its power to get a German expeditionary force for the conquest of Baku assembled and on its way. Two German brigades were shipped from the Ukraine to Georgia, and on September 10 Ludendorff sent word to Gen. Kress in Tiflis that the advance on Baku was to be started as soon as possible. Ludendorff also emphasized that the capture of the oil city was to be effected if at all possible without direct participation of Turkish or Azerbaijani troops. But Enver was in no mood to play Ludendorff's game.[52] On September 14 the Army of Islam, now reinforced by contingents of the Ottoman 36th Division, opened a concentric attack on Baku. In a massive push the next day the Turks and their Azerbaijani auxiliaries quickly crushed the

[51] *Ibid., aide-mémoire* by Talât, 10 Sept 1918; Hintze to Grünau, 13 Sept, No. 534 and enclosure.

[52] See *ibid.*, Bussche to Lersner, 10 Sept 1918, No. 1,065 and enclosures; Hintze to FO, 11 Sept, No. 2,069; Mühlmann, *deutsch-türkische Waffenbündnis*, p. 210. On September 10 the Wilhelmstrasse reminded Ambassador Joffe that German troops would have to be sent to Baku unless the Bolsheviks got their own operation against the city started very quickly. See FO, *Russland 97a*, Bd. 24, "Rücksprache mit Herrn Joffe," 10 Sept.

will to resistance among the city's defenders. While local Moslem elements started an orgy of pillage and massacre in the Armenian districts, Dunsterville's troops and thousands of local soldiers and civilians streamed toward the harbor to find refuge on the ships waiting there. On the morning of September 16, Nuri's regulars formally occupied the city and gradually restored a semblance of order.[53]

The Turkish move was resented almost as much in Berlin as it was in Moscow, and the chagrin in both capitals was heightened on September 17, when the Azerbaijani government officially installed itself in Baku under the protection of Nuri's troops. However, while the Soviet government reacted to these developments with vigorous diplomatic protests, the Wilhelmstrasse and the OHL decided to suppress their anger, and instead reopened the stalled talks with Talât.[54] After bargaining for a week Hintze and the grand vizier reached an uneasy compromise on the Baku question to the effect that the "administration" of the oil industry in Baku, of the pipeline to Batum, and of the Tiflis-Baku railroad would be assumed by German personnel. In a secret protocol of September 23 Talât, furthermore, agreed to a general withdrawal of Turkish troops from the Armenian and Azerbaijani Republics, while the German government committed itself to work for Soviet Russia's recognition of these two states upon completion of the Turkish pull-back. With regard to the northern Caucasus and Turkestan, Berlin formally reiterated its position that it could not support the Porte's plans in those areas.[55]

The rapid deterioration of the military situation in Syria

[53] Cf. Allen and Muratoff, pp. 494-95; Kadishev, pp. 153-56; Dunsterville, pp. 295-317. On the massacres in Baku see below, pp. 265-66. Fischer, *Weltmacht,* p. 749, claims Baku was captured with the help of German and Russian troops, but his account is misleading.

[54] See Mühlmann, *deutsch-türkische Waffenbündnis,* pp. 210-11; Kazemzadeh, p. 146; Zenkovsky, pp. 259-60; and Kheifets, pp. 67-69.

[55] FO, *Russland 97a,* Bd. 26, Hintze to Kress, 25 Sept 1918, No. 149; Ziemke, pp. 55-56, 475, note 11; Fischer, *Weltmacht,* pp. 749-50.

and the collapse of Bulgaria during the last week of September induced Talât's colleagues to accept without much ado the settlement he had made in Berlin. On October 1 the Porte notified Berlin that the evacuation of Transcaucasia had already begun, and that the Soviet government should immediately be apprised of Turkey's "voluntary" withdrawal behind the lines fixed at Brest-Litovsk. Two days later the new Ottoman ambassador in Berlin, Rifât Paşa, officially confirmed this decision in a meeting with Joffe, but the Soviet ambassador was not impressed. Instead, he handed Rifât a note in which the Soviet government formally declared the Brest-Litovsk peace settlement with the Ottoman empire as being null and void. Despite subsequent attempts by the Porte to reopen negotiations with Moscow the Soviet government stuck to its decision.[56]

In the meantime Gen. Kress had dispatched a delegation of German officers and petroleum experts to Baku to work out arrangements with Nuri and the Azerbaijani government concerning the exploitation of the oil resources there. On their arrival the German emissaries soon found out that they were not welcome. Since telegraphic communications between Tiflis and Berlin were as usual in utter disarray, the Wilhelmstrasse and the OHL did not learn of the seriousness of the situation in Baku until October 24. According to a dispatch from Kress which arrived in Berlin on that day, the German delegation in Baku had made no progress whatever. Kress added that Germanophobic sentiments were rampant at Nuri's headquarters, and that no settlement was feasible since "Nuri hides behind [the government of] Azerbaijan and the latter behind him."[57]

At the behest of the OHL the Wilhelmstrasse thereupon ap-

[56] FO, *Russland 97a*, Bd. 26, Bernstorff to FO, 1 Oct 1918, No. 1,622; Hauschild to FO, 7 Oct, No. 401; *Türkei 150*, Bd. 10, Bernstorff to FO, 1 Oct, No. 1,628; Kheifets, pp. 69-71; and *Dokumenty vneishnei politiki SSSR*, 1, Nos. 346, 358 and notes 60, 62.

[57] See Mühlmann, *deutsch-türkische Waffenbündnis*, p. 211; FO, *Russland 97a*, Bd. 26, Kress to FO, 26 Sept 1918; Bd. 27, same to same, n.d. (arrived in Berlin 24 Oct).

pealed to the Porte to do something about Nuri's obstruction-ism and reminded the Turks that the Baku oil was urgently needed for the German war effort. The Porte replied on October 30 that Germany could have the oil reserves stored in Batum, that Nuri had already been recalled, and that any further inquiries about the Baku oil should henceforth be directed to the Azerbaijani government.[58] The same evening representatives of the Porte signed the Armistice of Mudros with Britain.[59]

THE DISAGREEMENTS over the Transcaucasus question in 1918 strained the German-Turkish alliance more than any other event of the war. If the war had lasted much longer this issue might have caused an open break between the two allies. According to the testimony of one German staff officer the maps of the Ottoman Third Army in August 1918 identified the German sentry posts along Georgia's railroads as "enemy" positions, and there are numerous other indications that Germanophobia was rapidly spreading in the Turkish officer corps because of the Transcaucasian quarrel.[60]

Berlin's opposition to the Turks' expansion beyond their 1877 frontiers has often been ascribed to Germany's own imperialistic ambitions in that area.[61] Undoubtedly Berlin's desire for strategic footholds and raw materials in the Caucasus region played a significant role in its mounting quarrels with the Turks, but there are several other factors which need to be considered. First, there is ample evidence that Berlin's conduct was strongly influenced by fear of adverse Soviet reactions if the Reich did not put a stop to the conquering march of its Otto-

[58] *Ibid.*, Hintze to FO, 28 Oct 1918, No. 2,599; Bussche to Waldburg, 29 Oct, No. 1,839; Waldburg to FO, 30 Oct, No. 1,860.

[59] See Chapter XI.

[60] See Mühlmann, *deutsch-türkische Waffenbündnis*, p. 276, note 1, and *passim*.

[61] See, for example, Fischer, *Weltmacht*, pp. 733-34, 748, and *passim*.

man ally. Second, the OHL was no doubt militarily justified in demanding that the Turks should concentrate on the defense of their Mesopotamian and Palestinian fronts against the British instead of wasting manpower and materiel in their eastward expansion toward the Caspian Sea. Finally it should be noted that at least some of Germany's leaders, including Field Marshal Hindenburg, were genuinely concerned about the fate of the Transcaucasian Armenians and wished for that reason alone to get the Turks out of Transcaucasia as quickly as possible.[62]

[62] For a more thorough analysis of the Transcaucasian problem within the context of Berlin's over-all eastern policy, see Winfried Baumgart, *Deutsche Ostpolitik 1918. Von Brest-Litowsk bis zum Ende des Ersten Weltkrieges* (Vienna, 1966), pp. 174-207 and *passim*. Baumgart's excellent monograph appeared too late to be used in this book, but generally his findings agree with mine.

CHAPTER VII

The Armenian Persecutions

AFTER THE successful struggle of the various Balkan peoples for independence during the preceding hundred years, the largest Christian national group left in the Ottoman empire in 1914 were the Armenians, most of whom lived in the eastern portions of Anatolia.[1] After submitting for centuries to legal discrimination, harassment, and misgovernment—which earned them the designation of the "loyal community" (*Millet-i Sadika*) by their Turkish overlords—many Ottoman Armenians had become increasingly restive and nationalistic in the course of the 19th century. Since their requests for efficient and fair government, evenhanded justice, and local autonomy were repeatedly ignored by the Porte, and since the diplomatic efforts of the European powers on their behalf produced little more than paper reforms, some elements of the Armenian community turned to "nonlegal" and violent methods to throw off the Turkish yoke. After the 1860s a number of revolutionary societies and parties sprang up, and by the early nineties the radicalization of the Armenian revolutionary movement found outward expression in the emergence of the *Hunchakian* Party and the Armenian Revolutionary Federation or *Dashnaktsuthiun*. While the "Hunchaks" aimed for the creation of an independent Armenian state, the "Dashnaks" advocated radical political and social reforms within the framework of the Ottoman empire. Both groups hoped to attract energetic European support for the Armenian cause, but it was a hope that proved illusory.[2] When in the mid-1890s

[1] Counting Roman Catholics and Protestants as well as the Gregorian majority, there were an estimated 1.8 to 2.1 million Armenians in the Ottoman empire by 1914. For an excellent introduction to the history of the Armenian people see Hrant Pasdermadjian, *Histoire de l'Arménie* (Paris, 1949).

[2] Cf. A. O. Sarkissian, *History of the Armenian Question to 1885*

The Armenian Persecutions

Sultan Abdülhamid II responded to mounting Armenian agitation by ordering, or condoning, the massacre of thousands of Armenians in Constantinople and elsewhere in the empire, the European powers restricted themselves to largely ineffectual diplomatic protests and the protection of some Armenian conspirators.[3]

The overthrow of Abdülhamid's despotic regime and the formal resurrection of a constitutional form of government by the Young Turks in 1908 was initially greeted by many Ottoman Armenians as the dawn of a new era, but their hopes were quickly quashed. Though some Armenian groups were eager to collaborate with the new regime the Young Turks soon made it clear that they had no intention of granting the non-Turkish communities in the empire the political equality which they desired.[4] In 1909 thousands of Armenians were massacred by Moslem mobs in the so-called Cilician Vespers. Even though the central government in Constantinople was perhaps not directly involved in this new outrage, many Armenians did not trust the Young Turks thereafter.[5]

(Urbana, Ill., 1938); Louise Nalbandian, *The Armenian Revolutionary Movement* (Berkeley and Los Angeles, 1963); and Roderic H. Davison, *Reform in the Ottoman Empire, 1856-1876* (Princeton, 1963), and *passim*.

[3] On the shifting policies of the European powers on the "Armenian Question" in the latter half of the 19th century cf. Pasdermadjian, pp. 320-412, *passim*; William L. Langer, *The Diplomacy of Imperialism, 1890-1902*, rev. edn. (New York, 1951), Chapters v, vii, x; and A.O. Sarkissian, "Concert Diplomacy and the Armenians, 1890-1897," in *Studies in Diplomatic History and Historiography in Honour of G. P. Gooch*, A. O. Sarkissian, ed. (London, 1961), pp. 48-75.

[4] Cf. Pasdermadjian, pp. 438-41; Lewis, pp. 206-15; Ernest E. Ramsaur, Jr., *The Young Turks: Prelude to the Revolution of 1908* (Princeton, 1957), pp. 65-66, 70-75, 124-29; and Sarkis Atamian, *The Armenian Community* (New York, 1955), pp. 156-77.

[5] Cf. André Mandelstam, *Le sort de l'Empire Ottoman* (Paris, 1917), pp. 203-206; Simon Vratzian, *Armenia and the Armenian Question* (Boston, 1943), pp. 22-23; Atamian, pp. 174-75, 178, note 20; Lewis, p. 212.

The Armenian Persecutions

During the next few years the Porte officially improved the legal status of the Armenians and extended to them all the duties and privileges of military service, but in many provinces the traditional forms of harassment and sporadic acts of violence (especially by the Kurds) against the Armenian population continued virtually as before. After prolonged negotiations the Porte in February 1914 agreed in a treaty with Russia to institute yet another round of "reforms" in the Armenian provinces, but the two European inspectors-general who were to watch over the implementation of these reforms had just arrived when World War I broke out, and before the year was over the Porte unceremoniously sent them home.[6]

Although the Armenian Patriarch of Constantinople and various other spokesmen publicly announced at the beginning of the war that the Armenians in the Ottoman empire would loyally support the government, it seems fairly clear that many Ottoman Armenians disapproved of the Porte's interventionist course or actually hoped for an Entente victory over the Turks.[7] Contrary to the assertions of many writers there is also considerable evidence that some Armenians in the Ottoman empire engaged in subversion and espionage or deserted to the Russians.[8] On the other hand, it must be emphasized that the large majority of Ottoman Armenians were in no way involved in

[6] Mandelstam, pp. 30, 33, 50, 206-48; Pasdermadjian, pp. 440-44; Roderic H. Davison, "The Armenian Crisis, 1912-1914," *AHR*, 53 (1948), pp. 481-505; Lepsius, *Deutschland*, Nos. 9, 15.

[7] For widely differing appraisals of the attitude of the Ottoman Armenians toward the war and their own government, cf. Vratzian, pp. 25-27; Atamian, pp. 185-89; Pasdermadjian, pp. 452, 456-60; Emin, pp. 214-15; Tunaya, p. 397; Bayur, III:3, 12-20 and *passim*; Altemur Kilic, *Turkey and the World* (Washington, D.C., 1959), pp. 17-18; William Yale, *The Near East* (Ann Arbor, Mich., 1958), pp. 230-31; and Lenczowski, p. 48.

[8] Cf. Lewis Einstein, *Inside Constantinople* (London, 1917), pp. 163-64; Morgenthau, pp. 294-95; Pomiankowski, p. 159; Lepsius, *Deutschland*, Nos. 11, 17-22, 24-26, 31.

any overtly disloyal activities, and the contention of many Turkish authors that the Armenian districts behind the Turkish front in Transcaucasia were teeming with sedition is obviously wrong. Several German officers who were stationed in that area during the opening months of the war agree in their accounts that until April 1915 the Armenian districts were essentially quiet.[9]

1915: THE YEAR OF HORRORS

The eruption of street fighting between Turks and Armenians at Van and in some other places in April 1915 has been blamed by most Turkish and some Western historians on the alleged rebelliousness of the Armenian population—an interpretation that is at most a highly oversimplified version of what happened.[10] More important, even if it were true that there were some Armenian "provocations," this hardly warranted the kind of "countermeasures" the Ottoman authorities instituted. In fact most of the available evidence points to the conclusion that a systematic decimation of the Armenian population in the eastern provinces had already been decided on by the *Ittihad ve Terakki* regime, and that the troubles in Van and elsewhere merely served as a convenient excuse for getting a program of mass deportations and large-scale extermination started.[11]

[9] See, for example, Guse, pp. 27, 61-63, and *passim*; and the report of Gen. Posseldt, fortress commandant in Erzurum until April 1915, in Lepsius, *Deutschland*, No. 31. Cf. Bayur, III:3, 2-9, *passim*, for a representative sample of the Turkish point of view.

[10] See Viscount Bryce [and Arnold Toynbee], *The Treatment of Armenians in the Ottoman Empire, 1915-16* (London, 1916), pp. 638-39 and *passim*; Johannes Lepsius, *Bericht über die Lage des Armenischen Volkes in der Türkei* (Potsdam, 1916), pp. 81-88, and *passim*; Lepsius, *Deutschland*, pp. xiii-xvi; Onnig Mekhitarian, "The Defense of Van," *Armenian Review* (1948), I:1, 121-29; I:2, 131-43; I:3, 130-42; I:4, 133-42. Cf. Bayur, III:3, pp. 2-5.

[11] See Navasard Deyrmenjian, "An Important Turkish Document on the 'Exterminate Armenians' Plan," *Armenian Review*, 14:3 (1961),

The Armenian Persecutions

The gruesome details of the Armenian "deportations" of 1915 and the following years, during which probably more than a million men, women, and children perished, are well known and require little further elaboration.[12] Germany's role in this Armenian tragedy has, on the other hand, remained a subject of lively controversy and needs fresh examination.

Contrary to the assertions of several recent authors, the wartime persecution of the Ottoman Armenians was neither instigated nor welcomed by the German government.[13] However, there are certainly other grave charges which may be leveled against it, and for that matter, against the Austro-Hungarian government as well. The statesmen of both Central Powers and some of their representatives in Constantinople were guilty of extremely poor judgment, a considerable degree of moral callousness, and an altogether excessive concern with what was or seemed to be politically expedient. Despite mounting indications to the contrary they accepted far too long the spurious claims of the Porte that its anti-Armenian policies

---

pp. 53-55; Haigaz K. Kazarian, "Minutes of Secret Meetings Organizing the Turkish Genocide of Armenians," *Armenian Review*, 18:3 (1965), pp. 18-40; and E.K. Sarkisian and R.G. Sahakian, *Vital Issues in Modern Armenian History. A Documented Exposé of Misrepresentations in Turkish Historiography* (Watertown, Mass., 1965), pp. 26-38. Cf. Bayur, III:3, 7-9, who rejects the thesis that the Porte's action against the Armenians was premeditated.

[12] Probably the best work of synthesis on this subject is Johannes Lepsius, *Der Todesgang des armenischen Volkes in der Türkei während des Weltkrieges*, 4th edn. (Potsdam, 1930), which is an expanded version of his wartime *Bericht über die Lage des Armenischen Volkes in der Türkei*, cited in note 10 above. According to Lepsius' postwar calculations approximately 1.1 million Armenians died. Lewis, p. 350, speaks of "a million and half," but this figure is probably too high. Cf. Pasdermadjian, p. 453.

[13] For accusations of this sort, see, for example, Emil Lengyel, *Turkey* (New York, 1940), pp. 195-206; Atamian, pp. 180-81; Gottlieb, pp. 109-10; and Lothar Rathmann, *Stossrichtung Nahost 1914-1918* (Berlin, 1963), pp. 138-40.

were necessitated by widespread sedition in the eastern provinces. More importantly, even after it became apparent that the Ottoman "security measures," including the ruthless evacuation of entire provinces, were part of a deliberate effort to decimate and disperse the Armenian population in Asia Minor, the German and Austro-Hungarian governments steadfastly refused to do anything drastic about the matter. While they abhorred and were acutely embarrassed by the brutal policies of the Turks and directed numerous admonitions and protests to the Porte, the statesmen in both Berlin and Vienna were much too concerned with keeping the Turks in the war to risk alienating the Porte by really strong pressures. But it should be added that there were numerous German and Austro-Hungarian officials, particularly diplomatic and consular, who did not condone such a policy of expediency and whose efforts to stop or mitigate the brutal measures against the Armenians were a great deal more emphatic than has hitherto been assumed.

WHILE RUMORS and reports about isolated "incidents" between Turks and Armenians in some of the eastern *vilayets* had trickled into Constantinople from the very beginning of the war, it was only in March 1915 that the deterioration of Turkish-Armenian relations became patently obvious to the German and Austro-Hungarian observers in Constantinople.[14] After receiving a welter of conflicting reports about growing "unrest" in some Armenian areas and about an armed clash between Armenian "deserters" and government forces at Zeitun, Ambassador Wangenheim during the first half of April directed several appeals to the Porte and to the Armenian Patriarch for calmness and "the preservation of good mutual relations."[15] At the same time, he remained in steady contact with

[14] See FO, *Türkei 183*, Bd. 36, Rössler to Wangenheim, 16 Oct 1914, J. No. 2,480; Wangenheim to Bethmann Hollweg, 29 Dec, No. 341; 2 Feb 1915, J. No. 269; 22 Feb, No. 95; 9 March, No. 140; and Lepsius, *Deutschland*, Nos. 14, 17-25.

[15] FO, *Türkei 183*, Bd. 36, Wangenheim to Bethmann Hollweg, 15

various Armenian organizations in Constantinople and listened to their complaints about Turkish provocations and misdeeds, but when they suggested that Germany assume officially the "protection" of the Armenian *millet* (community) and assign additional consular officials to the eastern *vilayets*, Wangenheim refused them. As he explained to Bethmann Hollweg on April 15 the Armenians' desire for formal German protection was certainly understandable, especially since the Entente powers were no longer around to provide support for them, but if Germany complied with the Armenian requests she would undoubtedly incur the resentment of the Porte:

> The moment for such a move is all the less propitious in that the Porte has just now begun to wipe out the rights of protection which other foreign powers used to exercise over Turkish subjects. Moreover, it [the Porte] needs to consider the national feelings of the Turkish elements which have risen sharply because of the events in the past few years.

Wangenheim concluded that he could not recommend assigning additional German consuls to the eastern *vilayets*. To do so would probably not only strain Germany's relationship with the Porte but also "turn the authorities all the more against the Armenians and, thus, produce the very opposite" of what the Armenians themselves wanted.[16]

By the time this report reached Berlin (it was sent by diplomatic pouch and arrived on April 22), the first news about bloody Turkish-Armenian "clashes" at Van and the eruption of violence in certain other eastern areas were beginning to trickle into Constantinople.[17] On April 24 Wangenheim called

April 1915, No. 228. This dispatch was included in the document collection, *Deutschland und Armenien*, published by Lepsius in 1919. It is now clear, however, that someone deleted important passages from this document and a number of others, and whenever necessary the original rather than Lepsius' reproduction will be cited in this chapter.

[16] Wangenheim to Bethmann Hollweg, No. 228, *loc.cit.*

[17] See FO, *Türkei 183*, Bd. 36, Wangenheim to FO, 24 April 1915, No. 966; Lepsius, *Deutschland*, No. 27.

in person on the Ottoman ministry of interior and was told in strict confidence that a regular uprising had occurred at and near Van and that countermeasures were making progress. When the ambassador expressed hope that the government forces would maintain discipline and avoid anything that might "look like Christian massacres," the spokesman at the ministry replied somewhat sheepishly that the garrison at Van consisted of poorly trained draftees and that "excesses" might not be entirely avoidable.[18]

After receiving a number of new reports about growing tensions and mob violence in some Armenian districts, Wangenheim on April 28 authorized the German vice-consul at Erzurum, Max Erwin von Scheubner-Richter, to intervene against "massacres" and other excesses which might occur in his area, but cautioned him not to create the impression "as though we want to exercise a right of protection over the Armenians or interfere with the activities of the authorities."[19]

In the meantime several hundred Armenians in Constantinople itself had been arrested, and most of the prisoners— among them numerous professional people, clergymen, and politicians—had almost immediately been carried off to the interior of Anatolia. Talât explained to the First Dragoman of the German embassy a few days later that the deportation of these people was primarily a security measure, though he admitted that the Porte was in any case no longer willing to tolerate the existence of separate political organizations among any of the religious communities. The minister also conceded that many of the Armenian deportees were undoubtedly not guilty of anything, but hastened to add that corrective action

[18] FO, *Türkei 183*, Bd. 36, Wangenheim to Bethmann Hollweg, 24 April 1915, No. 260.

[19] Lepsius, *Deutschland*, Nos. 31, 33, 34, 36. Scheubner-Richter, like so many other German officials in wartime Turkey, later became a prominent figure in German politics. In the early years of the Nazi movement he was one of Hitler's closest advisers and was killed at his side in the Munich Putsch of November 9, 1923.

would soon be taken and that foreign "intervention" would be unnecessary and unwelcome.[20]

Wangenheim obviously got the point for there is no evidence that he did anything about the deportations from the capital. His Austro-Hungarian colleague adopted an equally passive attitude. When the American ambassador, Mr. Morgenthau, suggested to him that he intercede for the deportees at the Porte, Pallavicini wired to Vienna that he had no intention whatever of making such a move. As he put it, the Porte was unlikely to accept his advice and would surely resent such interference in its own affairs.[21] Two days later, however, Pallavicini decided that the Armenian issue called for some action after all, for numerous German and Austrian consular reports about outright massacres in the provinces were beginning to come in.

> In view of the political significance which the question has ... now assumed [he wired to Vienna on May 1], I believe I should at the earliest opportunity alert the Turkish statesmen in a friendly manner to the repercussions which an inhuman proceeding against Christians in Turkey might have on the general situation; for our enemies will be given a new pretext to move with all their might against Turkey.[22]

Evidently the "repercussions" really worried the ambassador, for he found an opportunity to buttonhole Talât the very same day. According to his subsequent report to the Ballhausplatz he pointed out that the repression of Armenian unrest should be handled carefully and that the "persecution of women and children" in particular should be avoided lest "the enemies of

[20] Lepsius, *Bericht*, pp. 187-94; FO, *Türkei 183*, Bd. 36, Wangenheim to Bethmann Hollweg, 30 April 1915, No. 267.

[21] *Foreign Relations of the United States, 1915 Supplement* (Washington, 1928), p. 981; AHFM, *Türkei, Berichte 1915*, Pallavicini to Burian, 29 April 1915, No. 32D/P.

[22] *Ibid.*, Pallavicini to AHFM, 1 May 1915, No. 347.

Turkey" be provided with a good propaganda issue. In his reply Talât admitted that several thousand people, "though not only Armenians," had perished in the provinces, but denied that any acts of violence against women and children had occurred. In conclusion the minister thanked the ambassador for his "warning" and assured him that the Porte would proceed only against "the guilty."[23]

During the next two weeks the Porte and the provincial authorities in the east made periodic disclosures of the evidence they had allegedly found concerning Armenian plots against the state. Since there was continued fighting between Armenians and government troops at Van and elsewhere, both Germans and Austro-Hungarians were only too willing to accept the theory that the Turks had an outright revolt on their hands. On the other hand, by the middle of May it became increasingly clear from the reports of the German consuls in the eastern provinces that the Turkish "pacification" program in many areas had become unjustifiably brutal.[24] On May 18 Scheubner-Richter wired from Erzurum that deportations in his area had caused "terrible" misery, with thousands of women and children camping outside the city without food, and that he wished to intervene with the Turkish military commander about these "senseless" expulsions. Wangenheim immediately authorized him to go ahead but apparently made no attempt to take up the matter at the Porte. Nor, for that matter, did Pallavicini see fit to intervene, as Morgenthau once again suggested to him.[25]

On May 24 the British, French, and Russian governments issued a joint public warning to the Porte that they regarded the recently begun persecutions and "mass murders" of Armenians in the Ottoman empire as a crime "against humanity

[23] *Ibid.*, Pallavicini to AHFM, 2 May 1915, No. 352.
[24] Lepsius, *Deutschland*, Nos. 41, 43-53, 56-58.
[25] *Ibid.*, Nos. 59, 60; AHFM, *Türkei, Berichte 1915*, Pallavicini to Burian, 20 May 1915, No. 37C/P.

and civilization," for which they would hold "all members" of the Ottoman government as well as their culpable subordinates personally responsible.[26] On June 4 the Porte, after consultation with Wangenheim, replied with a sharply worded public declaration of its own. Far from having condoned or organized mass murders, the Porte declared, it had merely exercised its sovereign right of self-defense against a revolutionary movement, and the responsibility for everything that had happened in the Armenian districts had to be borne exclusively by the Entente powers themselves, because they had organized and directed the revolutionary movement in the first place.[27]

A few days before this declaration was issued to the press Enver informed Wangenheim that he intended to intensify the counterinsurgency program in a number of ways: closing many Armenian schools, suppressing the Armenian press, banning the use of the mails by Armenians, and transferring all "suspect families" from the present centers of insurrection to Mesopotamia. Enver also expressed the hope that Germany would not try to interfere. Wangenheim, still obsessed with the idea that there was a gigantic Armenian underground movement which threatened the very existence of Turkey, promptly forwarded Enver's plan to the Wilhelmstrasse with the suggestion that, though it entailed "certainly great hardship for the Armenian population," it should not be contested.[28]

[26] The declaration originated in the Russian foreign office and was only reluctantly subscribed to by Sir Edward Grey. The French government saw to it that the originally proposed phrase, "crime against Christianity and civilization," was replaced by "crime against humanity and civilization," in order to spare the feelings of the Moslem population in the French colonies. See *Die Internationalen Beziehungen . . . ,* ser. 2, VII:2, Nos. 609, 724, 740, 797, 799. The English text of the declaration is reprinted in *Foreign Relations U.S., 1915 Supplement,* p. 981.

[27] See FO, *Türkei 183,* Bd. 37, Wangenheim to Bethmann Hollweg, 5 June 1915, No. 349; and *Schulthess,* v. 56, 1,151-54.

[28] FO, *Türkei 183,* Bd. 37, Wangenheim to FO, 31 May 1915, No.

The Armenian Persecutions

The Berlin foreign office, which had not shown very much interest in the Armenian troubles in the preceding weeks and was obviously quite content to let its man in Constantinople decide on the proper course of action, accepted Wangenheim's recommendation. Not so Dr. Johannes Lepsius, the president of the German-Armenian Society and of the "German Orient-Mission," who had good connections with some of the officials in the Wilhelmstrasse and was being given liberal access to the incoming dispatches on the Armenian situation. As soon as Lepsius learned of Enver's latest plan he decided that things had gone far enough and that he should go to Constantinople to look into the Armenian problem. His plan to "mediate" between the Turks and the Armenians was approved by the Berlin foreign office, but Wangenheim would not hear of it; as he explained to the Wilhelmstrasse on June 9 the anti-Armenian measures of the Porte were already fully underway, there was no chance that Lepsius could accomplish anything worthwhile, and his appearance in Constantinople would merely cause trouble for the embassy since the Porte did not want him to come.[29]

Despite this rebuff Lepsius refused to give up. With the support of the directors of the German-Armenian Society and the Orient-Mission, among them the well-known publicist Paul Rohrbach, he immediately renewed his request for a travel permit. On June 13 Zimmermann advised Wangenheim that

---

1,268. On the background story see Bayur, III:3, 37-42, who claims that Talât was the driving force behind the new repressive measures.

[29] See FO, *Türkei 183*, Bd. 37, Zimmermann to Wangenheim, 6 June 1915, No. 1,106; Wangenheim to FO, 9 June, No. 1,338; Lepsius, *Deutschland*, p. 79, note 1; Lepsius, "Mein Besuch in Konstantinopel Juli/August 1915," *Der Orient*, 1:3 (1919), 21. On Lepsius' background and meritorious efforts on behalf of the Ottoman Armenians since the days of Sultan Abdülhamid, see Jean Naslian, *Les mémoires de Mgr. Jean Naslian, Évêque de Trebizonde, sur les événements politico-religieux en Proche-Orient de 1914 à 1928*, 2 vols. (Beirut, 1955), I, 463-64.

Lepsius' trip might be useful and that the embassy should overcome the Porte's objections.[30]

In the meantime a whole string of reports about massacres or brutal mistreatment of Armenians in various places had reached the German embassy from the consulates at Erzurum, Aleppo, and Mosul. On June 17 Wangenheim therefore felt constrained to warn Bethmann Hollweg that the ruthless mass deportations in the eastern provinces were obviously no longer based on "military considerations alone." Talât, he added, had admitted as much in a recent conversation with an embassy official, and the Armenian Patriarch was now firmly convinced that the Porte meant to exterminate the entire Armenian population. When this disturbing report reached the Wilhelmstrasse somebody there drew a black line along the margin of the key paragraph, but this apparently was all the action that was taken on the matter.[31]

With no reply, let alone a policy directive, coming from Berlin Wangenheim during the remainder of June seems to have done little more on the Armenian problem than to read the gruesome consular messages coming in from the eastern *vilayets* and to send back notes to the consuls that they could and/or should protest to the provincial authorities about outrages which had occurred in their regions. On one occasion, it is true, Wangenheim assured the consul at Erzurum that he would support the latter's protests to the provincial governor by parallel efforts at the Porte, but whether he actually followed through is doubtful. All we know for certain is that Wangen-

---

[30] FO, *Türkei 183*, Bd. 37, Lepsius to German embassy Constantinople, 11 June 1915; petition, dated 11 June 1915, by Lepsius, Rohrbach, and five other directors of the *Deutsche Orient-Mission* and the *Deutsch-Armenische Gesellschaft*; Zimmermann to Wangenheim, 13 June, No. 461. See also Lepsius, "Mein Besuch in Konstantinopel . . . ," p. 22.

[31] See Lepsius, *Deutschland*, Nos. 73-76, 78-80; FO, *Türkei 183*, Bd. 37, Wangenheim to Bethmann Hollweg, 17 June 1915, No. 372.

heim applied for and got the Porte's formal approval for Lepsius to come to Constantinople, though Talât made it clear that the unwelcome visitor would not be allowed to venture into the provinces.[32]

Judging from the available evidence Wangenheim's Austro-Hungarian colleague did not get any policy directives on the Armenian question from his superiors either. All indications are that he too remained passive throughout the latter half of June. Finally, at the very end of the month, the two ambassadors got together and decided that without waiting for specific instructions from home they would have to do something about the reign of terror their common ally was unleashing in the Armenian districts. As Wangenheim later explained in a somewhat disjointed report to Bethmann Hollweg, the scope and nature of the deportation proceedings in the eastern provinces no longer left any doubt that the Porte was "actually" trying to "exterminate the Armenian race in the Turkish empire," and it was therefore essential for Germany to go on record that she disapproved of what the Turks were doing.[33]

Pallavicini made the first move. On July 1 he told Talât that the indiscriminate deportations of men, women, and children "seemed hardly justified," and that the whole anti-Armenian program was creating a very bad impression.[34] Wangenheim went one step further on July 4 by presenting the grand vizier

[32] See Lepsius, *Deutschland*, Nos. 84, 87-92, 94-100, 102, 103; FO, *Türkei 183*, Bd. 37, Wangenheim to FO, 24 June 1915, No. 1456. The passivity of the Wilhelmstrasse was interrupted twice by instructions from Zimmermann to the Constantinople embassy to prevent the execution of certain Dashnak leaders, but these were strictly limited cases of intervention which Lepsius had urged upon the foreign office. Lepsius, *Deutschland*, Nos. 82, 83, and 101.

[33] FO, *Türkei 183*, Bd. 37, Wangenheim to Bethmann Hollweg, 7 July 1915, No. 433. In an interview on June 26 with the Catholic-Armenian Patriarch of Cilicia, Wangenheim had promised to make an appeal to the Porte. Naslian, 1, 57-58, 503-504.

[34] AHFM, *Türkei, Berichte 1915*, Pallavicini to Burian, 1 July 1915, No. 51E/P.

with a diplomatically worded, but fairly straightforward, "memorandum" on the Armenian problem, copies of which he subsequently also sent to the Ottoman ministries of foreign affairs and interior. While the German government had no objections whatever, the memorandum read, to measures of repression which were "dictated by military reasons" and intended to enhance the internal security of the Ottoman empire, it could not ignore "the dangers" which were created by indiscriminate measures against, and mass deportations of, "the guilty and the innocent, particularly when these measures are accompanied by acts of violence, such as massacres and pillagings." Inasmuch as such incidents had not been prevented by "the local authorities," a very bad impression had been created abroad, particularly in the United States, and the German government felt duty-bound to notify the Porte that the whole matter might detrimentally affect their common interests, both now and the future. The German embassy, therefore, considered it a matter of urgency

that peremptory orders be issued to the provincial authorities so that they take effective action to protect the lives and property of the expatriated Armenians, both during their transportation and in their new homes.

It [the embassy] feels likewise that it would be prudent to suspend, for the time being, the execution of death sentences against Armenians which have already been or will be passed by the military courts in the capital or in the provinces, above all at Diyarbekir and Adana.

Finally, the embassy of Germany requests that the Ottoman government give due consideration to the manifold interests of German commerce and of the German welfare institutions in those provinces where the expulsion of Armenians is now being carried out. Since the precipitous departure of the latter entails serious damage to these interests, the embassy would be obliged if the Sublime Porte would, in certain cases, prolong the grace period accorded to deportees and permit those who belong to the personnel of the welfare institutions in question, as well as pupils, orphans, and other dependent persons, to stay in their former homes; except, of course, if they have been found culpable of acts which necessitate their removal.[35]

Neither this note nor Pallavicini's oral admonitions made the slightest impression on the Porte. On July 8 Pallavicini advised the Austro-Hungarian foreign minister, Stefan Count Burian, that, Talât's previous assurances notwithstanding, the brutal persecutions in the eastern provinces were going on as before. The ambassador concluded:

Unfortunately, the men in power here cannot be convinced of the incorrectness of their proceedings against the Armenians, and it is to be feared that more insistent admonitions to them will merely make the matter worse. Evidently, one is determined here to render the Armenian element, which has become so suspect here, harmless once and for all.[36]

With fresh reports of murder and rapine coming in from the German consulates in the east[37] Wangenheim delivered a new note to the Porte on July 12, in which he bluntly suggested that "measures be taken against" the vali of Diyarbekir, Dr. Reşid Bey, lest his murderous policies lead to the total extermination of the Christians in his area.[38] Once again, the Porte simply ignored the unwelcome advice, and on July 16 Wangenheim notified Bethmann Hollweg that inasmuch as further efforts to divert the Porte from its course were unlikely to produce any better results, "responsibility" for all the consequences of the

[35] FO, *Türkei 183*, Bd. 37, "Anlage zu Bericht No. 433." The text of the "Memorandum" can also be found in Lepsius, *Deutschland*, pp. 96-97.

[36] AHFM, *Türkei, Berichte 1915*, Pallavicini to Burian, 8 July 1915, No. 54C/P. Cf. Naslian, 1, 505.

[37] See, for example, Lepsius, *Deutschland*, Nos. 108-10, 116 *Anlage*.

[38] *Ibid.*, No. 112. Reşid committed suicide after the war.

Armenian persecutions would have to be "left" to the Turks. There was of course a possibility, the ambassador added, that "our enemies" would later try to make the German government equally responsible for what was happening to the Armenians, but his own reports of the preceding months could then surely be used to demonstrate that the Reich had "always emphatically condemned" the excesses of the Turks.[39]

Shortly after dispatching these recommendations Wangenheim went on sick leave to Germany. (According to Pomiankowski's memoirs the ambassador by this time was very urgently in need of medical attention, for in addition to suffering from a serious heart defect and arteriosclerosis he had become afflicted with a "clearly pathological" form of "nervousness.")[40] Wangenheim's temporary replacement at the embassy, Prince zu Hohenlohe-Langenburg, arrived in Constantinople on July 20 and lost no time in "reopening" the Armenian question.

Hohenlohe's increasingly outspoken criticism of the Porte's Armenian policy and his "untiring" efforts to stop the mass killings in the provinces have been attested to by several people who were in Constantinople at that time.[41] How much his concern for the Armenians was shared by the leading men at the Wilhelmstrasse is however quite another question, for the messages which he received from Berlin were usually more concerned with the propagandistic damage the Turks were doing than with the suffering of their victims. In fact, there is considerable evidence that Wangenheim's suggestion of July 16 that Germany should abandon the futile exhortations to the Porte

[39] See *ibid.*, No. 114; and FO, *Türkei 183*, Bd. 37, Wangenheim to Bethmann Hollweg, 16 July 1915, No. 449.

[40] Pomiankowski, pp. 174-75. See also AHFM, *Türkei, Berichte 1915*, Pallavicini to Burian, 7 Aug 1915, No. 64D/P; and Morgenthau, p. 373.

[41] For example, Lepsius, *Deutschland*, p. xxxi; and AHFM, *Türkei, Berichte 1915*, Pallavicini to Burian, 29 Oct 1915, No. 91A-C/P.

and concentrate instead on preparing a defense against the charge of complicity had fallen on fertile ground in German government circles. As Zimmermann wired to Hohenlohe on August 4 there was a good chance that the Entente and "unfriendly" neutrals would try to pin part of the blame for the Armenian persecutions on Berlin, and since such allegations might cause domestic unrest in Germany, particularly in "church and missionary circles," a public "justification of our attitude" might become necessary. The Constantinople embassy should therefore start with the collection of documentary evidence regarding Germany's efforts to "avert an excessively harsh treatment of the Armenians," though Zimmermann thought it even more important to gather "proof" that a "widespread subversive movement" had existed among the Ottoman Armenians and that the Entente had instigated their "treasonable activities."[42]

In the meantime, Lepsius had finally arrived in Constantinople.[43] After collecting information there on the Armenian situation from various sources, including the American embassy, Lepsius eventually managed to be received by Enver himself. In a lengthy interview with the latter on August 10, Lepsius learned to his dismay that the Porte would not permit

[42] FO, *Türkei 183*, Bd. 37, Zimmermann to Hohenlohe, 4 Aug 1915, No. 590. The worry of the Wilhelmstrasse that it might come under fire from German "church and missionary circles" was no doubt triggered by a lengthy communication from Lepsius, in which he denounced the Porte's anti-Armenian measures as "thinly veiled Christian massacres." *Ibid.*, Lepsius to FO, 22 June 1915.

[43] It is clear that both Wangenheim and the Wilhelmstrasse tried to dissuade him from the trip in early July, but no action was taken to prevent his departure from Germany. (See *ibid.*, Wangenheim to FO, 2 July 1915, No. 1,523; Zimmermann to Wangenheim, 4 July, No. 1,276.) According to Lepsius' testimony he arrived in Constantinople on July 24, after stopping over in Switzerland, Bucharest, and Sofia, where he had lengthy strategy talks with Armenian circles. Lepsius, "Mein Besuch in Konstantinopel . . . ," *Deutschland*, pp. 22-23.

him or any other foreigner to organize aid programs for the Armenian deportees, that the anti-Armenian proceedings would be continued, and that Enver himself had no intention of advocating a reversal of that policy. Moreover, Enver seems to have admitted that his colleagues at the Porte were out to "make an end of the Armenians now."[44]

Loaded with notes, affidavits, and excerpts from American consular reports, Lepsius shortly thereafter returned to Germany. From then on he spared neither time nor effort to drum up public opinion both in Germany and abroad against the inhuman policies of the Porte.

The unsatisfactory outcome of Lepsius' conversation with Enver seems to have strengthened Hohenlohe's resolve to express his disapproval of the Armenian persecutions in another formal note to the Porte. Like Wangenheim's note of the preceding month, Hohenlohe's "memorandum" to the Porte, which he personally delivered on August 11, had neither been suggested by, nor cleared with, the Wilhelmstrasse, and the ambassador was undoubtedly taking a risk in denouncing the Porte's Armenian policy as bluntly as he did. After pointing out in his note that the previous formal request by Wangenheim for the termination of massacres and other acts of violence had obviously been disregarded, and that the Porte had actually seen fit to broaden the geographic scope of the anti-Armenian measures, Hohenlohe informed the Turks that "by order of . . . [his] government" he had to "remonstrate once again *against these acts of horror* and to decline all responsibility for the consequences which might spring from them."[45]

Although both Talât and Halil, upon receipt of this note, assured the ambassador that the Porte would endeavor to curb

---

[44] Cf. Lepsius, *Deutschland*, No. 131; Lepsius, "Mein Besuch in Konstantinopel . . . ," pp. 23-27; Jackh Papers, No. 22, Rohrbach to Jäckh, 21 Sept 1915.

[45] FO, *Türkei 183*, Bd. 38, "Memorandum; Pera, le 9 août 1915" (italics added); Hohenlohe to Bethmann Hollweg, 12 Aug 1915, No. 501.

the excesses of "subordinate authorities," Hohenlohe was not impressed. The next day he proposed to Bethmann Hollweg that his own efforts to stop the Armenian holocaust should be supported by suitable pressures on the Ottoman embassy in Berlin, and that an official disavowal of the Porte's policies in the German press might very well be in order.[46]

That Hohenlohe was in earnest about the whole matter is confirmed by a report which Pallavicini subsequently sent to Vienna,[47] but the men in the Wilhelmstrasse, far away from the scene of the Armenian horrors, caught little if any of Hohenlohe's sense of outrage. With new reports about the murderous policy of the Turks coming in almost daily, Zimmermann responded to Hohenlohe's dispatch on August 18 in a singularly mealy-mouthed fashion. As the under-state secretary put it, Hohenlohe should express Germany's hope and "conviction" that the continuing anti-Armenian excesses in the provinces ran counter to the Porte's "intentions and instructions." Zimmermann continued:

> Our friends in the Turkish cabinet will surely understand that we have a lively interest in the energetic suppression of the excesses, all the more so since we have been accused of being the instigators.
>
> The high sense of humaneness and culture which has characterized the Turkish conduct of the war in contrast to that of the enemy warrants the expectation that our ally will see to it that the same principles are applied also in the interior [of the Ottoman empire].

As for a recent suggestion by the German consul in Aleppo, Rössler, that Berlin ought to do something drastic about the mistreatment of the Armenians, Zimmermann concluded

[46] See *ibid.*

[47] AHFM, *Türkei, Berichte 1915*, Pallavicini to Burian, 13 Aug 1915, No. 66B/P. See also *Foreign Relations U.S., 1915 Supplement*, pp. 985-87, for Morgenthau's comments on Hohenlohe's efforts.

rather unctiously, the embassy should seek to "enlighten" the consul, that despite the reprehensible "machinations" of the Armenians, efforts on their behalf had already been made.[48] Equipped with these worthless instructions Hohenlohe continued during the following weeks to direct admonitions and protests to the Porte, but the Turks paid little or no attention. While Talât, at the end of August, assured the ambassador that the anti-Armenian program was being terminated and subsequently even furnished copies of the requisite orders which the ministry of interior had sent out to the provincial authorities, reports from several German consuls soon indicated that in many areas the persecutions were continuing as before.[49] On September 11 Hohenlohe notified Berlin of this situation, but it was only a week and a half later that the Wilhelmstrasse responded—though this time, at least, Zimmermann did recommend that the ambassador admonish the Porte "in forceful fashion."[50]

While the Wilhelmstrasse was continuing to practice diplomatic restraint in regard to the Armenian problem,[51] Lepsius had meanwhile launched a massive campaign to acquaint clerical and journalistic circles in the Reich with the brutal conduct of the Turks. Needless to say, his blunt statements about the misdeeds of Germany's ally put the Berlin foreign office in a very awkward position, but surprisingly little was done by it or any other German government agency to keep Lepsius quiet.

[48] FO, *Türkei 183*, Bd. 38, Zimmermann to Hohenlohe, 18 Aug 1915, No. 1,547. For Rössler's dispatches of the preceding weeks see *ibid.*, Rössler to Bethmann Hollweg, 27 July 1915, K. No. 81; and Lepsius, *Deutschland*, Nos. 121, 125, 128, and 134.

[49] See *ibid.*, Nos. 133-34, 142, 145-48, 151-52, 157, 160-65; *Foreign Relations U.S., 1915 Supplement*, p. 987.

[50] FO, *Türkei 183*, Bd. 38, Hohenlohe to Bethmann Hollweg, 11 Sept 1915, No. 560; Lepsius, *Deutschland*, No. 174.

[51] See, for example, the memorandum by Rosenberg on a *démarche* he made on October 1 to the Ottoman embassy in Berlin, *ibid.*, No. 178.

The Armenian Persecutions

On September 22 the German consul-general in Basel informed Bethmann Hollweg that a recent Swiss press campaign against the Porte's Armenian policy had probably been inspired by Lepsius during a visit to Switzerland, and that Lepsius had reportedly also mentioned there that the Wilhelmstrasse knew about, but could not do anything against, the conduct of the Turks.[52] While this was embarrassing enough for the directors of Germany's foreign policy, the stir Lepsius was making in the Reich itself proved even more of a problem. Inquiries came in from various sides as to what the Wilhelmstrasse was going to do about the Armenian problem, and the chairman of the German *Zeitungsverlag*, Dr. Faber, wanted to know how the newspapers should treat the story—a matter all the more urgent in that some clerical circles were pushing for a public airing of the events in Armenia.

Suppressing his personal feelings about the Ottoman government (which were anything but friendly),[53] Zimmermann on October 4 penned the following answer to Faber, using several arguments which were henceforth to become the stock-in-trade in official declarations and explanations of the Berlin government:

> Without needing any prodding from church circles, the foreign office and the imperial representative agencies in Turkey have, of their own volition, already done all that was possible by diplomatic means to mitigate the sufferings of the Armenians. To bring about a break with Turkey on account of the Armenian question we did not and do not consider appropriate. For as regrettable as it is from the Christian standpoint that innocent people, too, must suffer under the Turkish measures, the Armenians are after all

[52] FO, *Türkei 183*, Bd. 38, Consul-General, Basel, to Bethmann Hollweg, 22 Sept 1915, J. Nr. 6,867. Cf. Lepsius, "Mein Besuch in Konstantinopel . . . ," p. 31.

[53] See, Kanner Papers, II, 276-84, "Besuch bei Zimmermann, 4. Oktober. . . ."

less close to us than our own sons and brothers, whose sacrificial, bloody struggle in France and Russia is being indirectly aided by the military help of the Turks.

Zimmermann emphasized that the regrettable misfortunes which had befallen the Ottoman Armenians were really the fault of the revolutionary elements among them—and of their friends "in Petersburg"—for the "Armenian uprising" behind the Ottoman lines had caused understandable resentment among the Moslems in the empire—all the more so in that "more than 150,000" Moslems had perished "within a few days" as a result of the uprising.[54]

While the first part of Zimmermann's statement deserves at least credit for its frankness, there is little excuse for his reference to the 150,000 slain Moslems. The story of their deaths hinged on the Porte's contention that approximately that many Moslem residents of the *vilayet* of Van were unaccounted for since the Russian army had conquered the region in the spring of 1915. However, since the Turks had meanwhile offered at least three different versions as to what had happened in that *vilayet*,[55] Zimmermann should have known better than to present the massacre of the Moslem population as an established fact. In the following months Lepsius did his best to disprove the Turkish charges, but how effective he was is difficult to tell since many Germans who attended his lectures or read his brochures considered him excessively partisan in his treatment of Turkish-Armenian relations.

Lepsius' hard-hitting style and the resistance he encountered may be gleaned from a report by the censorship bureau of the

[54] FO, *Türkei 183*, Bd. 39, Zimmermann to Faber, 4 Oct 1915.

[55] At first, in late June 1915, the Porte had merely claimed that the fate of 150,000 Moslems left behind in the *vilayet* (province) of Van was unknown and that they were "exposed" to murder by Russians and Armenians. In early August Enver asserted that the "Armenians" had killed them all, and two months later the number of alleged Moslem victims was raised by the Ottoman embassy in Berlin to "no less than 180,000."

OHL concerning a meeting with German newspaper executives which Lepsius arranged in Berlin early in October 1915. Lepsius opened the meeting with a lengthy speech in which he sharply denounced both what the Turks had done to the Armenians and the timidity with which the German government had so far reacted to the misconduct of its ally. By not forcing the Porte to stop its anti-Armenian policy, he asserted, Germany was not only allowing the ruination of its own "economic and cultural" influence in the Ottoman empire but was also exposing itself to propagandistic attacks from abroad which would be even more damaging than all that had been said about German conduct in Belgium. The fact of the matter was that, instead of making itself the "master of Turkey," as the British would have done under comparable circumstances, the German government, through its ineptitude, had actually become the "servant" of the Porte. This situation, Lepsius concluded, could be corrected once Germany had gained secure access to Constantinople via Serbia, and Berlin should then see to it that at least in the northern half of the Turkish empire Germany would have a controlling influence. The remainder of the empire would "undoubtedly" fall under British domination anyway.[56]

Lepsius' pronouncements were highly embarrassing to the Wilhelmstrasse (which had sent a representative to the meeting). Moreover, some of the newspaper executives, too, reacted unfavorably to Lepsius' speech. One Socialist editor, Max Grunwald, announced that he found Lepsius' arguments unconvincing: as Marx had taught, historical developments were following their own laws, and the application of European moral and political standards to the events in the

---

[56] Lepsius, "Mein Besuch in Konstantinopel . . . ," *Deutschland,* p. 31; Jackh Papers, No. 22, OHL (Main Censorship Bureau of the War Press Department, Berlin) to Jäckh, 1 Nov 1915, No. 2,610 O.Z., "Auszug aus dem Vortrage des Dr. Lepsius vom 5.10.15 über die Lage der türkischen Armenier."

Ottoman empire was therefore quite inappropriate. When Lepsius thereupon conceded that the problem should perhaps be discussed primarily in terms of its political and economic implications, Director Bernhard of the Ullstein Publishing House eagerly agreed and announced he was, indeed, worried about the economic consequences of the Armenian persecutions. The Turks, he asserted, were completely without talent in technical and economic matters, and by eliminating the highly capable Armenian population element they were creating a situation which would adversely affect Germany's own interests. To complete this rather curious discussion, another SPD (Social Democrats) editor, Julius Kaliski, seconded Bernhard's charge that Lepsius had painted the Armenian situation in excessively black colors; moreover, Kaliski added, there was a good chance that the business talents of the Armenians might be adequately replaced by those of the Jews.[57]

The charge that Lepsius was exaggerating the miseries of the Armenians was promptly repeated the next day by a spokesman of the Berlin foreign office on the occasion of a press conference. After rattling off most of the arguments which had already been used by Zimmermann in his letter to Dr. Faber, the spokesman added that the moral responsibility for the Armenian troubles had to be borne by all three Entente powers. Although the Turkish "countermeasures" had indeed been "rough and cruel," he continued, it would be "most deplorable if our missionary associations and our press were to let themselves be used as battering rams in the Armenian question." While diplomatic efforts to ease the lot of the Ottoman Armenians had been made all along, the German government was not prepared to risk a rift, let alone a break, with the Porte by championing the cause of the Armenians too militantly. Should the Entente attempt to construe a case against Germany, the spokesman concluded, it would not get very far—for its own record was replete with immoral acts—and it was

[57] *Ibid.*

therefore altogether preferable that the German press should abstain from any commentary on the Armenian question "for the time being."[58]

Privately the Wilhelmstrasse was becoming increasingly worried about the sharp criticism Germany was being subjected to abroad because of the Armenian persecutions. Charges that Berlin had instigated the Porte's anti-Armenian program, and that German officials had been directly involved in some of the Armenian massacres had been aired in various countries, particularly Britain. By October 8 Zimmermann decided that a simple German refutal would hardly be sufficient to convince the world that these accusations were untrue. He therefore wrote to Wangenheim who had meanwhile returned to his post in Constantinople, that it was high time for the Porte to declare publicly that the German representatives in the Ottoman empire had always exerted themselves on behalf of the Armenians.[59] Needless to say, the Turks found this request from Berlin most unpalatable, and despite repeated warnings by Wangenheim that Berlin would have to issue a declaration on this matter unilaterally if the Porte did not publish the desired refutal, Halil refused to oblige. After keeping Wangenheim waiting for over a week, the Ottoman foreign minister informed the embassy on October 21 that if Berlin really went ahead with a declaration of its own it should by all means cut out any references to the efforts it had made on behalf of the Armenians, for Turkish public opinion would react very unkindly to such news of "foreign" meddling in the internal affairs of the Ottoman empire.[60]

Faced with the choice of clearing Germany's name even if that aroused Turkish hostility or doing nothing, the Wilhelm-

[58] *Ibid.*

[59] FO, *Türkei 183*, Bd. 39, Zimmermann to Wangenheim, 8 Oct 1915, No. 1,918.

[60] *Ibid.*, Wangenheim to FO, 15 Oct 1915, No. 2,354; 16 Oct, No. 2,378; 18 Oct, No. 2,399; 21 Oct, No. 2,424.

strasse did the predictable thing. As Zimmermann wired to the Constantinople embassy rather sheepishly, "In order to oblige Halil, we will for the time being refrain from issuing our own *démenti* and continue to wait for the Turkish *démenti*." Moreover, contrary to previous instructions, Wangenheim was ordered not to press any longer for a written affidavit from the American embassy concerning Germany's noninvolvement in the Armenian massacres. For, as Zimmermann put it, the more this whole issue was made the subject of public controversy the more the Turks would take out their resentments on the helpless Armenians.[61]

This reversal in the Wilhelmstrasse's attitude might be interpreted as a sign that it had a guilty conscience and was no longer sure of its own case, but all available evidence points to the conclusion that it was actually fear of probable Turkish reprisals, against both Germany and the Armenians themselves, which induced Berlin to abandon its efforts at public exculpation for the time being. Whether Berlin's fears were objectively justified is of course quite another matter. The point is that they definitely existed and that they received new nourishment by several reports the Wilhelmstrasse received at that time. Wangenheim had reported on October 15 that recent complaints by him about new massacres in Mesopotamia had

---

[61] *Ibid.*, Zimmermann to Wangenheim, 21 Oct 1915, No. 2,016. In compliance with Berlin's instructions Wangenheim had previously approached Morgenthau and allegedly received unqualified oral assurances from the latter that he knew how Germany had tried "everything" to prevent the excesses against the Armenians and how the German consuls had "always and everywhere" exerted themselves for the Armenian population. See *ibid.*, Wangenheim to FO, 15 Oct, No. 2,359. Cf. the different version given by Morgenthau, p. 377.

Ralph Elliot Cook, "The United States and the Armenian Question, 1894-1924," unpub. ph.d. diss. (Fletcher School of Law and Diplomacy, 1957), p. 129, has pointed out that there are some discrepancies between what Morgenthau reported to the State Department at the time and the anti-German interpretation of the Armenian story in his published memoirs.

been rebuffed by Talât, and on October 26—shortly after Wangenheim's death—Neurath thought it advisable to warn Berlin that due to the sensitivity of the Turks to anything that smacked of interference in their domestic affairs even private German charity programs for the survivors of the Armenian deportations should be kept as small as possible.[62]

Thanks to the efforts of Lepsius, Rohrbach,[63] and other prominent figures in the German Orient-Mission and the German-Armenian Society, a large number of German Protestant pastors, university professors, and others with an active conscience had meanwhile been stirred into action. On October 15 about 50 of these Protestants, including several high-ranking church officials, addressed a formal petition to Bethmann Hollweg, in which they expressed their abhorrence of the "infamous" persecutions of the Armenians and called for prompt action by the German government to stop and reverse the policy of the Porte. In particular every conceivable effort should be made at once: (1) to prevent deportations in those areas (Constantinople, Smyrna, Aleppo, *et al.*) where the Armenian population had so far been spared; (2) to make sure the already deported Armenians were kept alive and safe from further atrocities; and (3) to make it possible for "Christians of other countries" to render aid and comfort to the suffering deportees. Moreover, the Berlin government should see to it at the end of the war that "the now forcibly Islamized Chris-

[62] See DZA, Reichskanzlei, *Kriegsakten 22*, Bd. 1, "G.A.," Zur Besprechung mit Pastor Weber"; FO, *Türkei 183*, Bd. 39, Wangenheim to Bethmann Hollweg, 15 Oct 1915, No. 618; Neurath to same, 26 Oct, No. 634.

[63] Contrary to French press reports, approvingly repeated in Morgenthau's memoirs, p. 366, Rohrbach was not anti-Armenian but rather a passionate critic of the measures taken against them. He consistently denounced the failure of the German government to do more for the Armenians and in 1916 even talked of turning his back on the "fatherland" that had tolerated such crimes by its Turkish ally. See Jackh Papers, No. 22, Rohrbach to Jackh, 21 Sept 1915; No. 23, same to same, 15 Aug 1916.

tians shall be able to return to Christianity, and that necessary guarantees are provided for a henceforth peaceful and loyal evolution of the Christian minorities in Turkey and for the unhampered continuation of Christian charitable and cultural work in the Orient."[64] Two weeks later Prelate Werthmann and two prominent figures of the Center Party, Matthias Erzberger and Karl Bachem, addressed a similar, though less strongly-worded, appeal to Bethmann Hollweg. Speaking on behalf of the "Mission Section of the Central Committee for the General Assemblies of the Catholics of Germany," they requested that the imperial government do everything "that can be done without endangering the military alliance relationship" to bring about an improvement in the situation of the Ottoman Armenians.[65]

Bethmann Hollweg responded to the two petitions on November 12, when he informed Director Schreiber of the *Deutsche Evangelische Missionshilfe* and Erzberger in identical messages that he would do "everything that is in my power" to solve the Armenian issue in accordance with the wishes communicated to him. Simultaneously the chancellor forwarded copies of the Protestant and Catholic petitions to the Constantinople embassy and instructed its *chargé*, Neurath, to continue with forceful appeals to the Porte on behalf of the Armenians and to make "particularly" sure that the Turkish measures of repression were not extended to yet some other Christian group in the empire.[66]

Bethmann Hollweg's belated instructions to Neurath were quite superfluous since the *chargé* had already bombarded the Porte with numerous admonitions and "warnings" against an extension of the anti-Armenian program. As Morgenthau later

[64] Lepsius, *Deutschland*, No. 197, *Anlage* 1.

[65] *Ibid.*, *Anlage* 2. On the background see Lepsius, "Mein Besuch in Konstantinopel . . . ," pp. 30-31.

[66] See Lepsius, *Deutschland*, Nos. 198, 199; FO, *Türkei 183*, Bd. 39, Bethmann Hollweg to Neurath, 13 Nov 1915, No. 857.

recalled, Neurath's indignation over the Turkish atrocities was so great that "his language to Talât and Enver became almost undiplomatic." But this was nothing compared to the lectures the newly appointed German ambassador, Wolff-Metternich, delivered to the Turks when he arrived in Constantinople.[67] Equipped with specific instructions from State Secretary Jagow, Wolff-Metternich took up the Armenian question with the grand vizier and other members of the Porte and made it clear that he detested the violent manner in which the government and its underlings had behaved. As previously mentioned, the Turks never forgot or forgave him. If they had known what he reported to Berlin in the following weeks they probably would have insisted on his recall much sooner than they did.[68]

Some of the best information about the disdainful fashion in which Wolff-Metternich treated the Turks comes from the correspondence of Pallavicini, whose own efforts on behalf of the Armenians were much more "inoffensive" in form, as well as being very sporadic. In fact there are some indications that the Austro-Hungarian embassy made hardly a stir in the Armenian question during September and October; it was only after Pallavicini returned from a brief leave in Vienna that he resumed his carefully worded admonitions to the Porte. During the first two weeks of November he repeatedly talked to the grand vizier and Halil Bey about the "dangerous consequences" of the Porte's anti-Armenian policy and the determination of the Central Powers to let the Turks carry the full responsibility for what they were doing, but as he subsequently informed Burian there was little hope that his remarks would do much good. Although both Said Halim and Halil seemed

---

[67] See Lepsius, *Deutschland*, Nos. 191, 194, 201; Morgenthau, p. 372.

[68] See FO, *Türkei 183*, Bd. 39, Jagow to Wolff-Metternich, 12 Nov 1915, No. 855; Jackh Papers, No. 4, "Zur Lage am 20. Dezember 1915"; AHFM, *Türkei, Berichte 1915*, Pallavicini to Burian, 18 Dec 1915, No. 103A-E/P; *Türkei, Berichte 1916*, same to same, 7 Oct 1916, No. 76C/P. Cf. Pomiankowski, pp. 175-76.

impressed by his arguments, he explained, Talât and other *Ittihad ve Terakki* leaders were obviously trying to "solve" the Armenian question in their own way. Since many provincial *valis* and other regional officials were in the habit of taking their instructions from the Party Central Committee rather than from the cabinet, the termination of the anti-Armenian program would be difficult to secure.[69]

Since Scheubner-Richter in Erzurum and various other informants continued to report anti-Armenian outrages in the eastern provinces and, even worse, widespread rumors among the Turkish population that Germany was squarely behind the Porte in that matter, Jagow at the end of November urged Wolff-Metternich to admonish the Porte that it must set the record straight about Germany's involvement and handle the Armenian question in accordance with the "advice" that it had been given. Alerted by Lepsius that the Turks had actually resumed deporting Armenians from Constantinople itself, Zimmermann followed up a few days later with instructions that Wolff-Metternich should emphatically remonstrate about that matter, too.[70] On December 7 the ambassador replied that he had expressed Germany's opposition to the continuing anti-Armenian campaign repeatedly and "in extremely sharp language," but that neither Enver nor Halil had shown much inclination to discuss the issue. Since protests were obviously "useless," the ambassador continued, it might be advisable to initiate a press campaign in Germany against the Armenian persecutions. In particular, a semi-official announcement in the *Norddeutsche Allgemeine Zeitung*, the traditional mouthpiece of the Berlin government, might now be in order, to the effect that the German government deplored the sufferings of the

---

[69] AHFM, *Türkei XLVII/3*, Pallavicini to AHFM, 1 Nov 1915, No. 830; 8 Nov, No. 842; same to Burian, 7 Nov, No. 93B/P. For indications of Pallavicini's basic inclination not to rock the boat on the Armenian issue, see also his dispatch to Burian, 10 Nov, No. 94B/P.

[70] Lepsius, *Deutschland*, Nos. 205, 206, 208.

Armenian people and was once again forced to "demand" that the Porte take corrective action to prevent further "deeply deplorable events." Undoubtedly, such a public chastisement would strain Germany's political relationship with the Turks, Wolff-Metternich concluded, but the risk of their deserting the alliance was not quite as great as Berlin might think; for it was extremely unlikely that the Entente powers, Britain in particular, would want to make a deal with the men who were presently running the Ottoman government.[71]

Both Jagow and Zimmermann thought Wolff-Metternich's proposal had some merit, but since the ambassador himself had requested that its implementation be postponed until Talât, "the soul of the Armenian persecutions," had returned from the provinces and been given a chance to react to the latest German steps, the project was shelved until then.[72]

Despite the obvious futility of his previous efforts Wolff-Metternich resumed his lectures to the Porte on December 9, this time choosing the grand vizier as the recipient of his strictures. Although, as the ambassador subsequently explained to Bethmann Hollweg, Said Halim was powerless to do anything about the Armenian persecutions, it was useful to supply the grand vizier with arguments he could then use on his colleagues. According to Wolff-Metternich there could be no doubt that Said Halim personally was opposed to what they were doing. Moreover there was some indication that Cemal Paşa, too, was ashamed of the atrocious treatment meted out to the Armenians and was actually making some headway in reversing the measures decreed by the central government.[73]

---

[71] FO, *Türkei 183*, Bd. 40, Wolff-Metternich to Bethmann Hollweg, 7 Dec 1915, No. 711.

[72] *Ibid.*

[73] *Ibid.*, Wolff-Metternich to Bethmann Hollweg, 9 Dec 1915, No. 714. For conflicting information about Cemal's role in the anti-Armenian program cf. Lepsius, *Deutschland*, Nos. 24, 25, 34, 107, 120, 135, 150, 163, 193; Bryce and Toynbee, No. 143 and *passim*; Djemal, pp. 277-81; Bayur, III:3, 224 and *passim*.

The Armenian Persecutions

About a week later Talât returned from his inspection tour to Constantinople. On December 18 Wolff-Metternich called on him for a "thorough" discussion of the Armenian situation. To the ambassador's surprise, the minister conceded that the anti-Armenian "security measures" of the preceding half year had hurt many innocent people, adding that the program had now run its course and that everything was being done to protect the deported families against further violence, hunger, and other misfortunes. Moreover, according to Talât, all provincial authorities had been instructed to publicize the fact that the German government had nothing to do with the anti-Armenian proceedings and that the Porte had assumed full responsibility for them. Although Wolff-Metternich was by no means fully convinced that the Porte had actually changed its course for good, he decided to accept Talât's assurances for the time being and to await further developments. As he wrote to the Wilhelmstrasse and Bethmann Hollweg, it was perhaps best to hold up the publication of the *Norddeutsche Allgemeine Zeitung* announcement, and to discontinue diplomatic steps for a while, especially since too-frequent protests would merely blunt their effectiveness.[74]

Wolff-Metternich's decision to give the Porte a chance to prove its good intentions was poorly rewarded, for exactly five days after Talât had made his soothing declarations the German embassy received a blistering note from the Porte—the first written communication concerning the Armenian issue ever received by the Germans. Referring to several official German steps of the preceding six months the Porte pointed out "first of all" that its policy towards the Armenians was a domestic issue and could therefore not be made the object of foreign diplomatic intervention except when foreign interests were directly affected. Inasmuch as the anti-Armenian measures had been and still were "dictated by military reasons and consti-

[74] FO, *Türkei 183*, Bd. 40, Wolff-Metternich to FO, 18 Dec 1915, No. 2,990; same to Bethmann Hollweg, 18 Dec, No. 725.

tute a means of legitimate defense" against subversion, the Ottoman government could not accept any responsibility for the damage which had thereby been caused to German economic interests—all the more so in that the deportation of "suspect persons" had been properly regulated by a "provisional law." German representations in this matter, the note concluded, were therefore unacceptable.[75]

There are no indications in the German government files that the Wilhelmstrasse ever tried to reply to the note. On the contrary, the ill-concealed demand of the Porte that the Germans should mind their own business appears to have confirmed the view of Germany's policy-makers, from Bethmann Hollweg on down, that they were risking entirely too much by their pleas for the Armenians. During the following months the exhortations and admonitions from Berlin became increasingly sporadic and insipid in character. More important, the timidity and passivity displayed by Wolff-Metternich's superiors seems to have affected his outlook and behavior as well. During the remainder of his tenure at Constantinople his pro-Armenian efforts were to be significantly less vigorous.

1916-17: The Policy of Expediency Continues

By the beginning of 1916 the mass deportations of the Armenian population from the east-Anatolian *vilayets* to Mesopotamian and Syrian desert regions and internment camps had largely been completed. Already a very large number of Ottoman Armenians had perished as the result of mass executions, popular massacres, maltreatment en route, undernourishment, and disease, but even the survivors of the deportation

[75] Lepsius, *Deutschland*, No. 218 and *Anlage*. The law cited by the Porte was promulgated on May 27, 1915. See *ibid.*, No. 71, and Bayur, III:3, 45-49. On the losses suffered by German firms due to the deportation of their Armenian employees or the "disappearance" of Armenian debtors, see, for example, FO, *Türkei 134*, Bd. 34, Director Gutmann (*Dresdener Bank*) to Zimmermann, 9 Dec 1915.

program faced a bleak future. Contrary to repeated Turkish assurances, little if anything was being done to provide the deportees with adequate food, clothing, and shelter, or to protect them from physical violence. Moreover, in several regions, particularly where the "evacuation" of Armenians had not been carried out completely, direct or indirect pressures were instituted by the local and provincial authorities to obtain "conversions" to the Islamic faith.[76]

Wolff-Metternich made repeated attempts in January 1916 to register his dismay with the continuing persecutions at the Porte but accomplished very little. His complaints were either treated as being groundless or brushed off with empty assurances that the Porte would look into the matter. The Wilhelmstrasse, which was regularly informed of the continuing outrages, especially by Consul Rössler in Aleppo, did absolutely nothing, nor did it bother to send any instructions to the Constantinople embassy.[77] In fact it was only in the latter half of February that the Berlin foreign office was briefly stirred out of its ostrich-like pose. Faced with a formal inquiry from the recently organized Swiss *Hilfswerk 1915 für Armenien* whether it could count on Berlin's official assistance with charitable work among the Armenian deportees, Zimmermann wrote back on February 26 that the Wilhelmstrasse would "gladly" help, though only insofar as this was possible without offending the Turks.[78] Berlin's determination not to have any more unpleasantness with the Porte over the Armenian question was even more clearly manifested when the German embassy in Washington sent word that the United States government might soon direct another appeal to the Porte concerning the Armenian persecutions. Zimmermann immediately instructed Wolff-Metternich to warn the Porte of what was coming and to counsel a

[76] Cf. Lepsius, *Der Todesgang des armenischen Volkes, passim*; Naslian, 1, 509 and *passim*.

[77] See Lepsius, *Deutschland*, Nos. 225-37.

[78] *Ibid.*, Nos. 239, 244.

conciliatory Turkish reply to the American note, but the ambassador himself was not to make any "remonstrances" of his own.[79]

Perhaps this admonition to Wolff-Metternich was not really needed. His correspondence of this time gives the distinct impression that his efforts to influence the Turks were becoming more and more perfunctory. One of his letters, addressed to Bethmann Hollweg, makes one wonder whether he had not become an outright convert to the Wilhelmstrasse's long-standing policy of caution and expediency. Recently, he wrote to the chancellor on February 14, Halil had intimated to him that Germany's failure to confer a decoration on Talât was viewed as a snub in some circles, especially since some Turks of lesser status had long since been so honored. In view of Talât's prominent role in the initiation of the "Armenian expulsions," the ambassador continued, he and his predecessors had hitherto thought it inadvisable to recommend any public honors for the minister, for they might have been interpreted as a sign that Germany approved of the Porte's Armenian policy. Now, however, such considerations "no longer" applied. On the contrary, since Talât was "the most influential minister" at the Porte, a "convinced supporter" of the alliance, and, together with Enver and Halil, particularly instrumental in keeping the Ententophile elements in the *Ittihad ve Terakki* Party at bay, the conferral of the (Prussian) Red Eagle Order First Class would be very much in order. It appears that Wolff-Metternich's superiors in Berlin, for once, had genuine scruples. It was only in 1917, after Talât had become the official head of the Ottoman cabinet, that the Kaiser deemed it politically necessary to grant him a German decoration.[80]

[79] See FO, *Türkei 183*, Bd. 41, Zimmermann to Wolff-Metternich, 23 Feb 1915, No. 268; *Foreign Relations U.S., 1916 Supplement* (Washington, 1929), pp. 847-48.

[80] FO, *Türkei 159 Nr. 2*, Bd. 14, Wolff-Metternich to Bethmann Hollweg, 14 Feb 1916, No. 67; Bd. 16, Kühlmann to FO, 22 March 1917, No. 379.

The Armenian Persecutions

After procrastinating for almost six months the Porte finally issued in early March 1916 an official denial that Germany had "suggested" or otherwise been involved in the proceedings against the Ottoman Armenians. In a lengthy declaration entitled *Vérité sur le mouvement révolutionnaire arménien et les mesures gouvernementales,* the Porte emphasized that it had "naturally" permitted no foreign "interference, in whatever form, in its internal affairs," and that this rule applied to its "friends and allies" as much as to any other foreign government.[81]

While the Wilhelmstrasse was no doubt pleased, some pro-Armenian groups in Germany and in Austria-Hungary immediately took exception to the Porte's claim that its domestic policies were its own business. On March 3 Erzberger, who had tried during a recent visit in Constantinople to dissuade both Enver and Talât from the continuation of their anti-Armenian policy, sent a memorandum to the Wilhelmstrasse, in which he listed a number of minimal demands which Berlin should "at once" press upon the Turks. Aside from the restoration of the religious institutions and privileges of the Armenians, Erzberger called for effective material assistance to the deportees, their "gradual" repatriation and "resettlement" in Asia Minor under the auspices of the Order of Maltese Knights, the suspension of the Porte's liquidation law inasmuch as it applied to Armenian property, and various other steps designed to normalize the situation of the Armenians in general and of the Roman Catholics among them in particular.[82]

Shortly after Erzberger had sent off his appeal to the Wilhelmstrasse, the archbishops of Prague and Vienna, Leon von

[81] See Lepsius, *Deutschland,* No. 245.
[82] *Ibid.,* No. 246. On Erzberger's efforts in Constantinople during the preceding month cf. *ibid.,* No. 238 and *Anlage;* his memoirs, *Erlebnisse im Weltkrieg* (Berlin, 1920), Chapter VI; and Epstein, pp. 141-42.

Skrbensky-Hrištič and F. G. Piffl, directed a similar note to the Ballhausplatz. Speaking "in the name of the entire Austrian episcopate," the two cardinals called for energetic efforts by the governments of both Central Powers to end the "horrible" situation in which "the Christian Armenians of Turkey, or rather the still surviving remnants of this nation," found themselves. To make sure that the Porte changed its policy, a mixed commission, with Turkish, Austro-Hungarian, and German members, should be established immediately to "watch over" the resettlement and adequate provisioning of the Armenian people and over the restoration of their "religious liberty." Moreover, the Porte should be reminded forcefully that it owed a change of policy not only to humanity but also to the Christian powers which happened to be its allies.[83]

Neither the Wilhelmstrasse nor the Ballhausplatz deemed it advisable to do anything with these unwelcome recommendations. The headaches of Germany's statesmen were further increased when both the Swiss *Hilfswerk* and a phalanx of German organizations—the *Orientmission, Das Notwendige Liebeswerk,* and the German-Armenian Society—moved in on the Wilhelmstrasse with concrete proposals for the launching of aid and assistance programs among the Armenian deportees. While the Swiss promoters were willing to channel their aid through Consul Rössler and other German officials already stationed in Syria and Mesopotamia, the German groups proposed the dispatch of a regular expedition to the Ottoman empire.[84]

The Wilhelmstrasse, knowing full well that the Turks would react rather unfavorably to the appearance of such an "expedition," held on to the proposal for several weeks before forwarding it to Constantinople. As for the plan of the Swiss *Hilfswerk,* it was duly transmitted to Consul Rössler (and warmly

[83] AHFM, *Türkei XLVII/4,* Cardinal von Skrbensky-Hrištič and Cardinal Piffl to AHFM, March 1916.
[84] See Lepsius, *Deutschland,* Nos. 249, 251.

approved by him), but his sanguine attitude was not shared by Wolff-Metternich. As he informed Bethmann Hollweg on March 21, the Turks had recently started with new anti-Armenian measures in various parts of the empire, and although he had already expressed his dismay at the Porte it was too early to tell how much good that would do.[85] Six days later the ambassador advised Berlin that the Swiss aid program had very little chance of success; for "despite all assurances to the contrary it looks more and more . . . as though the Porte is now getting ready to do away with the remaining deportees as well. . . ."[86]

Although his suspicions were amply confirmed in the following weeks by reports of wholesale massacres and new "Islamization" and deportation proceedings in various places, both the Wilhelmstrasse and the Ballhausplatz remained silent. It would appear that the Porte sensed the timid attitude in German and Austro-Hungarian government circles, for when the aid project of the German *Orientmission* and the other German organizations was finally brought to its attention in late April, it bluntly refused to assent to it. As Wolff-Metternich explained to Berlin on April 28, the Turks took the position that they could not permit any outside assistance programs for the Armenians, in whatever shape or form, since otherwise the "hopes" of the Armenians for help from abroad would once again increase.[87]

Despite periodic reports from Wolff-Metternich, Rössler, and other observers about continuing anti-Armenian outrages,[88] Berlin remained virtually silent throughout the following four months. With no specific instructions to go by, Wolff-Metter-

---

[85] *Ibid.*, No. 253.

[86] FO, *Türkei 183*, Bd. 41, Wolff-Metternich to Bethmann Hollweg, 27 March 1916, No. 131. See also Bd. 42, same to same, 29 March, No. 139.

[87] See Lepsius, *Deutschland*, Nos. 257, 259-61.

[88] See *ibid.*, Nos. 265, 267, 270, 275, 279-81, 283-84, 289-91, 293, 296-98.

The Armenian Persecutions

nich sent periodic admonitions to the Porte, which, of course, made no impression. Nor did the OHL have any more luck when it expressed its dismay over the deportation of Armenian work crews from the Bagdad railroad line—a Turkish measure which had caused nothing less than the complete stoppage of all construction work on the unfinished sections both in the Amanus and the Taurus regions.[89]

Although Wolff-Metternich sent Bethmann Hollweg explicit warning that "the Armenian persecutions in the eastern provinces" had entered their "final phase," he received no reply or new instructions from Berlin.[90] In Vienna, too, dead silence prevailed. When the Ballhausplatz received word from the Ottoman embassy that some clerical circles in the Hungarian Diet were reportedly planning to raise the Armenian issue on the floor of the House, and that the Primate of Hungary, Cardinal Janos Csernoch, was behind the project, Burian hastily wrote to Premier Tisza to remind him that "such an interpellation at the present time would be extremely inopportune."[91] Burian need not have worried, for Cardinal Csernoch promptly denied that he had ever thought of sponsoring such a move. He explained to Tisza that he was "incapable" of such "tactlessness," and the Ottoman embassy should be assured that "I sincerely wish to promote the good Hungarian-Turkish relationship and hope that the Turkish government persecutes none of its subjects on account of their religion, but protects them against fanaticism."[92]

[89] Ibid., Nos. 264, 268-69, 272-73, 276-78, 282, 285-86. On the vitally needed construction work on the Bagdad line see Chapter IX.

[90] FO, Türkei 183, Bd. 43, Wolff-Metternich to Bethmann Hollweg, 10 July 1916, No. 368. The major parts of this dispatch were subsequently brought to the attention of numerous German embassies abroad and also forwarded to the Prussian legations in Munich, Dresden, etc.

[91] AHFM, Türkei XLVII/4, Burian to Tisza, 28 June 1916, No. 3144.

[92] Ibid., Csernoch to Tisza, 7 July 1916; Tisza to Burian, 9 July.

In the meantime, Lepsius had completed work on a lengthy exposé of the background, course, and results of the Armenian persecutions. Printed as a manuscript, and designated as "strictly confidential" on the title page, *Bericht über die Lage des Armenischen Volkes in der Türkei* was distributed during the summer of 1916 to thousands of people in Germany, and it was only after 20,000 copies had been turned out by the Protestant *Tempelverlag* in Potsdam that the Turks found out about Lepsius' treatise. On September 9 the Wilhelmstrasse received a formal request from Ambassador Hakki to put a stop to Lepsius' "hostile agitation" and to prevent the further dissemination of his "most infamous" booklet. Apparently as a result, the German censorship authorities formally prohibited the printing and distribution of any further copies of the *Bericht*.[93]

Wilhelmstrasse compliance with the Ottoman embassy's request was understandable, for Lepsius' booklet contained a detailed and devastating account of what had happened to the Ottoman Armenians since the beginning of the war. Moreover, despite an explicit warning in the preface that the revelations in the *Bericht* must not be used for political propaganda purposes, the preface alone contained enough political dynamite to blow the whole German-Ottoman alliance to pieces—

> The oldest nation in Christendom [Lepsius informed his readers], as far as it lives under Turkish rule, is threatened by annihilation. Six-sevenths of the Armenian people have been robbed of their possessions, been expelled from house and home, and—except for those who converted to Islam— been killed or sent into the desert. Only one-seventh of the people have been exempted from deportation. . . . [Moreover], the Syrian Nestorians and, partially, the Greek Christians, too, have been plagued by persecution.[94]

[93] Cf. Lepsius, *Bericht*; "Mein Besuch in Konstantinopel," pp. 31-32; FO, *Türkei 183*, Bd. 44, Hakki to Jagow, n.d.

[94] Lepsius, *Bericht*, pp. v-vi.

These facts, Lepsius continued, were known to the German government, which had done "what it could" to stem the tide of disaster. The purpose of his *Bericht*, he said, was simply to promote an "extensive" aid program for the surviving Armenians, a program which had the full support of the Berlin government according to its own pronouncements—

> Among all the Christian nations it is primarily up to us Germans to perform Samaritan services for the unfortunate [Armenians]. We were not able to prevent the annihilation of half of the nation. Our conscience demands the rescue of the other half. Hitherto nothing could be done for those in need. Now something must be done.
>
> We ask for bread for starving women and children, for aid to the sick and dying. A people of widows and orphans stretch out their arms to the German people as the only one which is able to help them. To other Christian nations, which would be willing to help, the road to the unfortunate [Armenians] is barred.
>
> We ask not only for temporary but for permanent help. . . . We know how much the strength of all those who remained at home is taxed in meeting the most immediate requirements which are raised by the struggle for the fatherland. But this, too, involves a moral duty [*Ehrenpflicht*] for our people, and [we must give] proof that in our quest [*Willen*] for self-preservation and victory we cannot deny the dictates of humaneness and of the Christian conscience.[95]

Among the Germans whose "Christian conscience" was very acutely pricked by Lepsius' efforts was the Grand Duchess Luise of Baden, who promptly wrote to Bethmann Hollweg inquiring what was being done about the Armenian horrors. The chancellor replied on September 9 in a confidential letter to the Prussian representative at the Badensian Court, instructing him to point out to the grand duchess that the whole Ar-

[95] *Ibid.*, pp. vi-viii.

menian issue was an extremely delicate matter. As Bethmann Hollweg explained,

> During the relocation of the Armenians, which as such was probably necessary, horrible things have certainly happened, and our continuous and emphatic steps at the Porte have had only slight success. A discussion of this topic, however, could only do harm at the present moment. The already existing ill-humor against us in certain circles of Turkey—whose alliance is especially now of particular value to us—would increase still further, while the Armenians themselves would not be helped at all. On the contrary, a public discussion of the question would almost certainly incite the Moslems to new persecutions, against which we would be well-nigh powerless.[96]

Embarrassed by the noise Lepsius was making, the Wilhelmstrasse initiated steps in late September to have all his foreign travel permits revoked. As it turned out, the decision to keep Lepsius in Germany was made too late, for a full two weeks earlier he had legally crossed the Dutch border and taken up residence in Holland.[97]

Lepsius' associates in the German *Orient-Mission* and the German-Armenian Society seem initially to have been determined to follow up the *Bericht* with further pamphlets and newsletters on the plight of the Armenians, but thanks to the persuasive arguments of Ernst Jäckh they abandoned that plan. In an emotional meeting on September 15 Jäckh persuaded Rohrbach and two other leading figures of the German-Armenian Society (Pastor Stier and Dr. James Greenfield) that continued propaganda for the Armenians would do them more harm than good, and that the lot of the deportees could be im-

[96] DZA, Reichskanzlei, *Kriegsakten 22*, Bd. 1, Bethmann Hollweg to Eisendecher, 9 Sept 1916.

[97] Cf. FO, *Türkei 183*, Bd. 45, Zimmermann to Adm. von Holtzendorff, 6 Nov 1916; Lepsius, *Deutschland*, p. v.

proved much more effectively by diplomatic representations and aid programs on the part of the German government. The following day Rohrbach, Stier, and Greenfield notified Jäckh that they were willing to suspend their propagandistic efforts if everything possible was done by Berlin to help the Armenians. They added that an appeal to Lepsius and everyone else to remain silent henceforth would, however, have little chance of success unless all inculpating stories about the Ottoman Armenians disappeared from the German press and those who blamed the Armenians for their own troubles kept quiet as well.[98]

It is not entirely clear whether Jackh brought this *quid pro quo* arrangement to the attention of the Wilhelmstrasse, but it was probably more than coincidence that only a week or so later Zimmermann delivered his sharpest statement on the Armenian question. Using the presence of Halil Bey in Berlin, he told the Ottoman foreign minister to his face that while some of the deportations in the past might conceivably have been justified in terms of the then prevailing military situation, the currently "planned measures against women and children, who constitute the sad remnants of the Armenian people, could in no way be justified or excused."[99]

As previously mentioned, the Porte had meanwhile succeeded in obtaining Wolff-Metternich's recall. During the next six weeks the representation of German interests in Constantinople was left in the hands of Legation Counsellor von Rado-

---

[98] See Jäckh Papers, No. 23, Jäckh to Lepsius, 11 Sept 1916; Rohrbach to Jäckh, 16 Sept; Frau Lepsius to Jäckh, 22 Sept. On Jäckh's rather ambiguous role in the whole Armenian tragedy cf. his own statements in *Rising Crescent*, pp. 42-47 and *passim*; and in his memoirs, *Der Goldene Pflug* (Stuttgart, 1954), pp. 232-33 and *passim*.

[99] FO, *Türkei 183*, Bd. 44, Memorandum by Zimmermann, 25 Sept 1916. Regarding a similarly outspoken critique of the Porte's policies which Jagow presented to the budget committee of the Reichstag four days later, see *ibid.*, Rosenberg to Zimmermann, 27 Sept ("Aufzeichnung über die Armenierfrage . . . für den Reichstag"); Lepsius, *Deutschland*, No. 300.

witz. As *chargé*, Radowitz apparently did not think it advisable to get too deeply involved in the potentially explosive Armenian business and restricted himself to forwarding periodic reports on the subject to his superiors in Berlin.[100] The only ray of light in this somber spectacle of German passivity was provided by Liman von Sanders, who intervened energetically against the initiation of Armenian deportations in Smyrna. Using his authority as Fifth Army commander (some of his troops were garrisoned in Smyrna), Liman informed the *vali* of the province on November 10 that the mass movement of Armenians interfered with military security requirements, and that he would use troops to stop the police if it continued with the roundup of Armenians. When the *vali* notified Liman that the deportations were being carried out at the behest of the central government, the general reiterated his veto and suggested that the *vali* get himself some new instructions from Constantinople.[101]

At the Wilhelmstrasse Liman's unorthodox intervention in the "domestic affairs" of the Ottoman ally was welcomed, and Radowitz received instructions to back up the general by appropriate steps at the Porte. There are some indications, however, that the leading men at the Wilhelmstrasse did not really have much hope that the Turks would actually abandon their original project, for on November 15 Jagow sent an inquiry to the Constantinople embassy whether it might not be possible to send the Smyrna Armenians to Germany. Kühlmann, who had meanwhile arrived in Constantinople to take over the embassy, wired back two days later that the diversion of Armenian deportees to Germany could hardly be suggested to the Porte without arousing fresh "suspicions" among the Turks,

[100] See *ibid.*, Nos. 301-304.
[101] FO, *Türkei 183*, Bd. 45, Radowitz to Bethmann Hollweg, 13 Nov 1916, No. 703; Liman to Embassy Constantinople, 17 Nov, B. Nr. 1950 geh.

and that he would try his best to stabilize the situation in Smyrna. Whether he actually took up the matter at the Porte is doubtful, but a diplomatic move was for once not needed, since the Smyrna deportations were shortly thereafter officially cancelled.[102]

Faced with renewed appeals from the United States government and German clerical circles for forceful steps, the Wilhelmstrasse instructed the Constantinople embassy on November 14 and again on Christmas Day 1916 to point out to the Porte that a relaxation of its anti-Armenian policy was overdue.[103] On January 4, 1917 Legation Counsellor Göppert thereupon presented a note to Halil which once again expressed the regret and disapproval of the German government with regard to the continuing "acts of violence" and the forcible conversion of Armenians "in the provinces." In the ensuing conversation the Ottoman foreign minister agreed to work for the immediate cessation of forcible conversions but declared it impossible and impracticable to undo what had already been done in that sphere as this would probably entail "new deportations." Once the war was over, he consoled Göppert, the involuntary converts would certainly have an opportunity to return to the Christian faith, just as had happened after the persecutions in the time of Abdülhamid II.[104]

Although Talât's leading role in the Armenian persecutions of the preceding years was patently obvious to anyone who

---

[102] *Ibid.*, Zimmermann to Radowitz, 14 Nov 1916, No. 1,226; Jagow to Kühlmann, 15 Nov, No. 1,301; Kühlmann to Bethmann Hollweg, 17 Nov, No. 710; same to FO, 17 Nov, No. 1,209; Lepsius, *Deutschland*, No. 308.

[103] FO, *Türkei 183*, Bd. 45, Zimmermann to Kühlmann, 14 Nov 1916, No. 1,226; *Missionsdirektor* Karl Axenfeld to Bethmann Hollweg, 16 Nov; Kühlmann to Bethmann Hollweg, 25 Nov, No. 723; Zimmermann to Göppert, 25 Dec, No. 1,410.

[104] *Ibid.*, Bd. 46, Göppert to FO, 5 Jan 1917, No. 17; Lepsius, *Deutschland*, No. 311. (Kühlmann was on leave at this time.)

knew what was going on at the Porte, his elevation to the grand vizier's post on February 4, 1917 was at first greeted by Kühlmann as an event which might produce a drastic improvement for the Ottoman Armenians. His rather naïve reaction was mainly based on Talât's opening speech in Parliament on February 15, during which he had announced his cabinet's intention to provide "every Osmanli" with all the rights which "the Constitution grants to him and thus to secure the rule of law in the country." To heighten Kühlmann's euphoria Talât assured him on February 24 in a personal interview that he "intended to steer a new course in all questions" pertaining to the non-Turkish nationalities, and that he had already informed the leaders of the Armenian churches that the war-related measures of the past two years would be reversed.[105]

As so often before, the assurances of the Porte proved worthless. Although in most *vilayets* there were no further deportations, very little was changed in the policy of purposeful neglect of the destitute masses of deportees. Moreover, in several areas efforts at the forcible Islamization of Armenians continued much as before.[106]

The plight of the surviving Armenian deportees in Mesopotamia and Syria can be gleaned from a series of surveys which the German consulates in Aleppo, Beirut, Damascus, and Mosul undertook during the spring of 1917. In the Aleppo area Consul Rössler found about 45,000 deportees, 35,000 of whom were in "extreme need, many close to starvation." In the Beirut district the situation was less critical, though there was a large incidence of "conversions" to Islam. The consulate in Damascus estimated that approximately 30,000 Armenians in its sphere of authority were still alive, most of them being in a "deplorable condition." The number of Armenian deportees in the Mosul area, according to Consul Wustrow, amounted to about

[105] Lepsius, *Deutschland*, Nos. 317, 318. The text of Talât's speech is reproduced in *Schulthess*, v. 58:2, 815-16.
[106] Lepsius, *Deutschland*, p. xlv.

8,000, "mainly women and children." He understood, moreover, that many additional women and girls were living in
"semi-slavery" among some of the desert and mountain
tribes.[107]

Although most of the German consulates in the eastern provinces were by this time actively involved in various privately
financed charity programs—with the money coming from
German, Swiss, American, and other sources—these efforts to
keep the Armenian deportees alive were only partially successful. There were numerous cases of passive or active resistance
by the local or provincial officials, though in some areas the Ottoman authorities cooperated rather well and allowed the distribution of food and other aid measures.[108]

In August 1917 the military governor of the Syrian provinces, Navy Minister Cemal Paşa, came to Berlin on the invitation of the German government. Since Cemal was increasingly
being suspected by Enver and other key figures at the Porte of
spinning intrigues against them, the visit was at least partially
arranged to remove him temporarily from the Ottoman capital (where he had appeared in defiance of Enver's and Talât's
wishes). While staying in Berlin, Cemal received some of the
directors of the German *Evangelische Missionshilfe*, who appealed to him for support of their charitable work among the
Armenians. Cemal readily promised to help within his sphere
of authority—Syria—and assured them that he would also attempt to exert a positive influence in other regions. There is
reason to believe that Cemal's offer was sincere, but since he
gave up his Syrian command a few months later, the agreement bore very little fruit.[109]

---

[107] See *ibid.*, Nos. 329-33.

[108] Cf. *ibid.*, Nos. 315, 325-27, 336-44, 346-51, 357-59, 361; and Vahe
E. Sarafian, "World War I American Relief for the Armenians,"
Armenian Review, x:2 (June 1957), 121-36; x:3 (Sept 1957), 133-45,
and *passim*.

[109] FO, *Türkei 159 Nr. 2*, Bd. 17, Lersner to FO, 18 Aug 1917, No.

The Armenian Persecutions

With the disintegration of the Russian Caucasian Army in the autumn of 1917 and the Bolshevik request for a ceasefire agreement, the vexing "Armenian Question" assumed a new dimension; for hundreds of thousands of Armenians, including numerous refugees from the Ottoman empire, were sitting behind the crumbling Russian front.

Shortly before the conclusion of the Brest-Litovsk Armistice Talât "confidentially" informed Berlin that the Porte intended to grant a general amnesty and financial assistance to the Armenians "if it came to a separate peace with Russia." Although this was certainly good news, there were some circles in the Reich who were thoroughly disinclined to believe in any basic change of Turkish policy. On December 31 Reichstag deputy Reinhard Mumm of the *Deutsche Fraktion*, formally appealed to the Wilhelmstrasse to make sure that the Armenians in areas to be evacuated by the Russians would not be victimized by the Turks. Once the Ottoman army moved into those areas, he proposed, German officers and consular officials should probably go right along with them and thus keep an eye on the Turks. A week later, Rohrbach and other officers of the German-Armenian Society approached the new chancellor, Georg Count von Hertling, with an even more far-reaching proposal. They requested adequate German protection of the Armenians in the erstwhile Russian areas as well as positive German support for the establishment of Armenian autonomy. Since the Turks were pursuing a program of Pan-Islamism,

---

1,232; Waldburg to FO, 24 Aug, No. 1,017; Lepsius, *Deutschland*, No. 360. Regarding Cemal's previous efforts to soften the anti-Armenian measures in his sphere of authority, cf. above, note 73; and Sarafian, "World War I American Relief," x:2, 126 and *passim*. There is disappointingly little information on this question in Avedis K. Sanjian's recent *The Armenian Communities in Syria under Ottoman Dominion* (Cambridge, Mass., 1965).

they emphasized, it was essential for Germany to manifest its Christian solidarity with the Armenians.[110]

The situation in Transcaucasia in the weeks following the Brest-Litovsk Armistice was highly unstable; there were numerous clashes between armed Armenian bands and the Moslem populace in some districts. At the beginning of February 1918 the Ottoman news agency *Milli-Agence* issued a lengthy statement on the alleged atrocities the Armenians had committed in the areas behind the armistice line. At the behest of some of the pro-Armenian organizations in Germany, which suspected that the agency report was to serve as a pretext for a new wave of Turkish "countermeasures," the Wilhelmstrasse instructed Bernstorff on February 8 to warn the Porte emphatically against a revival of indiscriminate persecution. Once they marched back into the Russian-held part of the empire, Undersecretary Hilmar von dem Bussche said, the Turks must maintain "strictest discipline, refrain from all reprisal measures," and institute judicial proceedings solely against those Armenians who had actually "participated in crimes against the Moslem population." Bernstorff replied with a number of reassuring messages, pointing out that Gen. von Seeckt was keeping an eye on Enver and that Halil had assured him that the Ottoman troops were under strict orders not to engage in reprisals.[111]

On February 14, two days after Ottoman army units had begun crossing the Transcaucasian demarcation line, the Wilhelmstrasse forwarded to Bernstorff a petition from the German *Evangelische Missions-Ausschuss* which called for forceful steps to prevent renewed Turkish outrages against the Armenians. Two weeks later Bussche himself instructed Bern-

---

[110] FO, *Türkei 183*, Bd. 49, Bernstorff to FO, 11 Dec 1917, No. 1,617; Mumm to FO, 31 Dec; Rohrbach, Stier and Rade to Hertling, 6 Jan 1918.

[111] See above, pp. 171-73; and FO, *Türkei 183*, Bd. 49, Bussche to Bernstorff, 8 Feb 1918, No. 194; Bernstorff to FO, 10 Feb, No. 194; 11 Feb, No. 202.

storff to impress on Talât, Enver, and other Turkish leaders that it was definitely in their own interest to demonstrate to all the world that the Ottoman government meant to give "equal, mild, and just treatment" to all the people in the provinces which were now being reoccupied. Bussche thought a good start would be for the Porte to grant a general amnesty to the Armenians, including those who had hitherto borne arms.

> Quite aside from the fact that further, and possibly heavy, fighting could thus be avoided, [an amnesty] constitutes the only viable point of departure for converting the Armenians —who are an indispensable and valuable population element of those provinces—once again into loyal subjects of Turkey. ... It would also be desirable to take into consideration the repatriation of those Armenians who had been deported to the interior of the empire.

Bernstorff immediately wired back that he had been pushing that kind of program "for months," albeit so far without much success. However, it appeared that the Porte was gradually becoming more responsive, for Talât had just promised again that an amnesty would soon be proclaimed.[112]

Although little reliable information about conditions in the reoccupied Ottoman provinces had reached the outside world, the Vatican decided at the beginning of March to direct formal appeals to both the Reich government and the Porte on behalf of the Armenians in Transcaucasia. Four days after Pacelli had presented such an appeal to the Wilhelmstrasse, Monsignore Dolci, the papal representative in Constantinople, advised Bernstorff that he was about to deliver a similar note to the Porte. The ambassador immediately wired to Bucharest (where both Kühlmann and Talât were staying in connection with the Rumanian peace negotiations) and urged that the

---

[112] See Lepsius, *Deutschland*, Nos. 370-71; FO, *Wk 15*, Bd. 27, Bussche to Bernstorff, 2 March 1918, No. 322; Bernstorff to FO, 3 March, No. 300.

often promised Turkish amnesty decree or some other reassuring proclamation be issued forthwith. Talât refused to be "rushed" but finally assured Kühlmann that on his return to Constantinople he would definitely act on the matter.

In Germany, Chancellor Hertling had meanwhile drafted a fairly evasive reply to the appeal from the Vatican. He pointed out that Germany was as always intent on preventing Turco-Armenian troubles, but added that the existence of armed Armenian bands in Transcaucasia and their outrages against the Moslem population made it very difficult to keep the situation under control. Indeed, if the Vatican really wanted to help it should persuade the Entente governments to stop their agitation among the Armenians.[113]

On March 18, shortly after the Congress of Soviets in Moscow had formally ratified the Brest-Litovsk Peace, the German Reichstag began its discussion of the treaty. While the parties of the Right and the Center were openly jubilant at having achieved peace in the east on their own terms, the Majority Socialists and, more vociferously, the Independent Socialists (SPD) severely criticized the settlement. On March 19, in a scathing attack on the *Vergewaltigungsfrieden* that had been imposed on the Bolsheviks, the SPD deputy, Georg Ledebour, took issue with the de facto surrender of the Kars, Ardahan, and Batum districts to the Turks. Ethnographically, he emphasized, the Turks had no claim to these areas, and once they marched in they were likely to exterminate the "Armenian and Georgian population" there just as they had "nearly exterminated" the Armenians in Anatolia during the previous years. To prevent new massacres Berlin and Vienna should veto Ottoman occupation of the three districts and if necessary arrange for the protection of the native population by neutral troop contingents, such as from Sweden or Switzerland. Since there was some doubt whether the Reich government had the necessary determination to prevent renewed Armenian mas-

[113] FO, *Türkei 183*, Bd. 50, Bernstorff to FO, 13 March 1918, No. 350; Hertling to Pacelli, 14 March; Lepsius, *Deutschland*, No. 378.

sacres, Ledebour concluded, it was now up to the Reichstag to see to it that appropriate steps for "the protection of these threatened peoples" were taken.[114]

Possibly in response to this challenge, the staff of the Wilhelmstrasse drew up a lengthy memorandum on the Armenian question, which Bussche used in his talks with Reichstag leaders during the following days. In defining the standpoint of the foreign office, the memorandum noted (1) that everything possible had been done to prevent the renewal of Armenian persecutions; (2) that the Porte itself had repeatedly indicated its benign intentions; and (3) that the restoration of peace and order in the Armenian areas would ultimately depend on the willingness of the Armenians themselves to abandon "their striving for independence and to respond to the Turks' offer of reconciliation." Indeed, Berlin's official efforts to prevent any untoward developments in Transcaucasia could best be helped "if the German Armenophiles were to use their influence to warn the Armenians against useless resistance—which would be tantamount to suicide—and to induce them instead to negotiate with the Turks about their submission."[115]

While this official policy statement appears to have influenced a slight majority of the Reichstag's Main Committee in its ultimate decision not to demand the exclusion of Ottoman troops from the Kars, Ardahan, and Batum districts, the mood in the Finance Committee was considerably more pessimistic. According to the notes made by one of its members, Hans P. Hanssen, several of his colleagues manifested deep concern over the possibility of renewed Turkish outrages, while Gustav Stresemann expressed cautious hope that the Porte had changed its ways. The only speaker who tried to defend the Turks, according to Hanssen, was the *Mitteleuropa* proponent Friedrich Naumann.[116]

---

[114] *Verhandlungen des Reichstags*, vol. 311, pp. 4,483-84.

[115] FO, *Türkei 183*, Bd. 50, "Aufzeichnung," 19 March 1918.

[116] Cf. *Verhandlungen des Reichstags*, vol. 311, pp. 4,565-66; Hanssen, pp. 269-71.

The Armenian Persecutions

When the Reichstag resumed debate in plenary session on March 22 the USPD once again lashed out against the Transcaucasian clause of the Brest-Litovsk Treaty. Hugo Haase reminded the house of the mass slaughter the Turks had perpetrated in the preceding years and emphasized anew that the USPD would never accept the responsibility for "playing areas with an Armenian population into the hands" of the Porte. After Stresemann had argued in rebuttal that the troubles of the Ottoman Armenians had been caused largely by their own "conduct . . . in the border districts during the first months of this world war," and that Germany did not have the means or the right to force its will on the Ottoman ally, Haase reiterated his contention that the Reich must not "deliver new groups of Armenians" to the Turks, especially not by means of a "policy of annexations." His protest was forcefully supported by Ledebour, who declared that the "shame" of the Brest-Litovsk Treaty was nowhere more evident than in the clauses concerning Transcaucasia.

As the USPD had suspected all along, its protests were disregarded. After the official spokesman of the Main Committee had assured the House that the government possessed firm pledges from the Porte concerning the prevention of new anti-Armenian outrages, the debate moved to other parts of the treaty. In the final vote on the ratification of the Brest-Litovsk settlement only the USPD cast a negative vote, while the Majority Socialists abstained.[117]

While domestic opposition to the surrender of the Kars, Ardahan, and Batum districts had thus been overcome quite easily, the Wilhelmstrasse redoubled its efforts to keep the Turks on the straight and narrow. On March 24 Bussche reminded Bernstorff that he should do everything possible to stop the continuing campaign in the Ottoman press against

[117] *Verhandlungen des Reichstags*, vol. 311, pp. 4,543, 4,545, 4,553-54, 4,560-71, and *passim*; Wheeler-Bennett, pp. 304-308; Fischer, *Weltmacht*, pp. 662-65.

the Armenians of Transcaucasia. On April 3 he followed up with instructions to the ambassador that he should keep pressure on the Porte and make sure that the commanders of the advancing Ottoman troops in Transcaucasia were "again forcefully reminded" to maintain strict discipline and to accord "mild treatment to the peaceful population."[118]

Though the Wilhelmstrasse was by now certainly doing everything it could do diplomatically to remind the Turks of their obligations, some circles in Germany were obviously not convinced of the efficacy of such measures. On April 2 the Archbishop of Cologne, Felix Cardinal von Hartmann, sent a personal exhortation to Hertling to protect the Armenians in Transcaucasia and to assign a German officer to that area for purposes of supervision. The chancellor replied on April 13 that the Porte had already pledged itself to pursue a reasonable policy, but that it would be rather difficult to prevent all untoward incidents in view of the old animosities which existed between the various ethnic groups in Transcaucasia.[119]

No sooner had Hertling dispatched this rather pessimistic reply than Berlin received two radio messages from Soviet Foreign Commissar G. V. Chicherin and the "Armenian National Council" in Moscow accusing the Ottoman Caucasus Army of murderous outrages and demanding prompt German intervention. The Wilhelmstrasse ordered Bernstorff to check the Bolshevik charges and protest to the Porte if they proved to be accurate.

We must insist [Bussche wired] that Turkey shall treat the Christian population with fairness and respect their rights in every way. We are also entitled to be kept informed by the Turks about all developments in the areas in question. Your Excellency should speak in this sense to the grand vizier and

[118] FO, *Türkei 183*, Bd. 50, Bussche to Bernstorff, 24 March 1918, No. 430; 3 April, No. 482.

[119] *Ibid.*, Archbishop Hartmann to Hertling, 2 April 1918; Hertling to Hartmann, 13 April.

the minister of foreign affairs and remind Talât of his promise that an amnesty for the Armenians would be decreed soon after his return from Bucharest.[120]

Bernstorff replied within 24 hours that he "believed" the charges by Moscow to be false, and noted that Seeckt and several other German officials were presently en route to Transcaucasia with Enver. The Wilhelmstrasse, suspecting the worst, had meanwhile also contacted the OHL and requested the dispatch of some "influential" German officers to Transcaucasia to keep an eye on the Ottoman troop commanders there. The OHL sympathized with this proposal but later changed its mind when Seeckt made it clear that Gen. Vehib was highly unlikely to tolerate any German snooping in his area of command.[121]

More encouraging news came from Bernstorff on April 25. He reported Talât's assurance to him that an "amnesty for peaceful Armenians plus financial grants and permission for [their] return home" would soon be announced, and that Berlin could publicize these plans if it wished. Upon Bussche's request for more details the ambassador explained that the proposed amnesty would apply only to those Armenians who were already effectively under Ottoman control; to bring back the others, according to Talât, would be too "dangerous." As for the intended financial assistance to Armenian "returnees," the Porte meant to compensate those who had "lost their possessions."[122]

Once again the declarations by the Porte proved to be meaningless. Although there were some instances of official "mag-

---

[120] *Ibid.*, Chicherin and Karachan to FO, 13 April 1918; *ibid.*, Bd. 51, Bussche to Bernstorff, 15 April, No. 561; Lepsius, *Deutschland*, No. 382; Kadichev, p. 57.

[121] See FO, *Türkei 183*, Bd. 51, Bernstorff to FO, 15 April 1918, No. 527; 16 April, No. 535; Bussche to Lersner, 16 April, No. 690; Berckheim to FO, 7 May; Seeckt, pp. 25-26.

[122] Lepsius, *Deutschland*, Nos. 384-86.

nanimity," as exemplified by the release of captured Armenian soldiers in Batum, the promised resettlement of the Armenian deportees in their old homes never materialized; nor was there any noticeable improvement in the treatment and care of most of the deportees. Moreover, rumors and unconfirmed reports about Turkish brutality in some of the newly occupied areas continued to reach Berlin.[123]

Confronted with the swift disintegration of the Transcaucasian federative state, Kühlmann instructed Bernstorff on May 26 to remind the Porte that Germany was opposed to any further Ottoman advances into Transcaucasia and expected, in any case, proper treatment of the Armenians in all "Turkish-occupied territories." A few days later the state secretary inquired in Constantinople what was holding up the promised amnesty; since Berlin had already announced the impending Turkish step, it was high time for the Porte to act. Talât, predictably, did not respond.[124]

In the meantime the newly created Armenian Republic had opened an office of ill-defined diplomatic status in Berlin. Headed by Dr. H. Ohandjanian, this "Delegation of the Armenian Republic" initiated a lively correspondence with the Wilhelmstrasse concerning the protection of the new state by the Reich and succeeded in securing numerous interviews with Kühlmann's staff. On June 15 and again on July 2 the Delegation presented lengthy memoranda to the Wilhelmstrasse concerning the pressing need for German intervention in Transcaucasia. According to the note of July 2 an estimated 600,000 Armenians from the formerly Russian parts of Transcaucasia, as well as innumerable refugees of Ottoman citizenship, had crowded into the Armenian Republic in their flight from the advancing Turks. To prevent general economic chaos, famine, and epidemics, it was essential to get all these refugees

[123] Cf. *ibid.*, Nos. 391, 393, 395; FO, *Türkei 183*, Bd. 51, Bernstorff to FO, 2 May 1918, No. 632.
[124] Lepsius, *Deutschland*, Nos. 396-97.

back to their original homes, but this could be accomplished only if the Turks withdrew to the frontiers fixed at Brest-Litovsk. German pressure on the Turks would thus be highly welcome.[125]

On July 10 Gen. Kress in Tiflis supported the case of the Armenian government, especially since he had just received a reliable first-hand account of the critical situation in Armenia from the Bishop of Yerevan, Mesrop. There could be no doubt, Kress informed the Wilhelmstrasse, that the Turks intended "to starve the entire Armenian nation by sealing it off completely." All his efforts to secure the readmission of Armenian refugees into Turkish-occupied territory had been in vain, and "massive pressure by the Central Powers" on the Porte was therefore "an urgent commandment of humanity and policy." The next day Kress wrote directly to Chancellor Hertling, urging him to use every available means to force the Porte into a change of policy and to secure the following concessions:

> that [the Ottoman government] withdraws its troops from Armenia forthwith; allows the fugitive Armenians to return to their homeland; makes sure that the Armenians can bring in their harvest without hindrance or threat to their life and property; and that the Armenians who have been pressed into labor services shall be released to their homeland at once.[126]

By the time these messages from Tiflis reached Berlin several representatives of the Georgian, Armenian, and Azerbaijani governments had journeyed to Constantinople for a conference called by the Porte. While the Turks had initially indicated that they wished to discuss, and possibly to revise, the Batum peace treaties of June 4, the assembled delegations from Tiflis, Yerevan, and Elizavetpol soon found out that the Porte was

---

[125] See FO, *Türkei 183*, Bd. 52, Ohandjanian to FO, 2 July 1918.

[126] *Ibid.*, Bd. 53, Kress to FO, 10 July 1918; same to Hertling, 11 July.

actually in no hurry to deal with them.[127] While the Georgian government, under the protection of German troops, could well afford to wait, the isolated Armenian government in Yerevan was highly disturbed by the procrastinating tactics of the Turks. In response to its appeals for German support and the previously mentioned reports from Gen. Kress, the OHL proposed to the Wilhelmstrasse on July 15 that continued efforts should be made to secure some political stability in Transcaucasia. In particular it would be desirable to define "to some extent" the general relationship between the Central Powers bloc and the Armenian and Azerbaijani republics, whose status was as yet rather nebulous. Simultaneously Ludendorff announced the OHL's desire to concentrate henceforth solely on the "military aspects" of the Transcaucasian problem, while the Wilhelmstrasse should handle all pertinent political questions. As for the protection of the Armenian Republic against possible Turkish violence, Ludendorff thought it advisable to leave that job to the Dual Monarchy. Just as the Reich had done in Georgia, Austria-Hungary should send some battalions and batteries to the Armenian Republic to shield the population there against "Turco-Tartarian massacres." In addition the OHL found it desirable that the Armenian armed forces themselves be organized into an effective fighting instrument.[128]

While Ludendorff was inclined to leave the defense of Armenia to the Austrians and the Armenians themselves, the Berlin foreign office continued to investigate the feasibility of moving German troops to Yerevan as well. One problem, of course, was the likelihood of new complications with the Soviet government, though some officials at the Wilhelmstrasse were hopeful that Moscow would accept the presence of German soldiers in Armenia if it was made clear that they had the purely

---

[127] Cf. Kazemzadeh, p. 152; Pomiankowski, pp. 366-67; Avalishvili, pp. 87-88.

[128] Lepsius, *Deutschland*, Nos. 409-10. See also Nos. 407-408.

humanitarian task of "saving the remnants of the Armenian people." The deliberations on this subject were still in progress when Bernstorff sent word that the Armenian government delegates in Constantinople had approached him with the request for the dispatch of "Austrian or German police troops" to the Armenian Republic. A week later, the ambassador sent a follow-up message in which he noted that the Armenian calls for German or Austrian troops were becoming more and more insistent.[129]

From Tiflis Gen. Kress meanwhile bombarded the Wilhelmstrasse with urgent requests to do something about the repatriation of the destitute Armenian refugees, that is, to force the Porte into letting them move back to their original homes. On July 27 State Secretary Hintze therefore instructed Bernstorff to make "forceful representations" to the Porte. Two days later Field Marshal Hindenburg backed up Hintze's demand in a personal message to Enver. Half a million of his fellow Christians in Armenia, Hindenburg noted, were facing certain death by starvation unless the Ottoman authorities permitted them to return to their homes; "now that you have been informed of the situation among the Armenians by me, I am confident that Your Excellency shall not hesitate for a moment to give the strictest orders [permitting repatriation] and to supervise their implementation."[130]

The following day Bernstorff advised Berlin that the Porte had finally seen fit to clarify its stand on the Transcaucasian issues and was now willing—despite Enver's objections—to permit a selective repatriation of Armenian refugees. As for the border revisions desired by both Georgia and Armenia, the Porte had so far manifested a "completely intransigent" attitude, and further diplomatic pressures were obviously useless.

[129] See *ibid.*, No. 414; FO, *Türkei 183*, Bd. 53, Bernstorff to FO, 18 July 1918, No. 1,158; 25 July, no No.
[130] Lepsius, *Deutschland*, Nos. 417, 419.

If Germany did not wish to accept the existing situation, Bernstorff concluded, there was only one possible remedy, namely to "send more [German] troops to Armenia and Georgia."[131]

Concurrent with Bernstorff's dispatch, the Wilhelmstrasse received a formal note from the Armenian Delegation in Berlin, officially requesting German military help once again. With the Turks constantly moving into Armenian territory, the note emphasized, there was mounting misery among the refugees. The only solution was the "immediate evacuation of our territory by the Turks and the dispatch of German troops," whose task it would be to protect the population against the Turks and "organize and supervise the return of the refugees to their homes."[132]

As already noted, the OHL was unwilling to move German troops into Armenia—and that more or less settled the matter. On the other hand, Hindenburg and Ludendorff had already made it clear that they favored the prompt repatriation of Armenian refugees and that they expected Enver to act accordingly. They soon found out that the vice-generalissimo was in no mood to oblige them.

In a lengthy reply to Hindenburg's appeal Enver pointed out that large-scale repatriation measures were not possible since otherwise new turmoil in the rear areas of the Ottoman army would develop. Only in those places where there had been no previous "fighting between Moslems and Armenians" could one expect peace and order after the return of the refugees; elsewhere new bloodshed would surely materialize and force the Ottoman army to divert its forces for pacification tasks. The result would be the forced cessation of all military operations; "our war effort would be paralyzed," something the OHL surely did not want. As for the Armenians in Baku, Enver concluded sarcastically, he was glad to oblige Germany and to have them moved to the territory of the Armenian Re-

[131] *Ibid.*, No. 418.

[132] FO, *Türkei 183*, Bd. 53, Ohandjanian to FO, 29 July 1918.

public, for it would thus be all the easier for the Turks to come to an understanding with the remaining Russian elements in the oil city.[133]

While the OHL and the Wilhelmstrasse thus found themselves once again rebuffed, Gen. Kress and his Austro-Hungarian counterpart in Tiflis, Baron von Franckenstein, had meanwhile taken matters into their own hands and staged a personal appearance in the capital of the floundering Armenian Republic. After traveling by train through "Turkish-occupied territory without serious molestation," they arrived at Yerevan on July 30 and spent the next 24 hours in a hectic round of conferences and banquets with the political and ecclesiastic leaders of the republic. While Kress's subsequent reports to Berlin made it clear that his sympathies for the Armenians were reinforced by what he saw and heard, he did not consider it politic to remain in Yerevan for the opening of the Armenian Parliament. As he explained to Hertling after his return to Tiflis, his personal appearance at that solemn act would have aroused false hopes among the Armenians concerning the help they might get from Germany—and, after all, he himself did not even know what Berlin's "Armenian policy" was all about. One thing was certain, though, he continued, and that was the imminence of mass starvation in Armenia unless the Central Powers intervened and forced the Turks to relax their stranglehold. Moreover, it was indispensable to ship grain from the Central Powers' stores to Armenia, preferably, according to Kress, from stocks earmarked for the Turks, for the latter had caused all the trouble in the first place by preventing the Armenians from bringing in their harvest:

> The question as to what must be done in order to make Armenia a viable state and to enable it to lead an independent existence in affiliation [*unter Anlehnung*] with one of the Central Powers I should answer as follows: that Armenia

[133] *Ibid.*, Bernstorff to FO [Enver to Hindenburg], 3 Aug 1918, No. 1,255.

must get the borders of the Brest-Litovsk Treaty and that the border revisions desired by the Turks shall not be granted. Exactly these border revisions would deprive Armenia of its best border areas. If these areas are surrendered to the Turks, their production will drop immediately because of the economic inefficiency of the Turks and will thus be lost for the German market.[134]

While Kress was doing his best to direct Berlin's attention to the plight of the Armenian Republic, using economic arguments for good measure, representatives of the Yerevan government continued to bombard both Berlin and Vienna with requests for military assistance and—more importantly—for diplomatic recognition of Armenia's sovereignty. On August 10 Burian notified the Wilhelmstrasse that he was inclined to assign a diplomatic representative to Yerevan and thought Germany should do likewise. In line with previous decisions the Wilhelmstrasse politely refused. According to an internal office memorandum drawn up for Hintze's guidance, compliance with Vienna's proposal would entail new unpleasantness with the Porte and problems with Moscow, since Germany had committed herself by the Brest-Litovsk Treaty not to support separatist tendencies in the formerly Russian Empire. However, if Vienna sent both military aid and a diplomatic representative to Yerevan, Germany should certainly not object. Hintze agreed with this reasoning and Vienna was notified accordingly.[135]

Although it turned a deaf ear to Armenia's requests for diplomatic recognition, the Wilhelmstrasse continued to search for ways in which the physical plight of the Armenians could be alleviated. Aside from encouraging the Austrians to

[134] See *ibid.*, Bd. 54, Kress to Hertling, 4 Aug 1918; same to same, 5 Aug; Franckenstein to Burian, 4 Aug.

[135] Cf. *ibid.*, Bd. 53, Ohandjanian to FO, 5 Aug 1918; Burian to Hohenlohe, 9 Aug; Memorandum by Göppert (?) to Hintze, 11 Aug; Bd. 54, note by same, 20 Aug; Pomiankowski, pp. 369-70.

dispatch some of their own troops to Yerevan, Berlin suggested
to Kress on August 14 that the population pressure in the Armenian Republic might be reduced by channeling the refugees
there "toward the north," into Georgia. Six days later Hintze
sent an inquiry to Kress whether the transshipment of grain
for Armenia through Georgia would be politically feasible in
view of the fact that "we can supply the Georgians themselves
only with an amount smaller than originally promised."[136]

Confronted with new demands by Kress that Berlin do something about the stranglehold the Turks had forged around Armenia, Hintze instructed Bernstorff on August 22 to appeal
once again to the Porte for a change of policy. According to
all available evidence, Hintze noted, the Ottoman military
authorities in Transcaucasia were purposely sabotaging the
official program of selective repatriation, and Bernstorff should
therefore press for corrective action. Moreover, "You should
ask the Turkish government . . . to consider once more whether
there are not weighty reasons for opening the entire area up to
the Brest borderline for repatriation [of the Armenians]." That
Hintze did not really expect any tangible results from this new
diplomatic effort can be gathered from a note he subsequently
sent to Kress, advising him that the prevailing political and
military situation was hardly auspicious for securing concessions from the Porte.[137]

On August 28, one day after the signing of the Russo-German Supplementary Treaties, Bernstorff advised Berlin that
the Armenian delegation in Constantinople regarded the imminent recognition of Georgia's independence by Germany

[136] Lepsius, *Deutschland*, Nos. 428-30. See also FO, *Türkei 183*, Bd.
54, Axenfeld to FO, 16 Aug 1918, in which the dispatch of 300 carloads of wheat to Yerevan was proposed.

[137] *Ibid.*, Kress to FO and OHL, 10 Aug 1918, No. 46; Hintze to
Bernstorff, 22 Aug, No. 1,345; Lepsius, *Deutschland*, No. 433. See also
FO, *Russland 97a*, Bd. 23, Bernstorff to Hertling, 24 Aug, No. 216,
regarding a futile appeal by Seeckt to Enver to permit the partial
repatriation of Armenian refugees.

as a catastrophic blow to their own country, since it would thereby be totally isolated from Russia and become an easy prey for the Turks. In view of this mortal danger and the Porte's persistent refusal to commit itself on Armenia's future status, the Armenian delegation in Constantinople now was seriously interested in close affiliation of their country with Georgia. The crucial question was whether the Georgians themselves would agree to such a merger.[138]

It appears that Bernstorff sympathized with this Armenian project, but his superiors in Berlin were rather less impressed. As Hintze reminded the ambassador, neither a diplomatic recognition of Armenia nor assistance with a Georgian-Armenian merger were compatible with Germany's treaty obligations toward the Soviet government, quite aside from the fact that Talât, because of the recent Russo-German treaty, was furious enough already.[139]

Meanwhile Gen. Kress and his Austro-Hungarian colleague in Tiflis, Franckenstein, had traveled once again to Yerevan, this time in company with Enver's uncle, Gen. Halil Paşa, who had meanwhile replaced Vehib Paşa as commander of "Army Group East." The ostensible purpose of Halil's visit to the Armenian capital was a courtesy call, but Kress did his best to use that occasion for "enlightening" the Ottoman general about the true situation in Armenia. In particular, Kress noted in his report to Berlin, he had tried to demonstrate to Halil that the Armenians posed no real threat to the Ottoman army at all and that a more liberal policy in regard to their repatriation was entirely feasible. Unfortunately, Kress continued, the apparent headway he had made with Halil was liable to go for naught: "The Turkish troops in the Caucasus, from the army commanders on down to the last lieutenant . . . have been

[138] FO, *Türkei 183*, Bd. 54, Bernstorff to FO, 28 Aug 1918, No. 1,397.

[139] *Ibid.*, Hintze to Bernstorff, 2 Sept 1918, No. 1,432. Cf. above, p. 193.

so much stirred up against both Armenians and Germans by that wild beast [*Bestie*] Vehib Pasha that it will likely take a long time before Halil Pasha, who is far more reasonable, will succeed in enforcing his will." According to Kress, virtually every Turkish general under Halil's command was more or less opposed to his policy of moderation, and one—Şevki Paşa —had already protested against the alleged revival of German influence in the sphere of Halil's Army Group. To complicate the situation, Kress noted, a steady stream of false reports about Armenian "misdeeds" and gang warfare had been sent by these generals to Constantinople, and it was painfully obvious that Gen. Seeckt had been duped all along about what was going on in Transcaucasia. His apparent agreement with Enver that it would be too dangerous to permit large masses of Armenians to resettle behind the Ottoman lines was based on false premises; for these masses consisted almost entirely of old men and women and children: "The Turks and Tartars have seen to it with thoroughness that hardly any men capable of bearing arms are left for repatriation." As for the nefarious activities of one Armenian guerrilla band, led by Gen. Antranik, whose existence was indeed not just a figment of Turkish imagination, the Yerevan Government had nothing to do with it and had actually offered its help in the suppression of that band.[140]

Perhaps as a result of Kress's pleas Halil Paşa released several hundred Armenian soldiers from captivity during the following weeks, most of them being sent to Yerevan. This positive gesture was atypical, for in mid-September the Germans were confronted with a new wave of anti-Armenian violence during and after the capture of Baku by Nuri's Army of Islam. Although Turkish regular troops were probably not directly

[140] FO, *Türkei 183*, Bd. 54, Kress to Hertling, 3 Sept 1918; Waldburg to FO, 15 Sept, No. 1,516. On the guerrilla activities of Antranik's band see Allen and Muratoff, pp. 461, 472-75, and *passim*; Pasdermajian, pp. 462-66, and *passim*.

involved in the slaughter of several thousand Baku Armenians, Nuri and other Ottoman officers did very little to stop the local Moslem populace and Azerbaijani soldiers. Efforts by Gen. Halil's German chief-of-staff, Lt. Col. Paraquin, to restore order in the city were largely futile and eventually led to a heated argument between him and Nuri. Two days later Halil abruptly relieved Paraquin of his post and sent him back to Constantinople.[141]

Alerted by Paraquin about the turmoil in Baku and the precarious situation in which even German nationals there found themselves, Gen. Kress promptly addressed protests to the Ottoman and Azerbaijani diplomatic representatives in Tiflis and to Nuri himself. In a telegram to the latter, Kress demanded, moreover, that the transfer of a German battalion to Baku be permitted at once, so that it could "safeguard" the lives and property of all German nationals. Nuri replied five days later that the allegations of rampant disorder and bloodshed in Baku were largely without foundation, and that the dispatch of German troops would, therefore, be pointless.[142]

As a result of Nuri's opposition no German troops ever got to Baku. The Turks themselves pulled out of that city and all other Transcaucasian areas in the weeks following the conclusion of the Mudros Armistice, the evacuation being largely completed by the beginning of December. On November 17 British forces occupied Baku and in December spread over other parts of the Transcaucasian region.[143]

As soon as the Ottoman intruders had left, the Dashnak government in Yerevan raised territorial claims against both Georgia and Azerbaijan.[144] More importantly, in the winter of 1918-19 Armenian troops followed the retreating Turks and with Britain's approval occupied some parts of Eastern Ana-

---

[141] See Lepsius, *Deutschland*, Nos. 436, 442 (*Anlage* 1).

[142] *Ibid., Anlagen* 2-6; FO, *Russland 97a*, Bd. 26, Kress to FO, 26 Sept 1918.

[143] Kazemzadeh, pp. 163-73; Kheifets, pp. 74-75, 81.

[144] Kazemzadeh, pp. 174-83; Pipes, p. 210.

tolia. In May 1919 the Yerevan government formally proclaimed the inclusion of several provinces of the prewar Ottoman empire in a "United Armenia," but despite some Allied sympathies with the Armenian cause this triumph over the hated Turks was to be short-lived.[145] When the British withdrew from Transcaucasia in the spring and early summer of 1920, the Armenian Republic was left in dangerous isolation, facing the revolutionary expansionism of the Russian Bolsheviks on one side and the irredentist pressures of Mustafa Kemal's Turkish nationalists on the other.[146] In September 1920 the Kemalists marched into Armenia and within six weeks forced the Yerevan government to give up most of the territory it had annexed since late 1918. Simultaneously, Red Army troops moved into the eastern portions of the Armenian state and engineered its conversion into a Soviet Socialist Republic.[147]

Having jointly crushed the cause of Armenian national independence, the Soviets and Kemalists subsequently worked out a delineation of their respective spheres of influence in Transcaucasia. In March 1921 they concluded the Treaty of Moscow, by which Turkey's northeastern frontier was moved up to or even beyond the 1877 line except in the northern section of the Batum District.[148] With roughly 25,000 square

[145] Kazemzadeh, pp. 213-15; Pipes, p. 210. Text of the May 28, 1919 proclamation by the Armenian government in Poidebard, "Chronique: Le Transcaucase et la République d'Arménie," IV:1, 57-58.

[146] On the hesitant policies in 1919-20 of the Western powers regarding the Armenian question cf. Pasdermadjian, pp. 469-74; Kazemzadeh, pp. 253-65; Ziemke, pp. 80-123, and *passim*; Howard, pp. 217-49, and *passim*. See also Howard's recent study *The King-Crane Commission* (Beirut, 1963), and *passim*.

[147] Pasdermadjian, pp. 474-77; Kazemzadeh, pp. 286-93; Pipes, pp. 229-34. Cf. Kheifets, pp. 130-71, and *passim*. Text of the Turco-Armenian peace treaty of 2 December 1920 in Poidebard, "Chronique," IV:1, 70-72.

[148] See *ibid.*, pp. 72-77, for the text of the Turco-Soviet treaty, which was signed on March 16.

The Armenian Persecutions

kilometers of erstwhile Tsarist territory formally handed over to them, the Kemalists in effect acquired title to more Transcaucasian, and particularly Armenian, land than the *Ittihad ve Terakki* regime had gained for Turkey by the dictated Peace of Brest-Litovsk three years earlier. The Russo-Turkish border settlement of 1921 has remained intact to this day. Armenian efforts to undo this renewed partition of their traditional homeland have been and are likely to remain futile.

A REVIEW of the Armenian tragedy during World War I suggests the following conclusions. First, the decimation of the Ottoman Armenian population between 1915 and 1918 through physical violence, hunger, and disease was not the unfortunate by-product of an otherwise legitimate security program but the result of a deliberate effort by the *Ittihad ve Terakki* regime to rid the Anatolian heartland of a politically troublesome ethnic group. While there were undoubtedly some districts behind the Transcaucasian front where deportations and other precautionary measures were militarily justified, the sweeping geographic scope of the Porte's anti-Armenian program and its indiscriminate application to men, women, and children alike suggest that this was a politically inspired attempt to achieve a kind of "final solution" of the Armenian question in Anatolia. Although this interpretation is still being contested by most Turkish historians, at least some of them have acknowledged that the wartime "deportations" were accompanied by extraordinary savagery.[149]

Secondly, it is clear that the German government neither instigated nor approved of the Armenian persecutions in the Ottoman empire, though it had no objections to orderly and militarily necessary evacuation proceedings as such. Moreover, for reasons of political expediency, the statesmen in Berlin (and Vienna as well) steadfastly refused to go beyond admonitions and diplomatic protests to divert the Porte from its brutal

[149] Cf. Kilic, pp. 17-18; Bayur, III:3, 6.

· 268 ·

policy. Indeed, without the constant prodding by some German officials in the Ottoman empire and by private individuals like Lepsius, Berlin's efforts to secure the termination of the Armenian persecutions would probably have been even more timid. Whether more energetic protests would have induced the Turks to halt their anti-Armenian program is quite doubtful. Contrary to what has sometimes been claimed, direct protection of the Armenians was completely beyond Germany's capacity. At the height of the massacres, in 1915, there were practically no German troops in the Ottoman empire, and most of the individual German officers who were stationed in the eastern provinces had no command functions whatever.[150]

The decision of Germany's and Austria-Hungary's leaders not to risk a break with the Porte on account of the Armenians must of course be seen and judged in context. The massacres occurred in the midst of war. Continued Ottoman participation in it was deemed essential by both Central Powers. Modern history records no instance where humanitarian considerations induced a belligerent country to dispense with the active support of its ally on account of the latter's domestic misdeeds.

In evaluating the conduct of Berlin and Vienna it should finally be noted that the statesmen in most other countries were similarly reluctant to take drastic action in the Armenian issue. In the United States President Wilson authorized diplomatic and charitable efforts on behalf of the Ottoman Armenians but was never persuaded to include the *Ittihad ve Terakki* regime among America's declared enemies. In fact, if the Porte had not

[150] At the time of the mass deportations the Ottoman Third ("Caucasus") Army was commanded by Gen. M. Kâmil Paşa, who was succeeded by Gen. Vehib Paşa in March 1916. The Second Army, moved to eastern Anatolia in the spring of 1916, was until March 1917 under the command of Gen. Izzet Paşa. German officers in these two armies were mostly engaged in technical and staff functions; the most responsible position being held by a field grade officer, Maj. Guse, as chief-of-staff at Third Army HQ.

taken the initiative (under German pressure) and severed relations with the United States in April 1917, the Wilson administration would probably have continued normal diplomatic intercourse with the Ottoman government right to the end of the war.[151]

---

[151] On the Wilson administration's reserve on the whole Armenian issue cf. Robert L. Daniel, "The Armenian Question and American-Turkish Relations, 1914-1927," *MVHR*, 46 (1959-60), pp. 252-59; and John A. DeNovo, *American Interests and Policies in the Middle East, 1900-1939* (Minneapolis, 1963), pp. 98-109.

CHAPTER VIII

Germany's Financial Support

WHEN THE Ottoman empire entered the war in November 1914 its state treasury was virtually empty. Although the Porte had often demonstrated before that it could survive with a minimum of funds (the delayed payment or nonpayment of government officials and of the Ottoman armed forces was a frequently used device), the German government realized it would have to provide some financial assistance if the Turks were to launch a really serious war effort. What the leaders of the Reich did not at all foresee was just how costly and troublesome it would become to keep the Turks financially afloat. Throughout the war anguished cries were to be heard in Berlin that a disproportionate share of Germany's resources was being drained off by the seemingly insatiable junior ally.[1]

In October 1914 the German government agreed to loan the Porte T£ 5 million in gold if the Porte honored its alliance obligations without further delay. Because of the obstructionist tactics of Finance Minister Cavid Bey, the conclusion of a requisite loan contract was held up until after the Ottoman empire had intervened. By that time the Turks were no longer willing to accept the original German terms. When the Porte finally signed the loan agreement on November 10 it secured not only more favorable repayment terms but also a pledge from Wangenheim (which was most unwelcome to the Wil-

---

[1] The primary evidence for this chapter is derived mainly from the Berlin foreign office file *Türkei 110*, which contains thousands of official and private documents (including the internal correspondence of the *Deutsche Bank* and of other financial institutions). Because of limitations of space only the most important documents will be cited in the following. On the financial problems of the Porte in the pre-intervention period, see Bayur, III:1, 186-90.

helmstrasse) that in case of need a further gold loan with "analogous terms" would be granted by the Reich.[2]

Under the provisions of the November treaty Germany agreed to disburse immediately the T£ 2 million it had shipped to Constantinople the previous month, while the balance of the loan would be paid out in six monthly instalments after December 1. Berlin soon came to rue this commitment, for the transportation of such large amounts of gold through the Balkans, and more particularly through Ententophile Rumania, proved to be a complex and nerve-racking job. Although virtually all of the German gold transports dispatched prior to February 1915 got through without major delays or incidents, the Wilhelmstrasse became increasingly nervous about the political situation in Rumania and in March suspended all further shipments.[3] As a result the gold payable to the Porte in April and May, the last two instalments of the loan, had to be scraped together from the vaults of the *Deutsche Bank* and from other sources in Constantinople.[4]

In the meantime the Germans had made strenuous efforts to persuade the Turks that in order to stretch out their limited gold supplies they should finance part of their war effort by the issue of paper money. Prior to World War I most of the money circulating in the Ottoman empire consisted of gold

[2] FO, *Türkei 110*, Bd. 73, Wangenheim to FO, 30 Oct 1914, No. 1,168; 5 Nov, No. 1,230; 10 Nov, No. 1,306; Zimmermann to Wangenheim, 1 Nov, No. 1,089; 7 Nov, No. 1,171; Bd. 74, Wangenheim to Bethmann Hollweg, 14 Nov, No. 286; Bd. 76, Wangenheim to Said Halim, 27 Nov.

[3] *Ibid.*, Bd. 73, Zimmermann to Wangenheim, 7 Nov 1914, No. 1,173; 10 Nov, No. 1,204; Bussche to FO, 8 Nov, No. 566; 13 Nov, Nos. 598, 599; Bd. 74, Zimmermann to Bussche, 18 Nov, No. 707; Kühn to FO, 30 Dec; Bd. 75, Wangenheim to FO, 31 Jan 1915, No. 265.

[4] *Ibid.*, Bd. 76, Zimmermann to Helfferich, 15 March 1915; Wangenheim to Bethmann Hollweg, 18 March, No. 165; Bd. 77, Jagow to Wangenheim, 30 April, No. 854; Zimmermann to Helfferich, 4 May; Wangenheim to FO, 4 May, No. 1,048; 5 May, No. 1,051; Kaufmann to Talât, 12 May.

and silver coins and foreign metallic money, and the idea of diluting that hard currency with paper bills not fully covered by gold naturally did not appeal to the Porte.[5] What made matters after October 1914 even more difficult for the Germans was the fact that under the Constitution of the Ottoman empire the issue of paper money was reserved exclusively to the *Banque Impériale Ottomane* (BIO), an institution owned by French and British interests, with real headquarters in Paris and management in Constantinople by an Englishman named Nias and a French citizen named Steeg.[6]

A few days after the Turks had entered the war the leading figures of the German business community in Constantinople, among them Director Otto Kaufmann of the *Deutsche Bank* branch office and the vice-president of the Anatolian Railroad Company, Franz J. Günther, got together with Wangenheim's staff to figure out a basic policy on the paper money issue. They concluded that, given the Ottoman population's unfamiliarity with bank notes other than those issued by the BIO, the issuing of new paper money would have to be handled by that institution, though, of course, its present managers—two enemy nationals—would first have to be removed.[7]

To provide the Porte with expert advice on the reorganiza-

---

[5] According to Emin, p. 161, the currency circulating in the Ottoman empire in 1914 amounted to about T£ 60 million in coins and only about T£ 1 million in bank notes (all issued by the *Banque Impériale Ottomane*). Cf. Gustav Herlt, "Kriegswirtschaft in der Türkei," *Weltwirtschaftliches Archiv*, VIII (1916), Chronik und Archivalien, p. 472, who claims that the *Banque Impériale Ottomane* had T£ 4 million worth of notes in circulation.

[6] At the beginning of the war the rotating director-generalship of the BIO in Constantinople was held by Nias. His alternate, Steeg, was the brother of a prominent politician of the Third Republic, who held ministerial posts before and during the war.

[7] See FO, *Türkei 110 Nr. 2*, Bd. 8, Wangenheim to FO, 19 Sept 1914, No. 839; *Türkei 110*, Bd. 73, same to same, 5 Nov, No. 1,231; 10 Nov, No. 1,297; Bd. 74, Wassermann to Helfferich, 12 Nov.

tion of its enemy-owned "state bank" and related matters, the Wilhelmstrasse contracted the services of the German banker Eugen von Wassermann, who arrived in Constantinople during the second week of November.[8] To his amazement Wassermann found that nothing had as yet been done to get rid of Nias and Steeg, nor was it clear who, if anyone, was in charge of the Ottoman finance ministry. Although Cavid had formally resigned from the cabinet early in November there were some indications that he was still (or again) in control of the finance ministry, and that Talât, the "interim" minister of finance, was playing a more or less decorative role in that position.[9]

By November 17 the Germans finally figured out that Cavid was indeed the man they would have to deal with; a rather sobering discovery in view of the anti-interventionist record he had compiled during the preceding three months. The uneasy feeling that the ex-minister would give them nothing but

[8] Thanks to his largesse—he "lost" 104,000 marks in poker games with Cavid and other Ottoman dignitaries within four months—and his willingness to defend the Porte's point of view in some of the financial negotiations with Berlin, Wassermann quickly earned the trust of the Turks. In March 1915 he was formally assigned to the Constantinople embassy as a financial attaché but was dismissed at the end of the year because of his alleged tendency to see everything through Turkish glasses. See FO, *Türkei 139*, Bd. 34, Wangenheim to FO, 29 March 1915, No. 769; *Dt 135 Nr. 1 secr.*, Bd. 1, Berlin foreign office memo, 13 May 1915; Wassermann to Zimmermann, 31 May; "G. A.," November 1916; *Dt. 135 Nr. 1*, Bd. 5, Hohenlohe to Bethmann Hollweg, 11 Sept 1915, No. 561; Hohenlohe to FO, 18 Sept, No. 2,126; 27 Sept, No. 2,192; Wangenheim to FO, 12 Oct, No. 2,335; Jagow to embassy Pera, 24 Sept, No. 1,792; 15 Oct, No. 1,972; Neurath to FO, 7 Nov, No. 2,598; Zimmermann to embassy Pera, 9 Nov, No. 2,181; 22 Nov, No. 2,290.

[9] FO, *Türkei 110*, Bd. 74, Wassermann to Helfferich, 12 Nov 1914. The anomalous position of Cavid as the de facto head of the finance ministry from which he had officially resigned continued until February 1917, when he formally reentered the cabinet.

Germany's Financial Support

trouble was quickly confirmed. When Günther reminded Cavid that it was high time to dislodge Nias and Steeg and to place the BIO under Ottoman-German control, Cavid feigned utter surprise that this should be deemed necessary, but finally agreed to "study" the matter.[10]

A few days later the Germans learned to their surprise that Cavid had meanwhile directed an inquiry to the Paris headquarters of the BIO whether it was willing to supply the Porte with T£ 7.5 million of paper money if the Porte deposited T£ 5 million in gold with it and covered the remainder of the emission by tax pledges and other suitable guarantees. The Paris head office of the BIO replied negatively, but despite Talât's earlier promise that in such case the Porte would immediately put the bank under joint Turco-German management, nothing was actually done for the time being.[11]

The Germans, eager to get the issue of Turkish paper money underway in order to relieve the pressure on their own gold reserves, wrangled with the Porte throughout the following month and finally got a commitment after Christmas that the takeover of the BIO would be carried out. About two weeks later, a full two months after France and Britain had declared war on the Ottoman empire, Nias and Steeg were finally asked to leave and Ottoman nationals were put in their place, but this proved to be a Pyrrhic victory. Cavid coldly explained to the Germans that if any paper money was to be issued at all he would not allow the BIO to be used for that purpose; for it was his intention to do as little as possible to antagonize its French owners whose good will would be needed again once the war was over.[12]

[10] FO, *Türkei 110*, Bd. 74, Wassermann to Helfferich, 17 Nov 1914.
[11] *Ibid.*, Wassermann to Helfferich, 21 Nov 1914, 26 Nov, 30 Nov; Wangenheim to FO, 7 Dec, No. 1,545; Blaisdell, pp. 185-86, note 16.
[12] FO, *Türkei 110*, Bd. 74, Wangenheim to FO, 27 Dec 1914, No. 1,733; Bd. 75, same to Bethmann Hollweg, 13 Jan 1915, No. 32; same to FO, 24 Jan, No. 213; Günther to Gwinner, 12 Feb.

Germany's Financial Support

Chastened by past failures to undermine the ex-minister's influence or to make agreements behind his back with the senior officials in the finance ministry, the German representatives in Constantinople had no choice but to go along with the alternative proposal Cavid had thrown into the discussion ever since the end of November: to use the Ottoman Public Debt Administration (*Dette Publique*) temporarily as a bank of issue.

Created in the 1880s, the Public Debt Administration was an autonomous institution which represented the Porte's foreign creditors and collected a variety of state revenues in the Ottoman empire on their behalf.[13] Since the French and English representatives on the Council of this organization had left Constantinople upon the Turks' entry into the war, the decision whether the Public Debt Administration should accept Cavid's plan was left in the hands of the four remaining "delegates" (a German, an Austrian, an Italian, and the Turkish representative, Hüseyin Cahid Bey) and, more particularly, the creditor syndicates they represented.[14] The German delegate, Rudolph Pritsch, did not like Cavid's proposal at all, especially since only part of the issue was to be covered by gold. In explaining the situation to the Berlin head office of the *Deutsche Bank*, Pritsch pointed out that the proposed involvement of the *Dette Publique* in the issuing of paper money would undermine the credit and status of that institution and produce chaos in the Ottoman economy since the BIO notes and *Dette Publique* notes would not be treated as equal in value by the population at large.[15]

Faced with a probable veto from Pritsch—whose negative

[13] Lewis, p. 447, calls the Public Debt Administration quite appropriately "a second and independent exchequer" of Turkey, and notes that on the eve of the war it actually had a larger staff than the Imperial Ottoman finance ministry.

[14] See Günther to Gwinner, 12 Feb; Blaisdell, pp. 184-85.

[15] FO, *Türkei 110*, Bd. 75, Pritsch to Gwinner, 13 Feb 1915; 16 Feb.

attitude was fully approved by the German creditors' syndicate back home—Cavid agreed to modify his proposal to the extent that the Porte would offer *full* gold coverage for the issue of *Dette Publique* notes. This revision of the original project did much to mollify Pritsch and the monied interests in Germany which he represented. The German government, on the other hand, was still dissatisfied since it, and it alone, had the requisite amount of gold the Porte would need to cover the proposed issue.[16]

On February 23 Cavid and the Ottoman delegate on the Public Debt Council, Cahid, accompanied by Wassermann, set out for Vienna and Berlin to discuss the whole matter with the two allied governments.[17] Such a trip had been urged on Cavid for a long time by the German officials and businessmen in Constantinople, but their hope that personal contacts with the political leaders and financial magnates of Germany would have a beneficial effect on Cavid, that is, make him more cooperative and agreeable to German advice, was dashed rather quickly.

While Berlin was busily preparing a red carpet reception for the two Ottoman visitors, things did not go very well in Vienna, where Cavid and Cahid made their first major stop. When Cavid called on Burian and explained to him that the Porte was in serious financial straits and would need a joint German-Austrian gold loan of 150 million francs to carry on with the war, Burian promised sympathetic consideration of the request but suggested also that the Turks should grant

[16] See *ibid.*, Bd. 76, Zimmermann to Tschirschky, 20 March 1915, No. 229, for a concise review of these developments. Cf. Blaisdell, pp. 186-87.

[17] Since Cahid, like Cavid, was suspected of being an Ententophile at heart and had considerable influence as the editor of *Tanin*, Wangenheim suggested to Berlin that he be kept under surveillance and wooed at one and the same time. See FO, *Türkei 110*, Bd. 75, Wangenheim to FO, 23 Feb 1915, No. 441.

some economic concessions in return. This *quid pro quo* proposal did not appeal at all to Cavid, and he angrily informed the Austro-Hungarian foreign minister that such matters would have to be discussed after the war, when both Central Powers would in any case "find a rich field for activity" in the Ottoman empire.[18]

Forewarned of Cavid's sensitivity and of his determination to get a loan without strings attached, the Wilhelmstrasse gave him a splendid reception in Berlin and immediately agreed to put up two-thirds of the 150 million franc advance which he wanted from the two Central Powers. Cavid, in return, agreed to have the entire amount kept in a Berlin vault under the seal of the Public Debt Administration, which would thereby be enabled to issue fully-covered paper money of corresponding value to the Porte. This arrangement, subsequently approved by the Public Debt Council, finally laid the foundation for the Ottoman currency "reform" which the Germans had been demanding since November 1914 and had the added advantage that the Wilhelmstrasse would no longer have to worry about costly and hazardous gold transports through the Balkans.[19]

Although the procrastination of the Austro-Hungarian government in putting up its share of the loan and some minor technical problems produced several unpleasant moments between Cavid and the German negotiators, the second German-Ottoman loan treaty of the war was finally signed on April 20. The Ballhausplatz limped behind with its loan treaty about

[18] Cf. *ibid.*, Bd. 76, Austro-Hungarian embassy Berlin to FO, 3 March 1915; Tschirschky to FO, 4 March, No. 547. Concerning Cavid's resentment over Burian's "stupid" counterproposal, see also Wassermann to Wangenheim, 18 March.

[19] See *ibid.*, Zimmermann to Tschirschky, 20 March 1915, No. 229; Wangenheim to FO, 24 March, No. 719. The approval of the project by the Council of the Public Debt on March 25 was unanimous since the Italian delegate, Nogara, went along with his German, Austrian, and Turkish colleagues. Blaisdell, p. 187.

two weeks later, and the printing of new paper money for the Ottoman empire was at last started.[20] The actual issue of the new Public Debt notes took place three months later, accompanied by a law which made anyone discriminating against the new currency liable to a fine or imprisonment.[21]

With approximately 175 million marks in German gold already spent or obligated for the service of the November and April loans—and another 150 million payable to German firms for the materiel they had shipped to Turkey since the beginning of the war—the Wilhelmstrasse was unpleasantly surprised when the Turks came back within six weeks with a request for yet another gold loan. As Enver wired to the OHL, it was no longer possible to obtain supplies for the Ottoman army by means of unpaid requisitions, and German gold was urgently needed so that "at least part of the army's requirements can henceforth be paid for in cash."[22] General Falkenhayn immediately informed Berlin of Enver's predicament, but the head of the German treasury department, State Secretary Karl Helfferich, was extremely reluctant to take action on the matter. In several communications to Cavid he explained that it was just not possible for Germany to allocate so much

[20] FO, *Türkei 110*, Bd. 76, Zimmermann to Tschirschky, 25 March 1915, No. 1,010; Tschirschky to FO, 27 March, No. 610; Bd. 77, Zimmermann to Tschirschky, 6 April, No. 1,128; Tschirschky to FO, 7 April, No. 640; Austro-Hungarian embassy Berlin to FO, 10 April; Giesecke & Devrient *Typographisches Institut* to FO, 26 April; Blaisdell, p. 185.

For the original of the German-Ottoman treaty, see FO, *Verträge 95 (IE)*.

[21] See *Türkei 110*, Bd. 79, Pritsch to Wangenheim, 7 July 1915; "Convention entre le Gouvernement Impérial Ottoman . . . et le Conseil d'Administration de la Dette Publique," signed July 3, 1915, by Talât and Cahid; Blaisdell, pp. 187-89; Emin, p. 161.

[22] FO, *Türkei 110*, Bd. 77, Wangenheim to FO, 28 May 1915, No. 1,242. On German materiel shipments see Trumpener, "German Military Aid to Turkey in 1914," *Journal of Modern History*, 32 (1960), pp. 145-49; and below, pp. 282-83 and *passim*.

gold for the Porte and that serious thought should therefore be given to the issue of only partially covered bills; an operation which would of course require the creation of a new Ottoman bank of issue.[23] This proposal, coupled with assurances that German and Austro-Hungarian banks were willing to provide part of the capital for such an institution, was discussed at the Porte for several weeks, but was eventually turned down. Talât explained to Director Kaufmann at the end of July that the establishment of a new bank would require too much time, and the Porte was rather more inclined to buy the BIO and convert it into a bona fide state bank. Much of the capital for the purchase, he added, would have to be provided by German banks and the Berlin government, but, in return, the Germans would be given some representation on the governing board and Kaufmann himself could have the top manager's job if he wanted it.[24]

Since most German banks were not interested in investing their capital unless they were given some form of veto power in the administration of the projected Ottoman state bank, the whole issue hung fire during the next few months, while the Turks became ever more persistent in their demands for a new loan—bank or no bank. Well aware of Helfferich's determination to make the grant of further gold loans contingent on their full cooperation in the establishment of a new bank of issue, the Turks finally persuaded Hohenlohe to put pressure on the German treasury department. On September 7 Hohenlohe wired to Berlin that regardless of the obstinacy the Porte had shown on the bank and other issues, it was a matter of

---

[23] FO, *Türkei 110*, Bd. 78, Helfferich to FO, 22 June 1915; Treutler to FO, 29 June, No. 173; Helfferich to Falkenhayn, 30 June; Bd. 79, Enver to Falkenhayn, 8 July; Helfferich to Falkenhayn, 10 July.

[24] *Ibid.*, Hohenlohe to FO, 29 July 1915, No. 1,683. For evidence that Cavid, for one, was strenuously opposed to any tampering with the status of the BIO, see "Auszug aus einem Briefe Djavid Beys an Talaat Bey . . . 21.7.15."

urgency that its financial requests be satisfied. Hohenlohe pointed out that most of the Ottoman army had gone without pay since the beginning of the war, and the resultant morale problem was assuming serious proportions. Moreover, the provisioning of the troops on Gallipoli was made increasingly difficult by the lack of cash for necessary purchases, and unless Germany helped out immediately, mutinies in the army and unrest among the population might yet cause the loss of the Dardanelles.[25]

Faced with this grim news Berlin immediately changed its course. On September 9 Helfferich and the foreign office informed Ambassador Hakki that a new gold loan of 120 million marks (T £ 6 million) would be paid out before the end of the year. At the same time they pointedly reminded the Porte that it should do its share and establish at long last the necessary machinery for the issue of partially covered paper money.[26] Hardly had this new German grant been announced when the Turks notified Berlin that they needed yet another 40 million marks, and at once, to purchase supplies for the Gallipoli army. Under pressure from the OHL, Helfferich had to agree to that advance as well—once again without getting any commitment from the Turks that they would create a state bank of some sort which could furnish them with paper money not fully covered by gold.[27]

Since all further attempts to push the Porte in that direction proved futile, Berlin had to accept the perpetuation of the existing system, that is, the issue of fully covered paper money

---

[25] *Ibid.*, "Notiz, 3.8.15, Berlin"; Bd. 80, Hohenlohe to FO, 31 Aug, No. 1,953; 7 Sept, No. 2,024.

[26] *Ibid.*, Helfferich to FO, 10 Sept 1915, and enclosures.

[27] *Ibid.*, Bd. 81, Hohenlohe to FO, 13 Sept 1915, no No.; Treutler to FO, 14 Sept, No. 399; Helfferich to FO, 14 Sept; 15 Sept; same to Pritsch, 15 Sept; Hohenlohe to FO, 18 Sept, No. 2,125; 22 Sept, No. 2,147; 25 Sept, No. 2,174; Treutler to FO, 27 Sept, No. 437.

by and through the *Dette Publique*. The only concession Berlin did obtain was that henceforth it could substitute German treasury notes (redeemable after the war) for the gold with which the previous loans had been paid.[28] After lengthy negotiations between the Porte, the Wilhelmstrasse, and the Council of the Public Debt Administration, the whole matter was formally settled by a treaty which Jagow and Ambassador Hakki signed on November 9, 1915. Under its provisions the German government confirmed its previously given promise to loan the Porte T£ 8 million (160 million marks), with the stipulation that it would hand over treasury notes in that amount to the Public Debt Administration as cover for a new issue of paper money in the Ottoman empire. As with the previous two loan treaties the Porte was granted very liberal terms for the repayment of the loan after the war.[29]

Although subsequently Berlin tried repeatedly to have this costly and complicated subsidization system revamped, the Porte refused to budge. While the Turks did found a "National Credit Bank" early in 1917, they insisted until the end of the war on using the *Dette Publique* as their one and only bank of issue. As a result Germany found herself called on to provide full coverage, in treasury notes or hard cash, for virtually all of the wartime issues of paper money which were made in the Ottoman empire, an obligation which in all cost the German government close to 4 billion marks.[30]

[28] *Ibid.*, Hohenlohe to FO, 13 Sept 1915, No. 2,082; 14 Sept, No. 2,088; 27 Sept, No. 2,193; Helfferich to FO, 30 Sept.

[29] *Ibid.*, Bd. 82, Neurath to FO, 27 Oct 1915, No. 2,481; Jagow to Neurath, 31 Oct, No. 2,101; Neurath to FO, 2 Nov, No. 2,530, 5 Nov, No. 2,566, 7 Nov, No. 2,596. For the full text of the German-Ottoman treaty of November 9 and of a supplementary agreement that the Porte would use the new loan to pay off half of its debt with the Anatolian and Bagdad Railroad companies, see FO, *Verträge* 95 (IE).

[30] Cf. FO, *Türkei 110*, Bd. 109, Memorandum, 15 Oct 1918, by Dr. Greve re "Die der türkischen Regierung seit Kriegsbeginn . . .

Germany's Financial Support

In addition to underwriting the new paper currency of the Ottoman ally, the German treasury department in the course of the four war years spent well over half a billion marks on the procurement and delivery of war materiel to the Ottoman armed forces.[31] Moreover, close to another half billion in cash or credit were granted to the Porte for the importation of nonmilitary supplies from the Central Powers (grain, coal, machinery, etc.); for debt payments to German private creditors; and, most important of all, for the promotion of construction work on the unfinished sections of the Bagdad railroad line.[32]

The implementation of all of these assistance programs occasioned a good deal of friction between Berlin and Constantinople, the Germans being convinced that their "generosity" was being unduly exploited, the Turks feeling that they deserved more aid than they got. However, in most cases the ir-

---

bewilligten Vorschüsse"; Memorandum, 15 March 1919, of the Berlin foreign office about "Kriegsvorschüsse und Kriegslieferungen an die Türkei"; Blaisdell, p. 185; Emin, pp. 161-62; Mühlmann, *deutsch-türkische Waffenbündnis*, pp. 311-12; Borchard and Wynne, II, 482-83. See also DZA, Büro Staatsminister Dr. Helfferich, *Akten betr. Türkei*, Bd. I, "Leistungen und Verpflichtungen aus den mit der türkischen Regierung . . . geschlossenen Vorschussverträgen," n.d. (probably late 1917).

[31] Cf. *ibid.*, Bd. 3, "Notiz," 31 July 1918; FO, *Türkei 110*, Bd. 109, "Kriegsvorschüsse und Kriegslieferungen an die Türkei," 15 March 1919; Ernst von Wrisberg, *Wehr und Waffen 1914-1918* (Leipzig, 1922), pp. 179, 288, and *passim*; Emin, p. 163; Mühlmann, *deutsch-türkische Waffenbündnis*, pp. 296-97.

[32] Cf. Wrisberg, pp. 175-87; Mühlmann, *deutsch-türkische Waffenbündnis*, pp. 297-98. According to the computations of the Berlin foreign office in the spring of 1919 the total of German government loans and credits to its wartime Ottoman ally had amounted to T£ 235,056,344 (or roughly 4.7 billion marks at the frequently used exchange rate of 1:20). Of this total, T£ 148,581,400 had been advanced in German treasury notes, the remainder in marks, Turkish pound bills, gold, and silver. See FO, *Türkei 110*, Bd. 109, "Kriegsvorschüsse und Kriegslieferungen an die Türkei," 15 March 1919. Emin, p. 163, presents figures which are similar in most respects.

ritation between the two allies was of no great political consequence. A major exception to this rule, though, was the almost constant bickering which went on between them regarding the subsidization of the German railroad companies in the Ottoman empire and the financing of the latter's construction work. After 1914 disagreements on these two issues repeatedly led to serious problems between the two governments, and for that reason alone the wartime history of the Bagdad railroad enterprise merits somewhat closer attention than it has usually received.

CHAPTER IX

The Bagdad Railroad

A T THE OUTBREAK of World War I the principal traffic artery of the Ottoman empire, the German-built Bagdad railroad, was still far from completion. Traveling southeastward from Haydar Pasha (on the Asiatic side of the Bosporus) one encountered the first stop in the Taurus Mountains, where 37 kilometers of difficult terrain had yet to be cut or tunneled through. The next gap in the line, in the Amanus range, was even longer, with 97 kilometers of track remaining to be laid. From the southern slopes of the Amanus, trains operated as far as the partly built Euphrates bridge near Djerablus. On the other side of the river a track to Tell el Abyad (100 km east of Djerablus) was finished, the next section, to Ras el Ain, nearing completion. Beyond Ras el Ain, there were 536 km of right-of-way (to Samara) on which very little work had been done so far, and only a small part of the requisite building supplies had been assembled at either end of the long gap. From Samara on to Bagdad the line was almost completed, full service being started on it early in October 1914.[1]

While the two concessionaires of the Bagdad line, the *Anatolische-Eisenbahn-Gesellschaft* (*Anatolie*) and its subsidiary company, the *Bagdad-Eisenbahn-Gesellschaft* (B.E.G.),[2]

---

[1] These data are derived from FO, *Türkei 152*, Bd. 79, Memorandum by Otto Riese, 23 Nov 1914; undated memorandum about "Die Bagdadbahn," addressed to Zimmermann; Hennig, p. 9. See map, p. 286.

[2] The *Anatolie* (founded in 1888) and the B.E.G. (1903) were owned by an international syndicate dominated by the *Deutsche Bank* of Berlin. By an annually renewed contract the operational management of both companies was handled by the *General-Direktion* of the *Anatolie* in Constantinople which in turn was responsible to an Administrative Council (*Verwaltungsrat*) in Berlin. In 1914 the *General-Direktion* was headed by Eduard Huguenin and his deputy, Franz J.

had reaped handsome profits during much of the prewar period, they were facing a number of irksome financial problems by the summer of 1914. One of these derived from the fact that 119 million francs in Ottoman government bonds, the so-called Series III, had proved unsaleable during the preceding years, thereby undercutting the financial basis for much of the remaining construction work.[3] Another, more troublesome, problem confronting the B.E.G. stemmed from its being tied down by an "operational revenue formula" (*Betriebsschlüssel*) in the original concession which was increasingly working against the company. Under Art. 35 of the Bagdad Concession of 1903 the B.E.G. had been guaranteed by the Ottoman government an annual kilometric income of 4,500 francs. Any kilometric revenues in excess of this figure, up to 10,000 francs, had to be turned over in full to the Porte, while revenues above that ceiling were to be shared, with 60 percent of the sum in question going to the Porte. Because of mounting operating expenses which the company had not anticipated in 1903, this formula had begun to put a squeeze on its profits after 1911. Although negotiations with the Porte for an adjustment had been in progress for quite a while, nothing was settled when World War I broke out.[4] As will become apparent below, the

Günther, the Administrative Council by the directors of the *Deutsche Bank*, Arthur von Gwinner and Emil G. von Stauss.

[3] See Mühlmann, "Die deutschen Bahnunternehmungen," pp. 385-87 and *passim*; FO, *Türkei 152*, Bd. 91, "Kurze Aufzeichnungen über die Lage des Bagdadbahn-Geschäftes," Berlin, 24 Nov 1916; Bd. 94, Gwinner and Stauss to FO, 22 May 1917; "Die Bagdadbahn" (printed memorandum by the Administrative Council of the B.E.G., June 1917). Cf. Conker, pp. 28-29; Fischer, "Weltpolitik, Weltmachtstreben und deutsche Kriegsziele," pp. 319-21.

[4] Cf. Mühlmann, "Die deutschen Bahnunternehmungen," pp. 386-87; Chapman, pp. 41-43, 212-14; FO, *Türkei 152*, Bd. 91, "Kurze Aufzeichnungen," 24 Nov 1916; Bd. 95, Gwinner and Stauss to Oldershausen, 5 July 1917; Bd. 100, Gwinner to Goeppert, 2 Jan 1918; same to same, 19 Jan.

The Bagdad Railroad

Betriebsschlüssel handicap alone turned into a nightmare for the company during the ensuing years.

A foretaste of its wartime difficulties was experienced by the B.E.G. right after the war in Europe had started. Due to a government-decreed temporary stoppage of all bank payments the Mesopotamian branch of its subsidiary construction concern, the *Deutsche Gesellschaft für den Bau von Eisenbahnen in der Türkei*, was unable to meet its payroll requirements

THE BAGDAD RAILROAD, 1914-1918

▬▬ In operation, October 1914
ⵜⵜⵜⵜⵜⵜⵜ Completed during the war

and had to cope with a riot among its workers as a result. Some of the German managerial personnel were besieged in their homes, and Turkish troops had to be sent to get them out of the construction zones. Thus it was apparently only in October that orderly work on the Tell el Abyad-Ras el Ain section resumed. In the Taurus and Amanus sections no such disorders occurred, but there, too, construction slowed down markedly because of the induction of many workers into the army.[5]

[5] See *ibid.*, Bd. 79, Rössler to Bethmann Hollweg, 20 Oct 1914;

The Bagdad Railroad

With the intervention of the Ottoman empire in early November the Bagdad railroad of course assumed a vital role; for it, and it alone, provided a halfway viable transportation link between Constantinople and the various eastern theaters of war. Strangely enough only a handful of Germany's military and political leaders manifested much interest in how the Bagdad railroad, in its truncated state, might manage its increased responsibilities, though somebody in the Wilhelmstrasse did at least commission a study regarding the time and effort it would require to close the three gaps in the line. Late in November the head of the B.E.G.'s subsidiary construction concern, Privy Counsellor Otto Riese, responded with a lengthy memorandum, in which he pointed out that if a crash building program, with adequate quantities of money, personnel, and material, were instituted right away, the Taurus and Amanus gaps might be provisionally closed by April 1916, the much longer gap in Mesopotamia by May 1917.[6]

Riese's calculation that the Taurus and Amanus jobs alone would probably require an extra outlay of 45 million marks, and that it would take a relatively long time to finish the project, seems to have cooled whatever interest existed in German government circles; for no further action was taken for the next two months. When Ernst Jäckh, on a visit at imperial headquarters in mid-January 1915, intimated to the Kaiser how much the completion of the Bagdad line would facilitate the movement of German troops to the Suez Canal, Wilhelm

---

Memorandum by Riese, 23 Nov. Construction work on all sections of the Bagdad line was handled by a single contractor, the Philipp Holzmann G.m.b.H. of Frankfurt am Main. Pönicke, "Heinrich August Meissner-Pascha und der Bau der . . . Bagdadbahn," p. 203. On the background and repercussions of the Porte's moratorium decree, see Bayur, III:1, 182-83.

[6] FO, *Türkei 152*, Bd. 79, Rosenberg to Zimmermann, 27 Nov 1914, and enclosure.

brusquely retorted that *his* soldiers had no business there in the first place.[7] Gen. von Falkenhayn, the chief of the OHL, listened somewhat more attentively to Jäckh's talk about the strategic importance of the Orient in general, and of the Bagdad line in particular, but when Jäckh had to concede that work on the line would require about a year and a half, Falkenhayn smilingly informed him that "the war must and will be over before that time and will be decided here in the West near Calais." With Falkenhayn's blessings Jäckh thereupon approached Col. Wilhelm Groener, the head of the OHL's railroad section. According to Jäckh's own account of the interview, Groener basically agreed with all that he said, but the colonel's diary reveals that he was not at all converted. Sending German troops into a Near East campaign against the British, Groener jotted down after Jäckh's visit, was a rather unrealistic idea, and if Berlin had any money to spare it should use it to import food and not on the Bagdad railroad.[8]

Despite the prevailing indifference at the OHL, the Wilhelmstrasse decided in February 1915 to take a second look at the whole question of the Bagdad Railroad. The first step it took was to send the Constantinople embassy three alternative, crash building plans which Riese had drawn up in the meantime. One of these, *"Projekt* III," envisaged the completion of a highly improvised through-connection between the Bosporus and Aleppo within 11 months. Zimmermann explained to Wangenheim in a cover letter that the project would cost about 31 million marks, but that the Porte could probably get substantial assistance from the German treasury under certain circumstances:

[7] Cf. Jackh, *Goldene Pflug,* pp. 222-26; *Regierte der Kaiser?,* p. 82.
[8] Cf. Jackh, *Goldene Pflug,* pp. 226-28; Wilhelm Groener, *Lebenserinnerungen* (Göttingen, 1957), p. 530; FO, *Türkei 152,* Bd. 79, Jackh to FO, 21 Jan 1915.

Whether assistance by the Reich is warranted depends primarily on whether the military authorities [in Constantinople] regard the project as advantageous for a major German-Turkish operation against Egypt, which may conceivably become necessary later on. . . .

The OHL shows little interest as of now. To us [at the foreign office] the matter seems important; for after wrestling down Russia and France we may have to fight the English alone for quite some time, and they can be hit with effect only in Egypt.[9]

For some reason it took Wangenheim almost three weeks to collect the opinions of the "military authorities," but by February 28 he was able to assure the Wilhelmstrasse that they, as well as Vice-President Günther of the *Anatolie*, were very much in favor of a German-sponsored crash building program. The following day the ambassador forwarded to Bethmann Hollweg the written statements he had received from Liman, Goltz, and Lt. Col. Böttrich (the chief of the railroad section at Ottoman GHQ) and placed himself squarely behind their recommendations for prompt action.[10]

Of the three memoranda submitted, those by Liman and Böttrich contained sober analyses of the logistic problems facing the Turks and presented specific proposals for the elimination of the Taurus and Amanus bottlenecks, including the increased use of trucks and narrow-gauge equipment while work on the main line was pushed on.[11] Goltz' memorandum, on the other hand, was of a rather different character, reflecting his long-standing preoccupation with questions of grand strategy. As Goltz explained, he shared Liman's view

[9] *Ibid.*, Zimmermann to Wangenheim, 9 Feb 1915, No. 265. Cf. Mühlmann, *deutsch-türkische Waffenbündnis*, p. 113.

[10] FO, *Türkei 152*, Bd. 79, Wangenheim to FO, 28 Feb 1915, No. 486; same to Bethmann Hollweg, 1 March, No. 116.

[11] *Ibid.*, Report by Liman, 20 Feb 1915; "Kurzer Bericht über die Verbindung Konstantinopel-Suezkanal," 22 Feb 1915, by Böttrich.

that the jobs in the Taurus and Amanus ranges deserved priority, but some thought ought to be given also to getting the Mesopotamian gap closed. There was a good chance that the war would "go on for years," for the British would fight until either they or Germany were totally exhausted. To force Britain to her knees an invasion might become necessary, but there were viable alternatives, such as an attack on Egypt or a march on India, and for both of these the Bagdad line was needed. A march on India, Goltz declared, was not a "fairy tale adventure" by any means; for what Shah Nader of Persia had accomplished in the 18th century and others, like Alexander the Great and Tamerlane, before him, could certainly be done "with the perfected means of the modern age." Indeed, a carefully prepared campaign against India would constitute a "worthy and decisive conclusion" of the present world conflict.[12]

But Goltz' ideas did not make much impression in Berlin. On March 13, 1915 Zimmermann advised the OHL that the accelerated completion of the Bagdad line to Aleppo (but not beyond it) appeared most desirable "from the political standpoint" and submitted a modified crash building plan by Riese, "*Projekt* IV," for Falkenhayn's approval. Simultaneously the understate secretary reminded the OHL—as so often before —that it was essential to secure possession of Serbia's Negotin district so that a communication route around Rumania would at long last be available for materiel shipments to the Ottoman empire.[13]

While the OHL was still pondering these proposals Böttrich

[12] *Ibid.*, "Gutachten über die Wichtigkeit des beschleunigten Ausbaues des kleinasiatischen Eisenbahnnetzes," 26 Feb 1915, by Goltz.

[13] See *ibid.*, Bd. 80, Riese to B.E.G. Administrative Council, 11 March 1915; *Deutsche Bank* to Rosenberg, 12 March; Zimmermann to Treutler, 13 March, No. 11. On the wrangle between the Wilhelmstrasse and the OHL over the acquisition of a viable Balkan route to Turkey, cf. above, pp. 82-84.

sent a reminder from Constantinople that a decision on the Bagdad railroad issue should be made with dispatch. At the same time he pointed out that inasmuch as the completion of the Taurus line would take much more time than that of the Amanus section, the only efficient approach was to build up a high-capacity road transport system in the Taurus region and to restrict track-laying operations to the Amanus.

> If work trains and standard-gauge trains are used in combination, rail movements of large troop masses across the Amanus will become possible as early as the fall of 1915. The road across the Taurus can until then be fixed up for unlimited truck traffic. . . . Automobiles must be supplied by Germany. . . .
>
> Given Turkish conditions, the question for the war period boils down to this: Either no railroads—neither through the Taurus nor through the Amanus—or a railroad through the Amanus only, but that one for sure. . . .[14]

On March 22 Falkenhayn advised the Wilhelmstrasse that the OHL was all in favor of the "accelerated" creation of a high-capacity transportation route "through Asia Minor in the direction of the Suez Canal," and that Riese's *Projekt* IV, in conjunction with Böttrich's latest proposal, should be implemented for that purpose.[15]

The crash building program thus authorized got off to a very bad start. For one thing, the Administrative Council of the B.E.G., headed by *Deutsche Bank* directors Arthur von Gwinner and Emil G. von Stauss, was disinclined to get the company involved in that venture unless it was assured of adequate financial support. After three weeks of discussions, agreement was reached between the Wilhelmstrasse and the company that the Reich would advance the required sums, "up

---

[14] FO, *Türkei 152*, Bd. 80, Wangenheim to FO (Böttrich to general staff Berlin and OHL), 16 March 1915, No. 646.

[15] *Ibid.*, Treutler to FO, 22 March 1915, No. 210.

to 40,000,000 marks," to the Porte at an appropriate rate of interest, and that the latter would then "loan" the selfsame money, interest free, to the company to pay for the actual cost of construction and a surcharge of 15 percent. Moreover, this interest-free loan was to be left at the disposal of the B.E.G. until a "general revision" of the company's contractual arrangements with the Porte concerning the "construction and operation of the Bagdad railroad" had been effected—in other words, until the Concession of 1903 and supplementary contracts of later years had been modified to the company's satisfaction. On April 17 Jagow instructed Wangenheim to present these terms "confidentially" and informally to Enver and other appropriate authorities, informing him at the same time that a "definitive" settlement would have to be reached before the end of the month as "otherwise" the B.E.G. would terminate its building program altogether.[16]

In compliance with Jagow's instructions Wangenheim immediately spoke to Enver and the grand vizier and received their assurances that the proffered arrangement was agreeable and that Cavid, who was in Berlin at this time, would be instructed to close the deal. As might be expected, Cavid found the proposal most disagreeable and refused even to discuss the matter until after he had had a chance to hold consultations in Constantinople. By the time he got back to that city, which was in mid-May, his letters to the Porte had already produced a very definite shift in the latter's attitude. As Talât explained to Wassermann on May 12, the Porte could hardly be expected to borrow money at 6 percent interest to finance a construction project whose strategic value was just as important to Germany as it was to the Turks, but what irked the Porte even more was the attempt of the B.E.G. to get a revision of its concession tied into the whole arrangement.[17]

[16] *Ibid.*, Jagow to Wangenheim, 17 April 1915, No. 760.
[17] *Ibid.*, Wangenheim to FO, 23 April 1915, No. 953; 30 April, No. 1,010; 4 May, No. 1,042; 8 May, No. 1,077; 12 May, No. 1,119 (Wasser-

The Bagdad Railroad

Since a new arrangement would obviously have to be worked out, everyone concerned agreed to shift the negotiations back to Berlin. By the time Cavid returned there, now accompanied by Böttrich and the understate secretary in the ministry of public works, Ahmed Muhtar Bey, it was almost June. To participate in the talks, Huguenin of the *Anatolie* traveled to Berlin as well. With more than three precious months already wasted in fruitless talk, Böttrich presented the Wilhelmstrasse with a new memorandum in which he pointed out that, for military reasons, the Amanus line should be built as quickly as possible and "regardless of the expense involved." As for the Taurus line, its construction should be pushed, too, though only to the extent that it did not adversely affect the job in the other mountain range.[18]

Böttrich's call for prompt action and a warning by Riese that valuable summer time was fleeting away proved utterly in vain. Although, when on June 19 Bethmann Hollweg explicitly authorized State Secretary Helfferich of the treasury department to offer the Turks a more attractive loan contract and if necessary even some payments without collateral. Helfferich (a former *Deutsche Bank* director) was most reluctant to follow through. Cavid, in turn, showed no particular inclination either to get the matter settled quickly. As he eventually explained to the German negotiators, there was really not much point in the Porte contracting new debts if the borrowed money was then used to build all kinds of improvisations that would be of little or no use to the Ottoman state once the war was over. Germany should therefore increase the size of the proposed loan by another 15 or 20 million, so that the missing

---

mann to *Deutsche Bank*); Jagow to Wangenheim, 1 May, No. 858; Tschirschky to FO, 1 May, No. 708; 5 May, No. 723.

[18] *Ibid.*, Bd. 81, Wangenheim to FO, 17 May 1915, No. 1,154; Memorandum by Böttrich about "Militärische Forderungen für den Bau der Bahnen im Amanus und im Taurus," 1 June 1915.

sections of the Bagdad railroad in Asia Minor could be built from the start for "normal and permanent" use.

After weeks of fruitless parleys the German negotiators agreed to a compromise solution—40 million marks of German state funds would be made available with the understanding that the money would go into the construction of the main line. With two draft treaties in his pocket Cavid returned to Constantinople in the second week of August.[19] Contrary to what the Wilhelmstrasse had been led to believe, the Ottoman cabinet was still not fully satisfied and took another three months before the details in the draft treaties were ironed out. Finally, on November 6, 1915 the two treaties in question— one with the B.E.G., the other with the German government— were signed in Berlin by Ambassador Hakki. In essence the deal at long last concluded called for a German government loan of 40 million marks, at 5½ percent interest, to the Porte which in turn would advance most of the money, at 3 percent interest, to the B.E.G. for the construction of the permanent lines in the Taurus and Amanus.[20]

Since the completion of the "permanent" Taurus line was expected to take at least until late 1917—thereby making it virtually impossible to plan for a major campaign against Egypt until 1918—the Wilhelmstrasse, in agreement with the OHL, had meanwhile worked out an emergency solution with

[19] See *ibid.*, Zimmermann to Wangenheim, 14 June 1915, No. 1,151; "G.A." by Jagow, 19 June; Bethmann Hollweg to Helfferich, 19 June; Wangenheim to FO, 20 June, No. 1,415; *Türkei 110*, Bd. 78, "G.A." for Jagow, 5 July; Bd. 79, Zimmermann to Hohenlohe, 2 Aug, No. 1,452; 6 Aug, No. 1,471; Helfferich to Jagow, 9 Aug; Bd. 80, Jagow to Treutler, 17 Aug, No. 121.

[20] See FO, *Türkei 152*, Bd. 83, Zimmermann to Wangenheim, 8 Oct 1915, No. 1,919; Gwinner to Riese, 20 Oct; *Türkei 110*, Bd. 80, Hohenlohe to FO, 31 Aug, No. 1,953; Bd. 82, Neurath to FO, 2 Nov, No. 2,530. For copies of the Porte's treaties with the B.E.G. and the German government see *Türkei 152*, Bde. 84-85, and *Verträge 95 (IE)*, respectively. Cf. Herlt, "Kriegswirtschaft in der Türkei," p. 474.

the B.E.G.[21] In a separate treaty, signed by Jagow, Gwinner, and Stauss on November 6, the B.E.G. undertook to resort to improvisations in the building of the Taurus line so that a makeshift through-connection would be available by the end of 1916. In particular, the company agreed to make all tunnels just big enough for special, motor-driven engines and "open freight cars" to go through, and to erect emergency structures wherever the regular bridges, viaducts, etc., could not be completed in time. In return, the German government committed itself to pay for all extra expenses, up to five million marks, which the B.E.G. might incur in implementing this emergency program.[22]

The general settlement finally arrived at on November 6 proved to be extremely short-lived, for within the next three weeks Enver and his advisers at Ottoman GHQ decided the Taurus and Amanus sections should be built in a "provisional" manner after all. On December 1 Riese, Günther, and Huguenin were informed of this decision at a conference in Constantinople and, as they later explained to the Wilhelmstrasse, "yielded ... to the will" of the military authorities.[23]

From the standpoint of the German government Enver's conversion to a program of improvisation was of course highly welcome, but inasmuch as a formal new settlement with the Porte would obviously once again require endless preparatory negotiations, the Wilhelmstrasse decided to make another provisional arrangement with the B.E.G. alone. In a new treaty, signed by Zimmermann, Gwinner, and Stauss on January 14,

[21] FO, *Türkei 110*, Bd. 79, Helfferich to Jagow, 9 Aug 1915; Bd. 80, Jagow to Treutler, 17 Aug, No. 121; Herz to Jagow, 21 Aug; *Türkei 152*, Bd. 82, Jagow to Gwinner, 9 Sept; Gwinner to Jagow, 11 Sept; Treutler to FO, 11 Sept, No. 897; Bd. 83, Jagow to Gwinner, 16 Oct; Gwinner and Stauss to Jagow, 21 Oct.

[22] *Ibid.*, Bd. 84, "Vertrag zwischen dem Reichskanzler . . . und der Bagdad-Eisenbahn-Gesellschaft . . . ," 6 Nov 1915.

[23] See *ibid.*, Bd. 85, B.E.G. Administrative Council to FO, 24 March 1916.

1916, the B.E.G., taking cognizance of the wishes of the "German and the Turkish supreme commands," agreed to increase at once the length and capacity of its narrow-gauge work train line in the Amanus and to hasten the completion of the improvised rail connection through the Taurus. Although military transports were henceforth to have top priority, thus cutting into the movement of building supplies, the company further undertook to push the work on the regular line with all the means at its disposal. The Wilhelmstrasse, in turn, gave the B.E.G. a guarantee that the requisite funds for the job would be made available and that the company would be compensated by the Reich for all extra expenses not covered by the B.E.G. treaty with the Porte of November 6, 1915.[24]

Thanks to the conquest of Serbia in the fall of 1915, the shipment of German supplies to Constantinople on a route entirely controlled by the Central Powers had by now become possible. Although the rail line between Nish and Sofia had suffered extensive damage during the Serbian campaign, the first trains from Germany got through to Constantinople by January 1916, bringing some of the building supplies and a number of motor vehicles for the projects in the Taurus and Amanus.[25]

With material assistance from Germany now feasible, Goltz and Böttrich persuaded Enver that something could and ought to be done about closing the big gap in the Bagdad line in Mesopotamia. As a result, on February 11, 1916, the vice-generalissimo directed a formal inquiry to Riese whether the B.E.G.'s construction concern was prepared to build an exten-

[24] *Ibid.*, Bd. 84, "Vertrag zwischen dem Reichskanzler . . . und der Bagdad-Eisenbahn-Gesellschaft . . . ," 14 Jan 1916, and two appended "secret" letters signed by Zimmermann.

[25] Max Schwarte, ed., *Der grosse Krieg 1914-1918: Die Organisationen der Kriegsführung*, part 1 (Leipzig, 1921), p. 250; F.B., "Die militärischen Durchgangsfrachten zwischen Deutschland und der Türkei während des Weltkrieges," *Wissen und Wehr*, VII (1926), 346-47 and *passim*; Mühlmann, *deutsch-türkische Waffenbündnis*, p. 114.

sion of the line from Ras el Ain eastward. As Enver explained, the Ottoman High Command would finance the job; rails for the first 100 kilometers or so could be scavenged from the (French-owned) Tripoli-Homs railroad; and "workers battalions" would be made available.[26]

Neither Riese nor Gwinner were interested in this proposal. As they explained in a joint letter to Falkenhayn, the promise of Ottoman financial assistance could not be trusted in light of previous experiences, and if the B.E.G., in its exhausted financial condition, were to accept the job it would first need a guarantee from the German government.[27] Since Enver wanted an answer by February 17 Gwinner and his colleagues in Berlin next drew up a set of conditions which *Baurat* (Construction Councilor) Grages, the field director of the construction concern, was to present to the vice-generalissimo on that day. After expressing the company's basic willingness to do the job Grages was to stipulate that the B.E.G. expected (1) an interest-free advance of T£ 30,000 *before* the project was launched; (2) a guarantee that thereafter "each month on the 15th our expenditures of the previous month, plus 10%, will be reimbursed in cash"; and (3) the prompt conclusion of a formal treaty, which "shall include a stipulation" that the company need later return only that part of the money which would have been required to construct the line under normal conditions. Moreover—and here was the crux—the B.E.G. wished it to be understood that such repayments, after the war, would be contingent upon an appropriate "rearrangement" of the Bagdad Concession which would allow the company to

[26] FO, *Türkei 152*, Bd. 85, Enver to Holzmann Co. (via Prussian war ministry), 11 Feb 1916. On the responsibility of Goltz and Böttrich for getting Enver interested in the project, cf. *ibid.*, Grages to Holzmann Co., 26 Feb; Mühlmann, *deutsch-türkische Waffenbündnis*, p. 114.

[27] FO, *Türkei 152*, Bd. 85, Riese to *Deutsche Bank*, 11 Feb 1916; Gwinner and Riese to Falkenhayn, 14 Feb.

find a market for the previously unsaleable Ottoman government bonds.[28]

While Enver listened rather placidly to Grages' enumeration
of these points, both Understate Secretary Muhtar Bey and
Böttrich explained to the *Baurat* that the renewed attempt of
the B.E.G. to drag the concession question into the matter at
hand was most inappropriate, and that no settlement was possible until the company retreated on that point.[29] Böttrich's
decision to take sides with the Turks against the company
caused no great surprise in B.E.G. circles, for the colonel had
been feuding with the management of the *Anatolie* and B.E.G.
off and on since the beginning of the war. In fact, his disdainful refusal to listen to the various financial grievances of the
company and his repeated charges that it was not doing its
proper share in the war effort of the Ottoman empire had provoked a major storm in the fall of 1915, but an attempt by the
Wilhelmstrasse at that time to get him recalled had failed completely since both Falkenhayn and Groener declared that they
had no suitable man to replace Böttrich.[30]

Because Gwinner and his colleagues on the Administrative
Council of the B.E.G. refused to modify their terms, Enver
dropped several hints in the ensuing weeks that unless a settlement was reached soon the construction work in Mesopotamia would be handled without the company. When these
hints did not elicit any response from the B.E.G., Enver sent a

[28] *Ibid.*, Zimmermann to Wolff-Metternich (Gwinner, Günther, and
Riese to Huguenin), 15 Feb 1916, No. 230.

[29] *Ibid.*, Grages to Holzmann Co., 26 Feb 1916.

[30] See *ibid.*, Bd. 83, Günther to Hohenlohe, 1 Sept 1915; 25 Sept;
same to Gwinner, 8 Sept; Wangenheim to FO, 18 Oct, No. 2,398;
Treutler to Bethmann Hollweg, 19 Nov, No. 76; Groener, pp. 261-62.
Interestingly enough, Böttrich's predecessor, the Bavarian major
Kübel (also a member of Liman's military mission), had displayed a
similarly hostile attitude toward the B.E.G. and was eventually recalled at Bethmann Hollweg's insistence. See Hallgarten, II, 441-46,
561-74; Fischer, "Weltpolitik," pp. 315-17.

curt notice to Wolff-Metternich on March 19 that construction of the line from Ras el Ain would be started immediately under the auspices of the Ottoman war ministry. Needless to say, the prospect of having the B.E.G. frozen out of its concessionary rights in Mesopotamia caused considerable excitement both at the company's headquarters and at the German embassy, and the following day Wolff-Metternich directed a personal appeal to Enver to reconsider his decision. To the ambassador's relief the vice-generalissimo readily agreed to give the B.E.G. another chance and negotiations between the company's officials and representatives of the Porte and Enver's staff were hurriedly reopened the same day.[31] Duly impressed by the "warning shot" Enver had fired, Günther and Huguenin hastily agreed to scale down some of the original B.E.G. demands. On March 28 they accepted a so-called *Entente Préliminaire*, devoid of any signatures on the Turkish side, according to which the company would start construction as soon as it had received the T£ 30,000 advance. The other financial conditions originally raised by the B.E.G. directors in Berlin were also declared accepted by the Turks, but they made no commitment whatever regarding an eventual revision of the Bagdad Concession.[32]

Outwardly this "preliminary agreement" looked like a fair compromise settlement, but because the document bore no signatures by anyone representing the Porte it really put the B.E.G. in an untenable position. The company learned that lesson during the next few months. Work on the line east of Ras el Ain was started early in April. Since the Wilhelmstrasse

[31] Cf. FO, *Türkei 152*, Bd. 85, Wolff-Metternich to FO, 19 March 1916, No. 436; Lossow to Falkenhayn, 20 March; Wolff-Metternich to Bethmann Hollweg, 21 March, No. 124.

[32] See *ibid.*, Bd. 86, Günther to B.E.G. Administrative Council, 25 March 1916; "Entente Préliminaire entre le Gouvernement Impérial Ottoman . . . et la Société Impériale Ottomane du Chemin de fer de Bagdad," 28 March 1916; Bd. 88, "Kurze Darstellung des Verlaufs der in Konstantinopel geführten Verhandlungen. . . ."

had meanwhile committed itself to protect the B.E.G. against the contingency that the promised Turkish construction subsidies might not be forthcoming, the company could await with some lassitude the moment when the Porte would agree to sign a more definitive contract. Not so the German treasury department. As it made clear to the Porte on several occasions, an orderly contract regarding the Mesopotamian job should be signed so that everybody would know just who would pay for what. Simultaneously the Berlin treasury department sent a friendly reminder to Enver (via Falkenhayn) that a formal settlement regarding the Taurus and Amanus projects should be made as well; that is, the Porte should "join" the bilateral treaty between the German government and the B.E.G. of January 14 and assume its proper share of the financial burden.[33]

For almost two months the Porte simply did not respond to these messages, nor did it make any move to pay the monthly subsidies for the Mesopotamian project as the Preliminary Agreement of March 28 had stipulated. When the B.E.G. reminded the Porte of this default it was informed that the document no longer had any validity inasmuch as it was not drawn up in the Turkish language. Making reference to a language law which had been promulgated in April, the Turks politely suggested to the company that it had better sign a new "preliminary agreement" exclusively in Turkish if it ever wished to secure a definitive contract. Neither Wolff-Metternich nor the directors of the B.E.G. in Berlin took very kindly to this new twist, especially since no one of importance in Germany was linguistically qualified to read such a document without benefit of a translator's commentary. Moreover, Gwinner and Stauss grumbled, the Turkish language was just not "suffi-

[33] *Ibid.*, Bd. 86, Treutler to FO, 5 April 1916, No. 250; Wolff-Metternich to FO, 6 April, No. 508; Gwinner and Stauss to *Anatolie*, 8 April; Wolff-Metternich to FO (*Anatolie* to Gwinner and Stauss), 12 May, No. 645.

ciently developed" to serve as an acceptable medium for any kind of "modern treaty."[34]

Since the Porte made it clear during four weeks of negotiation that it would neither pay the Mesopotamian construction subsidies nor conclude a definitive treaty unless the preliminary agreement was first signed in its unilingual form, the B.E.G. gave in—though Wolff-Metternich simultaneously advised Halil Bey that the German government, because it was deeply involved in the whole matter, would insist that the definitive treaty be executed in the customary bilingual form.[35] (Berlin was to retreat on this point, too, before the year was out.)

Although the Porte proved to be quite accommodating in the ensuing negotiations for a "definitive" settlement, the talks were suspended in early September when the B.E.G. once again insisted that the "necessary" revision of the Bagdad Concession of 1903 be tied in with the rest of the issues.[36] To understand the obstinacy of the company in this question one must consider the rather hair-raising experiences which it had had since the beginning of the war in terms of operational expenses. As previously mentioned, the *Betriebsschlüssel* fixed in 1903 had assured the B.E.G. of an annual kilometric reve-

[34] *Ibid.*, Bd. 88, Treutler to FO, 30 June 1916, No. 402; 3 July, No. 422; Wolff-Metternich to FO, 3 July, No. 816; Gwinner and Stauss to *Anatolie*, 5 July; Zimmermann to Wolff-Metternich, 7 July, No. 634.
The new language law prescribed the use of Turkish by railroad companies and various other business concerns, but also provided for a grace period until July 1919. *Schulthess*, 57:2, pp. 455-56.

[35] FO, *Türkei 152*, Bd. 88, Jagow to Wolff-Metternich, 14 July 1916, No. 668; Stauss to *Anatolie*, 14 July; Grünau to FO, 14 July, No. 488; Bd. 89, Neurath to FO (*Anatolie* to Gwinner and Stauss), 17 July, No. 833; Neurath to FO, 1 Aug, No. 877; Stauss to *Anatolie*, 5 Aug; Wolff-Metternich to FO, 4 Aug, No. 117; 9 Aug, No. 126.

[36] Cf. *ibid.*, Bd. 90, Enver to Said Halim, 25 Aug 1916; Wolff-Metternich to Bethmann Hollweg, 7 Sept, No. 534.

nue of 4,500 francs, while virtually all revenues exceeding
that figure would be assigned to the Ottoman treasury (100
percent up to 10,000 francs, 60 percent of sums in excess of that
figure). This arrangement was predicated on the assumption
that the company would run its trains pretty much as it saw
fit, and that the passengers and freight shippers using its facilities would pay for the services rendered. Unfortunately for the
company, these rules no longer applied after the beginning of
the war. For one thing, the company was increasingly being
told by various Ottoman government agencies how to run its
trains, what equipment to use, etc. While the resulting deterioration of the rolling stock and other company assets was
bad enough, the whole revenue structure of the enterprise was
being torn apart by the Turks as well. Thus the government,
and particularly the Ottoman High Command, periodically
banned all shipments of "private freight" and forced the
B.E.G. to carry all sorts of goods at military rates (one-third of
standard rate) or altogether free. Similarly, a host of government bureaucrats, from the village level upwards, developed
the unpleasant habit of demanding free train rides, and since
much of the railroad's personnel consisted of Armenians and
Greeks, recalcitrant train crews and dispatchers would more
often than not be beaten up.[37] In short, the B.E.G. was forced
to run a high-speed, high-volume operation at drastically reduced rates and partly without any payment at all. The result
was that the company was losing more and more money while
the Porte, under the *Betriebsschlüssel* provisions, collected
rather sizeable sums each year. According to the company's
own calculations, which have a ring of truth, it finished the
business year 1914 with a net operating loss of 1.2 million

[37] Cf. *ibid.*, Bd. 80, Wangenheim to FO (*Anatolie* to Gwinner), 1
May 1915; No. 1,024; Bd. 83, Günther to Hohenlohe, 1 Sept; Falkenhayn to Helfferich, 2 Oct and enclosure.

francs and 1915 with an additional loss of 1.7 million, while the Porte collected over eight million during the same period under the *Betriebsschlüssel* arrangement.[38]

It was with this situation in mind that Günther and Huguenin informed the chief negotiators on the Ottoman side, Muhtar Bey and the understate secretary in the finance ministry, Tansin Bey, that unless the Porte agreed to a basic revision of the Concession very soon, only two alternatives remained: either the Turks nationalized the whole railroad (which, of course, would cost the Porte a great deal of money) or the company would declare its bankruptcy. When that warning did not produce any response from the Porte, Günther addressed himself directly to Abbas Halim Paşa, the minister of public works, advising him that the whole Bagdad enterprise was about to collapse catastrophically and that this would have the "most serious consequences" for Germans and Turks alike.[39]

Since the Porte proved totally unresponsive and, in violation of the "preliminary agreements" of March and August, had yet to pay a single monthly construction subsidy for the Mesopotamian job, the company finally obtained some official help from the embassy. On September 19, 1916 Lossow presented himself to Enver and pointed out to him that unless the company received the promised payments for its work east of Ras el Ain, the project would probably have to be terminated. This warning and a complaint by Wolff-Metternich to Talât finally produced some results, for a few days later the Ottoman finance ministry transferred about T£ 41,000 to the B.E.G.'s account as compensation for work done up to September 1.[40]

This, alas, was to be the first and last Mesopotamian con-

[38] *Ibid.*, Bd. 86, Wolff-Metternich to Bethmann Hollweg, 3 May 1916, No. 209 and enclosures.

[39] *Ibid.*, Bd. 90, Wolff-Metternich to Bethmann Hollweg, 7 Sept 1916, No. 534; Günther to Abbas Halim Paşa, 14 Sept.

[40] *Ibid.*, Wolff-Metternich to FO, 20 Sept 1916, No. 236; Zimmermann to Roedern, 30 Sept.

struction subsidy the Porte paid out. Although the company and the Porte finally agreed on and signed a "definitive" treaty in January 1917 regarding the extension of the Bagdad line from Ras el Ain toward Nusaybin and beyond, the agreed-upon compensation of the company for its monthly construction expenses remained a dead letter throughout the remainder of the war.[41] As a result the German government, as the guarantor of the job, had to reimburse the B.E.G. itself, a highly onerous obligation which was to cost the Berlin treasury well over 100 million marks before the war ended.[42]

WHILE THE Porte simply reneged on its contractual obligations in the Mesopotamian construction work, its position on the Taurus and Amanus projects was even stronger since the "emergency" construction there had never been the subject of any treaty to which it was a party. Despite the Wilhelmstrasse's efforts to remedy this defect and to make the Turks assume a share of the financial burden, the Porte successfully evaded all such invitations right down to the end of the war.[43]

[41] See *ibid.*, Bd. 92, Kühlmann to FO (Huguenin to Gwinner and Stauss), 11 Jan 1917, No. 47; 27 Jan, No. 116; 8 Feb, No. 164. The treaty followed essentially the pattern of the previous preliminary agreements and, at the Porte's insistence, was drawn up solely in the Turkish language.

[42] See DZA, Büro Staatsminister Dr. Helfferich, *Akten betr. Türkei*, Bd. 2, "Verpflichtungen des Deutschen Reiches . . . gegenüber der Bagdadbahn-Gesellschaft," (n.d., probably July 1918). For a partial list of the monthly payments made see FO, *Türkei 152*, Bd. 92, Dombois to Zimmermann, 12 March 1917; and Bd. 98, Roedern to FO, 29 Nov 1917.

[43] The Turks did offer repeatedly to conclude a separate treaty with the B.E.G. (which was to take the place of the company's contract with the Reich), but the B.E.G., naturally, refused. See *ibid.*, Bd. 92, Zimmermann to Kühlmann (Stauss to *Anatolie*), 31 Jan 1917, No. 110; Kühlmann to FO (Huguenin to Gwinner and Stauss), 3 Feb, No. 146; Zimmermann to Kühlmann, 7 Feb, No. 132; Gwinner to Zimmermann, 22 Feb; Bd. 98, Roedern to FO, 29 Nov; Bd. 100, FO to Bernstorff, 1 Feb 1918; Bd. 101, Stauss to FO, 29 Aug 1918.

The Bagdad Railroad

To increase Berlin's frustrations the Ottoman authorities indulged in a variety of practices which made the actual completion of the Taurus and Amanus jobs more costly and more time-consuming than Riese and others had originally calculated.

As previously mentioned, the first shipments of building supplies and motor vehicles for the Taurus and Amanus projects had arrived from Germany in January 1916, and by March several German motorized detachments were operating in the Taurus region. During the next three months sizeable quantities of building materials and an army railroad company were brought in from the Reich, but since the Ottoman authorities had meanwhile begun to arrest and deport many of the Armenian construction crews, work in both mountain ranges was actually reduced to a very slow pace during most of the summer. According to a report received by the OHL on October 1 the net effect of the Armenian deportations was that in both the Taurus and Amanus two-thirds of the originally scheduled work had been left undone, and estimated completion dates had to be revised significantly as a result of the Porte's anti-Armenian mania. Despite the assignment of additional German and Austro-Hungarian trucks to the Taurus route the average daily tonnage moved through that bottleneck was still distressingly low at this time (about 50 tons), resulting in the pile-up of enormous quantities of supplies at the railhead north of the Taurus.[44]

In spite of a variety of serious technical problems construction work both in the Taurus and the Amanus seems to have picked up speed during the first half of 1917. By August of that year improvised rail communications through both mountain ranges—via a narrow-gauge track in the Taurus and over a standard-gauge line in the Amanus—were fully operative.

[44] Cf. Reichskriegsministerium (Reichsarchiv), *Der Weltkrieg 1914 bis 1918,* x (Berlin, 1936), 616; Mühlmann, *deutsch-türkische Waffenbündnis,* pp. 185-86; Pomiankowski, pp. 259-60.

To increase the capacity of the main line east of the Taurus, a sizeable number of locomotives and about 600 freight cars had meanwhile been disassembled and moved across the mountains, but since there was a chronic shortage of fuel the newly opened routes never came close to peak efficiency.[45]

While 1917 was a relatively good year in terms of construction work accomplished, it also witnessed the de facto bankruptcy of the B.E.G., an event which caused much friction between the German government and the Porte before the year was over.

After the B.E.G. had incurred another net operating loss of several million marks for the business year 1916, Gwinner and Stauss early in 1917 cornered Cavid during one of his periodic appearances in Berlin and demanded that the *Betriebsschlüssel* clause in the 1903 Concession be adjusted at once to the realities of the day. Specifically, they proposed that the annual kilometric revenue retainable by the company be raised retroactively to 9,000 francs for the war period 1914-15 and to 10,000 for the year 1916; and that during the remainder of the war the company be allowed to keep all revenues on a cost-plus-10-percent basis. Cavid agreed that some corrective action regarding the distribution of revenues was in order, but before he could be pinned down on the details he was called back to Constantinople to join the newly-formed Talât cabinet.

Frustrated once again in their efforts to get rid of the obnoxious *Betriebsschlüssel*, Gwinner and Stauss notified the Wilhelmstrasse on February 16, 1917 that unless the Reich stepped into the breach and granted the company a "secret" subsidy for the "operation" of the Bagdad line, the B.E.G. could no longer vouch for the orderly movement of military transports. The directors pointed out that the increased cost of fuel alone ate up virtually the entire revenue the company was allowed to keep, the cumulative operational losses since

[45] Cf. Schwarte, p. 250; Mühlmann, *deutsch-türkische Waffenbündnis*, pp. 186-88.

the beginning of the war had meanwhile grown to about six million marks, and a Reich subsidy of about nine million would be just sufficient to keep the B.E.G. "above water" until the end of the year.[46]

While the German treasury had long since subsidized the operation of the Bagdad railroad in a roundabout way (since 1915 it had loaned the Porte virtually all the money which the latter owed to the company for the transportation of Ottoman troops), the idea of paying the B.E.G. a direct operational subsidy was unsympathetic to most of the governmental leaders in Berlin. When Gwinner tried to force the Wilhelmstrasse's hand a few weeks later by pointing out that the next Annual Report of the *Deutsche Bank* would necessarily have to reveal the catastrophic financial situation of the B.E.G. and ought to include some statement that help from the Reich was on the way, Zimmermann bluntly advised him that such an announcement would be inappropriate. The imperial government, the state secretary informed him on March 27, had every intention

> of supporting the Bagdad Railroad Company as much as possible [*nach Kräften*] in its efforts to create new foundations for the construction and operation of the line and to assist in the maintenance and growth of this enterprise, which is important for German and Turkish interests alike. However, it is too early to tell whether the German Reich will be in a position to lend its credit for the attainment of this goal. . . .[47]

Naturally the officialdom of the B.E.G. did not give up that easily. Vice-President Günther in Constantinople, in particular, kept up a steady barrage of warnings to various and sundry German government officials and finally persuaded Am-

[46] FO, *Türkei 152*, Bd. 92, Gwinner and Stauss to Zimmermann, 16 Feb 1917.
[47] *Ibid.*, Bd. 93, Zimmermann to Gwinner, 27 March 1917.

bassador Kühlmann, himself the son of a former *Anatolie* director, that the B.E.G. needed and deserved more help from the Reich. On May 19 Kühlmann wrote a cautiously worded letter to Bethmann Hollweg in which he pointed out that a possible financial collapse of the B.E.G. would entail a serious loss of prestige for the Reich. Since the Porte, despite all previous promises, was obviously unwilling to satisfy the company's requests for an adjustment of the *Betriebsschlüssel*, and since the prevailing political climate was hardly suitable for the exertion of diplomatic pressure, the temporary advance of German government funds seemed to be the only viable solution. In bailing the company out, Kühlmann concluded, Berlin might do well to remember that "neither the *Deutsche Bank* nor any other German financial institution would have touched the Bagdad railroad purely as a business venture if there had not been the hope and expectation in the background that important purposes of imperial policy were thereby being served."[48]

Judging from the available evidence, Kühlmann's recommendations did not elicit any response from Bethmann Hollweg. To get some action on the matter the ambassador and Gen. Lossow thereupon called a conference with the company's senior officers and several representatives of the Ottoman High Command, among them Böttrich and his deputy, Lt. Col. Pfannenstiel. After reviewing the unsatisfactory progress of the B.E.G.'s construction projects the conferees received a highly pessimistic report by Günther on the financial situation of the railroad. Günther pointed out that the B.E.G. had accumulated debts several times higher than its total capital stock, neither the *Deutsche Bank* nor any other institution was willing to advance any more money, and insolvency was imminent. Under German law, he emphasized, the company would be obliged to declare its bankruptcy, but for political

[48] *Ibid.*, Bd. 94, Kühlmann to Bethmann Hollweg, 19 May 1917, No. 291.

reasons this had not been done. What was needed now was prompt assistance from the German treasury, for even though a satisfactory settlement with the Porte would "no doubt" be achieved "some day," the B.E.G. could not survive without Berlin's help in the meantime.

Although Lossow went out of his way to impress upon Günther and Huguenin that the OHL was not interested in the *Betriebsschlüssel* problem as such or how the company ever solved it, he conceded that German governmental aid was in order; for the financial collapse of the B.E.G. would obviously affect the efficiency of the railroad and thereby hurt "military interests." Everyone else at the conference agreed with Lossow on this point, and recommendations for the grant of a German government loan to the B.E.G. were thereupon drafted and sent out to both the OHL and the chancellor's office in Berlin.[49]

It appears that these recommendations finally convinced the Berlin foreign office that some direct aid to the B.E.G. was indeed necessary. Relevant discussions with the B.E.G. Administrative Council were initiated at the end of June, but it soon became obvious that the B.E.G. really preferred to get its money from the Porte rather than from the German treasury. As Günther explained to the OHL (via Zimmermann), the crux of the problem was that operational subsidies from the Reich would sooner or later become known to the Porte, and the B.E.G. would then have even less leverage in getting the obnoxious *Betriebsschlüssel* adjusted than it had heretofore. Berlin should therefore initiate steps to force the Turks into a more accommodating policy toward the company. A few days later Gwinner and Stauss sent a similar appeal to the OHL. On July 9 Ludendorff obliged with a message to Enver, urging

[49] See *ibid.*, Report on "Sitzung am 8. Juni 1917 in Sachen Bagdadbahn . . . "; Kühlmann to Bethmann Hollweg, 15 June 1917, No. 336.

him to support the company's claims at the Porte, but the latter studiously ignored this new approach.[50]

In the meantime the B.E.G. Administrative Council had prepared a lengthy printed report on the history of the Bagdad railroad enterprise and the reasons for its steady drift toward bankruptcy. Obviously meant to impress the Berlin foreign office and the treasury department with the need for decisive action, the report pointed out that even before the war started the company had faced formidable financial problems, and that intervention by the Reich had meanwhile become all the more necessary. Although in theory there were several ways the company could be saved, the only viable solution obviously lay in the grant of a low-interest government loan of about 100 million marks, which would allow the B.E.G. "to pay off its big current debt" and survive the war years.[51]

With this report the desired impression was finally made in Berlin. On July 24, 1917 the Wilhelmstrasse formally agreed to the grant of a M 96,460,000 loan (*Amortisationsdarlehen*) by the Reich which was to enable the B.E.G. to reduce its debts to a level below the sum total of its capital stock. As security the B.E.G. assigned to the Reich–Ottoman government bonds of the Bagdad Series II and III at a nominal value of 118 million marks and agreed furthermore that under certain circumstances it would hand over more than half of the company's stock within a year's time.[52]

Although this big loan allowed the B.E.G. to wipe out much of its indebtedness, it did not materially improve the company's ability to cope with the ever mounting expenses for current

[50] Cf. *ibid.*, Zimmermann to Lersner, 30 June 1917, No. 1,224; Bd. 95, Gwinner and Stauss to Oldershausen, 5 July; Bd. 98, Bernstorff to FO, 13 Dec, No. 1,626.
[51] *Ibid.*, Bd. 94, "Die Bagdadbahn" (printed report by B.E.G. Administrative Council, June 1917).
[52] *Ibid.*, Bd. 96, Treaty between the Reich and the B.E.G.; Treaty between the Reich and the *Deutsche Bank*, 24 July 1917.

operations. With the *Betriebsschlüssel* still syphoning off its revenues the company quickly ran into new financial difficulties, and within three months the whole issue of operational expenses was once again brought to the fore by the company's officials. Since the Turks continued to be deaf to the company's complaints and the Wilhelmstrasse showed little inclination to enter the fray, the company directors once again took their problems to Ludendorff personally.[53] What followed was a rather curious tug-of-war between the OHL and the Ottoman government which, but for the intervention of the German embassy in Constantinople, might well have caused a serious rift in the alliance.

The opening shot in the new *Betriebsschlüssel* battle was made by Ludendorff on December 7, when he instructed Lossow to inform Enver that German military assistance in the recapture of southern Palestine would be problematical unless the B.E.G. was allowed to keep a much bigger share of its operating revenues. Before the *Militärbevollmächtigter* had a chance to deliver this message Günther appeared at the embassy to notify everyone concerned that Cavid had just offered the company a lump sum of five million marks, or roughly 50 percent of what the B.E.G. wanted, as compensation for its operational losses in 1915 and 1916.[54] Notified of this latest development, Ludendorff rescinded his original instructions to Lossow and ordered him to present the following substitute message to the vice-generalissimo:

To His Excellency Enver Pasha:

The long negotiations concerning the improvement of the Bagdad Railroad Company's financial situation have so far only resulted in ... [Cavid's offer] to pay M 5,000,000 to the company as compensation for its claims regarding the war years 1915/16. However, the company's claims for that pe-

---

[53] See *ibid.*, Bd. 98, Günther to OHL, 22 Oct 1917; Bernstorff to Michaelis, 1 Nov, No. 537; Ludendorff to Kühlmann, 6 Dec.
[54] *Ibid.*, Bernstorff to FO, 7 Dec 1917, Nos. 1,585, 1,588, 1,591.

riod amount to at least M 10,000,000. The financial situation of the Bagdad Railroad Company is becoming steadily more difficult and serious . . . [because of rapidly mounting operating expenses] which are not balanced by an appropriate increase in revenues. I see in the [financial] crisis a grave danger for the economic and especially for the military situation of Turkey. . . .

I, therefore, urge Your Excellency to see to it that the Bagdad Railroad Company (1) receives full compensation for the war years 1915/16, and (2) is allowed, from January 1, 1917, on, a 75% share of the incoming revenues . . . [above 10,000 francs], and that the base rate is raised from 4,500 to 6,000 francs per annum.

The Turkish quartermaster general has transmitted to me the wishes of Your Excellency regarding the continuation of operations [that is, Ottoman requests for German troops]. I can promise the probable fulfillment of these wishes only if the aforementioned demands for the Bagdad Railroad Company will be satisfied by the Turkish government. . . . I would appreciate a notification as soon as possible concerning the success of Your Excellency's efforts in this matter. With due regard for the critical military situation [in Palestine], I have ordered all preparations for the dispatch of the requested personnel and matériel to be made. However, I cannot give the final order for their dispatch until I have received . . . [word from you that the B.E.G. will be helped].[55]

Although it is most doubtful that Enver liked this piece of ill-concealed blackmail he did his best during the following weeks to promote a satisfactory settlement with the B.E.G. However, none of his colleagues in the cabinet, including Talât, showed the slightest inclination to help him out. As Lossow wired to the OHL on December 22, the Ottoman cabi-

[55] *Ibid.*, Bernstorff to FO, 13 Dec 1917, No. 1,626. For the complicated background story see also Ludendorff to Kühlmann, 9 Dec; Bd. 99, same to same, 13 Dec.

net was adamantly opposed to making any changes in the B.E.G.'s concessionary status while the war was on, and the proffered lump payment of five million was the most the company could hope to get. Two days later Enver himself notified Ludendorff that he was still trying to get a better settlement but simultaneously intimated that there was not much hope the cabinet would relent.[56]

Despite explicit and implicit warnings from Lossow and Ambassador Bernstorff that Enver's hands were obviously tied, Ludendorff refused to give up. On December 30 he wired Lossow that his personal views were immaterial. Instead Lossow should inform both Enver and Talât that the OHL was not going to invest German manpower and materiel in the preparation of a Palestinian campaign unless the B.E.G.'s financial grievances were taken care of first, that is, unless the *Betriebsschlüssel* was changed. Braving Ludendorff's wrath Lossow immediately got on the telephone to point out to his superior that an ultimatum of this sort would be both dangerous and futile. After prolonged discussion Ludendorff agreed to have a milder version presented to the Porte, namely, that general compensatory payments to the B.E.G., without any change in the *Betriebsschlüssel*, would be accepted by the OHL as a satisfactory solution.[57]

On January 5, 1918 Cavid (who had once again gone to Berlin for financial negotiations) formally assured representatives of the OHL that the Porte was prepared to compensate the B.E.G. for its operational losses in an equitable manner, and Ludendorff thereupon declared the issue settled.[58]

This dénouement was most disappointing to the B.E.G., but all subsequent attempts by its Administrative Council to re-

[56] See *ibid.*, Bernstorff to FO, 22 Dec 1917, No. 1,702; 24 Dec, No. 1,711; same to Hertling, 25 Dec and enclosure.
[57] *Ibid.*, Bernstorff to FO, 30 Dec 1917, Nos. 1,743, 1,745; 31 Dec, No. 1,750.
[58] Cf. FO, *Türkei 110 Nr. 5, Handakten*, unsigned memo, Berlin, 3 Jan 1918; *Türkei 152*, Bd. 99, Lersner to FO, 8 Jan, No. 53.

open the case were quickly squelched by the OHL. Since the company and the Porte could not agree as to how the B.E.G.'s operational losses were to be calculated, no compensatory payments ever materialized before the Turks left the war.

While the German treasury department continued to pour money into the construction projects along the Bagdad line, there is no extant evidence that the B.E.G. received any other aid from the Reich during the remainder of the war. Whether the steady decline in the railroad's performance during the summer of 1918 was causally related to the financial problems of the company will probably never be known. In any case, between May and August the daily tonnage moving to Syria shrank precipitously because of dwindling supplies of fuel.[59]

There were growing indications that the war was lost, but some of the construction work on the Bagdad line, particularly in the Taurus, was pushed on at the insistence of the military. On October 9, 1918—just three weeks before the Armistice of Mudros took the Ottoman empire out of the war—the standard gauge line through the Taurus was opened for provisional use, thus allowing for the first time uninterrupted train service between the Bosporus and Aleppo.[60]

BECAUSE OF fluctuations in the exchange rates for Turkish pounds and a variety of other problems, the sum total of German government expenditures between 1914 and 1918 for the extension and upkeep of the Bagdad line cannot be determined with exactitude. By the summer of 1918 the accounts of the

[59] *Ibid.*, Stein to Kühlmann, 8 Jan 1918; Bd. 100, Gwinner and Stauss to FO, 25 Jan; Goeppert to Gwinner, 10 Feb; Gwinner to Goeppert, 19 Feb; Bd. 101, Gwinner and Stauss to FO, 1 June; Bussche to B.E.G. Administrative Council, 3 Aug and 17 Aug; Oldershausen to War Ministry, 11 Aug; "Aufzeichnungen über die Besprechung am 13. August 1918"; Wrisberg to FO, 23 Aug; Bernstorff, pp. 191-96; Mühlmann, *deutsch-türkische Waffenbündnis*, p. 218.

[60] Earle, p. 289; Mühlmann, *deutsch-türkische Waffenbündnis*, p. 32; Richard Hennig, "Die Fortschritte im Eisenbahnwesen Nord- und Osteuropas und Asiens im Jahre 1919," *Weltwirtschaftliches Archiv*, XVI (1921), 127.

German treasury department showed an outlay of roughly 207 million marks for the Taurus-Amanus project and about 103 million for the construction work in Mesopotamia. Gen. von Wrisberg's subsequent testimony that by the end of 1918 "about 360 million marks" had been paid out altogether is probably accurate.[61] All this "investment" by the Reich was lost after the war, together with the concessionary rights held by the *Anatolie* and B.E.G.[62] In the long run, the completed part of the Bagdad line, from the Bosporus to Nusaybin, played an important role in the economic development of the new Turkish Republic, though it was only in 1948 that the nationalization of the whole line was completed. In July 1940, in the midst of another world war, the last unfinished section of the original "Berlin to Bagdad" railroad (in Iraq, south of Mosul) was completed, and through-train service all the way from the Bosporus to Bagdad finally became a reality.[63]

[61] DZA, Büro Staatsminister Dr. Helfferich, *Akten betr. Türkei*, Bd. 2, "Verpflichtungen des Deutschen Reiches . . . gegenüber der Bagdadbahn-Gesellschaft"; Wrisberg, p. 180. In computing the figures in the Helfferich file an exchange rate of 20 marks per Turkish pound was used by the author, though this of course is only an approximation.

Mühlmann, *deutsch-türkische Waffenbündnis*, p. 297, claims the total value of German supplies used during the war in the improvement and build-up of "Turkey's Asiatic railroad network" was 435 million marks, but gives no documentation or explanation how he arrived at that figure.

[62] On the Allies' disposition of the rights and properties of the two German railroad companies in the Versailles and Sèvres peace treaties and on Allied-Turkish arrangements regarding the status of the Bagdad line in the years thereafter, see Earle, pp. 300-302, 321-36; Conker, pp. 29-30, 75-76; Howard, p. 240.

[63] See Conker, pp. 85-90, 105-108, 157-61, and *passim*; Karl Krüger, *Die neue Türkei* (Berlin, 1963), pp. 85-87; Gotthard Jäschke, *Die Türkei in den Jahren 1942-1951. Geschichtskalender . . .* (Wiesbaden, 1955), pp. 79-81; Pönicke, "Heinrich August Meissner-Pascha . . . ," p. 208, E. Rossi, "Completamento della 'Ferrovia di Baghdad,'" *Oriente Moderno*, 20 (1940), p. 513.

CHAPTER X

German Efforts to Secure Economic Predominance

THE ECONOMIC penetration of the Ottoman empire by German business interests made very little progress between 1914 and 1918, nor was the German government very successful in harnessing the natural resources of its Turkish ally for the war effort of the Reich. While a great deal was said and written in wartime Germany about the feasibility and desirability of converting the Ottoman empire into a major market and raw materials supplier for the Reich,[1] attempts to implement such plans almost invariably ran into political or technical snags. Indeed, in some areas the positions and influence secured by German financial, industrial, and commercial interest groups prior to 1914 were actually eroded in the course of the war.

The promotion of Germany's multifarious economic interests in the Ottoman empire after the outbreak of World War I was of course hampered from the very start by the absorption of most of the German resources in the national war effort, but even if investment capital, export commodities, and suitable personnel had been in more plentiful supply, the net results would probably have been quite similar. As Ahmed Emin [Yalman] correctly observed more than thirty years ago,

[1] Most of the pamphlets, booklets, and scholarly monographs on this subject appeared during the latter half of the war. For representative samples see Albert Ritter, *Berlin-Bagdad: Neue Ziele mitteleuropäischer Politik* (Munich, 1916), a reprint of a pamphlet first published in 1913; Reinhard Junge, *Die deutsch-türkischen Wirtschaftsbeziehungen* (Weimar, 1916); Ernst Marré, *Die Türken und Wir nach dem Kriege. Ein praktisches Wirtschaftsprogramm* (Berlin, 1916); Max Blanckenhorn, *Syrien und die deutsche Arbeit* (Weimar, 1916); Josef Hellauer, ed., *Das Türkische Reich* (Berlin, 1918). For a review of the "*Orient-Propaganda*" in wartime Germany cf. Meyer, pp. 218-21 and *passim*; and Rathmann, *Stossrichtung*, pp. 41-61, 179-95, and *passim*, the latter highly polemical but rich in factual information.

all leading figures of the Union and Progress regime were united in their determination to whittle down foreign influence in the country, and throughout the war a "very acute suspicion of German post-war designs was dominant in all minds." The Germans were therefore forced to proceed very cautiously in their search for economic gain and power.[2]

The determination of the *Ittihad ve Terakki* Party to curtail the economic influence and privileges traditionally enjoyed by foreign interest groups was very clearly revealed by the unilateral abrogation of the capitulatory system in the fall of 1914, but this proved to be merely the beginning. Indeed, the longer the war lasted the more outspoken and energetic the Porte became in asserting itself to the outside world, and the brunt of this "aggressive nationalism"—to use Emin's phrase—was borne just as much by Turkey's allies as by her declared enemies.

Although during the first year of the war the Ottoman empire was for all intents and purposes physically isolated from the Central Powers, German business circles and journalists wasted no time in forging ambitious plans for the economic "development" of the Sultan's lands. Long before the collapse of Serbia opened a secure line of communication to Constantinople, several new private organizations had sprung up in the Reich whose avowed purpose it was to stimulate German-Ottoman trade and to secure valuable objects for exploitation by German firms. In March 1915 the *Deutsche Levante-Verband* was founded in Berlin to coordinate future efforts of that sort. Shortly thereafter a so-called *Deutsches Vorderasien-Institut* constituted itself under the patronage of prominent businessmen, journalists, and politicians, among them Director Albert Ballin of the HAPAG and Gustav Stresemann. In a mani-

[2] Emin, pp. 113-14. Cf. his wartime pamphlet for German readers, *Die Türkei* (Gotha, 1918), in which he warned, at least by implication, against underestimating the national pride and will to independence of his fellow Turks.

festo to the public the *Institut* expressed the hope that Germany's share in the "reorganization" of the Ottoman economy would increase greatly after the war and declared it more important than ever that the attention of all German circles who were "interested in the political, intellectual, and economic" opportunities for national action be directed to Asia Minor.[3]

To make sure that these and some of the older Orient-minded organizations in the Reich would not work at cross purposes to each other and to the imperial government, Ernst Jäckh proposed to the Wilhelmstrasse in July 1915 that all economic ventures in the Ottoman empire be supervised and coordinated by a special office. Jäckh's proposal to entrust his own German-Turkish Association (*Deutsch-Türkische Vereinigung*) with this task was subsequently approved, and by the end of 1915 a so-called *Deutsch-Türkische Wirtschaftszentrale* had been chartered as an affiliate of the *Vereinigung*.[4]

While the Wilhelmstrasse allocated an annual subsidy of 30,000 marks for the operation of the agency and otherwise took a lively interest in its activities, official government efforts to promote the penetration of the Ottoman economy by German interests remained low-keyed during the first year of the war. Although some conversations with individual members of the Porte were held regarding the future role of German business and industry in the Ottoman empire, there is no evidence that these approaches were very carefully prepared or that a basic plan or program had as yet been worked out by

[3] Subsequently a number of additional private organizations for the advancement of German trade and commerce in the Ottoman empire were founded, among them the *Deutsch-Orientalische Handelsgesellschaft*, the *Dresdener Orient- und Uebersee-Gesellschaft*, the *Mitteleuropäische Handelsvereinigung*, and the *Deutsch-Türkische Handelsgesellschaft*. Rathmann, *Stossrichtung*, pp. 145-47.

[4] *Ibid.*, pp. 147-55. The agency was subsequently renamed *Zentralgeschäftsstelle für Deutsch-Türkische Wirtschaftsfragen* and organized or sponsored seminars, lecture series, research projects, and so forth.

the imperial government. One project on which serious discussions were initiated in 1915 was the mobilization of German resources for the expansion of Ottoman shipbuilding facilities, but the initiative in this matter came from the Turkish side. Moreover these discussions never produced any results, for even though the *Reichsmarineamt* and all major German shipbuilding firms were more than eager to expand their influence at the Golden Horn, no agreement on the financial aspects of the project could be reached. As a result, the specially founded *Deutsch-Osmanische Werftenvereinigung*, representing Blohm & Voss, Krupp-Germania, Schichau, and other German shipyards, was still haggling with the Porte when the war ended, and no construction work ever materialized.[5]

The defeat of Serbia in the fall of 1915 and the subsequent opening of a secure line of communication between central Europe and Constantinople naturally ushered in a completely new phase in the military and economic relationship between the Central Powers and their Ottoman ally. The new situation at long last allowed the Turks to obtain badly needed supplies and military equipment from the Central Powers, while, conversely, Germany and Austria-Hungary were now able to draw some raw materials from Turkey.[6] Regarding the latter transaction a great deal has been written about the efficiency and ruthlessness with which the Germans stripped the Ottoman empire, but a review of the facts indicates that the Reich did by no means just pick up whatever it needed. From the beginning of 1916, when large-scale Ottoman ex-

[5] See FO, *Dt 128 Nr. 5 secr.*, Bd. 5, Jäckh to Zimmermann, 2 Jan 1915; Jäckh Papers, No. 4, Enver to Tirpitz, 10 Aug 1915; Tirpitz to Enver, 24 Aug 1915; DZA, Büro Staatsminister Dr. Helfferich, *Akten betr. Türkei,* Bd. 2, Memo about "Deutsch-Osmanische Werften-Gesellschaft," May 1918.

[6] On the movement of goods through the Balkans during 1916-18 and the technical problems attending thereto, see F. B., "Die militärischen Durchgangsfrachten . . . ," pp. 346-55.

ports to Germany first became possible, until the end of the war, Ottoman raw materials valued at 300 million marks were shipped to Germany—wool, cotton, ore, oil, and leather. All of these shipments (in contrast to most of Germany's deliveries to Turkey) were paid for in cash—often at inflated prices, since the Ottoman commissariat increasingly monopolized the management of exports and thereby made it impossible for the German purchasing agencies to strike bargains with competitive suppliers.[7] Moreover, while there was a great deal of public discussion in Germany about the actual and potential food-producing capabilities of the Ottoman empire, the actual export of Turkish foodstuffs to Germany during the war years never reached major proportions. On the other hand, during the last two war years sizeable shipments of grain were sent to Turkey, usually at German government expense, from the occupied parts of Rumania and other areas.[8]

While Germany's war industry definitely benefited from the Ottoman exports of various ores—over 12,000 tons were received during 1916 and 1917—the efforts of German firms to gain new concessions for the exploitation of mineral deposits in the Ottoman empire proved futile in all but a few cases. One of the exceptions was the Krupp Company, which was vitally interested in getting some of the chrome ore deposits in the Ottoman empire under its control. The company's head office explained to the Wilhelmstrasse in late November 1915 that Krupp's stockpile of chrome ore was rapidly shrinking, thereby endangering the continued production of armored plate, gun barrels, shells, and assorted other materiel for the German navy and army. About 3,000 tons of the ore had al-

[7] Cf. Pomiankowski, pp. 267-68; Wrisberg, pp. 175-86, 288-89; Emin, pp. 135-38; Mühlmann, *deutsch-türkische Waffenbündnis*, pp. 246-47.

[8] On the recurring food crises in Constantinople and German efforts to remedy the situation, cf. Pomiankowski, pp. 263-64, 319-20, 403-404; Emin, pp. 119-34; and the extensive correspondence, involving Ludendorff and other high-ranking figures, in FO, *Türkei 134*, Bde. 37 and 38.

Efforts Toward Economic Predominance

ready been located and purchased in the Ottoman empire, but the firm would need much more than that and was therefore endeavoring to obtain a regular mining concession. This project was all the more important in that

> even after the conclusion of peace the Krupp Company will probably have to wait for an extended period of time before it can obtain chrome ores from New Caledonia or South Africa. For the steel production of the Krupp Company it is nothing less than a question of life or death whether it succeeds in bringing in large quantities of chrome ore from Asia Minor or not.[9]

Fortunately for Krupp the Porte was for once in a cooperative mood (the fact that it owed the firm millions for armament deliveries in the prewar years may have helped), and on December 28, 1915 it formally granted a lease on three chrome mines.[10]

While the Wilhelmstrasse and other government agencies in Berlin had been relatively passive during the first year and a half of the war in questions relating to the exploitation of Turkey's mineral resources, they radically changed their stance in 1916. In February of that year the Prussian war ministry and the *Reichsmarineamt* drew up joint recommendations for the establishment of centralized controls over all German mining ventures in the Ottoman empire. In particular, they proposed the creation of a "Geological Bureau" in Constantinople and the dispatch of a fact-finding mission to the Ottoman provinces under the auspices of the Prussian *Königlich Geologische Landesanstalt*. Although these proposals were subse-

[9] See *ibid.*, Bd. 34, Zimmermann to Wangenheim, 20 Oct 1915, No. 783; Baur and Ehrensberger to FO, 30 Nov.

[10] *Ibid.*, Bd. 35, Wolff-Metternich to FO, 23 Dec 1915, No. 3,028; Neurath to Bethmann Hollweg, 30 Dec. On Krupp's financial claims against the Porte see, for example, *Türkei 142*, Bd. 40, *Direktorium Krupp Co.* to FO, 24 Sept 1914; Bd. 48, same to same, 27 April 1915.

quently debated in numerous interdepartmental conferences, nothing much ever came of them, particularly since it was becoming obvious that the Porte would react unkindly to any German moves resembling an organized raid on Ottoman natural resources. Aside from the appointment of an "economic advisor" at the Prussian war ministry's liaison office in Constantinople no progress was made in bringing the German search for mining concessions under centralized control, nor did the Porte show any inclination to open talks concerning the participation of German firms in the exploitation of the empire's untapped mineral wealth.[11]

While the recalcitrance of the Turks was disappointing enough, the Germans were even more disturbed by growing evidence that they would have to reckon with keen Austro-Hungarian competition throughout the Ottoman empire. Official Austro-Hungarian interest in the economic plums of the Ottoman empire had been minimal during the early part of the war, but with the opening of the Balkan route the Ballhausplatz quickly abandoned its passivity.[12] As Burian confided to Pallavicini in February 1916, the Dual Monarchy's task in the immediate future was to secure for itself an appropriate share of economic influence in the Ottoman empire and to exploit the Turks' obvious disinclination to allow the Germans

[11] See Rathmann, *Stossrichtung*, pp. 160-66.

[12] This passive attitude of Vienna during much of 1915 was doubtless the result of periodic reports from Pallavicini that the Turks had mixed feelings about their two allies and would certainly resist any attempts to tie them in more closely with the Central Powers, politically or economically. See, for example, AHFM, *Krieg 21a, Türkei*, Pallavicini to Berchtold, 23 Dec 1914, No. 76/P; same to Burian, 7 Dec 1915, No. 101A-E/P; *Türkei, Berichte 1915*, same to same, 25 Oct 1915, No. 90C/P; 20 Nov 1915, No. 97B/P. On Austria-Hungary's prewar efforts to broaden its economic influence in the Ottoman empire see Fritz Klein, "Die Rivalität zwischen Deutschland und Oesterreich-Ungarn in der Türkei am Vorabend des ersten Weltkrieges," in *Politik im Krieg 1914-1918*, Fritz Klein, ed. (Berlin, 1964), pp. 1-17 and *passim*.

a monopolistic hold on their country. To this end Austria-Hungary should aim to participate in due measure in the economic projects of German groups but also make it clear to the Turks that the Dual Monarchy did not sympathize with any German efforts to secure a predominant position in the Ottoman economy. Burian noted that if

> we keep our eyes open, and if we adjust ourselves early enough to the nationalistic sensitivity of the presently [ruling] Osmanlis, we shall—while fully maintaining our intimate alliance relationship with Germany—encounter quite a few opportunities for promoting the interests in Turkey which the [Dual] Monarchy has now and will have to an even larger extent henceforth.[13]

The determination of the Ballhausplatz and of Austro-Hungarian business circles to keep an "appropriate" share of the Ottoman market was soon noted by German agencies in Constantinople. On April 22, 1916 the German consulate-general there sent a complaint to Bethmann Hollweg that Austrian and Hungarian commercial firms were competing unscrupulously with German establishments, and that they were quite obviously trying to carve out a "hegemonial position" for themselves. Moreover, the Austro-Hungarian authorities in the Ottoman capital were displaying considerable ingenuity in impressing the Turks with their country's goodwill and generosity. Thus they had arranged a public display of the heavy artillery they had brought to Turkey, opened a hospital for free treatment of the natives, and initiated other similar projects. To counteract this pull, the consulate-general concluded, more German consumer goods should be shipped to Constantinople—perhaps 30 carloads per month—which should be assigned the same priority as military transports.[14]

[13] AHFM, *Türkei, Weisungen 1916*, Burian to Pallavicini, 9 Feb 1916, No. 592.

[14] Jackh Papers, No. 19, Renner to Bethmann Hollweg, 22 April 1916, No. 30.

Efforts Toward Economic Predominance

During the following months additional warnings and complaints about Austro-Hungarian "forwardness" and efforts to build up economic and cultural influence in the Ottoman empire reached Berlin from various sides, but it was only at the beginning of 1917 that the Wilhelmstrasse began to react in an official manner.[15] As State Secretary Zimmermann noted in a lengthy dispatch of March 25 to the Vienna embassy, there was some evidence that Austrian and Hungarian financial groups had their eyes on the Heraclea coal basin, the oil fields of Mesopotamia, and irrigation projects in the Plain of Adana—all three being objects in which the *Deutsche Bank* and its subsidiary companies had long since taken a keen interest. Zimmermann noted that the Reich welcomed Austro-Hungarian participation in the general "economic development" of the Ottoman empire, but an attempt to interfere with the long-standing "rights" of German interest groups would be regrettable.

> Through a now suddenly arising Austro-Hungarian competition both sides would . . . be harmed, and the continuation of enterprises which are so important for the economic recuperation of Turkey would be delayed and hampered.

Ambassador von Wedel should therefore drop a friendly hint to the Ballhausplatz that it ought to restrain the Austro-Hungarian financial groups in question, though Wedel should also make it clear that Germany had no objection to certain other Austro-Hungarian projects in the Ottoman empire, such as the development of a sugar-processing industry, the acquisition of brickyards, and the like. Moreover, Austro-Hungarian participation "to an appropriate degree" in some of the hitherto purely German development projects was by no means out of the question and might be made the subject of negotiations.[16]

[15] Cf. Pomiankowski, pp. 265-67; Rathmann, *Stossrichtung*, pp. 166-67.

[16] FO, *Türkei 152*, Bd. 93, Zimmermann to Wedel, 25 March 1917.

Efforts Toward Economic Predominance

About two weeks after this appeal the Prussian war ministry called a conference of interested government departments
regarding Germany's long-range economic plans in the Ottoman empire and the problems posed by Austria-Hungary's
competitive efforts there. It was agreed that the "economic
exploitation of Turkey" after the war required prompt preparatory measures, under the overall direction of the department
of the interior, and that governmental support of pertinent research would probably be in order. Direct financial assistance
from the Reich for "efforts to acquire concessions in hitherto
unexplored projects" was, however, "emphatically" ruled out
by the representatives of the treasury department. It was further agreed that it would be advisable to bring in the *Deutsche
Bank* right away since it was particularly familiar with Turkish conditions and had a strong interest in the area. Most of
the conferees also felt that Germany should proceed "in common with Austria-Hungary" and allow for Turkish participation in whatever was done. The war ministry was instructed
to inform the Vienna authorities of the German plan and to
propose "common action in conjunction with an appropriate
grant of credit."[17]

In Constantinople Kühlmann readily agreed with Berlin's
decision to proceed in common with Austria-Hungary. He
wrote to Bethmann Hollweg:

> The present situation with its mutual running matches
> [sic], underbidding, and intriguing of all sorts, must cease
> if we want to escape the danger of having perpetual business
> collisions with each other on the one hand, which also dis-
> turb our political relations quite considerably, and of work-

[17] *Ibid., Türkei 197,* Bd. 6, "Niederschrift über die am 7. April 1917
stattgehabte Besprechung wegen wirtschaftlicher Ausnutzung der
Türkei im Frieden." Cf. memorandum by Regedanz about "Studien-
syndikat für deutsche Bergwerksunternehmungen in der Türkei," n.d.
(probably April 1917).

ing, on the other hand, into the hands of the Turks, who are past masters at playing ... one party against the other.

An understanding [with Vienna] will bring us numerous advantages and will be all the more necessary in that after the war hostile and neutral, particularly American, capital [*Finanz*] will reappear on the scene, in competition with which we can only hope to succeed if both empires [Germany and the Dual Monarchy] proceed in complete unison.

As for the mode of cooperation Kühlmann thought a geographic division of the Ottoman empire or a division by economic categories would be unworkable; instead, all "objects" of interest to the two Central Powers would have to be worked on in common, preferably according to a prearranged formula fixing the share of each side in a particular enterprise. In this connection it should be made clear to Austria-Hungary that it could not really expect "us to return to second place in the Balkan and Orient business"; for aside from Germany's lead in terms of investments and her pivotal role in opening up the Ottoman market through the Bagdad railroad, her wartime assistance to the Turks, particularly in terms of money, certainly entitled Germany to get at least a position of parity.[18]

The desirability of coming to an agreement with Austria-Hungary on a division of labor in the Ottoman arena was underscored by the "infiltration" of Austro-Hungarian personnel into various governmental agencies in Constantinople. At the request of the Porte several German experts, civil servants, and others had been sent to the Ottoman capital in 1916 to serve as counsellors (*Beiräte*) at the ministries of education, justice, and commerce and agriculture. Though there was widespread doubt from the beginning whether the men would really be allowed to accomplish much in the way of "reform," the Dual Monarchy had never abandoned its efforts to place some Austro-Hungarian experts into the Ottoman administrative ap-

[18] See Rathmann, *Stossrichtung*, pp. 168-69.

paratus as well.[19] Now, in April 1917, Vienna landed its first major coup in that respect, for five Austro-Hungarian advisers were hired by the Ottoman commissariat to work in the areas of electrical engineering, hydraulics, mining, agriculture, and forestry (the latter field, it should be noted, having long since become a special preserve for Austro-Hungarian advisers at the ministerial level).[20]

While the Austro-Hungarian penetration of the Ottoman commissariat raised some eyebrows in Germany, Vienna's official reaction to Zimmermann's request of March 27 was even more disturbing. As the Ballhausplatz informed Ambassador von Wedel on May 7, it shared Berlin's view that "superfluous rivalry" between Austro-Hungarian and German economic groups in the Ottoman empire should be prevented. On the other hand, the Dual Monarchy could not forego the independent pursuit of its interests in the Orient. The question as to when common efforts were preferable to such independent action would have to be decided in each individual case. In any event, the particular objects of current Austro-Hungarian interest would be approached with due regard for any pre-established rights which Germany might happen to have in them.[21]

Aside from thus giving Berlin blunt notice that the Dual Monarchy meant to uphold its traditional economic influence in the Ottoman empire, Vienna supplied its representatives in Constantinople with a memorandum on how "German imperialism in Turkey" was to be resisted. According to Pom-

[19] See FO, *Türkei 139*, Bd. 38, Ottoman embassy Berlin to FO, 13 Nov 1915; Wolff-Metternich to Bethmann Hollweg, 4 Dec, No. 707; "Aufzeichnung," 10 Dec; AHFM, *Türkei LIII/2*, Pallavicini to Burian, 2 Nov 1915, No. 92B/P; 18 Dec, No. 103B/P; same to AHFM, 19 Dec, No. 940; same to Burian, 24 Dec, No. 104C/P; same to AHFM, 25 Sept 1916, No. 3578/A; Emin, p. 170.

[20] Pomiankowski, p. 320; Rathmann, *Stossrichtung*, p. 169.

[21] FO, *Türkei 152*, Bd. 94, AHFM to Wedel ("*Notiz*" by Gratz), 7 May 1917; Wedel to Bethmann Hollweg, 16 May.

iankowski's memoirs he replied to his superiors in Vienna that the promotion of Austro-Hungarian cultural, economic, and commercial influence in the Ottoman empire was somewhat hampered by the bigger means and the greater political influence the Germans had at their disposal, but that the balance was redressed somewhat by the Germans' "limited talent" in handling the Turks and the many "mistakes" they had already made in their policy.[22]

Pomiankowski's reference to the general "unpopularity" of the Germans was hardly news to Vienna. Pallavicini had been reporting along the same lines for a long time. Their assessments of Turkish public opinion on that subject were correct —indeed, several German representatives in Constantinople had long since come to similar conclusions—but it is also fairly clear that Austro-Hungarian hopes for exploiting the situation were largely unrealistic. In fact, at the same time that Pomiankowski was taking comfort in the "mistakes" the Germans had made, Talât intimated to Kühlmann that he had mixed feelings about Vienna's policies and regarded Germany, rather than the Dual Monarchy, as the principal partner of the Ottoman empire.[23]

As Rathmann has noted in his recent study, the efforts made by various German government agencies since the beginning of 1916 to place the economic penetration of the Ottoman empire under some form of centralized control were abandoned without result in the spring of 1917. But this did not mean that the imperial government retired from the scene. On the contrary, during the last year and a half of the war, it became for the first time really active in pushing for the acquisition of economic prizes in the Ottoman empire, most of the time with the direct encouragement of the OHL.

The decision of the OHL, and more particularly of its first

[22] Pomiankowski, pp. 323-24.

[23] FO, *Türkei 155*, Bd. 5, Kühlmann to Bethmann Hollweg, 14 May 1917, No. 279.

quartermaster general, to become involved in the question of economic concessions was somewhat justified by the needs of the German armed forces for raw materials, but Ludendorff soon made it clear that his interests went far beyond that. In this sphere of German policy, as in virtually every other sphere, he tried to set himself up as a mentor of the civilian government agencies and at times even as a policy-maker, an attempt which earned him a good deal of resentment in the Wilhelmstrasse, and a few rebuffs as well.[24]

Ludendorff's first major entry into the debate on the "development" of the Ottoman economy occurred in May 1917, when he sent a reminder to the Wilhelmstrasse that "our political collaboration with Turkey" both during and after the war would be "substantially furthered" if Germany's leading commercial firms could be persuaded to pay more attention to the Ottoman market. In a follow-up message to Bethmann Hollweg the quartermaster general pointed out that Germany's economic interests in the Ottoman empire were apparently being promoted in a rather haphazard fashion, and that the embassy in Constantinople ought to issue some guidelines to the various private interest groups concerned.[25]

Ludendorff's suggestion that the diplomatic representatives of the Reich were not doing a very good job was rejected out of hand by Zimmermann. As for the general's proposal to increase German commercial activities in the Ottoman empire, the Wilhelmstrasse engaged in lengthy correspondence on the matter but ultimately came up with nothing but negative responses from Constantinople. As the consulate-general there advised Bethmann Hollweg on July 16, the prospects for an intensification of German trade with the Ottoman empire were

[24] On the "rise of the OHL to political hegemony" in the Reich in 1916-17, see particularly the recent reassessment in Ritter, III, 253ff. Cf. Gordon A. Craig, *The Politics of the Prussian Army 1640-1945*, rev. edn. (New York, 1964), Chapter VIII.

[25] FO, *Türkei 158*, Bd. 17, Lersner to FO, 21 May 1917, No. 793; 22 May, No. 799.

dismal. German merchants without Orient experience would not find the business atmosphere congenial; also, official encouragement for German business ventures seemed most inappropriate in view of the unpredictable trend of Ottoman policy, the disappearance of the capitulatory system, etc. A week later Kühlmann chimed in with a report to Michaelis, pointing out that "confiscations, embargoes, and transportation problems" alike made the sale of German goods, "except for war matériel," most problematical, nor was there much room for German import firms, since all Ottoman export commodities were being handled by commissions and agencies of the government. On August 7 Zimmermann therefore coolly informed Ludendorff that his original proposal could not be acted upon for the time being.[26]

In the meantime the Wilhelmstrasse had initiated a much more ambitious policy project: to persuade the Turks that all British and French economic enterprises in their empire should be forcibly liquidated. The desirability of permanently dislodging the British and French firms in the Ottoman empire seems to have occurred to some government agencies in Berlin soon after the outbreak of war, but it was only in the spring of 1917 that a serious effort to that end was initiated.[27] Spurred on by Kühlmann (who later changed his mind drastically), and after lengthy discussion of the subject with other departments of the government, the Wilhelmstrasse drew up a policy paper in May 1917 in which the prompt liquidation of enemy firms by the Turks was declared desirable and feasible. Obviously meant for ultimate communication to the Porte,

[26] See *ibid.*, Zimmermann to Lersner, 23 May 1917, No. 961; same to Grünau, 24 May, No. 969; Lersner to FO, 5 June, No. 886; 10 June, No. 911; Zimmermann to Kühlmann, 27 June, No. 593; Daehnhardt to Bethmann Hollweg, 16 July; Kühlmann to Michaelis, 23 July, No. 391; Bd. 18, Zimmermann to Ludendorff, 7 Aug.

[27] Cf. FO, *Wk*, Bd. 53, "*Notiz*," 28 Oct 1914; Fischer, *Weltmacht*, pp. 780-81.

the paper first of all emphasized that such a measure was necessary for exerting counterpressures on the Entente bloc, some of whose member states had all but finished the liquidation of German and Austro-Hungarian firms in their sphere of influence. While the German government had already initiated suitable reprisals against British and French enterprises in the Reich, their total value was not large enough to equalize the damage:

> In order to hit the English and French effectively in the economic struggle unleashed by them, it will be necessary . . . to obtain the cooperation of the allied powers, among which only Bulgaria has so far followed the German example with a recently issued decree.
>
> The German government would, therefore, appreciate it if the Ottoman government, in whose sphere of power important English and French enterprises are located, should take a similar step as well. This seems all the more important in that it is a guiding principle of the German-Turkish alliance that in general an equalization of the gains and losses resulting from the war shall be arranged between the two countries. Such would hardly be the case if the enterprises of Germans in enemy countries are wiped out while [our] enemies would after the war find their own enterprises in German-allied Turkey intact.

But aside from the service the Porte could thus render to the Reich, the paper continued, it was in the Turks' own interest to carry out the proposed liquidation program. For one thing, they would thereby strengthen their position at the peace table. But even more important was the fact that they could thus rid themselves of the kind of outside interference in their affairs which massive British and French involvement in the Ottoman economy had hitherto entailed. As for the implementation of such a liquidation program, it would be essential to proceed in an orderly fashion and according to clearly-defined rules. In the case of the numerous public service enterprises now controlled by French and British interests, ownership should be transferred to private groups rather than the state; for the liquidation would thereby assume a much more permanent character and be less contestable at the peace conference. If the Porte so desired, it could of course secure an appropriate share in these enterprises in one form or another. The German government would in any event see to it that private German capital lent its support to the liquidation program. Indeed, if German capital should "succeed" in gaining a share in the liquidated public service enterprises, a way might conceivably be found to connect these transactions with the cancellation of the Porte's wartime debts to the Reich.[28]

Although Talât, during his visit to Germany the previous month, had left the impression with his hosts that he had no basic objections to the elimination of the British and French firms in the Ottoman empire, some German officials reacted to the Wilhelmstrasse's policy paper with well-advised caution. Dr. Köbner, of the Constantinople embassy staff, explained to the men in the Berlin foreign office that it was improbable that Cavid would ever agree to the proposed liquidation program; for his determination to spare the feelings and property of the French and British was patently obvious, and his resistance would be all the greater in that the proposed program was partly designed to benefit Germany. But even if he and his colleagues at the Porte should approve the passage of a liquidation law, it was highly unlikely that they would also agree to the participation of German capital in the implementation of the program, for even among otherwise German-ophile Turks any "endeavors on the German side which are directed toward an economic penetration of Turkey after the war" were being watched with suspicion.[29]

[28] FO, *Türkei 110 Nr. 5, Handakten,* "Denkschrift des Auswärtigen Amtes . . . 10.5.17"; Fischer, *Weltmacht,* pp. 781-83.

[29] FO, *Türkei 110 Nr. 5, Handakten,* "Bemerkungen des G. Köbner

Köbner's pessimistic judgment was quickly confirmed. When the Wilhelmstrasse officially presented its plan to the Ottoman embassy on May 17, Hakki made it clear that he did not like any part of it and would inform the Porte accordingly. Why, he argued, should the Porte oblige the Reich in this matter when even the Dual Monarchy had as yet done nothing to liquidate enemy firms in its sphere of influence? Moreover, he did not believe that Britain and France had initiated action against Ottoman assets, and it would be unwise for the Porte to make the first step—especially since it would probably face massive pressures at the peace conference to undo the whole program.[30]

Undaunted, the Wilhelmstrasse instructed Kühlmann to secure the Porte's approval of the German plan. The objections raised by Hakki and any other counterarguments, Zimmermann added, should be rejected with emphatic reference to the fact that "we attach great importance to this matter, and that a refusal of the proposal would disturb us very much indeed." The ambassador should furthermore make it clear that in view of the concessions Berlin had made in the capitulatory question it was entitled to expect the Porte's cooperation "in the area of economic reprisal measures," and that the participation of German experts in the proposed liquidation process would be an essential precondition for its successful completion.[31]

On June 22 Kühlmann wrote back that the proposed program went far beyond what he had originally suggested and what the Porte might be willing to concede. In theory it was desirable to have the enemy firms in the Ottoman empire

---

zu der Denkschrift vom 10. Mai 1917 . . . ," 14 May 1917. Köbner, an executive officer of the *Deutsche Bank* branch office in Constantinople, had just been posted to the embassy there as a kind of financial attaché.

[30] *Ibid.*, memorandum by Simons, 17 May 1917.

[31] *Ibid.*, Zimmermann to Kühlmann, 25 May 1917.

liquidated, both to put pressure on the Entente and open up new investment opportunities for German capital, but the Turks were not willing to go that far. Moreover, even if they were to prove cooperative it would be difficult to implement such a liquidation program. For instance, a good many so-called enemy concerns were actually owned in part by German interests—and experience had already shown that the Turks had little interest in such fine points of distinction. Altogether, Kühlmann concluded, it was advisable to scale down the original program and to ask the Porte for nothing more than the sequestration and forced administration of the enemy enterprises in question.[32]

On the same day Kühlmann also notified Bethmann Hollweg that he was opposed to certain other ambitious projects recently aired in German government circles. In particular he criticized a plan emanating from Ludendorff according to which all future railroad-building projects in "Asia Minor" should be handled exclusively by "German capital." Kühlmann noted that this plan and a concomitant demand by Ludendorff that the Turks should be prevented from building state railroads on their own were not realistic:

> Whether in the future we should place on the German national economy the heavy burden of supplying exclusively the capital for Turkish railroad construction, [and] whether we should really, beyond the absolutely necessary, place German capital on the Turkish card (which, if viewed *sub specie aeterni*, will always be a risky card), these are questions which in my opinion should not be decided without the most careful deliberation. . . .
>
> I believe that the Turkish urge for independence, which is presently directed toward the acquisition or creation of a

[32] *Ibid.*, Kühlmann to Bethmann Hollweg, 22 June 1917, No. 347. In contrast to Kühlmann, the German consul-general in Constantinople was quite sanguine about the project. See *ibid.*, Mertens to Bethmann Hollweg, 18 June.

state railroad network, cannot be successfully resisted in the long run.

Undoubtedly the Porte would eventually need—and accept—assistance from various foreign financial groups for the construction of new state-owned lines, but Ludendorff's objections to such a development were unsound. Any attempts

> to prevent or to hamper the resumption of economic relations between Turkey and our current enemies would be futile and actually harmful from Germany's point of view. These relations are the product of geography and the developments of many centuries. Just as Germany will have to try after the war to restore as quickly as possible its economic relations with England, America, France, and Russia, so Turkey will have to do the same.

Taking note of the relatively unimportant role the Ottoman empire had played in Germany's prewar trade (about 1.5 percent of the total trading volume), Kühlmann concluded:

> If a skillful policy is pursued [by us after the war], I do not believe that . . . [the revival of] foreign commercial and financial influence could jeopardize our political position at the Golden Horn. While I am opposed to the view of certain pessimists who would like us to drop Turkey after the war like a squeezed-out lemon, I would not wish to recommend on the other hand that we put more national assets into Turkey than is required for maintaining our previous political position there. . . .[33]

As Kühlmann, Köbner, and other German officials who were familiar with the political atmosphere in Constantinople had foreseen, the Porte at first simply ignored Berlin's official demand for the liquidation of enemy property. Finally, at the

[33] FO, *Türkei 152*, Bd. 94, Ludendorff to Lossow, 19 June 1917; Kühlmann to Bethmann Hollweg, 22 June.

beginning of August, word reached the Wilhelmstrasse via Eugen Wassermann, who had meanwhile become a director of the *Deutsche Bank*, that the Ottoman cabinet had turned down the German plan. As he explained after returning from a business trip to Constantinople, all Ottoman statesmen he interviewed had made it clear that they expected the Entente bloc to emerge from the war with greater economic unity and power than Germany could compete against, and that it was therefore advisable for the Ottoman empire to keep the door for renewed economic association with the Entente open. But quite aside from this and the rather precarious political position of the Talât cabinet because of food shortages in Constantinople, Wassermann continued, the program concocted in the Wilhelmstrasse was plainly unrealistic. The Smyrna-Aidin and Smyrna-Panderma railroads, for example, had already been sequestered by the Ottoman commissariat and the abuse they were suffering under this new management was such that no capitalist, Ottoman or German, would want to invest his money in them. As for the enemy enterprises not yet taken over by the Ottoman intendant-general, it was similarly unlikely that any buyers could be found. For Ottoman capitalists would be hard to convince that the liquidations were legal, and German investors would want much better terms than the Porte was willing to offer. Altogether, Wassermann warned the Wilhelmstrasse, it was advisable to forget about the liquidation program once and for all.[34]

Despite all the advice it had by now received, the Berlin foreign office refused to give up. Buoyed by hope that the Porte's need for more German money could yet be used to break the Turks' resistance, it continued to send reminders to Constantinople that the passage of a liquidation law was still very much at issue. In December 1917 Talât responded with a vague statement that such a law would be drawn up in the spring, and

[34] *Ibid., Türkei 110 Nr. 5, Handakten,* Memorandum by Simons, 4 Aug 1917.

Bernstorff advised Berlin that some headway might be made on the subject when Cavid came to Germany to secure another loan.[35]

Having encountered little sympathy among the civilians in Berlin with his proposals for intensified German commercial activities in Turkey, Gen. Ludendorff had meanwhile turned his attention to its mineral wealth. Buttressed with reports from the military mission on this and assorted other economic topics he called on Chancellor Michaelis on August 29 to see to it that German firms obtained concessions for the exploitation of Turkey's "valuable ore deposits." Once again Ludendorff found his suggestions turned aside by the civilian branch of the government. As Bernstorff wrote to the chancellor about seven weeks later, the idea of using diplomatic pressures to obtain mining concessions was simply not feasible. The Porte, and more particularly, Cavid, had made it clear on numerous occasions that the exploitation of the country's mineral wealth was to be handled primarily by the state and that foreign participation in mining ventures would be placed on a strictly competitive basis once the war was over. Hence, Bernstorff concluded, there was only one way in which the Reich could secure a preponderant position in the Ottoman mining industry, and that was by the private efforts of Germany's financial consortia, which would have to work with and through Ottoman financiers for purposes of camouflage.[36]

Ludendorff was not that easily turned aside this time. On November 10 he informed the new chancellor, Hertling, that the Austrians and Hungarians were apparently making headway with their own economic projects in Turkey, and since

---

[35] Cf. *ibid.*, Bernstorff to FO, 8 Dec 1917, No. 1,593; 12 Dec, No. 1,625; Bussche to Bernstorff, 12 Dec, No. 1,523; Kühlmann to same, 14 Dec, No. 1,537; Bernstorff, pp. 188-91.

[36] FO, *Türkei 134*, Bd. 38, Berckheim to Michaelis, 29 Aug 1917, No. 636; Bernstorff to same, 19 Oct, No. 500; FO to Berckheim, n.d., No. 687.

the Reich was actually doing so much more for the Turks than the Dual Monarchy, it ought to be possible to get some concessions—indeed, preferential treatment—in return. Inasmuch as the promotion of German economic interests in the Ottoman empire would be much more difficult once the war was over, something should be done at once while "our position is the strongest." Informed of Ludendorff's sentiments Bernstorff wrote back on December 13 that the general seemed to misunderstand the situation rather badly. For one thing, the Austro-Hungarians were not doing as well as all that, nor was the Porte inclined to admit that it owed the Reich anything for the financial and material assistance it had received. As a matter of fact, the ambassador explained, the Turks took the position that they had already made ample repayment by their successful defense of the Straits and by sending their troops to Galicia during the critical period of 1916. Moreover, given the military reverses they had recently suffered in Mesopotamia and Palestine, the Turks were even less inclined to feel "grateful" for the assistance they had received from Germany. Hence, if anything at all was to be extracted from them, it would have to be connected with the next loan request of the Porte, and that matter was best handled by the Wilhelmstrasse itself.[37]

At the time Bernstorff wrote this he had just received confirmation that another Ottoman loan application was imminent. As Cavid explained to Köbner on December 12, the amount needed to carry on for another six-month period would be at least $T£$ 42 million. When the financial attaché pointed out to him that Berlin's approval might be secured more easily if Germany's various wishes, such as the prompt promulgation of a liquidation law, were heeded by the Porte, Cavid retorted that such concessions could only be made if a satisfactory settlement on the Porte's wartime debts were

[37] *Ibid.*, Lersner to Hertling, 10 Nov 1917, No. 907; Kühlmann to Lersner, 15 Nov, No. 744; Bernstorff to Hertling, 27 Nov, No. 585.

reached simultaneously.[38] This counterproposal was a clever move on Cavid's part, for it was an open secret that the Berlin treasury department preferred to postpone all negotiations regarding the wartime loans until peace had been restored.

During the following two weeks Cavid dropped several hints at the German embassy that during his impending visit in Berlin he might be persuaded to make some concessions, even with respect to the liquidation law, but the leading men in the Wilhelmstrasse knew enough about his skill as a bargainer not to get their hopes up. Ludendorff was rather more optimistic. In his view, he wrote to Berlin shortly before Cavid's arrival, the "favorable development of the military situation on the eastern and Caucasus fronts" and the increased military support the Turks were getting from Germany justified driving a hard bargain with the Porte. Among the concessions which should by all means be extracted, the right of preemption on all Ottoman export products for "1 to 2 years after the conclusion of peace" was particularly important because the Entente would probably attempt to "exclude" Germany from the world market in the immediate postwar period. Similarly, a contractual agreement should be secured under which the Turks' postwar orders for "railroad construction materials, machines, etc." would be placed in Germany.[39]

Cavid arrived in Berlin shortly before New Year's Day and presented the Porte's loan requests to the Wilhelmstrasse on January 3, 1918. To take care of budgetary deficits, he explained, the Porte would need an advance of about T£ 32.5

[38] FO, *Türkei 110 Nr. 5, Handakten*, Bernstorff to FO, 13 Dec 1917, No. 1,631.

[39] Cf. *ibid.*, Kühlmann to Bernstorff, 18 Dec 1917, No. 1,562; Bernstorff to FO, 19 Dec, No. 1,669; 22 Dec, No. 1,698; Lersner to FO, 26 Dec, No. 1,991. Ludendorff's concern about possible anti-German trade restrictions after the war was justified. On Entente plans in this regard cf. Mayer, p. 20; and Pierre Renouvin, "Les buts de guerre du gouvernement français, 1914-1918," *Revue Historique*, 235 (Jan 1966), pp. 8-9.

million for the six-month period March-September. Part of that loan, moreover, would have to be paid out in effective gold, for he needed that to pay interest on a domestic loan which was to be raised in the near future. In addition, a credit of 110 million marks was needed from the Reich to finance grain purchases in Rumania, commodity imports from Germany, and various other projects.

Having made these requests, Cavid next turned to the more delicate question of how all of the Ottoman war debts were to be settled in the long run. He explained to his hosts that the Ottoman budget could never be expected to balance if Germany insisted on the repayment of its wartime loans; in fact, the interest payments alone would impose an "unbearable burden" on the Porte. This being so, it would be a nice gesture—and altogether in the spirit of the alliance treaty—if Germany simply forgave all the debts the Porte had incurred since 1914. In return, Cavid emphasized, he would see to it that the Reich got all the economic concessions it wanted, "especially regarding Heraclea [coal], oil fields, and railroads," and that a "big" economic development program for the Ottoman empire would be worked out and implemented in close collaboration with Germany. To demonstrate his goodwill he assured the German negotiators that the recently founded Ottoman National Credit Bank was not meant to finance any big projects, such as the exploitation of coal and oil fields, and that the *Deutsche Bank* was most welcome to join forces with the bank.[40]

Although the documentary record of the ensuing negotiations between Cavid and the Germans is spotty, it is clear that Cavid refused to make any firm commitments on the liquidation of enemy property or any of the other economic projects which Berlin had been interested in since the previous year. The Germans, in turn, reacted evasively to all of Cavid's ef-

[40] FO, *Türkei 110 Nr. 5, Handakten*, "Besprechung mit Djavid Bey am 3. Januar 1918"; and *"Aufzeichnung."*

forts to secure the diminution or outright cancellation of the Porte's wartime debts. As Helfferich, who headed the German negotiating team, explained to State Secretary Siegfried Count von Roedern of the treasury department, it was obvious that the Turks would sooner or later have to be granted less stringent repayment terms, but since no ironclad guarantees for the satisfaction of Germany's economic wishes in the Ottoman empire could presently be secured, it was best to keep the Porte dangling.[41]

On January 26 Bernstorff made a last-minute effort to push the German negotiators in Berlin into a more militant attitude. In a remarkable dispatch to Chancellor Hertling he asserted that despite of, or rather because of, the worsening military situation of the Turks in Palestine and elsewhere, the time for massive pressures on the Porte had now come:

> Only if Turkey is willing to let herself be economically dominated by us in the future shall the great sacrifices be worthwhile which we must presently make for her in military, financial, and diplomatic terms as a result of her deplorable condition. If Turkey does not accept our economic dominance, she has nothing more to offer us. Nor can she now hurt us, for even a Turkish separate peace would have little significance for us *after* the Russian [withdrawal from the war]....
>
> The moment has come for a last attempt to bind Turkey economically to us. If we are successful, it will then be worthwhile to make the necessary heavy sacrifices to maintain the [territorial] integrity of Turkey.[42]

Bernstorff's admonition went unheeded. After almost four weeks of fruitless discussions with Cavid, Helfferich and his

[41] See DZA, Büro Staatsminister Dr. Helfferich, *Akten betr. Türkei,* Bd. 1, "Ergebnis der Besprechung über türkische Finanzfragen . . . am 13. Januar 1918."

[42] FO, *Wk 15,* Bd. 25, Bernstorff to Hertling, 26 Jan 1918, No. 27.

fellow negotiators agreed to give the Porte a major portion of
the money it had originally asked for, about T£ 22 million,
and that without any strings attached.[43] Bernstorff was furious. "From the very outset," he wrote privately to Gwinner on
February 5,

> my view was that we should categorially refuse all Cavid's
> demands until he pledged himself in writing to fulfill our
> own. Our political position in regard to Turkey is now so
> strong that we can adopt this standpoint without misgiving.
> It was not done, and we have achieved nothing. . . .
>
> How can it be supposed in Berlin that we can achieve any-
> thing here, if all of our means of exerting pressure are to
> go for nothing in Berlin? . . . No one in Berlin has even any
> time for Turkish affairs, and they are ultimately dealt with
> in a rush *"inter pocula."*[44]

Two weeks later Bernstorff reiterated his disappointment
over the Wilhelmstrasse's attitude in another private letter to
Gwinner. In Berlin, he complained, it seemed to be believed
that

> our main effort must always be to keep the Turks in good
> humor. So long as this attitude prevails, we shall get no fur-
> ther. . . . I hope to get my view accepted that we should help
> the Turks in every direction, but demand in return that the
> country shall be entirely under our economic control. This
> program is the only one that meets the interests of both
> countries, as Turkey can never mend her fortunes on her
> own account. And it can be carried out, as Turkey is now
> wholly dependent on us, and can neither help nor harm
> us. . . .[45]

[43] See *ibid., Türkei 110*, Bd. 109, Memorandum by Greve, 15 Oct
1918, re "Die der türkischen Regierung seit Kriegsbeginn . . . bewilligten Vorschüsse."

[44] Bernstorff, pp. 193-94.

[45] *Ibid.*, pp. 194-95.

Efforts Toward Economic Predominance

Quite aside from Bernstorff's surprising lack of judgment—the contention that the Turks could neither help nor harm Germany's war effort was totally unrealistic—his characterization of Berlin's attitude was rather too simplistic. While the Wilhelmstrasse was indeed trying hard to keep the Porte in "good humor," it actually did not object to the preparation of a new set of economic demands by the *Reichswirtschaftsamt* which were to be presented to Cavid the next time he appeared in Berlin. By early March 1918 a "list of Turkish objects to be demanded" was ready for transmittal to and review by Bernstorff and his staff. As Understate Secretary von dem Bussche explained to the ambassador, the list had been purposely restricted to commercial operations which could be expected to return a profit "in the foreseeable future" without requiring an excessive amount of investment capital. Such operations, for which exploitation rights and/or control by German firms were to be secured, included the coal fields "of Heraclea and east of Heraclea"; the copper mines of Arghana Maden; the lead mines of Balia and Bulghar; the oil fields in upper Mesopotamia; phosphate and asphalt deposits in a number of areas; the boracite mines of Panderma; and the manganese ore deposits in the *vilayet* of Brusa. In addition, the *Société des Phares de l'Empire Ottoman* was to be liquidated "for Germany's benefit."[46]

Thanks to Cavid's success in raising an internal loan, the first of its kind in the Ottoman empire, the Porte was temporarily relieved of its most acute financial problems.[47] With this development in mind Bernstorff concluded in mid-May that the chance to secure concessions from Cavid in a new round of loan negotiations would probably not come until July. To make sure that his superiors in Berlin would be better pre-

[46] DZA, Büro Staatsminister Dr. Helfferich, *Akten betr. Türkei*, Bd. 2, Bussche to Bernstorff, 4 March 1918, No. 173.

[47] See *Schulthess*, v. 59:2, 521; Emin, *Turkey in the World War*, pp. 164-65.

pared than they had been during the last encounter, the ambassador sent a lengthy memorandum to Hertling on the course that should be taken. Bernstorff maintained that Berlin's refusal to make some tangible concessions in the question of the Porte's war debts had been a mistake. Since the Porte was most likely to go bankrupt if it had to pay full interest on the wartime loans, an adjustment would have to be made anyway, and now was the best time to strike a bargain with the Turks on this matter, that is, get some economic concessions in return. Though the sum total of such concessions would probably have a smaller monetary value than the loans the Reich had granted since 1914, that did not really matter as long as Germany succeeded in securing the "economic penetration and dependence of Turkey" and in ridding itself of onerous obligations such as its contractual commitment to redeem the treasury notes it had issued to the Ottoman Public Debt Administration since 1915. As for the entrenchment of German capital in the Ottoman empire Bernstorff agreed with Berlin that the liquidation of enemy firms was a central issue, but he thought that top priority should be given to getting the prospective German concessionaires organized. Indeed, to have any chance of success with Cavid it would be necessary first of all to weld together

> a big, high-capacity German capital consortium for the Orient business, which should include if possible all big German bank groups that have hitherto stood separately or in opposition to each other, and which is prepared to grant Turkish capital appropriate participation in the exploitation of the various objects.[48]

Bernstorff's proposals received only scant attention in Berlin,

[48] DZA, Büro Staatsminister Dr. Helfferich, *Akten betr. Türkei*, Bd. 2, Bernstorff to Hertling, 22 May 1918. Cf. FO, *Türkei 158*, Bd. 20, same to same, 11 May, No. 11.2,720.

especially since the independent course of the Turks in the Caucasus and various other signs of the Porte's assertiveness made it increasingly uncertain whether another bargaining session with Cavid was really worth the effort. The hesitancy in German government circles was clearly reflected in a major interdepartmental strategy session held under the chairmanship of Helfferich on June 29, 1918. Addressing himself to the assembled representatives from the OHL, the foreign office, the treasury department, the war ministry, the *Reichswirtschaftsamt* and the *Reichsbank*, Helfferich pointed out that Cavid would soon be back in Berlin to secure a new loan and, probably, also to push for a liberal settlement of the debt question. If Germany agreed to accommodate him on these questions it might be able to secure two things in return. One was a reduction of its contractual obligation to redeem within 11 years after the war all the treasury notes it had issued to the Public Debt Administration; the other was the kind of economic concessions in the Ottoman empire it had sought since the beginning of the war. To enter into negotiations on these matters, however, would only make sense if the German government were absolutely determined to get what it wanted— and such an approach might no longer be feasible in light of the current "political and military situation."

In the ensuing discussion most of the conference participants agreed that the situation was indeed not very suitable for a major showdown with the Porte, though all were hopeful some *quid pro quo* settlement could be worked out. Speaking for the foreign office Rosenberg thought the surrender of further redeemable treasury notes should perhaps be refused, but that the gold redemption obligations previously incurred by the Reich had better not be tampered with. The head of the treasury department, Count Roedern, said he was agreeable to a reduction of the Ottoman debt in return for financial and economic concessions by the Porte, though he emphasized that the Turks would definitely have to make full payment for the war materiel shipped to them under the auspices of the Prussian war ministry. Maj. Theodor Düsterberg, of the war ministry, agreed and furthermore announced that his ministry would no longer send any equipment to the Turks unless they paid for it in cash. This new policy, he emphasized, had the approval of the OHL, notwithstanding the possibility that it might cause a "break with the Turks."[49]

It would appear that the civilian leaders in Berlin were rather disturbed by this tough talk of the military. They soon found out that the OHL was indeed in a fighting mood. On July 12 Ludendorff notified both the foreign office and Helfferich that he expected them to treat all new loan requests from the Porte in a dilatory fashion so that the Turks could be pushed more effectively into a change of their Caucasus policy. In any event, the quartermaster general noted, the grant of a new loan and, possibly, minor concessions in the debt question should be made contingent on Ottoman cooperation in the following matters:

1. Expropriation of enemy property;
2. Mining concessions (especially chrome ores);
3. Concessions in the Mesopotamian oil fields;
4. Preferential deliveries of Turkey's wool, fatty oils, hides, pelts;
5. Railroad questions. Perpetuation and new grants of certain railroad concessions, participation and preferential treatment of German firms in the assignment of all new railroad construction projects, in the expansion of existing lines, and in the procurement of rolling stock as well as of building and operational equipment;
6. Oil deliveries from the captured stores in Batum.

[49] DZA, Büro Staatsminister Dr. Helfferich, *Akten betr. Türkei,* Bd. 2, "Aufzeichnung aus der Besprechung vom 29. Juni 1918."

To make sure Helfferich would display the necessary tough-ness in the impending negotiations with the Porte, Ludendorff sent a follow-up message to Berlin that "thumbscrews" should be used on Cavid, especially since evidence was mounting that the Turks were "continuously cheating" the Reich.[50]

Unfortunately for the OHL, Cavid was in no hurry to re-apply for a German government loan. When he finally ap-peared in Berlin for that purpose, in the second half of August, the military situation of the Central Powers had meanwhile deteriorated so much that no attempt was made to extract con-cessions from him. Instead, Cavid simply collected another ad-vance, this time $T\pounds$ 45 million, and returned to Con-stantinople.[51]

The decision of the German government not to insist on a *quid pro quo* arrangement was of course dictated exclusively by tactical considerations, that is, the need, now greater than ever, of preserving the Turks' allegiance to the cause of the Central Powers. That the ministerial bureaucracy in Berlin continued nevertheless to occupy itself with making plans for the economic penetration of the Ottoman empire is clear from scattered bits of evidence. According to Rathmann a proposal by Gen. von Seeckt (of February 1918) to bring together a consortium of German banks for the expansion of the Otto-man rail network in the postwar years was still being worked on in Berlin in August, though there is also evidence that the foreign office, for one, thought the project should be filed away for the time being.[52] A second topic on which governmental

[50] *Ibid.*, Bd. 3, Ludendorff to Berghes, 12 July 1918; Bartenwerffer to Brinckmann, 12 July.

[51] Cf. *Schulthess,* v. 59:2, pp. 523-24; FO, *Türkei 110,* Bd. 109, memorandum about loan payments, 15 Oct 1918, by Greve.

[52] Cf. FO, *Türkei 152,* Bd. 100, Seeckt to Hertling, 1 March 1918 and enclosure; FO to war ministry, June 1918 (draft); DZA, Büro Staatsminister Dr. Helfferich, *Akten betr. Türkei,* Bd. 1, Helfferich to Ludendorff, 22 March; Rathmann, *Stossrichtung,* pp. 175-77.

conferences in Berlin were held as late as August 1918 was the desirability of securing the oil fields of upper Mesopotamia for exploitation by Germany—a remarkable exercise in futility when one considers that at this time British troops were not more than a hundred miles from Mosul. It should be added, however, that none of the Berlin government departments were particularly sanguine about the acquisition of these oil fields, and recent assertions that even after the "Black Day" of the German army on the Western front Germany's statesmen were continuing to push for the "economic penetration" of the Ottoman empire, are somewhat misleading.[53]

THE WARTIME efforts of German governmental agencies and business groups to convert the Ottoman empire into an economic dependency of the Reich were singularly unsuccessful. Except for a few mining concessions Turkey granted no new rights to any German business interests and played havoc with some of the well-established firms, such as the Bagdad Railroad Company. Despite mounting pressures from Berlin and, more particularly, from the first quartermaster general of the OHL during the last two years of the war, the Porte never agreed to the forcible liquidation of the vast Entente enterprises in Turkey and repelled all other attempts by Germany to broaden its economic influence. Although the Porte was deeply in debt to the Reich by 1918, it is most unlikely that Berlin would have been able to derive much benefit from that situation even had the Central Powers won the war.

The appointment of German advisers to some Ottoman government ministries in 1916 brought the Reich no tangible

[53] Cf. FO, *Türkei 197*, Bd. 7, "Aufzeichnung über das Ergebnis der am 9. August 1918 . . . abgehaltenen Besprechung über die deutschen Mineralölinteressen in Mesopotamien"; Fischer, *Weltmacht*, p. 784.

advantages whatever. Contrary to the assertions in the most recent Marxist study of the German-Ottoman wartime alliance,[54] these German specialists had no policy-making powers nor did they in any other way "control" the Turkish government machinery.

Much of the credit for frustrating Germany's economic ambitions in the Ottoman empire belongs to Cavid. His expertise in financial and economic questions and his toughness as a negotiator made him a highly effective defender of Turkish interests and eventually earned him the grudging respect of Germany's officialdom. Cavid's determined efforts to keep Germany's economic ambitions in check obviously had the full backing of the more powerful *Ittihad ve Terakki* leaders, and whenever some of them, notably Enver, seemed to become too accommodating toward Germany, Cavid invariably succeeded in bringing them back to his own line of thinking.

Although virtually all prominent government figures in wartime Germany were at one time or another in sympathy with the expansion of German economic influence in the Ottoman empire, only a few of them were really militant on this issue. Gen. Ludendorff was one of them, Ambassador Bernstorff another. Kühlmann temporarily belonged to this group early in 1917 but later greatly moderated his views. After his frustrating experiences with the Turks in 1915, Helfferich, too, became a moderate, if only because he recognized that Germany did not actually have much leverage with the Porte. None of the wartime chancellors seems to have had much interest in the economic aspects of the Turkish question, nor is there any evidence that the Kaiser paid particular attention to this issue. Zimmermann, who practically ran the foreign office even before he succeeded Jagow as state secretary, was a militant proponent of the liquidation of enemy firms in Turkey

[54] Rathmann, *Stossrichtung*, p. 179.

but otherwise quite reserved in his support of German economic ambitions there.[55]

[55] Though both Bethmann Hollweg and Zimmermann expressed themselves quite passionately, before and during the Battle of the Straits, about the need to protect Germany's investments and opportunities for future economic activity in Turkey, their statements on the subject must be evaluated in context. That is, they were quite obviously colored by the Wilhelmstrasse's growing concern about the dangerous isolation of the Turks and its desire to impress the Kaiser and the OHL with the need for military action in the Balkans. Cf. above, pp. 82ff. The conclusions of Fritz Fischer—in *Griff nach der Weltmacht*, *passim*, and subsequently in *Weltmacht oder Niedergang. Deutschland im ersten Weltkrieg* (Frankfurt a. M., 1965), pp. 76-77—with respect to the consistency and success of Germany's wartime efforts to dominate the Ottoman empire economically and otherwise are altogether too sweeping.

CHAPTER XI

Collapse of the Alliance

ALTHOUGH the rapid decline of Germany's fortunes on the Western Front in July and August 1918 had not passed unnoticed in Constantinople, it was only in the following month that the imminence of general disaster became clear to the *Ittihad ve Terakki* leaders. The two most resounding blows to hit the Turks in September 1918 were the catastrophic rout of their Army Group F in Palestine and the great Allied victories in Macedonia. But there were numerous other danger signs which could no longer be ignored. Desertions from the Ottoman armed forces were rapidly increasing, there was mounting economic and administrative chaos in the interior of the empire, and the totally inadequate size of the Ottoman army facing the British in Mesopotamia made another fiasco on that front virtually inevitable.[1]

With Gen. Allenby's forces pushing northward toward Anatolia, neighboring Bulgaria in the throes of military collapse, and Constantinople itself becoming increasingly exposed to an Allied attack out of Thrace, the Porte readily accepted Germany's sudden decision in late September to sue for the cessation of hostilities and the initiation of peace talks "on the basis of the Fourteen Points." At the same time, however, the Porte cautioned Berlin that a Wilsonian peace settlement was

[1] Cf. Emin, pp. 261-67; Ahmed Emin Yalman, *Turkey in My Time* (Norman, Okla., 1956), pp. 60-62; Liman, *Five Years in Turkey*, pp. 268-305; Pomiankowski, pp. 380-84; Mühlmann, *deutsch-türkische Waffenbündnis*, pp. 225-37, and *passim*. For detailed analyses of the military developments in Palestine and Macedonia during the latter half of September see especially Cyril Falls, *Armageddon: 1918* (Philadelphia, 1964), pp. 35-125; and *Military Operations Macedonia*, 2 vols. (London, 1933-35), II, 147-253; Kriegsgeschichtliche Forschungsanstalt des Heeres, *Der Weltkrieg 1914 bis 1918*, XIII (Berlin, 1942), 407-17, 439-41, and *passim*; Mühlmann, *Oberste Heeresleitung*, pp. 228-38.

palatable to Turkey only if the President's call for the autonomous development of the non-Turkish nationalities in the Ottoman empire meant "autonomy . . . under republican [sic]
sovereignty" and, secondly, if the proposed "international
guarantees" of a new Straits regime extended to the continued
"Turkish possession" of Constantinople itself. To keep the
Balkan situation from getting any worse than it already was
the Porte further urged Berlin to surrender the Northern Dobruja to the Rumanians the moment Bulgaria's withdrawal
from the war was confirmed.[2]

On October 5, one day after Berlin had dispatched its first
peace note to President Wilson, the Porte addressed a virtually
identical message to the White House via the Spanish government. Apparently because of a breakdown in telegraphic communications, the Turkish note did not reach Madrid until October 12, and it was only on October 14 that it was delivered in
Washington.[3] The State Department duly informed the Allied
governments of the Turkish peace proposal and requested
their advice on how it should be answered. Since Britain, in
particular, did not respond, the American reply to the Porte
was delayed until October 31, by which time the Turks had
already signed the Armistice of Mudros.[4]

The Porte's peace note to Wilson was sent with Berlin's

[2] Harry R. Rudin, *Armistice 1918* (New Haven, 1944), pp. 44-55 and
passim; FO, *Türkei 150*, Bd. 10, Bernstorff to FO, 1 Oct 1918, No.
1,628. On the circumstances surrounding the decision of the German
government to sue for peace, new primary evidence may be found in
Matthias, II, 738-98, passim; Erich Matthias and Rudolf Morsey, eds.,
Die Regierung des Prinzen Max von Baden (Düsseldorf, 1962), pp.
3-123, *passim*; and Albrecht von Thaer, *Generalstabsdienst an der Front
und in der O.H.L.* (Göttingen, 1958), pp. 232-42, and *passim*.

[3] See *Schulthess*, v. 59:2, 524, 620; *Foreign Relations of the United
States, 1918, Supplement 1*, I, 359-60.

[4] See Laurence Evans, *United States Policy and the Partition of
Turkey, 1914-1924* (Baltimore, 1965), pp. 84-85. For text of Lansing's
reply to Turkey see *Foreign Relations of U.S., 1918, Supplement 1*, I,
428.

knowledge.[5] Three days after its dispatch, on October 8, Bernstorff notified the Wilhelmstrasse that Talât's cabinet was on its way out and that efforts were being made to assemble a new council of ministers which would be more acceptable to the Entente governments. Although Halil Bey, for one, assured Bernstorff that the *Ittihad ve Terakki* Party would certainly maintain sufficient influence in any new cabinet to prevent the conclusion of a separate peace, and that the Porte's future course would ultimately depend on the availability of adequate German help for the defense of the Straits area, the ambassador seems to have recognized that a major change in Turkish policy was in the offing. The only certain thing, he advised Berlin, was that the cabinet change would take some time, though it was already clear that Ahmed Tevfik Paşa (a former grand vizier) would take Talât's place, while Gen. Ahmed Izzet Paşa would succeed Enver as war minister.[6]

The imminence of a general change of personnel at the Porte was confirmed by Izzet himself in a farewell interview with Gen. von Lossow, who had just been ordered to return to Germany. Izzet confided to Lossow that the next cabinet would have little in common with the men who were about to step down or, for that matter, with the "circles" that had stood behind them, but this would not necessarily entail a general change in the alliance relationship with the Central Powers. In fact, the Porte would definitely decide against a "separate peace if Wilson rejected" Berlin's recent offer, provided only that the Dardanelles and Constantinople could be held "with

[5] See Pomiankowski, p. 385. Rudin's account, p. 129, is misleading.

[6] FO, *Türkei 158*, Bd. 21, Bernstorff to FO, 8 Oct 1918, No. 1,691. The replacement of Talât and Enver by Tevfik and Izzet appears to have been discussed in Turkish political circles as early as August 1918. See, for example, *ibid.*, *Russland 97a*, Bd. 23, same to same, 27 Aug, No. 1,389. On Izzet's background and wartime activities, see Inal, xiii, 1,973ff.

Germany's assistance" and Germany herself had some success in stabilizing the situation on the Western Front.[7]

Although there were about 25,000 German soldiers in the Ottoman empire at this time, most of them were dispersed in various parts of Asia and therefore not readily available for the defense of the Straits area. During the first week of October the OHL moved a German *Landwehr* division from Crimea to the Bosporus, a reinforcement which, of course, was not nearly enough to reassure the Turks. At the Kaiser's behest the Wilhelmstrasse therefore sent word to the Porte on October 12 that another German division was en route from the Crimea, that two additional divisions would be brought in from the Caucasus, and that all available German ships in the Black Sea would be sent to Constantinople.[8]

In the meantime Izzet had replaced Tevfik as the grand vizier-designate and had made considerably more progress than the latter in finding suitable men for a new cabinet.[9] On October 14 the transition of power from Talât to Izzet was formally completed. In the new cabinet Izzet was obviously the most important man. Aside from the grand vizirate, he took charge of the war ministry as well as of the general staff. Gen. Mustafa Kemal, who had aspired to the war minister's portfolio, was fobbed off with the explanation that his services were needed in the field until peace had been concluded. Other prominent ministers in the new cabinet included the former

[7] FO, *Türkei 158*, Bd. 21, Bernstorff to FO, 8 Oct 1918, No. 1,692.

[8] See *ibid.*, Grünau to FO, 12 Oct 1918, No. 604; Matthias and Morsey, No. 36; Seeckt, p. 49; Mühlmann, *deutsch-türkische Waffenbündnis*, pp. 236-37.

[9] On Tevfik's failure to form a viable cabinet (which was causally related to his refusal to include Cavid in it), and Izzet's appointment to the grand vizirate, see Inal, xiii, 1942; Seeckt, pp. 93-94; FO, *Türkei 161*, Bd. 5, Bernstorff to FO, 11 Oct 1918, No. 1,720; 12 Oct, No. 1,724; same to Max von Baden, 16 Oct, No. 248; and AHFM, *Türkei, Berichte 1918*, Pallavicini to Burian, 16 Oct, No. 86A-B/P.

envoy to Sofia, Ali Fethi Bey, for the interior, and the well-known naval officer, Hüseyin Rauf Bey, who took over Cemal's post. Of the former cabinet members only Cavid reappeared in the new cabinet—once again as finance minister. Halil moved back to his prewar position as president of the Chamber of Deputies. Enver, Talât, Cemal, and most other wartime leaders officially withdrew from public life.[10]

Shortly after Izzet's cabinet had been formally installed by the Sultan, Pallavicini received assurance from the new "interim" foreign minister, Mehmed Nabi Bey, that the Porte intended to maintain close relations with the Central Powers both in the immediate future and after the conclusion of peace. The next day, October 15, Nabi and Izzet himself expressed themselves in similar fashion to Bernstorff, though both men made it clear that the Porte was anxious for an armistice in view of Constantinople's exposure to an Allied attack from the Balkans.[11]

On October 17 Gen. Charles Townshend, who had received extraordinarily good treatment from the Turks since his capture at Kut-el-Amara and had offered to assist with the opening of Anglo-Turkish peace talks, met with Izzet. The result of their interview and of a supplementary conference with Navy Minister Rauf was Townshend's release from captivity and subsequent dispatch as a peace emissary to Adm. Sir Somerset A. Gough-Calthorpe, British Commander-in-

[10] For a complete roster of Izzet's cabinet see Gotthard Jäschke, "Beiträge zur Geschichte des Kampfes der Türkei um ihre Unabhängigkeit," *Welt des Islams*, n.s., v (1958), 61-62. On Mustafa Kemal's futile efforts to be included in the new cabinet cf. the same author's "Auf dem Wege zur Türkischen Republik," *ibid.*, pp. 206-207; Turkish National Commission for UNESCO, *Atatürk* (Ankara, 1963), p. 31; and Lord Kinross, *Ataturk* (New York, 1965), pp. 146-47.

[11] AHFM, *Türkei, Berichte 1918*, Pallavicini to AHFM, 14 Oct 1918, No. 618; FO, *Türkei 158*, Bd. 21, Bernstorff to FO, 15 Oct, No. 1,746. On the rather hesitant Allied advance toward Constantinople see Falls, *Military Operations Macedonia*, II, 254-65.

Chief, Mediterranean, whose flagship was anchored off Mudros. Townshend delivered the Porte's request for an immediate armistice with Britain on October 20. According to the armistice formula Rauf had outlined for him, the Porte desired Britain's friendship and protection, plus financial "help . . . if needed," as well as "financial, political, and industrial independence for Turkey." In return, the Porte would be prepared to "give autonomy to territories under the sovereignty of the Sultan [presently] occupied by the Allies. . . ."[12]

While Townshend was still en route to Mudros, on October 18 Izzet revealed to Gen. Seeckt that "negotiations with the Entente concerning a separate peace" had been initiated, and that in view of the "military situation and the impossibility of effective help from Germany" the Porte would accept the Allies' armistice terms. At the same time, the grand vizier assured Seeckt that the Porte would under no circumstances betray the German troops serving in the Ottoman empire, a promise which was well kept during the following weeks.[13]

To the relief of the Germans it took the Porte and the British almost a week to get their armistice negotiations started. By the time the Ottoman armistice delegation under Rauf reached Gough-Calthorpe's ship (October 26) Seeckt and other German officials in Constantinople had made considerable progress in organizing the withdrawal of German troops from the various Asian theaters of war, though the so-called *Yilderim* force on the Syrian front was left at Liman's disposal. At the same time German and Austro-Hungarian personnel already in or near Constantinople were being evacuated in stages to Russian or Rumanian Black Sea ports. On orders from Berlin Ambassador Bernstorff joined the general exodus on the evening of October 27. Before taking leave,

[12] Charles V. F. Townshend, *My Campaign*, 2 vols. (New York, 1920), II, 276-90, and *passim*.

[13] Cf. Mühlmann, *deutsch-türkische Waffenbündnis*, p. 237; Pomiankowski, p. 386; Seeckt, pp. 49-50, 95.

Bernstorff assured the Porte that his departure did not constitute a break in diplomatic relations.[14]

After four days of negotiations between Rauf's delegation and Adm. Gough-Calthorpe (during which the French tried in vain to secure a seat at the table), the Anglo-Turkish armistice agreement was signed on *HMS Agamemnon* October 30. Scheduled to become effective the following noon, the Mudros Armistice provided, among other things, for the opening of the Straits and Allied occupation of the forts guarding them; the immediate demobilization of the bulk of the Ottoman army; the surrender of Ottoman garrisons in some specified areas and their withdrawal in certain others; Allied occupation or control of certain strategic points and the right to occupy any other points "in the event of any situation arising which threatens the security of the Allies" (Art. vii); and Allied control of all Turkish railroads. Thanks to Rauf's insistence all German and Austro-Hungarian troops in the Ottoman empire were permitted to leave within a month's time, and an additional period of grace was to be given to those which had to be evacuated from remote areas (Art. xix). On the other hand, the Porte agreed to cease all relations with the Central Powers.[15]

On the same evening the armistice was signed Izzet wired Gen. Liman on the north Syrian front to surrender command of Army Group F to Mustafa Kemal and to return with his German soldiers to Constantinople. After an emotional fare-

[14] FO, *Türkei 158*, Bd. 21, Lersner to FO, 27 Oct 1918; *Dt 135 Nr. 1*, Bd. 6, Solf to Bernstorff, 25 Oct, No. 1,810; Bernstorff to FO, 27 Oct, Nos. 1,936, 1,937; Mühlmann, *deutsch-türkische Waffenbündnis*, p. 238; Bernstorff, pp. 239-42; Pomiankowski, pp. 389-91; Seeckt, pp. 49-52 and *passim*.

[15] See Rudin, pp. 192, 410-11; Ali Türkgeldi, *Mondros ve Mudanya Mütarekelerinin Tarihi* [History of the Armistices of Mudros and Mudania] (Ankara, 1948), and *passim*, especially pp. 44-46; and David Lloyd George, *War Memoirs*, 6 vols. (Boston, 1933-37), vi, 276-80.

well party with his Turkish associates and subordinates, Liman and a few of his staff officers left by train for Constantinople, where they arrived on November 4. The bulk of the German troops who had served under his command encountered numerous delays on their trip back, and most of them were still en route by the middle of the month.[16]

When Liman arrived in the Ottoman capital Gen. von Seeckt and his officers, the German naval personnel, and the German troops in the vicinity of Constantinople had already been evacuated to Odessa, Sevastopol, and other Russian ports. Two of the German ships used in the evacuation program had meanwhile, on November 2, also picked up a more controversial set of passengers, namely Enver, Talât, Cemal, Dr. Nazim, the former intendant-general, Ismail Hakki Paşa, along with several other prominent *Ittihad ve Terakki* figures.[17] Their unauthorized departure caused an uproar in Constantinople and entailed some rather unpleasant moments for the German and Austro-Hungarian officials who were still in the capital.

[16] Liman, *Five Years,* pp. 319-21; Papen, pp. 109-10; Kinross, pp. 151-52. Liman remained in the Constantinople area until January 1919 to supervise the repatriation of German troops coming in from the Asian provinces. On his way back to Germany he was placed under arrest by the British at Malta and held for six months as a suspected war criminal; in August 1919 he was released. See Carl Mühlmann, "Liman von Sanders," in *Deutsches Biographisches Jahrbuch,* xi (Stuttgart, 1932), 187-88; and the relevant documents in FO, *Türkei 139,* Bde. 48-49.

[17] All of the fugitives, except Ismail Hakki, gathered in the house of Enver's aide-de-camp, Kâzim Bey, on the night of November 2 and subsequently boarded a German torpedo boat which delivered them in Sevastopol the next day. Cf. Rustow, "Enwer Pasha," pp. 699-700; Inal, xiii, 1,943-44; FO, *Türkei 159 Nr. 2,* Bd. 20, Berchem to FO, 4 Nov 1918, No. 2,258. According to Seeckt, p. 95, he had promised German assistance to Enver, Talât, and "a few others" as early as Oct 20.

Collapse of the Alliance

It appears that Ismail Hakki left several hours before the others and on a different ship, and it was his flight which was discovered first. Since an Austro-Hungarian officer had allegedly assisted Hakki in his escape, the grand vizier called Pomiankowski during the night and informed him that unless the Austro-Hungarian military authorities in Odessa arrested the fugitive and turned him over to the commander of a Turkish torpedo boat which had just been sent after him, the repatriation of Austro-Hungarian personnel might run into serious difficulties. Though he disliked getting involved in this manhunt, Pomiankowski notified the authorities in Odessa of Izzet's ultimatum but, whether because of Austrian *Schlamperei* (muddling) or German intervention, the message seems to have been lost somewhere along the line.[18]

The discovery that Enver, Talât, Cemal, and several other wartime leaders had left the country as well was apparently made early on November 3. Izzet immediately notified the German embassy that the Porte expected prompt German cooperation in the return of the fugitives. Embassy Counsellor Count von Waldburg, acting as *chargé d'affaires* since Bernstorff's departure, knew very well where the fugitives were but feigned complete surprise. To soothe the Porte's feelings, Waldburg next sent an inquiry to the Wilhelmstrasse whether he could issue a statement to the effect that "we will initiate an investigation into the whereabouts" of the missing Turkish leaders, but Berlin rejected the proposal. On the other hand, it agreed with Waldburg that Enver's apparent intention to join his brother Nuri in the Caucasus was fraught with dangerous political consequences. On November 5 the Wilhelmstrasse therefore asked the German military authorities in the

---

[18] Pomiankowski, pp. 409-11. Cf. Gotthard Jäschke and Erich Pritsch, "Die Türkei seit dem Weltkriege. Geschichtskalender 1918-1928," *Welt des Islams*, x (1927-29), 7, who list Oct 31 as the date of Hakki's flight.

Ukraine to prevent Enver's departure for the Caucasus and to make it clear to him that he would be welcome in Germany, where Talât and the other fugitives were already expected.[19]

Since Waldburg, under instructions from Berlin, refused even to talk about the extradition of the fugitives, the Ottoman cabinet tried to apply pressure on Liman. Izzet pointed out to him that public opinion might force the Porte to treat all remaining German soldiers in the Ottoman empire as "hostages" unless at least Enver and Cemal, the two military figures among the fugitives, were returned to Constantinople. Since more than 12,000 German soldiers were at stake Liman promptly notified Berlin of what he had been told but studiously refrained from making any particular recommendation. The next day, November 6, Izzet himself addressed a lengthy note to Chancellor Prince Max von Baden. He pointed out that several of the fugitive leaders were wanted for malfeasance in office as well as for their involvement in "the Armenian affairs," and unless they were returned to Turkey there was danger of a major political crisis in Constantinople and of Allied intervention according to Art. VII of the Mudros Armistice.[20]

For some obscure reason Ambassador Rifât did not deliver the grand vizier's note to the Wilhelmstrasse until November 11, by which time the imperial regime in Germany had been overthrown and Izzet himself had been replaced by Tevfik as

[19] FO, *Türkei 159 Nr. 2*, Bd. 20, Waldburg to FO, 3 Nov 1918, No. 1,877; FO to Waldburg, 5 Nov, No. 1,879; same to Berchem, 5 Nov, No. 1,645.

[20] *Ibid.*, Waldburg to FO (Liman to Max von Baden), 5 Nov 1918; Izzet to Reich Chancellor, 6 Nov. It should be noted that Waldburg both then and later regarded the Porte's demands for the return of the fugitive *Ittihad ve Terakki* leaders primarily as a maneuver to satisfy public opinion and to divert attention from the Porte's own negligence in keeping the former wartime leaders under surveillance. See *ibid.*, Waldburg to FO, 6 Nov, No. 1,897; same to same, 12 Feb 1919.

head of the Ottoman cabinet. The available evidence indicates, however, that the Kaiser's government would not have yielded on the extradition issue in any case. It should be added that none of the fugitive *Ittihad ve Terakki* leaders had as yet actually crossed the borders of the Reich, and it was only in December that they moved from the Ukraine to Berlin, some in disguise.[21]

Enver, who had been officially advised by the new republican authorites in Berlin to stay away, was apparently the last to slip into Germany. Since he (like several of the other fugitive *Ittihad ve Terakki* leaders) was wanted both by the Porte and the Entente governments, Enver adopted the name "Ali Bey" for camouflage. His subsequent moves are a matter of scholarly controversy. It appears that in April 1919, possibly with Gen. von Seeckt's assistance, he secured the services of a pilot and airplane for a trip to Moscow, but the plane was forced down in Lithuania by mechanical trouble. After being detained there for several weeks, Enver eventually returned to Germany.[22] In August 1919 he visited the Bolshevik leader, Karl Radek, in his Berlin prison cell, and was thus the first one to establish this curious kind of contact with Moscow (which was subsequently used by a variety of German political, military, and industrial figures).[23] Early in 1920 Enver once again

[21] *Ibid.*, "G.A. zu A47482," 7 Nov 1918; Berchem to FO, 9 Nov, No. 2,307; Bd. 21, Rifât to Solf, 11 Nov, and enclosure; Rustow, "Enwer Pasha," p. 700; Wipert von Blücher, *Deutschlands Weg nach Rapallo* (Wiesbaden, 1951), p. 130.

[22] See FO, *Türkei 159 Nr. 2*, Bd. 20, FO to Diplomatic Representative in Kiev, 17 Dec 1918, No. 1,875; Rustow, "Enwer Pasha," p. 700; Blücher, p. 132; Gustav Hilger and Alfred G. Meyer, *The Incompatible Allies* (New York, 1953), pp. 192-93. Cf. Lionel Kochan, *Russia and the Weimar Republic* (Cambridge, 1954), pp. 20-21; Freund, pp. 47, 79; Rosenfeld, pp. 299-300; and John W. Wheeler-Bennett, *The Nemesis of Power*, 2d edn. (London, 1964), p. 126, note 2, who all postdate to October 1919 Enver's abortive attempt to reach Moscow.

[23] Rustow, "Enwer Pasha," p. 700; Kochan, pp. 17-18; Freund, pp. 46-48.

set out for the Soviet capital and this time reached it safely. During the following months he established contacts with the *Narkomindel,* Lenin himself, and eventually also with Mustafa Kemal's nationalist movement in Anatolia.[24] In August 1920 he also endeavored to arrange for a rapprochement between Germany and Soviet Russia (specifically for talks between Seeckt and a group around Trotsky), but his mediatory efforts were apparently futile.[25] The next month Enver appeared in Baku at the Soviet-sponsored Congress of the Peoples of the East as the "Delegate of the Revolutionaries of Libya, Tunisia, Algeria, and Morocco," then moved back to Berlin. After prolonged and ultimately futile efforts to secure a place in Mustafa Kemal's regime, Enver concluded his odyssey in the autumn of 1921 by going to Uzbekistan, where he joined some Moslem groups in their fight against Soviet Russian infiltration. He was killed in August 1922 while leading a cavalry charge on Red Army troops.[26]

Cemal, who like Enver and Talât was sentenced to death in absentia by an Ottoman court-martial in July 1919, concluded his life in a similarly exotic fashion. After initial sojourns in Germany and Switzerland he took service with the Emir of Afghanistan and subsequently moved to Moscow, where he acted on several occasions as a kind of mediator between the Soviet government and the Turkish Kemalists. Upon serving for about a year as the inspector-general of the Afghan army, Cemal returned to the Soviet capital in September 1921 for further negotiations with the Bolsheviks, the Kemalists, and Enver (whom he tried to dissuade from going to Uzbekistan). According to a rather garbled account given by the German

[24] Rustow, "Enwer Pasha," p. 700.

[25] F. L. Carsten, "The Reichswehr and the Red Army, 1920-1933," *Survey,* Nos. 44-45 (Oct 1962), pp. 117-18. Cf. Freund, pp. 79-83, *passim;* Seeckt, pp. 306-307; Otto Gessler, *Reichswehrpolitik in der Weimarer Zeit,* Kurt Sendtner, ed. (Stuttgart, 1958), p. 191.

[26] Rustow, "Enwer Pasha," pp. 700-702; Olaf K. Caroe, *Soviet Empire* (London, 1953), pp. 123-27.

diplomat, Wipert von Blücher, Cemal seems to have paid a brief visit to Berlin as well, where he had a meeting with Ago von Maltzan, the head of the foreign office's eastern division. On his way back to Afghanistan, in July 1922, Cemal was shot to death by two Armenians in Tiflis. He was eventually reburied on Turkish soil, in Erzurum.[27]

Talât, whom Sazonov later called the "most infamous figure of our time," lived at first semi-legally and then openly in Berlin, where he was assassinated in March 1921 by an Armenian student.[28] At the height of World War II, in February 1943, Talât's remains were moved from a Berlin cemetery to Istanbul, and he was reburied there with full military honors on the "Hill of Liberty."[29] Several of the other fugitive *Ittihad ve Terakki* leaders eventually returned to Turkey. Dr. Nazim, along with Cavid Bey, Halil Bey, and two other prominent wartime figures, was tried and executed there in 1926 for alleged conspiratorial activities against Mustafa Kemal's regime.[30] Prince Said Halim, the official signatory of the original alliance treaty with Germany, was arrested by the Turkish government in March 1919 and subsequently interned by

[27] Rustow, "Djemal Pasha," p. 531; Blücher, pp. 132, 136; Caroe, pp. 122-23.

[28] Inal, xiii, 1944-48; Sazonov, p. 133; Blücher, pp. 134-36; Jäckh, *Goldene Pflug*, pp. 232-33. The continued presence of Talât and other *Ittihad ve Terakki* leaders in Germany was publicly denounced in a pamphlet by the Turkish emigré, Mehmed Zeki Bey, *Raubmörder als Gäste der deutschen Republik* (Berlin [1920]), but to no effect.

[29] Jackh, *The Rising Crescent*, p. 95; Jäschke, *Die Türkei in den Jahren 1942-1951*, p. 13. Inal, xiii, 1948, incorrectly dates Talât's solemn reburial in 1944. On Talât's disputed reputation in modern Turkey cf. *ibid.*, pp. 1,948-72, *passim*; Cemal Kutay, *Talât Paşayi nasil vurdular?* [How Did They Shoot Down Talât Paşa?] (Istanbul, 1956), *passim*; Yalman, pp. 62-63.

[30] See Ziemke, pp. 389-94; Lewis, pp. 269-70; Kinross, pp. 483-93; Dankwart Rustow, "Djawid," *Encyclopaedia of Islam*, rev. edn., ii, 497-98.

the British. On his release in March 1921 he moved to Rome, where he too was assassinated by an Armenian nine months later.[31]

[31] Inal, XII-XIII, 1893-1932, *passim*; Jäschke and Pritsch, "Die Türkei seit dem Weltkriege . . . ," pp. 12, 15, 21, 47, 56.

CHAPTER XII

Summary

ALTHOUGH the cultivation of Turkish goodwill and the expansion of German economic influence in the Ottoman empire had been basic ingredients of Wilhelmian *Weltpolitik* for many years, the World War I alliance of the Ottoman empire with the Central Powers was not the culmination of carefully laid German plans but instead a diplomatic improvisation. Faced with the likelihood of a general European war, Germany's leaders in late July 1914 abruptly set aside their misgivings about a close association with the decrepit Ottoman state and accepted the proffered military help of the Turks. Once a formal alliance treaty with the Porte had actually been signed Berlin naturally did its best to secure the promised Turkish assistance at the earliest possible moment and, having finally achieved that objective in late October, to make the most effective use of the military power and strategic location of its newly gained ally. Whether Germany's leaders in the following years expected too much of the Turks and burdened them with strategic tasks beyond their strength is an issue on which military historians have never been able to agree. It is beyond question, though, that the intervention of the Turks and their war effort during the following four years greatly helped the Central Powers to hold out as long as they did.[1]

During the first year and a half of the war German policy toward the Ottoman empire revolved almost exclusively around purely military considerations. To keep the Turkish armies in the field and have them supplement as effectively as

---

[1] For appraisals of the Turks' overall contribution to the war effort of the Central Powers, cf. Larcher, pp. 636-37; Mühlmann, *deutsch-türkische Waffenbündnis*, pp. 243-47 and *passim*; and Germany's official military history, *Der Weltkrieg 1914 bis 1918*, XIII, 442-43.

possible the general war effort of the Central Powers were practically the only issues the OHL and civilian leaders in Berlin cared about. Hence their reluctance to do anything drastic about the anti-Armenian outrages of the Turks and their passivity regarding various other domestic developments in the Ottoman empire. It was only in 1916, and particularly after Ludendorff's entry into the German High Command, that German official interest in the Ottoman empire once again broadened. While the immediate military requirements of the war continued to be the central concern of Germany's leaders, some of them now also began to plan and to push for an expansion of German economic and political influence in the Ottoman empire. Because of the skillful and determined countermoves of the Porte, but also because of perpetual dissensions among the Germans themselves, these expansionistic efforts of the Reich produced only modest results. Among the few positive achievements were the conclusion of the German-Ottoman Military Convention (which implicitly committed the Turkish armed forces to rely primarily on German equipment and supplies in the postwar period) and the assignment of a few mining concessions in Turkey to German firms. On most other economic issues the Germans made no headway at all. Despite persistent coaxing by the OHL and the Wilhelmstrasse the Porte never made any binding commitments concerning Germany's share in the future economic development of the Ottoman empire and stubbornly refused to liquidate the vast Entente holdings in Turkey for the benefit of German interest groups. German banks and business establishments already entrenched in the Ottoman empire gained little or nothing from the wartime partnership of the two countries; some of them, notably the Bagdad Railroad Company, were actually brought close to bankruptcy.

In financial and monetary matters, also, the Turks kept Berlin's ambitions effectively in check. They persistently refused to tamper with the privileged status of the Franco-British

Summary

Banque Impériale Ottomane, declined to use uncovered paper money as Berlin would have preferred, and successfully resisted all attempts by the German and Austro-Hungarian governments to attach strings to the loans they granted to the Porte. By the spring of 1918, at the latest, many responsible German leaders were beginning to realize that the loans would probably never be repaid, though most of them hoped that the indebtedness of the Porte might some day at least be exploited as a lever for extracting some economic concessions from the Turks.

Both before and during the war the presence of Gen. Liman von Sanders' military mission in the Ottoman empire was far less of an advantage to Germany than has often been alleged. Liman and his officers did contribute substantially to the general improvement of the Turkish army in the prewar months and to the relative success of Ottoman mobilization after July 1914, but their involvement in the Turkish policy-making process was mostly of marginal significance. Neither before nor after the conclusion of the German-Ottoman alliance did Liman or any other member of his mission command or control the Turkish military establishment or possess the means to impose their will on the Porte, and the same generalization applies to the hundreds of German officers who were added to the mission or otherwise entered Ottoman service during the last three years of the war. Gen. Liman's successful intervention in the Armenian deportations at Smyrna may, of course, be cited as proof that the German officers in Turkey did have extensive political power, but this incident was atypical. As a rule, intervention in the internal political affairs of the Ottoman empire by German officers was either useless or counterproductive, and some of them, like Lt. Col. Paraquin, paid for their boldness by being summarily relieved of their duties.

During its five years' stay in the Ottoman empire the German military mission participated vigorously in Berlin's search for new investment opportunities and raw materials in the Turkish provinces but accomplished very little beyond the collection of information. Moreover, it is now clear that on a number of occasions the military mission was anything but helpful to German business interests, as is witnessed especially by the unfriendly treatment some of Liman's officers gave to the Anatolian and Bagdad Railroad Companies.

THE DECISION of the dominant men in the *Ittihad ve Terakki* Party in July 1914 to make common cause with the *Dreibund* and the eventual active participation of the Ottoman empire in the European war on the side of the Central Powers cost the Turks dearly and ultimately destroyed their empire. It is not to be wondered then that the wartime rulers of the Ottoman empire were later widely denounced by Turkish and foreign critics alike as irresponsible, incompetent, and ruthless adventurers or even as the corrupt minions of Germany. Some of these accusations are justified. Enver Paşa and some of his colleagues at the Porte did indeed miscalculate the military strength of the Central Powers and, after bringing the Ottoman empire into the war against the Entente, repeatedly overextended the slender resources of their country in the pursuit of various expansionist goals. Moreover, in their domestic policies, particularly in their treatment of the Armenians, the *Ittihad ve Terakki* Party leaders displayed a ruthlessness inexcusable under any circumstances. And yet, the record of the Union and Progress regime contains a number of positive features which have often been overlooked.[2]

Though some of the leading Turkish statesmen were undoubtedly corrupt in that they enriched themselves by illegal means, there can no longer be any question about their basic patriotism. The reason that Enver, Talât, and their supporters in the *Ittihad ve Terakki* Party threw in their lot with the

[2] See Lewis, pp. 222-33, for a fresh assessment of the Young Turks' domestic achievements.

Summary

Central Powers and stayed on their side through four years of bitter fighting was their conviction that the Ottoman empire could thereby regain its status as a fully sovereign power, reconquer some of its previously lost possessions, and perhaps even acquire new territories in the Caucasus and Russian Central Asia. During most of the war period, specifically until the spring of 1918, the majority of the Turkish leaders, and Enver in particular, were prepared to collaborate closely with the Reich in the military conduct of the war, but they vigorously and, on the whole, effectively resisted all German attempts to meddle in the internal affairs of the Ottoman empire. Aside from keeping Berlin's economic and political ambitions in check the Turks slowly but surely pushed their more powerful ally into a number of important concessions, particularly with regard to the capitulations question. Simultaneously, they made it abundantly clear that after the war they meant to remain masters in their own house, and that the continued alignment of the Ottoman empire on the side of the Central Powers in the postwar period would have to be based on absolute Turkish equality. Although some German leaders, notably Ludendorff, hoped to the end that they might yet convert the Ottoman empire into a satellite of the Reich, at least in the economic sense, there is every reason to conclude that these ideas were utterly unrealistic. Indeed, the record of Turkish policies from 1914 to 1918 demonstrates that even if Germany had won the war it could not have secured control of the Ottoman empire short of occupying that country by military force.

Since the appearance in 1961 of Professor Fritz Fischer's massive study, *Griff nach der Weltmacht*, the origins of the First World War and the war aims of imperial Germany have once again become the subjects of heated debate. Fischer's principal theses, which he has expanded in several subsequent publications, can perhaps be summarized as follows: First, in July 1914 the Kaiser's government, confident of German mili-

Summary

tary superiority, wanted the Dual Monarchy to take military action against Serbia and was quite willing to have a major war with the Entente; second, Germany's policy was shaped by the determination to attain, by force if necessary, a "world power" status (that is, one at least equal to that of the British empire, Russia, and the United States); and third, this goal dominated the thinking and action of the Reich government throughout the war itself.

While this book has been concerned only with a relatively narrow aspect of Germany's wartime policies, it raises a number of questions about Fischer's theses. As far as the July Crisis is concerned, German policies toward the Ottoman empire do not fit very well into his conceptual scheme. Berlin's failure to seek an alliance commitment from the Turks, Wangenheim's cold reception of Enver's overtures on July 22, and Bethmann Hollweg's hesitancy on the alliance issue at the end of the month were no doubt primarily reflections of the low opinion in which Ottoman military power had been held by most of Germany's leaders. Yet it must also be noted that all of them became suddenly very insistent on prompt Turkish assistance once hostilities with Russia and France had actually begun, a change of attitude which would suggest that Berlin's expectation of and psychological readiness for a major war was not as pronounced as Fischer has claimed.

His generalizations about the imperialistic mood which characterized both the governing circles and the large majority of the German nation during the war itself are similarly open to criticism. While he has presented a very persuasive case that practically all of Germany's leaders and large segments of German society desired the aggrandizement of the Reich—territorially, economically, and otherwise—Fischer's treatment of German wartime ambitions and policies in regard to the Ottoman empire is far too simplistic. There was demonstrably less "continuity" in the formulation, and far less unanimity in the execution of these policies than he has asserted, and his description of what the Germans were doing in the Ottoman empire during the war years is marred by a number of factual inaccuracies. These observations are primarily meant as a caveat against the uncritical acceptance of all of Fischer's theses and are not intended to belittle the significance of his work. Indeed, besides presenting a wealth of new information, it has forced historians everywhere to reassess issues which seemed to have been settled long ago.

A. Staff Assignments at Ottoman GHQ, January 1918

Vice-Generalissimo:	Gen. Enver Paşa
Chief of General Staff:	Lt. Gen. von Seeckt*
Central Department:	Lt. Col. Dunst*

Departments

I	(Operations)	Lt. Col. von Feldmann*
II	(Intelligence)	Lt. Col. Seifi Bey; Lt. Col. Sievert*
III	(Railroads)	Lt. Col. Pfannenstiehl*
IV	(Quartermaster)	Maj. Gen. Bischof*
V	(Weapons and Munitions)	Maj. Gen. Schlee*
VI	(Communications Zone Inspectorate)	Lt. Col. Rüşdi Bey; Lt. Col. Endres,* attached
VII	(Medical)	Maj. Gen. Süleyman Numan Paşa
VIII	(Traffic)	Col. Potschernik*
IX	(HQ Commandant)	Lt. Col. Mahmud Bey
X	(Central Files)	Maj. Ziya Bey
XI	(Coal)	Maj. Niemöller*
XII	(Engineering and Fortresses)	Maj. Gen. Langenstrass*

* Indicates German officers. Their ranks are those held in the Ottoman army, customarily one higher than their German rank.
SOURCE: Mühlmann, *Das deutsch-türkische Waffenbündnis*, p. 326.

B. Major Unit Commands in the Ottoman Army Held by German Generals During World War I

Name	Unit Commanded	Approximate Dates
Liman von Sanders	First Army	Aug 1914-March 1915
	Fifth Army	March 1915-Feb 1918
	Army Group F	Feb 1918-Oct 1918
von der Goltz	First Army	April 1915-Oct 1915
	Sixth Army	Oct 1915-April 1916
von Falkenhayn	Army Group F	June 1917-Feb 1918
Kress von Kressenstein	Eighth Army	Oct 1917-Dec 1917

C. German-Ottoman Military Convention of October 18, 1917 (Excerpts)

ART. I. UNIFORM PRINCIPLES CONCERNING PEACETIME
STRENGTH AND MILITARY SERVICE OBLIGATIONS.

The high contracting parties obligate themselves to use the human resources of their countries for national defense in approximately equal fashion and to regulate to that end the *peacetime strength* of their armies and the *military service obligations* according to the same principles. . . .

The peacetime strength of the army shall amount to about 1% of the population.

The high contracting parties obligate themselves to allocate as much as possible the funds (army budget) which are annually required for the maintenance, clothing, equipment, payment, training, weaponry, medical services, etc., of the peacetime army as well as for war preparations (procurement of war materiel stocks of all types), for fortifications, for strategic railroads, roads, etc.

The military education and invigoration of the youth . . . shall be introduced and carried out in both countries according to similar principles.

ART. 2. UNIFORMITY IN THE ORGANIZATION OF THE ARMY
AND THE ORDER OF BATTLE.

The experiences of this war have shown the necessity of having the infantry divisions . . . in the allied armies constitute as much as possible identical types of troop units. . . . The high contracting parties, therefore, obligate themselves to [adopt uniform principles in the formation of divisional units]. . . .

ART. 3. UNIFORMITY OF WAR MATERIEL.

The replenishment of ammunition as well as the replacement and mutual loaning of weapons and weapons parts make it absolutely necessary for the allied armies to have *uniform* armaments and munitions.

The high contracting parties, therefore, obligate themselves to adopt as standard models those firearms with ammunition which have proved themselves in the war or been designed in consonance with the latest experiences of the war, [and] to procure new weapons only of these models. . . .

[To facilitate] mutual loans of equipment, particularly of spare parts . . . the Ottoman army shall use as much as possible passenger cars, trucks, airplanes, etc., only of the standard types adopted by the allied armies. . . . [Similar uniform standards to apply to various other types of equipment.]

ART. 4. UNIFORMITY OF TRAINING.

(1) The use of troops of the allied armies in joint operations . . . requires uniform training to the greatest possible extent. The high contracting parties, therefore, obligate themselves to retain or introduce . . . uniform regulations . . . for troop training, firing practice, field exercises, and tactical leadership; and to regulate the training of general staff officers at the Great General Staff and official procedures in the higher staffs . . . according to uniform principles, so that the work of Turkish officers on German staffs and of German officers on Turkish staffs will be facilitated.

(2) The German army administration will make available, upon request by the Turkish army administration, a stipulated number of selected officers for assistance in the expansion of the Ottoman army—provisionally for a period of five years. These officers will be given leave without pay by the German army administration, [they] will transfer into Turkish service and be paid by the Turkish army administration.

In all matters relating to their official duties and assignments these German officers will be subordinates of the Turkish war minister and their superior officers. Pending other arrangements between the two army administrations, they will, however, remain subject exclusively to the judicial and honor codes and the disciplinary authority of their own country. The disciplinary authority will be exercised . . . by the ranking German officer in the Turkish army, who shall have his official residence in Constantinople. Analogous rules shall apply to the Turkish officers and cadets who are posted to the German army.

All further details on this subject will be regulated by a special agreement between the two army administrations and by the contract which the Turkish war ministry will conclude with each German officer who transfers into Turkish service.

(3) . . . . .

(4) . . . . [Concerning implementation of officer exchanges.]

(5) The high contracting parties obligate themselves not to dispatch officers, etc., to the armies of France, Great Britain, Italy, Russia, the United States of America, or Japan, nor to employ in their own army any officers, etc., from any of these powers. . . .

(6) . . . . [Both Germany and the Ottoman empire shall promote the study of each other's languages in their respective armies.]

ART. 5. MILITARY PENAL CODES.

. . . . .

ART. 6. UNIFORM WORLD RADIO NETWORK.

. . . . The high contracting parties will . . . construct in their territories several major radio telegraphy stations of uniform type to serve their common interests. . . .

ART. 7. UNIFORM DIRECTION OF OPERATIONS.

The agreements on a "Supreme *War Command*" made during this war shall automatically come again into effect in the event of another common war, provided that no other arrangements have been made upon common consultations under Article 8c. . . .

Appendix C

In order to implement the above agreements and to work out all military questions which touch upon common interests,

(a) the military plenipotentiaries or military attachés at the Berlin and Constantinople embassies shall receive requisite staffs for their expanded sphere of work and shall be invited regularly to major maneuvers, inspection trips, etc.,

(b) . . . . [Appropriate offices shall be opened in each country's war ministry and general staff,]

(c) . . . . [At least one annual meeting shall be held between the war ministers and the heads of the general staffs of the two countries, or their representatives, to confer on military issues, plans, etc.]

ART. 9.

This Military Convention, which is to be kept secret, enters into force upon the conclusion of peace.

This convention shall be automatically voided upon the termination of the alliance treaty. The high contracting parties, furthermore, have the right to withdraw from this convention after 10 years upon giving notice one year in advance. If a cancellation notice is not given, the convention shall be considered extended for another 10 years. . . .

> Signed, Constantinople, October 18, 1917
> Gen. Hermann von Stein
> Lt. Gen. Enver Paşa

Source: FO, *Dt 128 Nr. 5 secr.*, Bd. 7.

D. Major Personnel Changes in the German Foreign Service, 1914-18

	Approximate Dates	*Remarks*
AMBASSADORS IN CONSTANTINOPLE		
von Wangenheim	1912-Oct 1915	von Kühlmann attached, Oct-Nov 1914
Prince zu Hohenlohe-Langenburg	July 1915-Sept 1915	Temporary replacement for Wangenheim
Count Wolff-Metternich	Nov 1915-Sept 1916	
von Kühlmann	Nov 1916-July 1917	
Count Bernstorff	Sept 1917-Oct 1918	
FOREIGN OFFICE, BERLIN, STATE SECRETARIES		
von Jagow	1912-Nov 1916	
Zimmermann	Nov 1916-Aug 1917	
von Kühlmann	Aug 1917-July 1918	
von Hintze	July 1918-Oct 1918	
Solf	Oct 1918-	
UNDER STATE SECRETARIES		
Zimmermann	1911-Nov 1916	
von dem Bussche (1)	Nov 1916-	
von Stumm (2)	Nov 1916-	

E. Major Personnel Changes in the Ottoman Cabinet, 1914-18

	Approximate Dates	Remarks
GRAND VIZIER		
Said Halim Paşa	1913-Feb 1917	
Talât Paşa	Feb 1917-Oct 1918	
Izzet Paşa	Oct 1918-Nov 1918	
FOREIGN MINISTER		
Said Halim Paşa	1913-Oct 1915	
Halil Bey	Oct 1915-Feb 1917	Subsequently Minister of Justice
Nessimi Bey	Feb 1917-Oct 1918	Previously Minister of Commerce
Nabi Bey	Oct 1918-	"Interim" Appointment
MINISTER OF INTERIOR		
Talât Bey (Paşa)	1913-July 1918	Paşa from Feb 1917
Canbulat Bey	July 1918-Oct 1918	
Fethi Bey	Oct 1918-	
WAR MINISTER		
Enver Paşa	Jan 1914-Oct 1918	
Izzet Paşa	Oct 1918-	
NAVY MINISTER		
Cemal Paşa	March 1914-Oct 1918	In Syria, Nov 1914-Dec 1917
Rauf Bey	Oct 1918-	

Appendix E

	Approximate Dates	*Remarks*
FINANCE MINISTER		
Cavid Bey	March 1914-Nov 1914	
Talât Bey	Nov 1914-Feb 1917	"Interim" Appointment
Cavid Bey	Feb 1917-	

BIBLIOGRAPHY

The following listing is confined with a few exceptions to items cited in the footnotes of this book. It therefore omits many books and some sources which provided useful background information.

Primary Sources

I. UNPRINTED MATERIALS

German Foreign Office Archives (*Akten des Auswärtigen Amts*), 1867-1920. Auswärtiges Amt, Bonn. Microfilm collections of the University of California, Berkeley; the University of Michigan, Ann Arbor; St. Antony's College, Oxford; The National Archives, Washington, D.C.

Files of *Abteilung IA*

Bulgarien

6	Die Militärangelegenheiten Bulgariens, Bde. 17-18.
6 Nr. 1	Bulgarische Waffen- und Munitionsbestellungen, Bde. 7-8.
17	Beziehungen Bulgariens zur Pforte, Bde. 20-24.
17 *secr.*	Bd. 1.
17 adh. 1 *secr.*	Die türkisch-bulgarische Grenzregulierungskommission, Bd. 1.

Deutschland

127 Nr. 6	Die türkische Botschaft in Berlin, Bde. 3-4.
128 Nr. 1 *secr.*	Bündnisvertrag zwischen Deutschland, Oesterreich und Italien, Bde. 33-51.
128 Nr. 2 *secr.*	Beitritt Rumäniens zum Bündnisvertrage zwischen Deutschland und Oesterreich, Bde. 13-32.

Bibliography

128 Nr. 5 *secr.*	Beitritt der Türkei zu dem Bündnisvertrage zwischen Deutschland, Oesterreich und Italien, Bde. 2-7.
128 Nr. 8 *secr.*	Frage des Anschlusses Bulgariens an den Dreibund, Bde. 1-12.
135 Nr. 1	Die deutsche Botschaft in Konstantinopel, Bde. 5-6.
135 Nr. 1 *secr.*	Bd. 1.

Italien

90	Die Beziehungen Italiens zur Türkei, Bd. 6.

Orientalia Generalia

2	Die Herstellung eines Balkanstaaten-Bundes, Bd. 6.
5	Die Politik der Mächte bezüglich der Balkanhalbinsel und der Meerengen, Bde. 95-96.
5 *secr.*	Bd. 18.

Russland

97a	Russisch-Asien: Kaukasus, Bde. 9-27.

Tripolis

1	Allgemeine Angelegenheiten von Tripolis, Bde. 15-17.

Türkei

110	Türkische Finanzen, Bde. 72-109.
110 Nr. 2	Die Europäische Kommission zur Sicherstellung der türkischen Staatsgläubiger, Bde. 8-10.
110 Nr. 5	Die deutsch-türkischen Vorschussverträge, Bde. 1-6.
——	Handakten betr. die Finanzverhandlungen mit Djavid Bey.
134	Allgemeine Angelegenheiten der Türkei, Bde. 33-40.

Bibliography

139	Ueberlassung von preussischen Offizieren und Finanzbeamten an die Pforte zu Reorganisationszwecken, Bde. 33-49.
142	Die Militär- und Marineangelegenheiten der Türkei, Bde. 39-65.
142 *secr.*	Bd. 3.
150	Die Durchfahrt fremder Schiffe durch die Dardanellen, Bde. 9-10.
150 *secr.*	Bd. 1.
152	Eisenbahnen in der asiatischen Türkei, Bde. 78-102.
153	Die Beziehungen Russlands zur Türkei, Bd. 9.
154	Die Beziehungen Englands zur Türkei, Bd. 7.
155	Die Beziehungen Oesterreich-Ungarns zur Türkei, Bde. 4-5.
158	Das Verhältnis der Türkei zu Deutschland, Bde. 14-21.
158 *secr.*	Bd. 2.
158 Nr. 1 *secr.*	Verhandlungen über ein deutsch-türkisches Bündnis, Bd. 1.
159 Nr. 2	Türkische Staatsmänner, Bde. 12-20.
159 Nr. 3	Türkische Militärs, Bd. 4.
161	Türkische Ministerien, Bde. 4-5.
167 *secr.*	Die türkische Presse, Bd. 3.
168	Die Beziehungen der Türkei zu Griechenland, Bde. 11-16.
169	Die Beziehungen der Türkei zu Frankreich, Bd. 8.
171	Die Beziehungen der Türkei zu Rumänien, Bd. 3.
179	Die Eventualität eines Zusammenbruchs der Türkei, Bd. 1.
181 *secr.*	Allgemeine türkische Politik, Bd. 2.

183   Armenien, Bde. 36-55.
197   Deutsche wirtschaftliche und industrielle Unternehmungen in der Türkei, Bde. 5-7.
198   Die Jungtürken, Bde. 7-8.
204   Die seitens der Türkei angeregte Frage, ob durch ihre Beteiligung am Weltkriege 1914ff. der 1. Pariser Meerengenvertrag vom 30.3.1856, . . . als erloschen anzusehen sind, Bd. 1.

Weltkrieg

Wk   Der Weltkrieg, Bde. 11-74.
Wk Nr. 11u   Unternehmungen und Aufwiegelungen gegen unsere Feinde. Die Senussi. Bde. 1-3.
Wk Nr. 15   Material zu den Friedensverhandlungen, Bde. 24-29.
Wk Nr. 16   Entsendung von Offizieren pp. für die deutschen Schiffe in der Türkei, Lieferung von Kriegsmaterial durch die deutsche Heeres- und Marineverwaltung an die Türkei, Bde. 1-11.

Verträge IE

Nr. 94   1. Deutsch-türkischer Bündnisvertrag vom 2.8.1914, . . .
Nr. 95   Deutsch-Türkische Vorschuss-Verträge.
Nr. 98   I. Friedensvertrag zwischen Deutschland, Oesterreich-Ungarn, Bulgarien und der Türkei einerseits und Russland andererseits d.d. Brest-Litowsk, 3.3.1918. II. Deutsch-russischer Zusatzvertrag zu obigem d.d Brest-Litowsk, 3.3.1918.
Nr. 100   I. Die am 7.V.1918 in Bukarest unterzeichneten Verträge und Protokolle . . . zwischen Deutschland pp. und Rumänien. . . .
Nr. 102   I. Deutsch-russischer Ergänzungsvertrag zu

Bibliography

dem Friedensvertrag zwischen Deutschland, Oesterreich-Ungarn, Bulgarien und
der Türkei einerseits und Russland andererseits d.d. Berlin, 27.8.1918. . . .

Nr. 103   6 deutsch-georgische Abkommen d.d Poti,
28.5.1918.

Nachlässe: Nachlass, Paul Weitz (1862-1939).

Deutsches Zentralarchiv, Potsdam

Files of Reichskanzlei 1878-1945

Kriegsakten (1914-1922)

1   Allgemeines-Nr. 2398.
15   Vorschläge zu Friedensverhandlungen-Nr.
2442/10ff.
22   Türkei-Nr. 2458/9.

Registratur 1900-1918-Auswärtige Angelegenheiten

7   Türkei-Nr. 11.

Files of Büro Staatsminister Dr. Helfferich, 1917-1918.

100-102   Akten betr. Türkei-Nr. 19,315-19,317.

Austro-Hungarian Foreign Ministry Archives
(*Staatskanzlei, Ministerium des Aeussern*).
Oesterreichisches Staatsarchiv, Abt. Haus-,
Hof- und Staatsarchiv, Vienna

Files of Politisches Archiv
P.A. 1
Karton rot
941-948   Krieg 21a, Türkei.
P.A. xii
Karton 208   Türkei, Weisungen.
Karton 209-212   Türkei, Berichte.
Karton 463   Türkei XLVII/3-Die Armenier-Verfolgun-
gen . . . 1915-1918.
Karton 464   Türkei XLVII/4-Unsere Massnahmen zum

· 387 ·

Bibliography

Schutz der katholischen Armenier, Okt.
1915-1918.

Karton 466   Türkei LII/1-Abschaffung der Kapitulationen und Kündigung diverser Verträge durch die Türkei, 1914-1918.
Türkei LII/2-Reise des türkischen Minister des Aeussern Halil Bey . . . Sept. 1916-Okt.

Bundesarchiv-Militärarchiv, Koblenz

File K 07-4/1   "Erlebnisse des Admiral a.D. von Nordeck auf S.M.S. *Breslau* während des 1. Weltkrieges," typescript, dated 20 June 1945.

The Papers of Ernst Jäckh. Yale University Library, Historical Manuscripts Collection, drawer 69

The Papers of Dr. Heinrich Kanner of Vienna. Hoover War Library, Stanford, California

II. PRINTED MATERIALS
Published Public Documents

Browder, Robert P., and Alexander F. Kerensky, eds. *The Russian Provisional Government 1917. Documents.* 3 vols. Stanford, 1961.

Deyrmenjian, Navasard. "An Important Turkish Document on the 'Exterminate Armenians' Plan." *Armenian Review*, XIV:3 (1961), 53-55.

France. *Documents diplomatiques français (1871-1914).* 42 vols. Paris, 1929-59.

Gatzke, Hans W. "Dokumentation: Zu den deutsch-russischen Beziehungen im Sommer 1918." *Vierteljahreshefte für Zeitgeschichte*, 3 (1955), pp. 67-98.

Germany. *Die deutschen Dokumente zum Kriegsausbruch. Vollständige Sammlung der von Karl Kautsky zusammengestellten amtlichen Aktenstücke.* . . . 4 vols. Berlin, 1919.

Bibliography

Great Britain. *The Treatment of Armenians in the Ottoman Empire 1915-16. Documents presented to Viscount Grey of Fallodon.* Viscount Bryce [and Arnold J. Toynbee], eds. London, 1916.

Hurewitz, Jacob C., ed. *Diplomacy in the Near and Middle East: A Documentary Record.* 2 vols. Princeton, 1956.

Italy. *I Documenti Diplomatici Italiani.* Ser. 5, Vol. 1. Augusto Torre, ed. Rome, 1954.

Jäschke, Gotthard. "Urkunden: Osmanisch-Aserbeidschanischer Zusatzvertrag vom 4. Juni 1918." *Welt des Islams,* new series, 6 (1959), pp. 133-36.

Lepsius, Johannes, ed. *Deutschland und Armenien 1914-1918. Sammlung diplomatischer Aktenstücke.* Potsdam, 1919.

Matthias, Erich, ed. *Der Interfraktionelle Ausschuss 1917/18.* 2 vols. Düsseldorf, 1959.

—— and Rudolf Morsey, eds. *Die Regierung des Prinzen Max von Baden.* Düsseldorf, 1962.

Poidebard, A. "Chronique: Le Transcaucase et la République d'Arménie dans les textes diplomatiques du Traité de Brest-Litovsk au Traité de Kars, 1918-1921." *Revue des Études Arméniennes,* III:3 (1923), 63-78; IV:1 (1924), 31-98.

Russia. *Das Zaristische Russland im Weltkriege. Neue Dokumente aus den russischen Staatsarchiven. . . .* M. Pokrovski, ed. Berlin, 1927.

——. *Die europäischen Mächte und die Türkei während des Weltkrieges: Konstantinopel und die Meerengen. Nach den Geheimdokumenten des ehem. Ministeriums für Auswärtige Angelegenheiten.* E. A. Adamov, ed. 4 vols. Dresden, 1930-32.

——. *Die Internationalen Beziehungen im Zeitalter des Imperialismus. Dokumente aus den Archiven der Zarischen und der Provisorischen Regierung. . . .* M. Pokrovski, ed. Ser. 1 and 2. 11 vols. Berlin, 1931-36.

——. *Iswolski im Weltkriege. Der Diplomatische Schriftwechsel Iswolskis aus den Jahren 1914-1917.* Friedrich Stieve, ed. Berlin, 1925.

Bibliography

Russia. Ministerstvo Inostranich Del SSSR. *Dokumenty vneishnei politiki SSSR* [Documents on the Foreign Policy of the USSR]. Vol. 1. Moscow, 1957.

Scherer, André and Jacques Grunewald, eds. *L'Allemagne et les problèmes de la paix pendant la première guerre mondiale. Documents extraits des archives de l'Office allemand des Affaires étrangères.* Vol. 1. Paris, 1962.

Scott, James Brown, ed. *Official Statements of War Aims and Peace Proposals, December 1916 to November 1918.* Washington, D.C., 1921.

United States. *Papers Relating to the Foreign Relations of the United States. Supplements 1915-1918, The World War.* Washington, D.C., 1928-33.

Parliamentary Records

Germany. *Verhandlungen des Reichstags. XIII. Legislaturperiode. . . . Stenographische Berichte.* Vols. 306-14. Berlin, 1916-19.

Great Britain. *The Parliamentary Debates. . . . House of Commons.* Ser. 5, Vol. 93. London, 1917.

Memoirs, Diaries, and Personal Correspondence

Avalishvili, Zourab [Zurab D. Avalov]. *The Independence of Georgia in International Politics, 1918-1921.* London [1940].

Bernstorff, Johann. *Memoirs of Count Bernstorff.* New York, 1936.

Bethmann Hollweg, Theobald von. *Betrachtungen zum Weltkriege.* Part II. Berlin, 1921.

Blücher, Wipert von. *Deutschlands Weg nach Rapallo.* Wiesbaden, 1951.

Conrad von Hötzendorf, Franz. *Aus meiner Dienstzeit 1906-18.* Vols. IV-V. Vienna, 1923-25.

Demirhan, Pertev. *General-Feldmarschall Colmar Frhr. von der Goltz. . . . Aus meinen persönlichen Erinnerungen.* Göttingen, 1960.

Bibliography

Djemal Pasha [Cemal Paşa], Ahmed. *Memories of a Turkish Statesman, 1913-1919.* London [1922].

Dunsterville, L. C. *The Adventures of Dunsterforce.* London, 1932.

Einstein, Lewis. *Inside Constantinople.* London, 1917.

Erzberger, Matthias. *Erlebnisse im Weltkrieg.* Berlin, 1920.

Gessler, Otto. *Reichswehrpolitik in der Weimarer Zeit.* Kurt Sendtner, ed. Stuttgart, 1958.

[Goltz, Colmar Frhr. von der]. *Denkwürdigkeiten.* Friedrich Frhr. von der Goltz and Wolfgang Foerster, eds. Berlin, 1929.

Groener, Wilhelm. *Lebenserinnerungen. Jugend, Generalstab, Weltkrieg.* Friedrich Frhr. Hiller von Gaertringen, ed. Göttingen, 1957.

Guse, Felix. *Die Kaukasusfront im Weltkrieg bis zum Frieden von Brest.* Leipzig, 1940.

Hanssen, Hans P. *Diary of a Dying Empire.* Ralph H. Lutz *et al.*, eds. Bloomington, Ind., 1955.

Helfferich, Karl. *Der Weltkrieg.* Karlsruhe, 1925.

Hentig, Werner O. von. *Mein Leben eine Dienstreise.* Göttingen, 1962.

Hilger, Gustav and Alfred G. Meyer. *Incompatible Allies. A Memoir-History of German-Soviet Relations, 1918-1941.* New York, 1953.

Hoffmann, Max. *Die Aufzeichnungen des Generalmajors Max Hoffmann.* Karl F. Nowak, ed. 2 vols. Berlin, 1929.

Izzet Pasha [Paşa], Ahmed. *Denkwürdigkeiten des Marschalls Izzet Pascha.* Karl Klinghardt, ed. Leipzig, 1927.

Jäckh, Ernst. *Der Goldene Pflug.* Stuttgart, 1954.

Kannengiesser, Hans. *The Campaign in Gallipoli.* London [1928].

Kopp, Georg. *Das Teufelsschiff und seine kleine Schwester. Erlebnisse des Goeben-Funkers Georg Kopp.* Leipzig, 1930.

Kress von Kressenstein, Friedrich Frhr. *Mit den Türken zum Suezkanal.* Berlin, 1938.

Bibliography

Kühlmann, Richard von. *Erinnerungen*. Heidelberg, 1948.

Liman von Sanders, Otto. *Five Years in Turkey*. Annapolis, Md., 1927.

Lloyd George, David. *War Memoirs*. 6 vols. Boston, 1933-37.

Ludendorff, Erich. *Meine Kriegserinnerungen 1914-1918*. 3rd edn., Berlin, 1919.

Morgenthau, Henry. *Ambassador Morgenthau's Story*. New York, 1918.

[Müller, Georg A. von]. *Regierte der Kaiser? Kriegstagebücher, Aufzeichnungen und Briefe des . . . Admiral Georg Alexander von Müller, 1914-1918*. Walter Görlitz, ed. Göttingen, 1959.

Mutius, Gerhard von. "Die Türkei 1911-1914." *Preussische Jahrbücher*, 236 (1934), pp. 212-20.

Nadolny, Rudolf. *Mein Beitrag*. Wiesbaden, 1955.

Naslian, Jean. *Les mémoires de Mgr. Jean Naslian, Évêque de Trebizonde, sur les événements politico-religieux en Proche-Orient de 1914 à 1928*. 2 vols. Beirut, 1955.

Nekludoff, A. *Diplomatic Reminiscences, . . . 1911-1917*. New York, 1920.

Papen, Franz von. *Der Wahrheit eine Gasse*. Munich, 1952.

Pomiankowski, Joseph. *Der Zusammenbruch des Ottomanischen Reiches. Erinnerungen. . . .* Vienna, 1928.

Poincaré, Raymond. *Au service de la France*. Vol. VI. Paris, 1930.

Sâbis, Ali Ihsan. *Harb Hâtiralarim* [My War Memoirs]. 3 vols. Istanbul and Ankara, 1943-52. Vol. II. Ankara, 1951.

Sazonov, Serge. *Fateful Years, 1909-1916*. New York, 1928.

[Seeckt, Hans von]. *Aus seinem Leben, 1918-1936*. Friedrich von Rabenau, ed. Leipzig, 1940.

Seignobosc, Henri. *Turcs et Turquie*. Paris, 1920.

Steuber, Werner. *Jilderim. Deutsche Streiter auf heiligem Boden* [Schlachten des Weltkrieges, v. 5]. Oldenburg, 1922.

[Talaat Pasha (Talât Paşa), Mehmed]. "Posthumous Memoirs of Talaat Pasha." *Current History*, 15 (1921), pp. 287-95.

Bibliography

Thaer, Albrecht von. *Generalstabsdienst an der Front und in der OHL.* Siegfried A. Kaehler, ed. Göttingen, 1958.

Tirpitz, Alfred von. *Erinnerungen.* rev. edn., Leipzig, 1920.

Townshend, Charles V. F. *My Campaign.* 2 vols. New York, 1920.

Wrisberg, Ernst von. *Wehr und Waffen 1914-1918* (Erinnerungen an die Kriegsjahre im Königlich Preussischen Kriegsministerium, v. 3). Leipzig, 1922.

Yalman, Ahmed Emin. *Turkey in My Time.* Norman, Okla., 1956.

Wartime Pamphlets and Other Contemporary Publications

Alp, Tekin [M. Cohen]. *Türkismus und Pantürkismus.* Weimar, 1915.

Benson, E. F. *Deutschland über Allah.* London, 1917.

Blanckenhorn, Max. *Syrien und die deutsche Arbeit.* Weimar, 1916.

Emin, Ahmed. *Die Türkei.* Gotha, 1918.

Hassert, Kurt. *Das Türkische Reich. Politisch, geographisch und wirtschaftlich.* Tübingen, 1918.

Hellauer, Josef, ed. *Das Türkische Reich.* Berlin, 1918.

Hennig, Richard. *Die deutschen Bahnbauten in der Türkei, ihr politischer, militärischer und wirtschaftlicher Wert.* Leipzig, 1915.

Herlt, Gustav. "Folgen des Krieges für das wirtschaftliche und finanzielle Leben der Türkei." *Weltwirtschaftliches Archiv,* 6 (1915), pp. 147-64.

——. "Kriegswirtschaft in der Türkei." *Ibid.,* 8 (1916), pp. 466-76; 9 (1917), pp. 107*-12*, 285*-88*.

Hoffmann, Walter. "Deutsche Banken in der Türkei." *Ibid.,* 6 (1915), pp. 410-21.

Hurgronje, Christian S. *The Holy War "Made in Germany."* New York, 1915.

Jäckh, Ernst. *Die deutsch-türkische Waffenbrüderschaft.* Stuttgart, 1915.

Jäschke, Gotthard. *Die Entwicklung des Osmanischen Verfassungsstaates von den Anfängen bis zur Gegenwart.* Berlin, 1917.

Jastrow, J. *Die Weltstellung Konstantinopels in ihrer historischen Entwicklung.* Weimar, 1915.

Junge, Reinhard. *Die deutsch-türkischen Wirtschaftsbeziehungen.* Weimar, 1916.

Kaukasielli, K. *Der Kaukasus im Weltkriege.* Weimar, 1916.

Kunke, Max. *Die Kapitulationen der Türkei.* Munich, 1918.

Lehmann, Walther. *Die Kapitulationen.* Weimar, 1917.

Lepsius, Johannes. *Bericht über die Lage des Armenischen Volkes in der Türkei* (Als Manuskript gedruckt. Streng vertraulich). Potsdam, 1916.

Mandelstam, André. *Le sort de l'Empire Ottoman.* Paris, 1917.

Marré, Ernst. *Die Türken und Wir nach dem Kriege. Ein praktisches Wirtschaftsprogramm.* Berlin, 1916.

Mehrmann-Coblenz, Karl. *Der diplomatische Krieg in Vorderasien.* Dresden, 1916.

Naumann, Friedrich. *Mitteleuropa.* Berlin, 1915.

Ostrorog, Leon. *The Turkish Problem.* London, 1919.

Riba, Theodor Ritter von. *Der türkische Bundesgenosse.* Berlin, n.d.

Ritter, Albert. *Berlin-Bagdad.* 17th edn., Munich, 1916.

Schaefer, C. A. *Die Entwicklung der Bagdadbahnpolitik.* Weimar, 1916.

Schmidt, Hermann. *Das Eisenbahnwesen in der asiatischen Türkei.* Berlin, 1914.

Schwarzhaupt, Paul. *Die Wahrheit über die Türkei.* Berlin, 1919.

Stuermer, Harry. *Two Years in Constantinople.* New York, 1917.

Zeki Bey, Mehmed. *Raubmörder als Gäste der deutschen Republik.* Berlin [1920].

Bibliography

Newspapers

Hilal. Stambul, 1915ff.

Le Moniteur Oriental. Constantinople, 1914ff.

Osmanischer Lloyd. Constantinople, 1915ff.

Stamboul. Constantinople, 1914.

Secondary Works

OFFICIAL AND SEMI-OFFICIAL MILITARY HISTORIES

Austria. *Oesterreich-Ungarns letzter Krieg 1914-1918.* E. Glaise-Horstenau, ed. 8 vols. Vienna, 1931-38.

———. *Oesterreich-Ungarns Seekrieg 1914-1918.* Hans Sokol, ed. 3 vols. Vienna, 1929-33.

Germany. Reichsarchiv und Kriegsgeschichtliche Forschungsanstalt des Heeres. *Der Weltkrieg 1914 bis 1918.* 14 vols. Berlin, 1925-44.

———. Marine-Archiv und Kriegswissenschaftliche Abteilung der Marine. *Der Krieg zur See 1914-1918: Der Krieg in den türkischen Gewässern.* Hermann Lorey, ed. 2 vols. Berlin, 1928-38.

Great Britain. *History of the Great War: Military Operations Egypt and Palestine.* Sir George MacMunn and Cyril Falls, eds. 3 vols. London, 1928-30.

———. *Military Operations, Gallipoli.* C. F. Aspinall-Oglander, ed. 2 vols. London, 1929-32.

———. *The Campaigns in Mesopotamia, 1914-1918.* F. J. Moberly, ed. 4 vols. London, 1923-27.

———. *Military Operations Macedonia.* Cyril Falls, ed. 2 vols. London, 1933-35.

———. *Naval Operations.* Sir Julian S. Corbett and Sir Henry Newbolt, eds. 5 vols. London, 1920-31.

Turkey. État-Major général turc. *Campagne des Dardanelles* (Historique des opérations ottomanes dans la guerre mondiale). Translated by M. Larcher. Paris, 1924.

Bibliography

OTHER BOOKS, ARTICLES, AND
DISSERTATIONS CITED

Albertini, Luigi. *The Origins of the War of 1914.* 3 vols. London, 1952-57.

Allen, W. E. D. and Paul Muratoff. *Caucasian Battlefields. A History of the Wars on the Turco-Caucasian Border, 1828-1921.* Cambridge, 1953.

Ancel, Jacques, *Manuel Historique de la question d'Orient, 1792-1925.* 2d edn., Paris, 1926.

Anchieri, Ettore. *Constantinopoli e gli stretti nella politica russa ed Europea.* Milan, 1948.

Anderson, M. S. *The Eastern Question, 1774-1923.* London, 1966.

Andrew, Christopher. "German World Policy and the Reshaping of the Dual Alliance." *Journal of Contemporary History,* 1:3 (1966), 137-51.

Antonius, George. *The Arab Awakening.* Philadelphia, 1939.

Atamian, Sarkis. *The Armenian Community.* New York, 1955.

F. B. "Die militärischen Durchgangsfrachten zwischen Deutschland und der Türkei während des Weltkrieges." *Wissen und Wehr,* 7 (1926), pp. 346-55.

Baumgart, Winfried. *Deutsche Ostpolitik 1918. Von Brest-Litowsk bis zum Ende des Ersten Weltkrieges.* Vienna, 1966.

Bayur, Yusuf Hikmet. *Türk inkilâbi tarihi* [History of the Turkish Reform]. 3 [9] vols. Istanbul and Ankara, 1940-57.

Becker, Otto. *Der Ferne Osten und das Schicksal Europas, 1907-1918.* Leipzig, 1940.

Bestuzhev, I. V. "Russian Foreign Policy February-June 1914." *Journal of Contemporary History,* 1:3 (1966), 93-112.

Blaisdell, Donald C. *European Financial Control in the Ottoman Empire.* New York, 1929.

Borchard, Edwin, and William H. Wynne. *State Insolvency and Foreign Bondholders.* 2 vols. New Haven, 1951.

Bibliography

Brünner, E. R. J. *De Bagdadspoorweg . . . 1888-1908*. Groningen, 1957.

Cameron, Rondo E. *France and the Economic Development of Europe, 1800-1914*. Princeton, 1961.

Carlgren, W. M. *Neutralität oder Allianz. Deutschlands Beziehungen zu Schweden in den Anfangsjahren des ersten Weltkrieges*. Stockholm, 1962.

Caroe, Olaf K. *Soviet Empire. The Turks of Central Asia and Stalinism*. London, 1953.

Carsten, F. L. "The Reichswehr and the Red Army, 1920-1933." *Survey*, Nos. 44-45 (1962), pp. 114-32.

Chapman, Maybelle K. *Great Britain and the Bagdad Railway 1888-1914*. Northampton, Mass., 1948.

Conker, Orhan. *Les chemins de fer en Turquie et la politique ferroviaire turque*. Paris, 1935.

———— and Emile Witmeur. *Redressement économique et industrialisation de la Nouvelle Turquie*. Paris, 1937.

Cook, Ralph E. "The United States and the Armenian Question, 1894-1924." Unpublished ph.d. dissertation, Fletcher School of Law and Diplomacy, 1957.

Craig, Gordon A. *The Politics of the Prussian Army, 1640-1945*. rev. edn. New York, 1964.

Dallin, Alexander *et al*. *Russian Diplomacy and Eastern Europe, 1914-1917*. New York, 1963.

Daniel, Robert L. "The Armenian Question and American-Turkish Relations, 1914-1927." *Mississippi Valley Historical Review*, 46 (1959-60), pp. 252-75.

Davison, R. H. "The Armenian Crisis, 1912-1914." *American Historical Review*, 53 (1948), pp. 481-505.

————. *Reform in the Ottoman Empire, 1856-1876*. Princeton, 1963.

DeNovo, John A. *American Interests and Policies in the Middle East, 1900-1939*. Minneapolis, 1963.

Dranov, B. A. *Chernomorskiye prolivy* [The Black Sea Straits]. Moscow, 1948.

Bibliography

Earle, Edward Mead. *Turkey, the Great Powers, and the Bagdad Railway.* New York, 1923.

Edmonds, Sir James E. *A Short History of World War I.* London, 1951.

Emin, Ahmed. *Turkey in the World War.* New Haven, 1930.

Epstein, Klaus. *Matthias Erzberger and the Dilemma of German Democracy.* Princeton, 1959.

Evans, Laurence. *United States Policy and the Partition of Turkey, 1914-1924.* Baltimore, 1965.

Evans-Pritchard, E. E. *The Sanusi of Cyrenaica.* Oxford, 1949.

Falls, Cyril. *Armageddon: 1918.* Philadelphia, 1964.

Feis, Herbert. *Europe, the World's Banker, 1870-1914.* New Haven, 1930.

Fischer, Fritz. *Griff nach der Weltmacht.* Düsseldorf, 1961.

———. *Weltmacht oder Niedergang. Deutschland im ersten Weltkrieg* (Hamburger Studien zur neueren Geschichte, 1). Frankfurt, 1965.

———. "Deutsche Kriegsziele, Revolutionierung und Separatfrieden im Osten 1914-1918." *Historische Zeitschrift,* 188 (1959), pp. 249-310.

———. "Weltpolitik, Weltmachtstreben und deutsche Kriegsziele." *Ibid.,* 199 (1964), pp. 265-346.

Fisher, Sidney N. *The Middle East.* New York, 1959.

Freund, Gerald. *Unholy Alliance. Russian-German Relations from the Treaty of Brest-Litovsk to the Treaty of Berlin.* London, 1957.

Gehrke, Ulrich. *Persien in der deutschen Orientpolitik während des Ersten Weltkrieges.* 2 vols. Stuttgart [1960].

Gottlieb, W. W. *Studies in Secret Diplomacy during the First World War.* London, 1957.

Guinn, Paul. *British Strategy and Politics, 1914-1918.* London, 1965.

Hallgarten, George W. F. *Imperialismus vor 1914.* 2 vols. 2d edn., Munich, 1963.

Hauser, Oswald. "Die englisch-russische Konvention von 1907 und die Meerengenfrage." In *Geschichtliche Kräfte und*

Bibliography

Entscheidungen. Festschrift Otto Becker. Martin Göhring and Alexander Scharff, eds. Wiesbaden, 1954.

Henderson, W. O. *Studies in German Colonial History.* London, 1962.

Hennig, Richard. "Die Fortschritte im Eisenbahnwesen Nord- und Osteuropas und Asiens im Jahre 1919." *Weltwirtschaftliches Archiv,* 16 (1921), pp. 125*-30*.

Herzfeld, Hans. "Die Liman-Krise und die Politik der Grossmächte in der Jahreswende 1913/14." *Berliner Monatshefte,* 11 (1933), pp. 837-58, 973-93.

Higgins, Trumbull. *Winston Churchill and the Dardanelles.* New York, 1963.

Holborn, Hajo. "Deutschland und die Türkei 1878/90." *Archiv für Politik und Geschichte,* 5 (1925), pp. 111-59.

Hölzle, Erwin. *Der Osten im ersten Weltkrieg.* Leipzig, 1944.

————. "Das Experiment des Friedens im Ersten Weltkrieg 1914-1917." *Geschichte in Wissenschaft und Unterricht,* 8 (1962), pp. 465-522.

————. "Deutschland und die Wegscheide des ersten Weltkriegs." In *Festschrift Otto Becker.* Wiesbaden, 1954.

Howard, Harry N. *The Partition of Turkey. A Diplomatic History, 1913-1923.* Norman, Okla., 1931.

————. *The King-Crane Commission. An American Inquiry in the Middle East.* Beirut, 1963.

Hüber, Reinhard. *Die Bagdadbahn* (Schriften zur Weltpolitik, 6). Berlin, 1943.

Inal, Ibnülemin Mahmud Kemal. *Osmanli devrinde son sadriazamlar* [The Last Grand Viziers of the Ottoman Period]. 14 vols. Istanbul, 1940-53.

Jackh, Ernest [Ernst Jäckh]. *The Rising Crescent. Turkey Yesterday, Today, and Tomorrow.* New York, 1944.

James, Robert R. *Gallipoli.* New York, 1965.

Janssen, Karl-Heinz. *Der Kanzler und der General. Die Führungskrise um Bethmann Hollweg und Falkenhayn 1914-1916.* Göttingen, 1967.

Jäschke, Gotthard. "Geschichte der Türkei seit dem Waffen-

Bibliography

stillstand von Mudros." In *Handbuch der Orientalistik*. B. Spuler, ed. Erste Abteilung, Vol. VI, Part 3. Leiden-Cologne, 1959.

———. "Der Turanismus der Jungtürken. Zur osmanischen Aussenpolitik im Weltkriege." *Welt des Islams*, 23 (1941), pp. 1-54.

———. "Mitteilungen: Zum Eintritt der Türkei in den Ersten Weltkrieg." *Ibid.*, new series, 4 (1955), p. 51.

———. "Beiträge zur Geschichte des Kampfes der Türkei um ihre Unabhängigkeit." *Ibid.*, new series, 5 (1958), pp. 1-64.

———. "Auf dem Wege zur Türkischen Republik." *Ibid.*, new series, 5 (1958), pp. 206-18.

Jerussalimski, A. S. *Die Aussenpolitik und die Diplomatie des deutschen Imperialismus Ende des 19. Jahrhunderts.* 2d edn., Berlin, 1954.

Kadishev, A. B. *Interventsiya i grazhdanskaya voina v Zakavkaze* [Intervention and Civil War in Transcaucasia]. Moscow, 1960.

Kann, Robert A. *Die Sixtusaffäre und die geheimen Friedensverhandlungen Oesterreich-Ungarns im ersten Weltkrieg.* Munich, 1966.

Kazarian, Haigaz K. "Minutes of Secret Meetings Organizing the Turkish Genocide of Armenians." *Armenian Review*, 18:3 (1965), pp. 18-40.

Kazemzadeh, Firuz. *The Struggle for Transcaucasia, 1917-1921.* New York, 1951.

Kerner, Robert J. "The Mission of Liman von Sanders." *Slavonic Review*, 6 (1927-28), pp. 12-27, 344-63, 543-60; 7 (1928), pp. 90-112.

———. "Russia, the Straits, and Constantinople, 1914-15." *Journal of Modern History*, 1 (1929), pp. 400-15.

Kheifets, A. N. *Sovetskaya Rossiya i sopredelnye strani vostoka v godi grazhdanskoi voini, 1918-1920* [Soviet Russia and the Adjacent Countries of the East during the Civil War, 1918-20]. Moscow, 1964.

Bibliography

Kilic, Altemur. *Turkey and the World*. Washington, D.C. 1959.

Kinross, Lord. *Ataturk*. New York, 1965.

Klein, Fritz. "Die Rivalität zwischen Deutschland und Oesterreich-Ungarn in der Türkei am Vorabend des ersten Weltkrieges." In *Politik im Krieg 1914-1918*. Fritz Klein, ed. Berlin, 1964.

Kochan, Lionel. *Russia and the Weimar Republic*. Cambridge, England, 1954.

Korsun, N. G. *Pervaya mirovaya voina na Kavkazkom fronte* [The First World War on the Caucasian Front]. Moscow, 1946.

Kruck, Alfred. *Geschichte des Alldeutschen Verbandes, 1890-1939*. Wiesbaden, 1954.

Krüger, Karl. *Die neue Türkei*. Berlin, 1963.

Kutay, Cemal. *Talât Paşayi nasil vurdular?* [How Did They Shoot Down Talât Paşa?]. Istanbul, 1956.

Lafeber, C. V. *Vredes- en Bemiddelingspogingen uit het eerste jaar van Wereldoorlog I*. Leiden, 1961.

Landes, David S. *Bankers and Pashas: International Finance and Economic Imperialism in Egypt*. Cambridge, Mass., 1958.

Lang, David M. *A Modern History of Soviet Georgia*. New York, 1962.

Langer, William L. *The Diplomacy of Imperialism, 1890-1902*. 2 vols. rev. edn., New York, 1951.

Larcher, M. *La guerre turque dans la guerre mondiale*. Paris, 1926.

Lazarev, M. S. *Kruchenye turetskogo gospodstva na Arabskom vostoke 1914-1918 gg.* [The Shattering of Turkish Rule in the Arabian East, 1914-1918]. Moscow, 1960.

Lenczowski, George. *The Middle East in World Affairs*. 3d edn., Ithaca, 1962.

Lengyel, Emil. *Turkey*. New York, 1941.

Lepsius, Johannes. *Der Todesgang des armenischen Volkes in der Türkei während des Weltkrieges.* 4th edn., Potsdam, 1930.

―――. "Mein Besuch in Konstantinopel Juli/August 1915." *Der Orient,* 1:3 (1919), 21-33.

Lewis, Bernard. *The Emergence of Modern Turkey.* London, 1961.

Marder, Arthur J. *From the Dreadnought to Scapa Flow. The Royal Navy in the Fisher Era, 1904-1919.* London, 1961- .

Marriott, J. A. R. *The Eastern Question.* 4th edn., Oxford, 1940.

Mayer, Arno J. *Political Origins of the New Diplomacy, 1917-1918.* New Haven, 1959.

Mehlan, Arno. "Das deutsch-bulgarische Weltkriegsbündnis." *Historische Vierteljahresschrift,* 30 (1935), pp. 771-805.

Mekhitarian, Onnig. "The Defense of Van." *Armenian Review* (1948), 1:1, 121-29; 1:2, 131-43; 1:3, 130-42; 1:4, 133-42.

Meyer, Henry Cord. *Mitteleuropa in German Thought and Action, 1815-1945.* The Hague, 1955.

Miller, A. F. *Pyatidesyatiletye mladoturetskoi revolutsii* [The Fiftieth Anniversary of the Young Turk Revolution]. Moscow, 1958.

Moorehead, Alan. *Gallipoli.* New York, 1956.

Mühlmann, Carl. *Deutschland und die Türkei 1913-1914.* Berlin, 1929.

―――. *Das deutsch-türkische Waffenbündnis im Weltkriege.* Leipzig, 1940.

―――. *Oberste Heeresleitung und Balkan im Weltkrieg 1914/1918.* Berlin, 1942.

―――. "Die deutschen Bahnunternehmungen in der asiatischen Türkei, 1888-1914." *Weltwirtschaftliches Archiv,* 24 (1926), pp. 121-37, 365-99.

―――. *Der Kampf um die Dardanellen* (Schlachten des Weltkrieges, Bd. 16). Oldenburg, 1927.

―――. "Liman von Sanders." In *Deutsches Biographisches Jahrbuch,* XI. Stuttgart, 1932.

Bibliography

———. "Die deutsche Militärmission in der Türkei." *Wissen und Wehr*, 19 (1938), pp. 847-55.

Nalbandian, Louise. *The Armenian Revolutionary Movement*. Berkeley and Los Angeles, 1963.

Nebioglu, Osman. *Die Auswirkungen der Kapitulationen auf die türkische Wirtschaft*. (Probleme der Weltwirtschaft, Universität Kiel, v. 68). Jena, 1941.

Notovich, F. I. *Diplomaticheskaya borba v godi pervoi mirovoi voini* [The Diplomatic Struggle in the Years of the First World War]. Vol. 1, Moscow, 1947.

Novichev, A. D. *Ekonomika Turtsii v period mirovoi voini* [Turkey's Economy in the Period of the World War]. Leningrad, 1935.

Pasdermadjian, Hrant. *Histoire de l'Arménie depuis les origines jusqu'au traité de Lausanne*. Paris, 1949.

Pipes, Richard. *The Formation of the Soviet Union*. 2d edn., Cambridge, Mass., 1964.

Pönicke, Herbert. "Heinrich August Meissner-Pascha und der Bau der Hedschas- und Bagdadbahn." *Welt als Geschichte*, 16 (1956), pp. 196-210.

Ragey, Louis. *La question du Chemin de Fer de Bagdad*. Paris, 1936.

Ramsaur, Ernest E., Jr. *The Young Turks: Prelude to the Revolution of 1908*. Princeton, 1957.

Rathmann, Lothar. *Berlin-Bagdad. Die imperialistische Nahostpolitik des kaiserlichen Deutschland*. Berlin, 1962.

———. *Stossrichtung Nahost 1914-1918. Zur Expansionspolitik des deutschen Imperialismus im ersten Weltkrieg*. Berlin, 1963.

———. "Zur Legende vom 'antikolonialen' Charakter der Bagdadbahnpolitik in der wilhelminischen Aera des deutschen Monopolkapitalismus." *Zeitschrift für Geschichtswissenschaft, Sonderheft*, 9 (1961), pp. 246-70.

Renouvin, Pierre. *Le XIXe siècle. II: De 1871 à 1914* (Histoire des relations internationales, 6). Paris, 1955.

Bibliography

Renouvin, Pierre. "Les buts de guerre du gouvernement français, 1914-1918." *Revue Historique*, 235 (Jan. 1966), pp. 1-38.

Ritter, Gerhard. *Staatskunst und Kriegshandwerk*. 3 vols. Munich, 1954-64.

Rosenfeld, Günter. *Sowjetrussland und Deutschland 1917-1922*. Berlin, 1960.

Rossi, E. "Completamento della 'Ferrovia di Baghdad.' " *Oriente Moderno*, 20 (1940), p. 513.

Roumani, Adib. *Essai historique et technique sur la Dette Publique Ottomane*. Paris, 1927.

Rudin, Harry R. *Armistice 1918*. New Haven, 1944.

Rustow, Dankwart A. "The Army and the Founding of the Turkish Republic." *World Politics*, 11 (1959), pp. 513-52.

———. "Djawid." In *Encyclopaedia of Islam*, rev. edn. (1960–), 11, 497-98.

———. "Djemal Pasha." *Ibid.* 11, 531-32.

———. "Enwer Pasha." *Ibid.* 11, 698-702.

Sanjian, Avedis K. *The Armenian Communities in Syria under Ottoman Dominion*. Cambridge, Mass., 1965.

Sarafian, Vahe. "World War I American Relief for the Armenians." *Armenian Review* (1957), x:2, 121-36; x:3, 133-45.

———. "The Formation of the Armenian Independent Republic." *Ibid.* (1959), xii:2, 106-20; xii:3, 97-107.

Sarkisian, E. K. and R. G. Sahakian. *Vital Issues in Modern Armenian History*. Watertown, Mass., 1965.

Sarkissian, A. O. *History of the Armenian Question to 1885*. Urbana, Ill., 1938.

———. "Concert Diplomacy and the Armenians, 1890-1897." In *Studies in Diplomatic History and Historiography in Honour of G. P. Gooch*. A. O. Sarkissian, ed. London, 1961.

Schmitt, B. E. *The Coming of the War, 1914*. 2 vols. New York, 1930.

Schwarte, Max, ed. *Der grosse Krieg 1914-1918. Die Organisationen der Kriegsführung*. Part 1. Leipzig, 1921.

Bibliography

Shotwell, James T. and Francis Deák. *Turkey at the Straits.* New York, 1940.

Shukov, E. M., editor-in-chief. *Vsemirnaya istoriya* [Universal History]. 10 vols. Moscow, 1955-65.

Silberstein, Gerard E. "The Central Powers and the Second Turkish Alliance 1915." *Slavic Review,* 24 (1965), pp. 77-89.

Smith, C. Jay, Jr. *The Russian Struggle for Power: 1914-1917.* New York, 1956.

———. "Great Britain and the 1914-1915 Straits Agreement with Russia . . ." *American Historical Review,* 70 (1965), pp. 1,015-34.

Sousa, Nasim. *The Capitulatory Regime of Turkey.* Baltimore, 1933.

Stadelmann, Rudolf. "Friedensversuche im ersten Jahre des Weltkrieges." *Historische Zeitschrift,* 156 (1937), pp. 485-545.

Stravrianos, L. S. *The Balkans since 1453.* New York, 1958.

Steglich, Wolfgang. *Bündnissicherung oder Verständigungsfrieden.* Göttingen, 1958.

———. *Die Friedenspolitik der Mittelmächte 1917/18.* Vol. 1. Wiesbaden, 1964.

Sweet, Paul. "Leaders and Policies: Germany in the Winter of 1914-1915." *Journal of Central European Affairs,* 16 (1956), pp. 229-52.

Torrey, Glenn E. "German Policy toward Bulgaria, 1914-1915." Unpublished m.a. thesis, University of Oregon, 1957.

———. "Rumania and the Belligerents, 1914-1916." *Journal of Contemporary History,* 1:3 (1966), 171-91.

Townsend, Mary E. *The Rise and Fall of Germany's Colonial Empire, 1884-1918.* New York, 1930.

Trumpener, Ulrich. "German Military Aid to Turkey in 1914." *Journal of Modern History,* 32 (1960), pp. 145-49.

———. "Liman von Sanders and the German-Ottoman Alliance." *Journal of Contemporary History,* 1:4 (1966), 179-92.

Bibliography

Tunaya, Tarik Z. *Türkiyede siyasî partiler 1859-1952* [The Political Parties of Turkey, 1859-1952]. Istanbul, 1952.

Türkgeldi, Ali. *Mondros ve Mudanya Mütarekelerinin tarihi* [History of the Armistices of Mudros and Mudania]. Ankara, 1948.

Turkish National Commission for UNESCO. *Atatürk*. Ankara, 1963.

Ullman, Richard H. *Anglo-Soviet Relations, 1917-1921*. Vol. 1. Princeton, 1961.

Vratzian, Simon. *Armenia and the Armenian Question*. Boston, 1943.

Warth, Robert D. *The Allies and the Russian Revolution*. Durham, N.C., 1954.

Weltman, Saadia. "Germany, Turkey, and the Zionist Movement, 1914-1918." *Review of Politics*, 23 (1961), pp. 246-69.

Wheeler-Bennett, John W. *Brest-Litovsk. The Forgotten Peace*. London, 1938.

———. *The Nemesis of Power. The German Army in Politics, 1918-1945*. 2d edn., London, 1964.

Wolf, John B. *The Diplomatic History of the Bagdad Railroad*. Columbia, Mo., 1936.

Wolfslast, Wilhelm. *Der Seekrieg, 1914-1918*. Leipzig, 1938.

Yale, William. *The Near East*. Ann Arbor, Mich., 1958.

Zechlin, Egmont. *Die türkischen Meerengen—Brennpunkt der Weltgeschichte*. Hamburg, 1964.

———. "Friedensbestrebungen und Revolutionierungsversuche." *Aus Politik und Zeitgeschichte* (1961), B20/61, B24/61, B25/61; (1963), B20/63, B22/63.

Zeine, Zeine N. *Arab-Turkish Relations and the Emergence of Arab Nationalism*. Beirut, 1958.

Zenkovsky, Serge A. *Pan-Turkism and Islam in Russia*. Cambridge, Mass., 1960.

Ziemke, Kurt. *Die neue Türkei. Politische Entwicklung 1914-1929*. Stuttgart, 1930.

Bibliography

HISTORICAL CALENDARS

Jäschke, Gotthard and Erich Pritsch. "Die Türkei seit dem Weltkriege. Geschichtskalender 1918-1928." *Welt des Islams,* 10 (1927-29), pp. 1-154.

Jäschke, Gotthard. *Die Türkei in den Jahren 1942-1951. Ge-schichtskalender.* . . . Wiesbaden, 1955.

Schulthess' Europäischer Geschichtskalender. Vols. 53-59 [1912-18]. Munich, 1913-22.

INDEX

Note: Turkish surnames that were adopted after 1934 and the modern names of certain localities are listed in brackets.

Index

Index

Index

Index

Ottoman military operations, 69-70, 84ff, 101ff, 279, 369-70; political influence during the war, 70-71, 123-24, 129, 150, 156-57, 235, 247, 350; and Transcaucasian campaign of 1914/15, 75ff, 141; and revision of military mission system, 97-99; signs military convention with Germany, 99-100, 379; and Falkenhayn, 102-103; war aims of, 114; and North Africa, 115, 119ff; frictions with Wolff-Metternich, 126-28; peace question, 132, 151n, 162; and Transcaucasia, 168-70, 173, 178-80, 183-85, 188-89, 191, 195; and Armenian deportations, 210-11, 217-18, 222n, 229-30, 236, 249-50, 259-61, 263n, 265; and Bagdad railroad, 293, 296-301, 304, 310-14; resigns from all offices, 354-56; leaves Turkey, 359-60; exile and death, 361-63

Ernst Ludwig, Grand Duke of Hesse, 144n

Erzberger, Matthias (*Zentrum* politician), 160, 185n, 228, 236

Erzinjan, 171, 173

Erzurum, 167, 203n, 207, 209, 212, 230

Estonia, 170, 190

Euphrates River, 7, 63, 68, 285

Faber, Friedrich (German publisher), 221

Falkenhayn, Erich von, Gen. (chief, OHL), 52-53, 70, 91, 128, 132, 279; and Turkey's isolation, 82, 82n, 84; and Liman, 88-89, 92, 95-96; service in Tur-

key, 102-103, 105n, 106-107, 374; and attack on Suez Canal, 121n, 122; and Bagdad Railroad, 289, 291-92, 298-99

Feldmann, von, Lt. Col., 373

Ferdinand I, King of Bulgaria, 155

Fethi Bey [Okyar], Ali (Ottoman officer-diplomat), 356, 380

Fischer, Fritz (German historian), 16n, 22n, 118n, 147n, 196n, 351n, 370-72

Flanders, 133

Flotow, Johannes von (German diplomat), 116

France, vii, 21, 47, 60, 78, 110, 112-13, 160-61, 290, 336, 371, 377; and Eastern Question, 3, 5ff; prewar economic influence in Turkey, 9-12, 298; Turkish prewar attitude toward, 19-20; and Ottoman capitulations, 38-39; military operations, 26-27, 62, 65, 81, 83, 141, 352; Straits agreement with Russia, 141-42, 154; peace feelers, 148-49, 154; and Armenian persecutions, 209-10, 210n; German economic measures against, 332ff; and Mudros armistice, 358

Franckenstein, Georg Frhr. von und zu (Austro-Hungarian diplomat), 261, 264

Franz Joseph I, Emperor of Austria, 143

freedom of the seas, 160, 162-63

Galicia, 66, 131-32, 339

Gallipoli, 65-66, 81, 86-92, 105, 149-50, 281

Ganja, *see* Elizavetpol

Index

Index

Index

Index

Index

Index

Mehmed VI Vahideddin, Sultan, 104, 356

Mensheviks, 171, 176, 187

Mertens, Josef (German consul-general, Constantinople), 335n

Mesopotamia (and Iraq), 132f, 164, 166n; military operations in, 63, 68, 106, 122, 179f, 184, 199, 339, 352; Armenian deportations and, 210, 226, 233, 238, 246; railroad construction in, 285, 287f, 291, 297f, 299ff, 316; oil fields, 325, 341, 344, 347f

Mesrop (Armenian bishop), 257

Messina, 26f

Metternich, see Wolff-Metternich

Meyer, Henry Cord (American historian), 10n

Michaelis, Georg (German chancellor), 161, 163, 331, 338

Midilli, see Breslau

Militärkabinett, 75, 93

military mission, see German military mission

military operations in Europe: Western front, 21, 44, 289, 349, 352, 355; Balkans, 23ff, 52, 66, 82, 84, 297, 352, 356n; Eastern front, 36, 44, 52, 66, 131, 167, 340. See also naval operations; Turkish theaters of war

Miliukov, Paul (Russian politician), 155, 159

Miller, Anatolii F. (Soviet historian), 7n

minorities in Ottoman empire, 3, 67, 124f, 240, 246, 303. See also Armenians

Mitteleuropäische Handelsvereinigung, 319n

Mittelmeer-Division: escapes to the

Dardanelles, 25-30; fictitious sale of, 31f; and question of Turkish intervention, 35f, 39-43, 46; attacks Russian coast, 55; subsequent operations, 66; agreement on postwar status, 158

Moltke, Helmuth Count von, Gen. (chief, Prussian general staff), 14, 22, 36

Montenegro, 161

Morgenthau, Henry (American ambassador to Turkey), 14, 151n; and Armenian deportations, 208f, 226n, 228f

Morocco, 363

Moslems in: Baku, 187, 196, 266; British and French colonies, 113, 118f, 210n; Entente armies, 117f; Macedonia, 50; Ottoman empire, 201, 222, 222n, 242; Russian empire, 28, 113; Thrace, 133; Transcaucasia, 172f, 178ff, 182, 187, 249, 260; Turkestan, 194, 363. See also Islam

Mosul, 63, 246f, 316, 349

Mühlmann, Carl (German historian), 68, 112n

Muhtar Bey, Ahmed (under secretary, Ottoman public works ministry), 294, 299, 304

Muhtar Paşa, Mahmud, Gen. (Ottoman ambassador to Germany), 19, 42, 45, 123, 142f

Müller, Georg A. von, Adm. (chief, Marinekabinett), 142

Mumm, Reinhard (Reichstag deputy), 248

Mustafa Kemal Paşa [Atatürk], Lt.Col. (later Gen.), 86n, 267f, 355, 358, 363f

Index

Index

Index

Index

Index

Index

Index

Index

WITHDRAWN